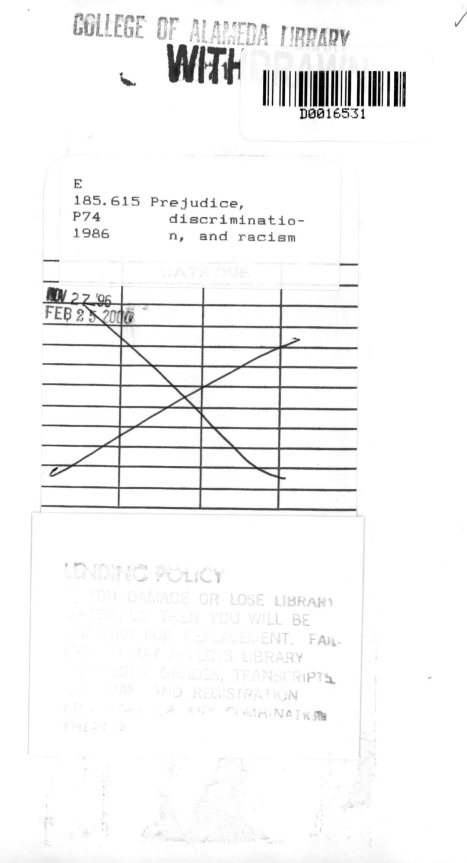

PREJUDICE,
DISCRIMINATION,
AND RACISM

PREJUDICE, DISCRIMINATION, AND RACISM

Edited by

JOHN F. DOVIDIO
Department of Psychology
Colgate University
Hamilton, New York

SAMUEL L. GAERTNER
Department of Psychology
University of Delaware
Newark, Delaware

1986

ACADEMIC PRESS, INC.
Orlando, Florida 32887

United Kingdom Edition published by
ACADEMIC PRESS INC. (LONDON) LTD.
24–28 Oval Road, London NW1 7DX

Library of Congress Cataloging in Publication Data

Prejudice, discrimination, and racism.

Includes index.
1. Racism—United States. 2. United States—Race
relations. I. Dovidio, John F. II. Gaertner,
Samuel L.
E185.615.P74 1986   305.8'00973   86-10720
ISBN 0–12–221425–0 (alk. paper)

PRINTED IN THE UNITED STATES OF AMERICA

86 87 88 89   9 8 7 6 5 4 3 2 1

To our children:
Alison, Michael, Lowell, and Robin

CONTENTS

    MODERN RACISM SCALE   91
    John B. McConahay

    Introduction   91
    The Tenets of Modern Racism..............................   92
    The Modern and Old-Fashioned Racism Items   93
    White Ambivalence and the Theoretical Relationship of the
        Two Scales   98
    The Empirical Relationship between the Two Scales.......... 102
    The Relative Reactivity of the Two Scales 110
    The Validity of the Modern Racism Scale.................... 115
    Future Research... 120
    References 124

5. STEREOTYPES AND STEREOTYPING: AN OVERVIEW
    OF THE COGNITIVE APPROACH   127
    David L. Hamilton and Tina K. Trolier

    Introduction 127
    The Categorization Process in Social Perception............... 128
    Cognitive Origins of Social Categories 133
    The Nature of Social Categories............................ 137
    The Use of Social Categories: Cognitive Consequences
        of Stereotypes.. 142
    The Cognitive Approach: Implications and Extensions 151
    References 158

6. STEREOTYPING AND PERCEIVED DISTRIBUTIONS OF
    SOCIAL CHARACTERISTICS: AN APPLICATION TO
    INGROUP–OUTGROUP PERCEPTION   165
    *Patricia W. Linville, Peter Salovey,
    and Gregory W. Fischer*

    Introduction 165
    Ingroup–Outgroup Perception: The Evidence for Outgroup
        Homogeneity... 167
    Social Categorization Processes 177
    Empirical Evidence: Ingroup–Outgroup Differentiation 189
    Empirical Evidence: Increasing Differentiation over Time 196
    Conclusion 198
    References 206

7. CATEGORIZATION EFFECTS ON INGROUP AND
    OUTGROUP PERCEPTION   209
    Norman Miller and Marilynn B. Brewer

    Introduction 209
    Levels of Intragroup Differentiation 215

Group Boundaries and Projected Similarity 224
Summary.. 227
References 229

8. CAUSES AND CONSEQUENCES OF THE
   COLORBLIND PERSPECTIVE   231
   Janet Ward Schofield

   Introduction 231
   The Research Site: Wexler Middle School.................... 233
   Data Gathering... 235
   The Colorblind Perspective and Its Corollaries............... 236
   The Functions and Consequences of the Colorblind Perspective
      and Its Corollaries 242
   Conclusions 250
   References 250

9. RACISM IN THE COURTROOM   255
   Stephanie Nickerson, Clara Mayo,
   and Althea Smith

   Introduction 255
   Racial Bias in Verdicts and Sentencing...................... 256
   The *Voir Dire* Procedure and Social Psychological Implications.. 263
   Application of Empirical Literature......................... 265
   Empirical Analysis of *Voir Dire* Questions................... 268
   Conclusion 272
   References 275

10. RACISM: A CULTURAL ANALYSIS OF THE PROBLEM   279
    James M. Jones

    Introduction 279
    A Look at the Problem 280
    Ways of Understanding the Problem....................... 288
    Black Culture: The TRIOS Approach 294
    TRIOS.. 296
    Conclusion: Multidimensional Approach to Cultural Diversity ... 306
    References 311

11. PREJUDICE, DISCRIMINATION, AND RACISM:
    PROBLEMS, PROGRESS, AND PROMISE   315
    Samuel L. Gaertner and John F. Dovidio

    Introduction 315
    Reasons to be Concerned 315
    Reasons to be Optimistic................................ 320

introduction

This book is about the nature of prejudice, discrimination, and racism among white Americans. While there is substantial evidence that blatant forms of racial bigotry are declining, subtle but insidious types are still pervasive. Because of the unequal distribution of socioeconomic and political power and the fact that racial prejudices are embedded in social norms, institutional policies, and the cognitive and affective systems of white Americans, racism has a significant impact on black Americans. In the United States, blacks are disadvantaged relative to whites in almost every important aspect of life: Blacks have a higher infant mortality rate, a shorter life expectancy, a lower level of educational attainment, a higher rate of unemployment, and a lower standard of living. Racism continues to have negative effects on the lives, hopes, and dreams of black Americans.

The idea for this book evolved from the formal and informal interactions that occurred during a symposium on "The Nature and Consequences of Contemporary Racial Attitudes" at the 1981 Eastern Psychological Association Convention and a symposium on "Contemporary Racial Attitudes: Motivational and Cognitive Approaches" at the 1981 American Psychological Association Convention. It was clear from the diversity of opinions expressed during our discussions that the causes and consequences of prejudice and racism are complex. Thus, this book represents an eclectic view of the forces that perpetuate racism. The focus of the book is not on questioning whether social *or* intergroup *or* intraindividual factors contribute most to prejudice, discrimination, and racism, but rather on examining how these factors operate, often in concert.

In particular, *Prejudice, Discrimination, and Racism* reviews motivational, cognitive, social, and cultural factors involved in racism. The first chapter examines historical trends and provides an overview of current psychological approaches. The next three chapters present motivational explanations of contemporary forms of prejudice. In general, these motivational explanations emphasize the socialization of attitudes and values. Katz, Wackenhut, and Hass (Chapter 2) discuss racial ambivalence and its consequences; Gaertner and Dovidio (Chapter 3) examine aversive racism, a subtle form of prejudice among people who genuinely hold egalitarian values; and McConahay (Chapter 4) focuses on modern racism, another type of prejudice which is less obvious than "old-fashioned" bigotry. Chapters 5, 6, and 7 present cognitive approaches to understanding prejudice and racism. Cognitive approaches emphasize the role of social categorization and biases in information processing as mediators of stereotyping and intergroup conflict. Hamilton and Trolier (Chapter 5) provide an overview of the cognitive perspective, and Linville, Salovey, and Fischer (Chapter 6) critically examine the hypothesis that people are more complex and differentiated in their thinking about members of their own group than about members of other groups. Miller and Brewer (Chapter 7) propose that the features of interracial contact situations that are instrumental in promoting intergroup acceptance are effective because they reduce the salience of group boundaries and promote personalized interactions. In Chapters 8, 9, and 10, the consequences of prejudice, discrimination, and racism are considered. Schofield (Chapter 8) studies interracial interactions in a desegregated school, and Nickerson, Mayo, and Smith (Chapter 9) review the impact of racism in the American courtroom. Jones (Chapter 10) examines the consequences of racism on the well-being of blacks and emphasizes cultural factors in contemporary race relations. In the concluding chapter, Gaertner and Dovidio discuss reasons for both continued pessimism and renewed optimism concerning the elimination of prejudice, discrimination, and racism.

This book is intended for our professional colleagues in psychology, sociology, education, and political science. It is also written for people who formulate and implement social policy. Beyond collegial communication, the primary use of this book is in graduate and advanced undergraduate courses where the range of approaches represented in the chapters will give students an appreciation of the complexity of the problem and the formidable challenges that must be faced if racism is to be eliminated.

ACKNOWLEDGMENTS

We gratefully acknowledge the significant contributions that many people have made to this book. Because an edited volume is truly a group effort, we would like to thank all our contributors for their dedication, patience, receptiveness to our editorial suggestions, and openness to thinking about and responding to each other's views. We also would like to express our gratitude to the organizations and people who supported our work on this book. In particular, we acknowledge the financial assistance provided by the Colgate University Research Council, the University of Delaware Research Foundation, and the Office of Naval Research, Division of Organizational Effectiveness. These organizations funded much of the research discussed in our chapters. We are grateful as well to a large number of support personnel: Shelley Sykes and Mark Sibicky for typing portions of the manuscript; Jeff Mann, Shelley Gaertner, Valarie Hans, Kris Anderson, and Richard Tyler for reading parts of the manuscript and offering helpful suggestions; and Erving Pfau, Jeannie Kellog, Rich Grant, and Cathy Toglia of the Colgate Computer Center, whose generosity in resources and time was invaluable in preparing the manuscript. In addition, we sincerely appreciate the patience and support that Academic Press showed at every stage of the development of this volume. Finally, we want to thank our wives, Linda and Shelley, and our children, Alison, Michael, Lowell, and Robin, for their understanding and tolerance. We are deeply indebted to Linda and Shelley for their special efforts to give us time, their helpful comments and suggestions on our work, and their encouragement.

John F. Dovidio
Samuel L. Gaertner

PREJUDICE, DISCRIMINATION, AND RACISM: HISTORICAL TRENDS AND CONTEMPORARY APPROACHES

John F. Dovidio

Samuel L. Gaertner

Department of Psychology
Colgate University
Hamilton, New York 13346

Department of Psychology
University of Delaware
Newark, Delaware 19711

INTRODUCTION

The United States is a country whose fundamental values demand "liberty and justice for all." It is a nation founded on "the proposition that all men [sic] are created equal." Nevertheless, it is also a country with racist traditions and contemporary manifestations of racial prejudice and discrimination. It was not until the Civil Rights Laws were passed in the early 1960s, over 175 years after human rights were proclaimed in the Declaration of Independence and guaranteed by the Constitution, that the United States formally recognized that black and white people were equal before the state. Furthermore, although civil rights legislation and subsequent affirmative action policies have been important steps toward these egalitarian precepts, they cannot quickly redress hundreds of years of mistreatment, nor can they immediately change people's attitudes and values. Over two-thirds of the current population lived during a time when it was legal and customary in some parts of this country to require that blacks sit in the back of a bus, give up their seats to whites, use different rest rooms, and drinking fountains, and eat at different restaurants. Also, more subtle, but equally pernicious forms of de facto discrimination thrived in other parts of the country. The process of abandoning racist traditions and prejudiced beliefs may be especially difficult because of their deep-seated nature in American culture (Feagin & Feagin, 1978; Knowles & Prewitt, 1969). Grier and Cobbs (1968) note, "The black man today is at one end of a psychological continuum that reaches back in time to his enslaved ancestors" (p. 24).

1

The historical coexistence of egalitarian values and racist traditions seems paradoxical. Myrdal (1944) addressed this "American dilemma" more than 40 years ago. According to Myrdal, the dilemma involves

> the ever-raging conflict between, on the one hand, the valuations preserved on the general plane which we shall call the "American creed," where the American thinks, talks, and acts under the influence of high national and Christian precepts and, on the other hand, the valuations on specific planes of individual and group living, where personal and local interests; economic, social, and sexual jealousies; consideration of community prestige and conformity; group prejudice against particular persons or types of people; and all sorts of miscellaneous wants, impulses, and habits dominate his outlook. (p. xliii)

The American dilemma of 1944 was thus between egalitarian ideals and personal and social forces that promote prejudice and discrimination. Although the United States is currently more conscious of racial issues and more committed to racial equality, we are still a nation struggling with the American dilemma. Prejudice, discrimination, and racism continue to exist despite personal, social, and political pressures to eradicate them. There is evidence, however, that because of contemporary egalitarian forces, changes in racial attitudes have occurred. In our view, these changes represent more qualitative shifts in attitudes than quantitative changes in the degree of prejudice. Thus, this book is about these contemporary forms of prejudice, discrimination, and racism directed by whites toward blacks and about current approaches to studying these issues.

PREJUDICE, DISCRIMINATION, AND RACISM DEFINED

Although several different definitions of prejudice, discrimination, and racism have been proposed, there has been general agreement about the essential meanings of these concepts. Allport (1954) defined *prejudice* as "an antipathy based on a faulty and inflexible generalization. It may be felt or expressed. It may be directed toward a group as a whole, or toward an individual because he is a member of that group" (p. 9). Sixteen years later, Ashmore (1970) defined it as "a negative attitude toward a socially defined group and toward any person perceived to be a member of that group" (p. 253). Jones, in Chapter 10 of this book, uses the term *prejudice* to refer to "a faulty generalization from a group characterization (stereotype) to an individual member of the group irrespective of either a) the accuracy of the group stereotype in the first place, and b) the applicability of the group characterization to the individual in question." Prejudice is generally conceptualized as having a cognitive component (e.g., irrationally based beliefs about a target group), an affective component (e.g., dislike), and a conative component (e.g., a behavioral predisposition to avoid the target group) (Harding, Proshansky, Kutner, & Chein, 1969).

Whereas prejudice is an attitude, discrimination is a selectively unjustified negative behavior toward members of the target group. According to Allport (1954), *discrimination* involves denying "individuals or groups of people equality of treatment which they may wish" (p. 51). Jones (1972) defines discrimination as "those actions designed to maintain own-group characteristics and favored position *at the expense* of the comparison group" (p. 4). Allport (1954) describes an intuitively based continuum of discrimination: antilocution, avoidance, discrimination, physical attack, and extermination. It is important to note that prejudice does not always lead to discrimination and that discrimination may have causes other than prejudice.

Racism is a term whose popularity stems from its use in the *Report of the National Advisory Commision on Civil Disorders* (1968). Jones (1972) identifies three uses of the term *racism.* The first is *individual racism,* which is similar in meaning to race prejudice, but places more emphasis on biological considerations and also encompasses discriminatory acts. The second is *institutional racism,* which refers to the intentional or unintentional manipulation or toleration of institutional policies (e.g., poll taxes, admissions criteria) that unfairly restrict the opportunities of particular groups of people. The third use of racism concerns cultural racism. *Cultural racism* includes elements of individual and institutional racism. According to Jones (1972): "Cultural racism can generally be defined as the individual and institutional expression of the superiority of one race's cultural heritage over that of another race" (p. 6).

TRENDS IN RACIAL ATTITUDES AND STEREOTYPES

White America is apparently becoming more liberal and egalitarian in its attitude toward blacks. Much of the data on whites' attitudes toward blacks and toward policies aimed at eliminating social inequality come from work conducted between 1940 and 1978 at the National Opinion Research Center (NORC) (Greeley & Sheatsley, 1971; Hyman & Sheatsley, 1956, 1964; Sheatsley, 1966; Taylor, Sheatsley, & Greeley, 1978) and from research sponsored by the National Advisory Committee on Civil Disorders (Campbell, 1971). The results of various public opinion polls are effectively summarized by Erskine (1967a,b; 1968a,b,c,d; 1969a,b), Rothbart (1976), and Smith and Dempsey (1983). We briefly highlight some of these findings.

An egalitarian trend in the expressed racial attitudes of whites is evident in the responses to NORC surveys conducted in 1942, 1956, 1963, 1970, 1972, and 1976. Between 1942 and 1970, both northerners and southerners showed dramatic shifts in their stances toward integration. For example, in 1942, only 2% of the southerners agreed that blacks and whites should go to the same schools, whereas in 1970, 45% of the southern respondents supported integrated schools. In 1942, 40% of the northerners believed that blacks and whites should go to the same schools; by 1970, 83% of the northerners expressed this view. By 1963, most respondents endorsed egalitarian and pro-integration statements concerning blacks' obtaining jobs (82%); riding street cars and buses (77%); using parks, restaurants, and hotels (71%); and attending schools (63%). Acceptance of blacks in each of these areas further increased by about 10% in 1970.

The results of more recent NORC surveys and Harris polls show that the egalitarian trend continued throughout the 1970s. The results of the NORC surveys (Taylor et al., 1978) are presented in Figure 1. Pro-integration sentiments concerning bringing a black person home for dinner, allowing blacks into the neighborhood, and permitting interracial marriage were at unprecedented highs in 1976. The results of the Harris poll (Newsweek, 1979) appear in Table 1. Progress has been slow but consistent; in 1978, compared to any previous time, whites were less likely to ascribe negative traits (e.g., violent, inferior, criminal, unintelligent) to blacks. In addition, the percentage of people stating that they would *not* vote for a well-qualified black candidate for president declined from 54% in 1958 to 16% in 1984 (Sigelman & Welch, 1984; Smith & Dempsey, 1983). Thus, on the basis of these survey data, whites in the United States are becoming more accepting of blacks and of egalitarian policies.

The traditional technique for assessing racial stereotypes has involved an adjective checklist procedure (Gilbert, 1951; Karlins, Coffman, & Walters, 1969; Katz & Braly, 1933). In this technique, subjects are given a list of adjectives and are asked to select characteristics that are most typical of whites and most typical of blacks. Although this approach has been criticized (Brigham, 1971; McCauley, Stitt, & Segal, 1980), the results of these studies are important because comparable samples were tested with identical instruments at three different times across a 33-year span (Gilbert, 1951; Karlins et al., 1969; Katz &

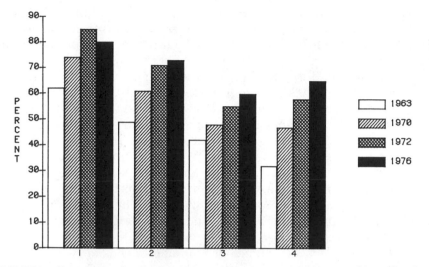

FIGURE 1. Proportion of pro-integration responses to questions on racial attitudes that were administered to a nationwide sample of white respondents in 1963, 1970, 1972, and 1976. (Adapted from Taylor, Sheatsley, & Greeley, 1978.)

Questions:
1. Do you think white students and black students should go to the same schools or to separate schools?
2. How strongly would you object if a member of your family wanted to bring a black friend home to dinner?
3. White people have a right to keep blacks out of their neighborhoods if they want to, and blacks should respect that right.
4. Do you think there should be laws against marriages between blacks and whites?

TABLE 1 Whites' Attitudes toward Blacks

	Percentage of white respondents agreeing in each year					
	1963	1966	1967	1971	1976	1978
Blacks tend to have less ambition than whites.	66	65	70	52	50	49
Blacks want to live off the handout.	41	43	52	39	37	36
Blacks are more violent than whites.	—	—	42	36	35	34
Blacks breed crime.	35	33	32	27	31	29
Blacks have less native intelligence than whites.	39	36	46	37	28	25
Blacks care less for the family than whites.	31	33	34	26	22	18
Blacks are inferior to whites.	31	26	29	22	15	15

Note. From *Newsweek*, February 26, 1979.

Braly, 1933). We used this procedure in 1982 with a sample of Colgate students that was demographically similar to the Princeton samples. The results of the Princeton studies and our research are presented in Table 2.[1]

As indicated in Table 2, whites' stereotype of blacks has changed considerably since 1932. There has been a consistent decrease in the frequency with which several negative traits are selected in the description of blacks: superstitious, lazy, ignorant, and stupid have shown a strong and steady decline across time. In contrast, whites' stereotype of themselves (see Table 2) is consistently becoming less favorable and progressive. The frequency with which intelligent is selected has declined from 47% in 1932 to 10% in 1982, and materialistic has increased from 33% in 1932 to 65% in 1982. New items among the 10 most frequently selected traits in 1982 include stubborn and conservative.

Not only are black stereotypes becoming more favorable and white stereotypes becoming less favorable, but also black and white stereotypes are becoming more similar in content across time. In 1933, there was 0% overlap between black and white stereotypic traits; in 1950, there was 6% overlap; and in 1967, there was 10% overlap in stereotypic characteristics. In our 1982 sample, there was a 22% overlap in black and white stereotypic traits. Thus, in terms of content and favorability, stereotypes of blacks and whites are becoming less distinct.

Increases in racial consciousness and changes in racial stereotyping have also been observed in the mass media. Specifically, blacks have appeared more frequently in magazine and television advertisements and have become more prominent in network programming. A series of studies on magazine advertisements revealed that in 1949–1950 only 0.5% of the advertisements showed blacks; in 1967–1968, 2% depicted blacks; in 1970, 7% pictured blacks; and by 1982, 9% showed blacks (Colfax & Sternberg, 1972; Cox, 1969–1970; Humphrey & Schuman, 1984; Shuey, 1953). How blacks are portrayed has also changed. In 1949–1950, virtually all of the blacks that appeared in magazine advertising were in low-skilled labor categories, and 80% were maids, cooks, or servants to whites; in 1980, only 14% of blacks

---

[1] It should be noted that because of changing cultural labels the term "Black Americans" was used in place of "Negroes" and the term "White Americans" was used instead of "Americans." Thus, the specific stimulus (label)–response (trait) connection is different in 1982 from that in the previous adjective checklist studies. It was assumed, however, that the concept (racial category)–trait connection would be fundamentally similar.

TABLE 2   Changes in Racial Stereotypes across Time: Percentage of Subjects Selecting Traits

For Negroes (1933, 1951, 1969) or black Americans (1982)

Trait	1933	1951	1969	1982
Superstitious	84	41	13	6
Lazy	75	31	26	13
Happy-go-lucky	38	17	27	15
Ignorant	38	24	11	10
Musical	26	33	47	29
Ostentatious	26	11	25	5
Very religious	24	17	8	23
Stupid	22	10	4	1
Physically dirty	17	—	3	0
Naive	14	—	4	4
Slovenly	13	—	5	2
Unreliable	12	—	6	2
Pleasure loving	—	19	26	20
Sensitive	—	—	17	13
Gregarious	—	—	17	4
Talkative	—	—	14	5
Imitative	—	—	13	9
Aggressive	—	—	—	19
Materialistic	—	—	—	19
Loyal to family	—	—	—	39
Arrogant	—	—	—	14
Ambitious	—	—	—	13
Tradition loving	—	—	—	13

For Americans (1933, 1951, 1969) or white Americans (1982)

Trait	1933	1951	1969	1982
Industrious	48	30	23	21
Intelligent	47	32	20	10
Materialistic	33	37	67	65
Ambitious	33	21	42	35
Progressive	27	5	17	9
Pleasure loving	26	27	28	45
Alert	23	7	7	2
Efficient	21	9	15	8
Aggressive	20	8	15	11
Straightforward	19	—	9	7
Practical	10	—	12	14
Sportsmanlike	19	—	9	6
Individualistic	—	26	15	14
Conventional	—	—	17	20
Scientifically minded	—	—	15	4
Ostentatious	—	—	15	6
Conservative	—	—	15	—
Stubborn	—	—	—	15
Tradition loving	—	—	—	19

Note. From Karlins, Coffman, and Walters, 1969.

in advertisements held low-skilled labor jobs. In 1950, blacks were presented in subordinate role relationships with whites 62% of the time, whereas, in 1980, 89% of the advertisements showing blacks and whites together depicted equal-status interactions.

In one of the earliest studies of minority representation in television programming and advertising, Plotkin (1964) reported that blacks were portrayed on TV only once every 2.5 hours. Almost always, blacks were seen in a position of subordinate status to whites. More recent work on television advertising by Dominick and Greenberg (1970) and Greenberg and Mazingo (1976) indicates a consistent increase in black presence in commercials from 1967 (4% showing blacks) to 1968 (6%) to 1969 (10%) to 1973 (14%). Although, as Greenberg and Mazingo (1976) pointed out, the first starring role for a black in a prime-time dramatic series (Bill Cosby in "I Spy") did not occur until 1965, by 1967 34% of all dramas included blacks. In 1968 and 1969, 52% of all dramas had black characters, and, in 1973, 43% had black characters. Greenberg and Mazingo (1976) also note that giving and taking orders were equalized for blacks and whites by 1973. The ratio of blacks giving orders to taking orders was 0.58 in 1967, 0.72 in 1968, 0.57 in 1969, but 0.92 in 1973. Liebert, Sprafkin, and Davidson (1982) also observe that "the formal social–occupational status of blacks has also been elevated since the early days of television. While they used to be cast as servants and entertainers, blacks in the late 1960s and early 1970s were presented as 'regulators' of society in positions such as teachers or law enforcers" (p. 162). In 1984, Bill Cosby's top-rated situation comedy portrayed Cosby as a caring obstetrician married to an attorney who together with their five children faced typical problems of middle-class family life. Thus, mass media portrayals of blacks have become more frequent and increasingly positive.

Although the research that we have presented shows egalitarian trends in racial attitudes, stereotyping, and mass-media portrayals, these figures may overestimate the degree to which white America has truly reversed its disaffection for blacks and other minorities. That is, these changes in attitude may be more superficial than real. Thus, attitudes and stereotypes may actually be less favorable than what the data seem to show. McConahay, Hardee, and Batts (1981; also see Chapter 4 by McConahay in this volume) found, for example, that many of the traditional prejudice items that have been used in the opinion surveys are highly susceptible to social desirability influences. Subjects often systematically alter their responses on these items to appear to be more egalitarian than they are. It is important to recognize, however, that what may have changed is what people regard as a socially desirable position rather than their racial attitudes per se. Research on stereotyping further indicates that people's responses on self-report measures are often systematically distorted to appear less biased than they are. Sigall and Page (1971), using the bogus pipeline procedure, found that white subjects who believed that their truthfulness was being monitored through their physiological responses gave more negative evaluations of blacks and more positive evaluations of whites than did control subjects who believed that they were not being physiologically monitored. In addition, people may behave in relatively favorable ways toward minorities so as to maintain a nonprejudiced image rather than out of a genuine interest for their well-being (Dutton & Lake, 1973). Gaertner and Dovidio (see Chapter 3) suggest that many people who are sincerely committed to egalitarian ideals do not recognize the extent to which they are racially prejudiced.

Also, the more favorable portrayal of blacks in the media may not entirely be a reflection of genuine positive regard. Liebert et al. (1982) suggest that the increases in the proportion of blacks on television are in part "due to pressure from black groups" (p. 162). In addition, despite the apparent gains blacks have made in the mass media, there continues to be evidence of tokenism. Colfax and Sternberg (1972) report that a large proportion of the blacks who appeared in print advertisements were token blacks, appearing with 5 to 1000 white people, or were children interacting with a white teacher, counselor, or superior. Even into the 1980s (Humphrey & Schuman, 1984), white authority figures are frequently shown helping poor blacks or supervising black children. Greenberg and Mazingo (1976) observe that much of the increased presence of blacks in television advertisements between 1967 and 1973 can be accounted for by increases in the number of blacks in background or walk-on roles rather than in major parts. Also, McNally (1983) found that blacks portrayed on television received more negative consequences for their behaviors than did whites. Liebert et al. (1982) further state that although black characters on television shows in the 1970s were "good and likeable, they were neither forceful nor powerful" (p. 162). It is therefore unclear how much of the shift toward egalitarianism over the past 40 years can be attributed to a sincere personal commitment to egalitarian values.

Even if the self-report data on prejudice and stereotyping are accepted at face value, a significant amount of bias still exists even after a 40-year trend toward egalitarianism. For example, in 1970, 16 years after the Supreme Court ruled against segregated schools (Brown v.

Board of Education, 1954), less than half of the southerners in the National Opinion Research Center survey endorsed the statement that blacks and whites should go to the same schools (Greeley & Sheatsley, 1971); in 1976, only about 80% of the respondents overall endorsed integrated schools (D. Taylor et al., 1978). In addition, on items involving some degree of intimacy between blacks and whites, relatively high proportions of respondents continue to show racial biases. In 1978, 54% of the white people questioned disapproved of marriage between blacks and whites and, in 1981, 31% preferred not to have blacks as neighbors (Smith & Dempsey, 1983). The Harris poll in 1978 indicated that only 35% of white respondents favored full integration (another 42% favored integration "in some areas"). The Harris poll also revealed that in 1978 blacks still perceived a significant amount of discrimination against them: 74% felt discriminated against in obtaining white collar jobs, 73% in getting managerial positions, 68% in getting skilled labor positions, 58% in obtaining housing, and 61% in receiving equitable wages. Although 71% of the whites reported that they believed the government was committed to racial equality, only 39% of black respondents felt that was true.

Although white college students' stereotypic descriptions of whites and blacks have become more similar over time, it is important to note that stereotypes of blacks are still less favorable than are stereotypes of whites. In 1967, a quarter of the college students sampled described blacks as lazy and ostentatious, and 10% described them as ignorant. In 1982, even though many positive characteristics were selected, over 10% of the sample described blacks as lazy, ignorant, aggressive, and arrogant. The most negative characteristics associated with whites in 1967 and 1982 were materialistic and aggressive (both of which were also associated with blacks), and stubborn, conventional, and conservative. Thus even with the egalitarian influences in the United States today, blacks remain some distance from being fully accepted as equals by whites. The question of whether or not this social distance is reflected in differences in the quality of life of blacks and whites is considered in the next section.

TRENDS IN THE QUALITY OF LIFE
OF BLACKS AND WHITES

Because the issue of the consequences of prejudice, discrimination, and racism is considered in more detail in Jones' chapter (Chapter 10), we only briefly review some trends in these data here. Quality of life

长寿

is reflected in health and longevity as well as in education and socio-economic status. Overall, the quality of life in the United States has improved both for blacks and for whites. Compared to previous years, median family income is higher, life expectancy is longer, infant mortality is less frequent, and higher education is more common. Furthermore, the U.S. Commission on Civil Disorders (1978) found that blacks and other minorities have shown considerable gains *relative* to whites in education, in terms of both basic education (i.e., completing at least 8 years of schooling) and higher education (i.e., completing college). In the health and economic areas, however, the data on blacks' gains relative to whites are mixed. Blacks and other minorities showed some relative gain in life expectancy: In 1944, the life expectancy for whites was 66.2 years and for blacks and other minorities was 56.6 years, a white : black ratio of 1.17; in 1974, the life expectancies were 72.7 and 67.0, a more equal ratio of 1.09. In terms of infant mortality, though, blacks are now worse off relative to whites: In 1944, the infant mortality rate was 1.63 times the rate for whites, but in 1982, the rate was 1.94 times higher. In addition, although blacks have consistently made gains relative to whites in median family income (see Jones' chapter), unemployment has generally gotten worse. An analysis of the unemployment rates of black and white males and females reveals that in 1983, blacks across all age groups from 18 to 64 were generally less well off than whites. Furthermore, compared to data from 1955, the ratio of black to white unemployment has become even more disproportionate for males aged 18–19, 20–24, and 45–54 and for females aged 18–19, 20–24, 25–34, 35–44, and 45–54 (Bureau of Labor Statistics, 1983).

In summary, the data on educational attainment, economic status, and personal well-being show that, in absolute terms, blacks are better off now than they have been in previous years, and, at least in some areas, they have shown improvements relative to whites. The trends toward equality in the quality of life, however, are less consistent and less dramatic than are the trends toward egalitarianism in racial attitudes. Important differences still remain. A report from the National Urban League (Vaughn-Cooke, 1984) revealed that in 1983, 26.5% of all white men in the labor force were managers or professionals, whereas only 13.4% of black men in the labor force were employed in these occupational categories. Another analysis, which controlled for educational attainment, indicated that in 1980, black males who worked full-time and had a college education made about 10% less than the earnings of white males with a high school education. Furthermore, other findings by the Urban Institute and by the Center on

Budget and Policy Priorities (summarized by Cordes, 1985) indicate that between 1981 and 1983, the gap between whites and blacks has widened in some economic areas. The black poverty rate in 1983 was the highest in 15 years and almost three times the rate for whites. In addition, between 1981 and 1983, the average disposable income increased 4.1% for white families but *decreased* 2.1% for black families. The Urban Institute report adds, "the income gap between the wealthiest two-fifths of U.S. society (where blacks are few in number) and the poorest two-fifths (where most of the black population is found) is now wider than any time since 1947" (Cordes, 1985, p. 10). Given the trends in racial attitudes and the data on the quality of life, theoretical questions arise about the nature of prejudice, discrimination, and racism. In the next section, we examine trends in research on racial biases.

TRENDS IN RESEARCH ON PREJUDICE

Phyllis Katz (1976) summarized trends in research on prejudice up to 1967 by content analyzing the bibliography of the Harding et al. (1969) review article, "Prejudice and ethnic relations," that appeared in *The Handbook of Social Psychology*. We have updated her work by content analyzing Stephan's (1985) review chapter, "Intergroup relations," that appears in the most recent edition of the *Handbook*. The combined results of Katz's work and our analysis are presented in Table 3.

On the basis of her content analysis, Katz (1976) suggests that there are four discernible research periods. In the first research phase, which occurred during the late 1920s and the 1930s, work primarily involved attempts at measuring ethnic attitudes and prejudice. In the second period, the "theory decade" of the 1940s, there was a dramatic increase in theory development. Studies concerning attitude measurement were frequently related to tests of theories, and there was considerable effort to develop general conceptual frameworks for studying prejudice. In the third phase, which occurred in the 1950s, theory and measurement were still important, but an interest in attitude change also emerged. This interest was largely stimulated by developments in cognitive dissonance theory (Festinger, 1957) and other general theories of attitudes and attitude change. Katz states, "In some ways, the decade of the 1950s is a flowering one for race relations research . . . a tremendous sense of optimism and productivity is evident. Social scientists behaved during this period as if their work

TABLE 3   Trends in Research on Racial Attitudes: Content Analyses of the
Bibliographies of Review Articles by Harding et al. (1969) and by Stephan (1985)

	Decade					
	1920–1930	1931–1940	1941–1950	1951–1960	1961–1970	1971–1980
Theoretical articles	0	3	27	14	1	6
Direct attitude measurements	7	14	34	45	13	13
Indirect attitude measurements	0	3	3	8	4	7
Behavioral measures	0	3	4	19	10	22
Descriptions of prejudice	2	4	2	4	1	1
Experimental manipulations	0	7	4	9	8	9
Attitude change studies	0	3	4	14	4	23
Total number of citations	9	37	78	113	41	81

Note. Analysis of the years from 1920 to 1970 is from P. Katz (1976).

might actually make a difference" (p. 10). Katz notes, however, that
during the 1960s, interest in prejudice and discrimination waned.
During this research phase, there was a dramatic decline in the number of references on prejudice.

The decline in interest in research on prejudice and race that Katz
observed in the 1960s did not, however, carry over into the 1970s.
Jones (1983), who charted the number of articles on race and ethnicity
in seven mainstream social psychology journals, reports a significant
increase in research activity on these topics from the late 1960s (39
articles in 1968) to the mid-1970s (82 articles in 1973 and 80 in 1974).
Moreover, our analysis of Stephan's (1985) bibliography revealed an
increase in the number of studies in almost every one of Katz's content
categories (see Table 3). Compared to the 1960s, the 1970s were characterized by more theoretical articles, attitude measurement studies,
experimental studies, and behavioral assessments. Probably due to
political and public concerns about desegregation policies (e.g., busing), there was also unprecedented interest in attitude change. Jones
(1983), however, notes that research on race, culture, and ethnicity
showed a consistent decline from the mid-1970s to the end of the
decade (30 articles in 1979 and 44 in 1980).

The research on prejudice and discrimination that has been conducted in recent years seems to represent a major shift in emphasis.
The work in the 1950s and 1960s, including the Harding et al. (1969)
review article, emphasized a social problems approach. This orientation focuses on "the behavior of discrimination, the attitude of preju-

dice, and the consequences for the minority and majority groups of both of these" (Rose, 1964, p. 571). In contrast, much of the research since the late 1960s emphasizes general processes involved in prejudice rather than the social issues related to specific prejudices. For example, Stephan's (1985) review chapter in the current edition of *The Handbook of Social Psychology* has a much broader focus than the Harding et al. (1969) chapter in the previous edition. According to Stephan, *intergroup relations* concerns "relations between individuals as they are affected by group membership," (p. 599) and *prejudice* is defined simply as "negative attitudes toward social groups" (p. 600). Whereas 56% of the Harding et al. (1969) references deal directly with racial and ethnic issues, 39% of Stephan's (1985) sources are directly related to these topics.

Much of the impetus for this change in empirical focus in the study of bias and discrimination can be attributed to the influence of Tajfel. Tajfel (1969, 1970) outlined a cognitive approach to intergroup behavior that has had a significant impact on the field (see Ashmore & Del Boca, 1981). The study of prejudice is now typically embedded in the larger theoretical context of the role of cognitive processes in intergroup behavior. Thus, although the overall number of papers on prejudice per se is smaller now than in 1960, the number of articles on the cognitive processes that may contribute to prejudice has shown a dramatic increase. Ashmore and Del Boca's (1981) overview of research on cognitive processes and intergroup behavior demonstrates a geometrical progression in the number of articles published on stereotyping. There were no entries on stereotypes in *Psychological Abstracts* between 1927 and 1929; there were 15 in the 1930s; 29 in the 1940s; 74 in the 1950s; and 174 in the 1960s. In the first 7 years of the decade of the 1970s, there were 783 entries! Clearly, researchers have not lost all interest in studying prejudice. Rather, interest is being focused on general psychological processes that contribute to prejudice.

Emphasis on general processes involved in bias and concern for experimental rigor are of obvious value in the development of psychology as a science. It does not necessarily follow, however, that an approach that is *generally* good for the discipline is the only or the best approach for studying a *specific* issue. Jones (1983), in fact, argues that the current concern for methodology and the focus on the behavior of the individual have distracted researchers from many important issues that would enrich the study of race. Jones comments about the impact of the recent developments in social psychology:

The rising emphasis on methodology inadvertently discouraged a sophisticated analysis of race-related issues. The experimental method, combined with enthusiasm for quantification and causal hypotheses, made it desirable to assign subjects randomly to experimental treatment and control groups. Since it is impossible to assign subjects randomly to races, race was forced to join other culture- and social system-related variables on social psychology's back burner. Moreover, the mass movement into university social psychology laboratories encouraged an emphasis on *molecular* levels of analysis. Modern equivalents of concepts such as group mind and *Volkgeist* rarely appeared in accounts of social behavior once the experiment took center stage. Instead, analogies between the individual mind and computers dominated the field. (p. 122)

Because race is confounded with ethnicity, culture, and social class and cannot readily be experimentally manipulated, Jones suggests that it is a "second-class" variable in contemporary social psychology. In the next section, we review traditional and emerging approaches that focus on both general processes and special forces in racial prejudice and discrimination.

CONCEPTUAL APPROACHES TO PREJUDICE

Researchers have proposed several ways to organize the different approaches to understanding racial prejudice and racism. Allport (1954, 1958), for example, identifies six approaches: the (1) historical approach, (2) sociocultural approach, (3) situational approach, (4) personality structure and dynamics approach, (5) phenomenological approach, and (6) stimulus–object approach. The basic assumption of the *historical approach* is that contemporary prejudice has its roots in slavery, carpetbagging, and failures during the reconstruction period following the Civil War. It is hypothesized that prejudice typically has the goal of allowing the exploitation of blacks. In the *sociocultural approach,* the emphasis is on the total social and cultural context within which prejudiced attitudes develop, are supported and reinforced, and are transmitted. The focus of the *situational approach* is immediate social forces; history is only relevant in how it shapes the current context. According to this perspective, types of intergroup contact (e.g., cooperation or competition) critically affect prejudice and discrimination. The *personality structure and dynamics approach* is represented by the classic work of Adorno, Frenkel-Brunswik, Levinson, and Sanford (1950) on the authoritarian personality. In their psychodynamic model, antecedent child-rearing practices set in motion underlying intrapsychic processes and create personality dispositions that result in ethnocentrism and specific prejudices. According to Allport (1954), the basic theme in the *phenomenological approach* is that "a person's conduct proceeds immediately from his view of the situation confronting him. His response to the world conforms to his definition of the world" (p. 216). Historical, cultural, social, personality, and immediate contextual forces converge to influence a person's experience, perceptions, and hypotheses, and thus together they shape attitudes and behavior. The emphasis in the *stimulus–object approach* is on earned reputation. Actual differences between groups provide the basis for dislike, discrimination, and hostility.

Although many researchers (e.g., Jones, 1972) still subscribe to Allport's general framework of the causes of prejudice, cognitive processes involved in prejudice currently receive greater attention. Allport argued that stereotypes are not an integral part of prejudice and are essentially a *consequence* of prejudice and discrimination rather than a fundamental *cause* of bias. He proposed that stereotypes develop in order to rationalize or justify one's prejudice and discriminatory acts. Allport (1954) wrote that stereotypes are "primarily rationalizers. They adapt to the prevailing temper of prejudice or the needs of the situation. While it does no harm (and may do some good) to combat them in schools and colleges, and to reduce them in mass media of communication, it must not be thought of that this attack alone will eradicate the roots of prejudice" (p. 204). In contrast, stereotypes now occupy a central role in many contemporary theorists' explanations of prejudice and discrimination (see Hamilton, 1981; Stephan, 1985).

Ashmore and Del Boca (1976), like Allport, organize theories of prejudice according to the level of analysis. Specifically, Ashmore and Del Boca categorize the work into two levels: societal-level and individual-level explanations. *Societal-level* approaches focus on how prejudice is shaped by the nature of the relationship between groups. *Individual-level* approaches emphasize how an individual living in a particular culture acquires and manifests prejudice.

Societal-level explanations generally suggest that prejudice and racism develop and are maintained for the purpose of exploiting minority groups or because of the nature of interaction between groups. Exploitation theories focus on economic and status self-interest factors among white workers (van den Berghe, 1967), control and self-interest motives of white elite managers or owners (Cox, 1948, 1959), and attempts by the majority white society to "colonize" the black community (Carmichael & Hamilton, 1967; Hechter, 1975). Theories that explain prejudice on the basis of the functional nature of intergroup interaction propose that positive intergroup interdependence (e.g., cooperation) promotes positive attitudes, whereas negative interactions (e.g., competition) create negative attitudes (Boulding, 1962; Sherif, Harvey, White, Hood, & Sherif, 1961). Ashmore and Del Boca conclude, "This generalization, particularly that aspect dealing with the effects of negative interdependence, has been supported by a large body of historical, sociological–anthropological, and psychological research . . . and consequently is the most solid 'principle' of the psychology of prejudice" (pp. 75–76).

Individual-level approaches explain prejudice in terms of basic intrapersonal or interpersonal factors. Intrapersonal factors involve personality, cognitive, and motivational processes. In terms of personality, much of the work is based on a Freudian psychoanalytic model. Specifically, Ashmore and Del Boca (1976) identify three major "symptom theories of prejudice" that assume prejudice is an indicator of an underlying intrapsychic conflict. These theories involve (1) projection (Jordan, 1968), (2) displacement (Allport & Kramer, 1946), and (3) the authoritarian personality (Adorno et al., 1950). In a nonpsychoanalytic model, Ehrlich (1973) has proposed that a negative self-concept predisposes an individual to become prejudiced. In terms of cognitive processes, the act of simply categorizing people into groups can form the basis for bias and discrimination (Brewer, 1979; Tajfel, 1970). With respect to motivation, cognitive consistency needs can contribute to prejudice. Rokeach and his colleagues (e.g., Rokeach & Mezei, 1966) propose that because of perceived group differences (based on racial characteristics), people assume that members of outgroups hold dissimilar attitudes compared to their own. This assumed belief dissimilarity, in turn, leads to negative attitudes.

The interpersonal factors in prejudice that Ashmore and Del Boca identify are socialization, conformity, and attribution processes. According to the socialization perspective, prejudice is acquired in the same manner as are other aspects of culture. Consequently, although there are large differences in prejudices across cultures, there are relatively consistent patterns of prejudice across time within a culture (Rose & Rose, 1965). Pettigrew (1958), in studies of attitudes in South Africa and the United States, provides evidence of the role that norms play in creating and maintaining prejudice. The attribution explanation (Ashmore & McConahay, 1975) suggests that, because humans have a need to explain the causes of behavior and tend to make dispositional attributions for others' behaviors, people tend to attribute the relatively low economic and social status of blacks to personality characteristics such as laziness or lack of ability.

Chesler (1976) uses a classification scheme for theories of racism that is quite different than the level-of-analysis frameworks used by Allport and by Ashmore and Del Boca. He organizes theories of prejudice and racism in terms of their position along two basic dimensions: (1) victim–system control, and (2) embeddedness. The concept of *victim–system control* refers to the degree to which responsibility for one's social position is assigned to internal or external causes. In relating this dimension to Ryan's (1971) work, *Blaming the Victim*, Chesler (1976) notes that Ryan "documents a number of theories of social organization that seem to blame relatively powerless victims of social injustice for creating their own problems" (p. 24). Theories that explain differences in economic well-being on the basis of a minority group's family or cultural pathology are strongly emphasizing victim control. The concept of *embeddedness* refers to the extent to which a theory emphasizes that racism is an isolated, peripheral, or abnormal element of society (low embeddedness) or is an integral part of the existing social system (high embeddedness). Theories of institutional racism, for example, are high in their degree of embeddedness.

Although Chesler (1976) presents victim–system control and embeddedness as theoretically independent dimensions, within various theoretical understandings of racism they are correlated. Theories that tend to be high in the degree of victim control (vs. system control) tend to be low in the degree of embeddedness. Theories of racism that emphasize characteristics of blacks such as an unwillingness to delay gratification (Riessman, 1962) or family psychopathology (Parsons, 1965), even though they do not assume genetic causes, are high in victim control and low in embeddedness. In the moderate–moderate range of victim–system control and embeddedness are theories that emphasize economic and status competition (van der Berghe, 1967) and cultural and normative theories (Kovel, 1970). Theories that are high in embeddedness and low in victim control (i.e., high in system control) emphasize internal colonization involving economic exploitation, political control, and a self-justifying ideology (Carmichael & Hamilton, 1967). In the next section, we review the specific themes and principles that are discussed within the remaining 10 chapters of this book.

ORGANIZATION OF THE BOOK
AND CHAPTER OVERVIEWS

This book examines the causes and consequences of contemporary forms of prejudice, discrimination, and racism. The emphasis is pri-

marily on the processes that contribute to the development and maintenance of prejudice at the individual level, which we assert contributes partially to the operation and tolerance of racism at the
institutional level. In terms of Allport's framework, the chapters represent sociocultural, personality, situational, and phenomenological approaches; in Ashmore and Del Boca's terms, they reflect intrapersonal
and interpersonal processes. All of the chapters share the common
theme that prejudice is highly embedded in individual and social
processes: Contemporary prejudice and racism seem to be rooted in
cultural norms and belief systems (see Chapters 2, 3, and 4) and develop from fundamental biases in the way people process information
(see Chapters 5, 6, and 7). Thus, contemporary forms of racial prejudice typically have a pervasive, but often unrecognized, influence on
the implementation of social policies (Chapter 8), the legal process
(Chapter 9), and society in general (Chapter 10), and they are difficult
to eradicate (Chapter 11).

One approach to studying prejudice that is represented in this book
is the motivational perspective. Basically, the motivational approach
assumes that prejudice originates and is perpetuated in order to
achieve desired goals (e.g., control of resources) or to satisfy needs, or
it occurs as a result of negative feelings or beliefs acquired through
socialization. The motivational approach encompasses personality
theories that emphasize the role of authoritarian personality structure
(Adorno et al., 1950) or negative self-concept (Ehrlich, 1973) and
downward comparison (Wills, 1981), interpersonal theories that focus
on status threat (Harding et al., 1969), intergroup theory that involves
striving for positive identity (Tajfel & Turner, 1979), and societal-
level explanations that concern economic or political exploitation
(Cox, 1948) or internal colonization (Hechter, 1975). In the present
volume, Chapter 2 on ambivalence theory, Chapter 3 on aversive racism, and Chapter 4 on modern racism emphasize the importance of
value structure and self-image and thus are motivational theories.

In Chapter 2, Irwin Katz, Joyce Wackenhut, and Glen Hass propose
that whites' racial attitudes generally have become more complex and
differentiated, containing both positive and negative components.
This chapter is based on Katz's previous work (see Katz, 1981) that
posits that racial ambivalence, which is caused by the simultaneous
existence of both positive and negative feelings toward blacks, "creates in the person a high vulnerability to emotional tension in situations of contact with the attitudinal object" (Katz, 1981, p. 25). From a
Freudian perspective (Freud 1923/1961), the conflict between positive and negative sentiments can be resolved by reactive displace-

ment of *cathexis,* energy from one source combining with energy from
the other source. Thus, depending on the nature of the contact, people
who experience ambivalence are likely to react more positively or
more negatively than are people who do not have conflicting feelings.
In this chapter, Katz, Wackenhut, and Hass review evidence of both
problack and antiblack attitudes, describe the relationship between
racial attitudes and general values, present research on ambivalence
and behavior, and summarize work in progress involving individual
differences in ambivalence.

In Chapter 3, Samuel Gaertner and John Dovidio use the term *aver-*
sive racism (also see Kovel, 1970) to describe the type of racial attitude that characterizes many white Americans who possess strong
egalitarian values. Specifically, Gaertner and Dovidio propose that
aversive racism represents a particular type of ambivalence in which
the conflict is between feelings and beliefs associated with an egalitarian value system and unacknowledged negative feelings and beliefs concerning blacks. These authors are not as convinced as are Katz
and his colleagues of the widespread existence among whites of genuinely positive affect toward blacks which are independent of egalitarian values. Aversive racists are very concerned about their nonprejudiced self-images; they are strongly motivated in interracial contexts
to avoid acting in recognizably unfavorable or inappropriate ways.
The negative component of the racial attitude, however, is often manifested in subtle and rationalizable ways. In support of this framework,
Gaertner and Dovidio report evidence that when norms prescribing
appropriate behavior are clear, whites do not exhibit bias against
blacks; but, when norms are ambiguous or conflicting, whites do discriminate. In addition, even when norms are clear, whites continue,
probably unwittingly, to be sensitive to apparently nonracial factors
that would allow them to discriminate against blacks but to attribute
their behavior to factors other than race. Thus, aversive racists discriminate against blacks, but they do so in ways that do not threaten or
challenge their nonprejudiced self-images.

Chapter 4 by John McConahay focuses on modern racism. The theory of modern racism builds upon McConahay's earlier work on symbolic racism (McConahay & Hough, 1976) and is related to attempts to
develop a measurement instrument for racial attitudes that could explain or predict voting behavior (Kinder & Sears, 1981), community
conflict (McConahay, 1982), opposition to busing as a means of
achieving integration (Sears & Allen, 1984), and jury behavior (Mc-
Conahay, Mullin, & Frederick, 1977). McConahay distinguishes modern racism from *old-fashioned racism,* which involves traditional,

stereotypic beliefs about black intelligence, industry, and honesty; support for segregation; and acceptance of open discrimination. The basic tenets of modern racism are that racism is bad, discrimination is a thing of the past, blacks are making unfair demands, and blacks are currently receiving more attention and resources than they deserve. In his chapter, McConahay outlines modern racism theory, reviews the development of the Modern Racism and Old-Fashioned Racism Scales, shows that the Modern Racism Scale is a less reactive measure of prejudice than the Old-Fashioned Racism Scale, and demonstrates the validity of the Modern Racism Scale for predicting simulated hiring decisions.

Although ambivalence, aversive racism, and modern racism theories share assumptions about the complex and conflicted nature of the contemporary racial attitudes of whites, there are also some basic differences in these motivational approaches. One fundamental difference concerns how the nonnegative component of the racial attitude is conceptualized. Katz, Wackenhut, and Hass describe it as a problack feeling, reflecting sympathy and favorable stereotypes; but, McConahay considers it to be a rejection of overtly racist beliefs, and Gaertner and Dovidio suggest that aversive racists sincerely embrace egalitarian ideals. How distinct the conceptualizations of the nonnegative component actually are, however, is not clear. The problack scale used by Katz and his colleagues contains several items concerning egalitarianism and correlates highly with an egalitarian scale. Ambivalence theory also differs from modern racism and aversive racism theories in the extent to which people acknowledge their negative feelings toward blacks. In previous work (e.g., Katz, Glass, & Cohen, 1973), ambivalent people scored high on prejudice scales and thus appeared to be aware of their negative racial attitudes. Gaertner and Dovidio, in contrast, believe that, because aversive racists do not recognize their negative racial feelings, aversive racists score low on prejudice inventories. McConahay proposes that because modern racism involves the rejection of traditional racist beliefs and the displacement of antiblack feelings onto more abstract social and political issues, modern racists are also relatively unaware of their racist attitudes. Scores on McConahay's Modern Racism Scale, however, are positively correlated with scores on the Old-Fashioned Racism Scale.

Although both McConahay's modern racism approach and Gaertner and Dovidio's aversive racism perspective propose that contemporary forms of racism are more subtle and indirect than traditional forms, these approaches developed with emphases on two different types of people. They therefore make different assumptions about underlying causes. In particular, Gaertner and Dovidio's work on aversive racism originated from observations of how liberals behaved in interracial situations. In Gaertner's (1973) wrong-number telephone experiment, Conservative party members exhibited a traditional form of discrimination against blacks, whereas Liberal party members showed a more subtle type of bias. Gaertner and Dovidio's subsequent research has examined a relatively liberal segment of the population: college students attending northern universities. They thus believe that aversive racism reflects the ambivalence of political *liberals*. McConahay's theory of modern racism developed from his work on symbolic racism. The focus of symbolic racism was on *conservatives*. Specifically, Mc-Conahay and Hough (1976) proposed that "symbolic racism rests upon anti-black socialization and conservative political and value socialization" (p. 23). In two studies reported by McConahay and Hough (1976), symbolic racism was positively correlated with political conservatism and religious conventionalism. Therefore, at least as initially formulated, symbolic racism represented subtle prejudice originating from the political right, whereas aversive racism reflected a type of racial bias of people who endorse the ideology of the political left.

In contrast to the motivational frameworks represented by ambivalence, aversive racism, and modern racism theories, a cognitive perspective to understanding prejudice and racism is shared by Chapters 5, 6, and 7. This cognitive approach (Hamilton, 1981; Stephan, 1985) emphasizes the roles of categorization and biases in information processing involved in stereotyping and intergroup interaction. Information processing approaches focus on the role of mental representations in encoding, storing, and retrieving information about persons and social events; categorization approaches emphasize the perceptual and affective consequences of simply categorizing people into social groups (Brewer & Kramer, 1985). Hamilton (1979; see also Chapter 5 in this volume) proposes that categorization and cognitive biases result *in* stereotypes and that intergroup biases result *from* stereotypic conceptions. Considerable evidence (see Brewer, 1979; Stephan, 1985) indicates that the mere categorization of persons into ingroup and outgroup membership is sufficient to affect interpersonal perception and behavior. There is a strong bias favoring ingroup members at the expense of outgroup members in the allocation of rewards (Allen & Wilder, 1975; Billig & Tajfel, 1973). People also attribute greater belief similarity (Allen & Wilder, 1979) and more favorable characteristics (Doise, Csepeli, Dann, Gouge, Larsen, & Ostell, 1972) to ingroup than to outgroup members. Another important result of the categorization process is that within-group differentiations, particularly among outgroup members, are more difficult to make than between-group discriminations (Taylor, Fiske, Etcoff, & Ruderman, 1978). Consequently, people tend to see members of the outgroup as similar to one another and as different than themselves. Furthermore, attention to salient or distinctive features (e.g., race) facilitates categorization (Taylor & Fiske, 1978) and leads to extreme evaluations (Linville & Jones, 1980; McArthur & Soloman, 1978). According to the cognitive perspective, this categorization process and the differential perceptions that accompany it form the bases of racial prejudice.

Biases that result from stereotypic conceptions also contribute to racial prejudice. Hamilton (1979) suggests that when an observer encodes information about ambiguous stimuli, stereotype schemas may "lead a perceiver to go beyond that information in certain specifiable ways . . . and may result in the perceiver 'seeing' certain things which are not part of the stimulus configuration" (p. 68). Duncan (1976), for example, found that witnesses to the same event perceived greater aggressive intent on the part of black actors than white actors. Rothbart, Evans, and Fulero (1979) also found that people tend to remember information that is consistent with their stereotypes better than information that contradicts their stereotypes. Thus stereotypes, operating as cognitive schemas, systematically influence information encoding, processing, and retrieval. Furthermore, these biases, which generally support the original stereotype, tend to perpetuate prejudice (Snyder, 1981). In the present volume, Chapter 5 reviews research on the cognitive approach to intergroup behavior, Chapter 6 examines the differential complexity of schemas concerning ingroup and outgroup members, and Chapter 7 investigates factors influencing the categorization process.

David Hamilton and Tina Trolier, in Chapter 5, provide a thorough overview of the cognitive approach to studying stereotypes and stereotyping. They consider why stereotypes develop, how cognitive mechanisms contribute to the development of stereotypes, and how cognitive processes help perpetuate stereotypic beliefs. First, Hamilton and Trolier emphasize the role of categorization in the development of stereotypes. Categorizing people into groups affects interpersonal perception, information processing, and retention of information. Second, the authors describe how cognitive mechanisms "lay the foundation for the development of stereotypic belief systems." Third, Hamilton and Trolier consider the nature of social categories and how the beliefs that compose stereotypes are represented in memory. Specifically, they examine assumptions underlying traditional trait measures and more recent reaction-time measures borrowed from cognitive psychology (relating, for example, to prototype models). Fourth, Hamilton and Trolier discuss the cognitive consequences of stereotypes: Activation of a stereotype influences what stimulus information people attend to, how that information is interpreted, and what information will be retrieved from memory. How these expectancies translate into behavior and result in a self-fulfilling prophecy is also reviewed. The chapter concludes with discussions of how the cognitive orientation relates to motivational and sociocultural approaches and how it fits with recent theoretical developments in intergroup behavior.

In Chapter 6, Patricia Linville, Peter Salovey, and Gregory Fischer propose that category differentiation is a critical feature in stereotyping. Category differentiation refers to the extent to which people perceive various types within a category, view these types as being equally likely, and see many distinctions among category members. The authors' basic hypothesis is that "greater category familiarity leads to greater category differentiation." Because people are more familiar with members of their own group than with members of other groups, it is predicted that perceivers are more differentiated in their thinking about ingroups than about outgroups – a prediction commonly known as the *outgroup homogeneity hypothesis*. Linville, Salovey, and Fischer review previous research on the outgroup homogeneity hypothesis and discuss the consequences of relatively undifferentiated thinking about outgroups. White people, for example, are more polarized in their evaluations of blacks than of whites (Linville & Jones, 1980). The authors then introduce a measure of variability and a new index of differentiation and empirically demonstrate, using both age and nationality as social categories, the outgroup homogeneity effect.[2] A third experiment, which involved students' perceptions of other members of their psychology class, directly supported the prediction that greater familiarity leads to greater differentiation.

In Chapter 7, Norman Miller and Marilynn Brewer examine the effects of categorization on perceptions of ingroup and outgroup members. Miller and Brewer outline three different theoretical approaches to understanding intergroup conflict and prejudice. In the first model, a functionalist approach, intergroup competition is viewed as a source of prejudice, and intergroup cooperation is viewed as the key to re-

---

[2] Using a procedure similar to that used by Linville, Salovey, and Fischer, we found that white subjects perceived blacks as more homogeneous than whites.

ducing intergroup conflict. The second model is similar to the first, except that it hypothesizes that any type of positive intergroup interaction, not just cooperation, will be effective in reducing prejudice. In the third model, the approach adopted by Miller and Brewer (also see Brewer & Miller, 1984), "perceptual processes are given greater weight and are viewed as antecedents to effects observed in cognitive, emotional, and behavioral systems" (p. 6). According to this model, changing category-based, undifferentiated responding (actions based only on the crude perception of category membership) to personalized, individuated responding (behavior based on the perception that a person is unique and complex) is a necessary step for reducing prejudice. Miller and Brewer report two experiments, which were conducted within this framework, that examine how the salience of ingroup–outgroup boundaries influences people's perceptions of ingroup and outgroup members. One study replicates Wilder's (1978) finding that the presence of a dissenter in an outgroup eliminates ingroup favoritism, but it demonstrates that this effect occurs only when the dissenter is highly likeable or of neutral likeability. The authors assert that the presence of a dissenting member alters affective responses to the outgroup but that these responses occur in an undifferentiated, category-based manner. The second study reported in this chapter shows that increases in the salience of intergroup conflict create perceptions of greater similarity among ingroup members. Miller and Brewer conclude that the two experiments that they report in this chapter support their "general view that category boundaries suppress interpersonal differentiation and limit the generalizability of interventions aimed at individuating group members."

The cognitive views presented in Chapters 5, 6, and 7 of this book share the theme that social categorization fundamentally affects the way people encode, process, and retrieve information about ingroup and outgroup members. Even in minimal intergroup situations, social categorization produces systematic biases: People show more positive attitudes toward ingroup than outgroup members; they also perceive the membership of the outgroup as more homogeneous than the membership of the ingroup. Linville, Salovey, and Fischer (Chapter 6) and Miller and Brewer (Chapter 7) propose that the perception of outgroup homogeneity is a central element in stereotyping and prejudice. Although these authors seem to agree that individuated or differentiated responses to outgroup members are important for eliminating intergroup conflict, their approaches have different implications for how this can be accomplished. Linville and her colleagues find support for their basic hypothesis that greater experience produces greater differentiation. Miller and Brewer's work, however, suggests a critical qualification. Familiarity with an outgroup should lead to greater differentiation (and hence reduce stereotyping and prejudice) primarily when these experiences involve personalized or individuated responding, and not when they involve category-based responding. The experiment reported by Linville, Salovey, and Fischer does not directly address this issue. Subjects in this study showed greater differentiation as they had more experience with other class members. It remains an empirical question whether this effect would occur toward blacks or other distinguishable minority groups, for whom the salience of physical characteristics and the effects of traditional socialization would likely produce category-based thinking even across several interactions.

It is important to note that prejudice, discrimination, and racism are not the result of cognitive *or* motivational factors. Rather, they are the manifestations of cognitive, motivational, *and* sociocultural forces operating often in concert with one another. For example, as Hamilton and Trolier note in their chapter, Tajfel's most recent formulation of intergroup behavior incorporates both cognitive and motivational factors (Tajfel, 1982; Tajfel & Turner, 1979). Tajfel and Turner (1979) propose that social categorization initiates a social comparison process. Because people desire positive self-esteem, in terms of both their personal and group identity, there is a tendency to seek positive distinctiveness for the ingroup over the outgroup. This need for positive distinctiveness then leads to intergroup competition and motivates prejudice and intergroup discrimination. In support of this framework, Turner (1981) summarizes research on categorization and bias and concludes that it is

difficult to explain discrimination of ingroup–outgroup divisions solely in terms of cognitive processes; motivational factors need to be superimposed (see Brewer, 1979; Turner, 1975). The simplest solution is to assume that categorization and the social comparison process are complementary. There are many possible complexities in such complementarity, but we shall do no more than suggest that the former is the necessary and the latter is the sufficient condition for competitive intergroup differentiation . . . . The categorization process produces the perceptual accentuation of intragroup similarities and intergroup differences and thus makes salient or perceptually prominent the criterial or relevant aspects of ingroup or outgroup membership. In this way it selects the specific dimensions for self-evaluation and social comparison in the given setting. It also ensures that intergroup comparisons focus on perceptual discontinuities between ingroup and outgroup members so that positive differences (distinctiveness) and not similarities contribute to self-esteem. The social comparison process transforms simple perceptual or cognitive discriminations into differential actions favouring the ingroup over the outgroup. (p. 82)

Thus, according to this *social identity principle,* social categorization causes intergroup discrimination through motivations for positive esteem. Furthermore, sociocultural and racial factors can mediate intergroup social comparison. To the extent that these forces reduce an individual's social mobility, they will increase a person's social identity and set in motion intergroup rather than interpersonal processes (Tajfel & Turner, 1979).

Whereas Chapters 2 through 7 outline motivational and cognitive factors that contribute to racism at the individual level, Chapters 8, 9, and 10 consider the consequences of prejudice, discrimination, and racism on society in general and blacks in particular. Given the cognitive processes that provide a foundation for bias, the motivational forces that perpetuate racism even among well-intentioned people, and antiblack traditions that have shaped contemporary society, we believe that racism is pervasive and reaches into even the most fundamental social institutions. Chapter 8 discusses racial desegregation in the schools; Chapter 9 examines racial attitudes in the courtroom; and Chapter 10 reviews the effects of racism on the personal, social, and economic well-being of blacks.

In Chapter 8, Janet Schofield examines the effects of the colorblind perspective (Rist, 1974), a belief system that emphasizes that racial group membership should be irrelevant to the ways in which people are treated. The basis of this chapter is a 4-year ethnographic study of peer relations in a desegregated school. The adoption of the colorblind perspective by both teachers and students at the school is evident in their behavior. People rarely acknowledged, and often denied, that they noticed the race of an individual; race was a taboo subject; and emphasis was on interpersonal, not intergroup, relations in the social life at the school. Schofield observes that the colorblind perspective made initial interracial contacts smoother and more harmonious. It also reduced the potential for overt interracial conflict by reducing the likelihood that behaviors (e.g., disciplinary actions) would be attributed to racist motivations. Although Schofield notes that the colorblind perspective is "understandable and, from a social policy standpoint, it seems laudable," it has several, typically unrecognized, negative consequences. First, the colorblind perspective does not necessarily reflect the reality of a situation: Schofield's observations and experiments demonstrated that race did significantly affect social interactions. Second, it ignores the reality of subjective culture. Third, it prevents capitalizing on personal and cultural diver-

sity. Thus, although the colorblind perspective has short-term benefits, it may have long-term consequences that may inhibit the development of genuinely positive interracial relations.

Chapter 9 by Stephanie Nickerson, Clara Mayo, and Althea Smith
relates research on racism with the study of legal processes in the
courtroom. First, the authors review the literature on racial bias in
verdicts and sentencing. Both simulated juror experiments (typically
from social psychology laboratories) and archival research (from actual
court records) are reported. Second, Nickerson, Mayo, and Smith apply social psychological research to procedures used in the selection
of jurors. They note, for example, that the nature of the questions
asked, the status of the judge, and the methods used (e.g., questioning
people in large groups) may reduce the likelihood that racial prejudice is exposed. Third, the authors present a study that examines the
underlying dimensions determining the types of questions allowed or
disallowed by the court in selecting jurors. In particular, questions
about prospective juror's attitudes toward the law and criminal acts
were more likely to be allowed in trials involving black defendants
than were questions asking about personal experiences with black
people. In their conclusion, the authors emphasize the importance of
a reciprocal interchange in which social psychological knowledge is
applied in the courtroom and information obtained by studying legal
procedures is used to extend our understanding of racial attitudes.

In Chapter 10, James Jones examines the relationship between race
and health, education, crime, and income in the United States. He
shows that although blacks have made some gains relative to whites,
particularly in terms of education, blacks are still disadvantaged and,
in health and economic areas, have lost some ground relative to
whites. Having demonstrated that racial differences exist, Jones then
considers approaches and models that attempt to account for these
data. One approach places responsibility on the majority group and
the system, whereas another model attributes cause to characteristics
of the victims. Jones suggests that in addition to individual-level influences in racism the effects of culture and social power must be considered. In particular, he argues that racism persists, in part, because race
is rarely seen in the context of culture. Racial issues, however, are
often actually cultural issues involving conflict between Euro-American and Afro-American perspectives. He presents the concept of
TRIOS, an acronym representing five basic aspects of cultural orientation on which blacks and whites may differ. These five aspects are
time, rhythm, improvisation, oral expression, and spirituality. Jones
observes, "With the addition of the power of definition and resources,

1. HISTORICAL TRENDS AND CONTEMPORARY APPROACHES

the Afro-American perspective will necessarily lose out." He concludes by proposing that an approach toward the amelioration of racism should involve recognizing ethnic diversity and pluralism, acknowledging black Americans as an ethnic group, and learning ways to incorporate diversity as a strength in the concept of society.

Chapters 8, 9, and 10, which focus on applied issues, demonstrate the effects of individual, institutional, and cultural racism in situations of consequence to blacks and whites. These chapters also provide illustrations of principles discussed in previous chapters. For example, Schofield's work that documents the effects of the colorblind perspective in a desegregated school reflects both motivational and cognitive factors. In essence, the colorblind perspective is rooted in the desire to appear, and probably actually to be, egalitarian. The colorblind perspective can also be seen as an attempt to promote integration by replacing category-based reponding with personalized responding. Nickerson, Mayo, and Smith's chapter shows how social pressures to appear nonprejudiced cannot ensure a legal system without racial biases. Subtle prejudices among jurors and judges exist, and racial stereotypes influence legal decisions. In addition, the applied work in Chapters 8, 9, and 10 raise important issues that go beyond those considered in previous chapters. Schofield considers the potential negative effects that can result from a system in which an appreciation of cultural diversity is sacrificed by focusing only on interpersonal relations and ignoring group identity. Nickerson, Mayo, and Smith suggest a new dimension of racial attitudes that relates to legal issues. Finally, Jones emphasizes that cultural issues and social, political, and economic power must be considered in any attempt to understand the nature of contemporary prejudice, discrimination, and racism in the United States.

In Chapter 11, Samuel Gaertner and John Dovidio review the causes and consequences of prejudice, discrimination, and racism. On the basis of the analyses presented in the preceding 10 chapters, they discuss reasons for both pessimism and optimism about the prospects for racial equality. Gaertner and Dovidio note that because racism is so embedded in cognitive processes, belief structures, affective responses, and social institutions, it is very difficult to combat. The authors observe, however, that significant progress toward an egalitarian society has been made over the past few decades, and the authors conclude their chapter by outlining strategies for reducing intergroup tensions and facilitating positive interactions that could lead to more harmonious race relations.

REFERENCES

Adorno, T. W., Frenkel-Brunswik, E., Levinson, D. J., & Sanford, R. N. (1950). *The authoritarian personality.* New York: Harper.

Allen, V. L., & Wilder, D. A. (1975). Categorization, belief similarity, and intergroup discrimination. *Journal of Personality and Social Psychology, 32,* 971–997.

Allen, V. L., & Wilder, D. A. (1979). Group categorization and attribution of belief similarity. *Small Group Behavior, 10,* 73–80.

Allport, G. W. (1954). *The nature of prejudice.* Reading, MA: Addison-Wesley.

Allport, G. W. (1958) *The nature of prejudice.* New York: Doubleday-Anchor.

Allport, G. W., & Kramer, B. M. (1946). Some roots of prejudice. *Journal of Psychology, 22,* 9–39.

Ashmore, R. D. (1970). Prejudice: Causes and cures. In B. E. Collins (Ed.), *Social psychology: Social influence, attitude charge, group processes, and prejudice* (pp. 245–339). Reading, MA: Addison-Wesley.

Ashmore, R. D., & Del Boca, F. K. (1976). Psychological approaches to understanding intergroup conflicts. In P. A. Katz (Ed.), *Towards the elimination of racism* (pp. 73–123). New York: Pergamon.

Ashmore, R. D., & Del Boca, F. K. (1981). Conceptual approaches to stereotypes and stereotyping. In D. L. Hamilton (Ed.), *Cognitive processes in stereotyping and intergroup behavior.* Hillsdale, NJ: Erlbaum.

Ashmore, R. D., & McConahay, J. B. (1975). *Psychology and American's urban dilemmas.* New York: McGraw-Hill.

Billig, M., & Tajfel, H. (1973). Social categorization and similarity in intergroup behavior. *European Journal of Social Psychology, 3,* 27–52.

Boulding, K. E. (1962). *Conflict and defense: A general theory.* New York: Harper.

Brewer, M. B. (1979). In-group bias in the minimal intergroup situation: A cognitive-motivational analysis. *Psychological Bulletin, 86,* 307–324.

Brewer, M. B., & Kramer, R. M. (1985). The psychology of intergroup attitudes and behavior. *Annual Review of Psychology, 36,* 219–243.

Brewer, M. B., & Miller, N. (1984). Beyond the contact hypothesis: Theoretical perspectives on desegregation. In M. B. Brewer & N. Miller (Eds.) *Groups in contact: The psychology of desegregation* (pp. 281–302). New York: Academic Press.

Brigham, J. C. (1971). Ethnic stereotypes. *Psychological Bulletin, 76,* 15–33.

Brown v. Board of Education (1954). 347 U. S. 483.

Bureau of Labor Statistics (1983). *Employment and earnings.*

Campbell, A. (1971). *White attitudes toward black people.* Ann Arbor, MI: Institute for Social Research.

Carmichael, S., & Hamilton, C. (1967). *Black power.* New York: Vintage Books.

Chesler, M. A. (1976). Contemporary sociological theories of racism. In P. A. Katz (Ed.), *Towards the elimination of racism* (pp. 21–71). New York: Pergamon.

Colfax, D., & Sternberg, S. (1972). The perpetuation of racial stereotypes: Blacks in mass circulation magazine advertisements. *Public Opinion Quarterly, 36,* 8–18.

Cordes, C. (1985). At risk in America. *APA Monitor, 16,* 10–12, 27.

Cox, K. (1969–1970). Changes in stereotyping of Negroes and whites in magazine advertisements. *Public Opinion Quarterly, 33,* 603–606.

Cox, O. C. (1948). *Caste, class and race: A study in social dynamics.* New York: Doubleday.

Cox, O. (1959). *Caste, class and race.* New York: Monthly Review Press.

Doise, W., Csepeli, G., Dann, H., Gouge, C., Larsen, K., & Ostell, A. (1972). An experimental investigation into the formation of intergroup representations. *European Journal of Social Psychology, 2,* 202–204.

Dominick, S., & Greenberg, B. (1970). Three seasons of blacks on television. *Journal of Advertising Research, 10,* 21–37.

Duncan, B. L. (1976). Differential social perception and attribution of intergroup violence: Testing the lower limits of stereotyping of blacks. *Journal of Personality and Social Psychology, 34,* 590–598.

Dutton, D. G., & Lake, R. (1973). Threat of own prejudice and reverse discrimination in interracial behavior. *Journal of Personality and Social Psychology, 28,* 94–100.

Ehrlich, H. J. (1973). *The social psychology of prejudice.* New York: Wiley.

Erskine, H. (1967a). The polls: Negro housing. *Public Opinion Quarterly, 31,* 655–677.

Erskine, H. (1967b). The polls: Demonstrations and race riots. *Public Opionion Quarterly, 31,* 655–677.

Erskine, H. (1968a). The polls: Negro unemployment. *Public Opinion Quarterly, 32,* 132–153.

Erskine, H. (1968b). The polls: World opinion of U.S. racial problems. *Public Opinion Quarterly, 32,* 299–312.

Erskine, H. (1968c). The polls: The speed of racial integration. *Public Opinion Quarterly, 32,* 513–524.

Erskine, H. (1968d). The polls: Recent opinion on racial problems. *Public Opinion Quarterly, 32,* 696–703.

Erskine, H. (1969a). The polls: Negro philosophies of life. *Public Opinion Quarterly, 33,* 147–158.

Erskine, H. (1969b). The polls: Negro finances. *Public Opinion Quarterly, 33,* 272–282.A

Feagin, J. R., & Feagin, L. B. (1978). *Discrimination American style: Institutional racism and sexism.* Englewood Cliffs, NJ: Prentice-Hall.

Festinger, L. (1957). *A theory of cognitive dissonance.* New York: Row, Peterson.

Freud, S. (1923/1961) *The ego and the id.* In J. Strachey, (Trans. and Ed.), *The standard edition of the complete psychological works of Sigmund Freud,* (Vol. 19). London: Hogarth Press, 1961. (Originally published, 1923)

Gaertner, S. L. (1973). Helping behavior and racial discrimination among liberals and conservatives. *Journal of Personality and Social Psychology, 25,* 335–341.

Gilbert, G. M. (1951). Stereotype persistence and change among college students. *Journal of Abnormal and Social Psychology, 46,* 245–254.

Greely, A. M., & Sheatsley, P. B. (1971). Attitudes toward racial integration. *Scientific American, 225,* 13–19.

Greenberg, B. S., & Mazingo, S. L. (1976). Racial issues in the mass media. In P. A. Katz (Ed.), *Towards the elimination of racism* (pp. 309–339). New York: Pergamon.

Grier, W., & Cobbs, P. M. (1968). *Black rage.* New York: Basic Books.

Hamilton, D. L. (1979). A cognitive-attributional analysis of stereotyping. In L. Berkowitz (Ed.). *Advances in experimental social psychology,* Vol. 12, (pp. 53–84). New York: Academic Press.

Hamilton, D. L. (Ed.), (1981). *Cognitive processes in stereotyping and intergroup behavior.* Hillsdale, NJ: Erlbaum.

Harding, J., Proshansky, H., Kutner, B., & Chein, I. (1969). In G. Lindzey and E. Aronson (Eds.), *The handbook of social psychology* (2nd ed.) (pp. 1–76). Reading, MA: Addison-Wesley.

Hechter, M. (1975). *Internal colonialism.* Berkeley: University of California Press.

Humphrey, R., & Schuman, H. (1984). The portrayal of blacks in magazine advertisements: 1950–1982. *Public Opinion Quarterly, 48*, 551–563.

Hyman, H. H., & Sheatsley, P. B. (1956). Attitudes toward desegregation. *Scientific American, 195*, 35–39.

Hyman, H. H., & Sheatsley, P. B. (1964). Attitudes toward desegregation. *Scientific American, 211*, 16–23.

Jones, J. M. (1972). *Prejudice and racism*. Reading, MA: Addison-Wesley.

Jones, J. M. (1983). The concept of race in social psychology: From color to culture. In L. Wheeler & P. Shaver (Eds.), *Review of personality and social psychology* (Vol. 4) (pp. 127–149). Beverly Hills, CA: Sage.

Jordan, W. D. (1968). *White over black: American attitudes toward the Negro, 1550–1812*. Chapel Hill, NC: University of North Carolina Press.

Karlins, M., Coffman, T. L., & Walters, G. (1969). On the fading of social stereotypes: Studies in three generations of college students. *Journal of Personality and Social Psychology, 13*, 1–16.

Katz, D., Braly, K. W. (1933). Racial stereotypes of 100 college students. *Journal of Abnormal and Social Psychology, 28*, 280–290.

Katz, I. (1981). *Stigma: A social psychological analysis*. Hillsdale, NJ: Erlbaum.

Katz, I., Glass, D. C., & Cohen, S. (1973). Ambivalence, guilt, and the scapegoating of minority group victims. *Journal of Experimental Social Psychology, 9*, 423–436.

Katz, P. A. (1976). Racism and social science: Towards a new commitment. In P. A. Katz (Ed.), *Towards the elimination of racism*, (pp 3–18). New York: Pergamon.

Kinder, D. R., & Sears, D. O. (1981). Symbolic racism versus racial threats to the good life. *Journal of Personality and Social Psychology, 40*, 414–431.

Knowles, L. L., & Prewitt, K. (Eds.). (1969). *Institutional racism in America*. Englewood Cliffs, NJ: Prentice-Hall.

Kovel, J. (1970). *White racism: A psychohistory*. New York: Pantheon.

Liebert, R. M., Sprafkin, J. N., & Davidson, E. S. (1982). *The early window: Effects of television on children and youth*, (2nd ed) New York: Pergamon.

Linville, P. W., & Jones, E. E. (1980). Polarized appraisals of out-group members. *Journal of Personality and Social Psychology, 38*, 689–703.

McArthur, L. Z., & Soloman, L. K. (1978). Perceptions of an aggressive encounter as a function of the victim's salience and the perceiver's arousal. *Journal of Personality and Social Psychology, 36*, 1278–1290.

McCauley, C., Stitt, C. L., & Segal, M. (1980). Stereotyping: From prejudice to prediction. *Psychological Bulletin, 87*, 195–208.

McConahay, J. B. (1982). Self-interest versus racial attitudes as correlates of anti-busing attitudes in Louisville: Is it the buses or the blacks? *Journal of Politics, 44*, 692–720.

McConahay, J. B., Hardee, B. B., & Batts, V. (1981). Has racism declined in America? *Journal of Conflict Resolution, 25*, 563–579.

McConahay, J. B., & Hough, J. C. (1976). Symbolic racism. *Journal of Social Issues, 32*, 23–45.

McConahay, J. B., Mullin, C. J., & Frederick, J. (1977). The uses of social science in trials with political and racial overtures: The trial of Joan Little. *Law and Contemporary Problems, 41*, 205–229.

McNally, D. P. G. (1983). *Blacks and television: A comparison of the portrayal of black and white characters on television*. Unpublished doctoral dissertation, University of Maryland, College Park.

Myrdal, G. (1944). An American dilemma: The Negro problem and modern democracy. New York: Harper.

Newsweek, February 26, 1979.

Parsons, T. (1965). Full citizenship for the Negro American? A sociological problem. Daedalus, Fall, 1009–1054.

Pettigrew, T. F. (1958). Personality and sociocultural factors in intergroup attitudes: A cross-national comparison. Journal of Conflict Resolution, 2, 29–42.

Plotkin, L. (1964). The frequency of appearance of Negroes on television. New York: The Committee on Integration, New York Society for Ethical Culture.

Report of the National Advisory Commission on Civil Disorders (1968). New York: Bantam Books.

Riessman, F. (1962). The culturally deprived child. New York: Harper & Row.

Rist, R. C. (1974). Race, policy, and schooling. Society, 12, 59–63.

Rokeach, M., & Mezei, L. (1966). Race and shared belief as factors in social choice. Science, 151, 167–172.

Rose, A. M. (1964). Race and minority group relations. In J. Gould and W. L. Kolb (Eds.). A dictionary of the social sciences (pp. 570–571). New York: Free Press.

Rose, A. M., & Rose, C. B. (Eds.). (1965). Minority problems. New York: Harper & Row.

Rothbart, M. (1976). Achieving racial equality: An analysis of resistance to social reform. In P. A. Katz (Ed.), Towards the elimination of racism (pp. 341–375). New York: Pergamon.

Rothbart, M., Evans, M., & Fulero, S. (1979). Recall for confirming events: Memory processes and the maintenance of social stereotypes. Journal of Experimental Social Psychology, 15, 343–355.

Ryan, W. (1971). Blaming the victim. New York: Pantheon.

Sears, D. O., & Allen, H. M., Jr. (1984). The trajectory of local desegregation controversies and whites' opposition to busing. In N. Miller & M. B. Brewer (Eds.), Groups in contact: The psychology of desegregation (pp. 123–151). New York: Academic Press.

Sheatsley, P. B. (1966). White attitudes toward the Negro. Daedalus, 95, 217–128.

Sherif, M., Harvey, O. J., White, B. J., Hood, W. R., & Sherif, C. W. (1961). Intergroup cooperation and conflict: The Robber's Cave experiment. Norman, OK: University of Oklahoma Press.

Shuey, A. (1953). Stereotyping of Negroes and whites: An analysis of magazine pictures. Public Opinion Quarterly, 17, 281–287.

Sigall, H., & Page, R. (1971). Current stereotypes: A little fading, a little faking. Journal of Personality and Social Psychology, 18, 247–255.

Sigelman, L., & Welch, S. (1984). Race, gender, and opinion toward black and female presidential candidates. Public Opinion Quarterly, 48, 467–475.

Smith, T. W., & Dempsey, G. N. (1983). The polls: Ethnic social distance and prejudice. Public Opinion Quarterly, 47, 584–600.

Snyder, M. (1981). On the self-perpetuating nature of social stereotypes. In D. L. Hamilton (Ed.), Cognitive processes in stereotyping and intergroup behavior (pp. 183–212). Hillsdale, NJ: Erlbaum.

Stephan, W. G. (1985). Intergroup relations. In G. Lindzey & E. Aronson (Eds.), The handbook of social psychology (3rd ed., pp. 599–658). New York: Random House.

Tajfel, H. (1969). Cognitive aspects of prejudice. Journal of Social Issues, 25, 79–97.

Tajfel, H. (1970). Experiments in intergroup discrimination. Scientific American, 223, 96–102.

Tajfel, H. (1982). Social psychology of intergroup relations. *Annual Review of Psychology, 33*, 1–39.

Tajfel, H., & Turner, J. C. (1979). An integrative theory of intergroup conflict. In W. Austin & S. Worchel (Eds.), *The social psychology of intergroup relations* (pp. 33–47). Monterey, CA: Brooks/Cole.

Taylor, D. G., Sheatsley, P. B., & Greeley, A. M. (1978). Attitudes toward racial integration. *Scientific American, 238*, 42–49.

Taylor, S. E., & Fiske, S. T. (1978). Salience, attention, and attribution: Top of the head phenomenon. In L. Berkowitz (Ed.), *Advances in experimental social psychology*, Vol. II, (pp. 249–288). New York: Academic Press.

Taylor, S. E., Fiske, S. T., Etcoff, N., & Ruderman, A. (1978). The categorical and contextual bases of person memory and stereotyping. *Journal of Personality and Social Psychology, 36*, 778–793.

Turner, J. C. (1975). Social comparison and social identity: Some prospects for intergroup behavior. *European Journal of Social Psychology, 5*, 5–34.

Turner, J. C. (1981). The experimental social psychology of intergroup behavior. In J. C. Turner & H. Giles (Eds.), *Intergroup behaviour* (pp. 66–101). Chicago: University of Chicago Press.

United States Commission on Civil Disorders (1978). *Report of the U.S. Commission on Civil Rights*. Washington, DC: Government Printing Office.

van den Berghe, P. (1967). *Race and racism: A comparative perspective*. New York: Wiley.

Vaughn-Cooke, D. (1984). The economic status of black America: Is there a recovery? In *The state of black America 1984*. Washington, DC: National Urban League, Inc.

Wilder, D. A. (1978). Reduction of intergroup discrimination through individuation of the outgroup. *Journal of Personality and Social Psychology, 36*, 1361–1374.

Wills, T. A. (1981). Downward comparison principles in social psychology. *Psychological Bulletin, 90*, 245–271.

RACIAL AMBIVALENCE, VALUE DUALITY, AND BEHAVIOR*

Irwin Katz
Joyce Wackenhut

Doctoral Program in Psychology
Graduate Center of the
City University of New York
New York, New York 10036-8099

R. Glen Hass

Department of Psychology
Brooklyn College of the
City University of New York
Brooklyn, New York 11210

INTRODUCTION

To follow the course of race relations in the United States since the 1950s is to be struck by a fundamental duality in white America's reactions to blacks and the civil rights movement. On one hand, there is ample documentation of almost unanimous public support for a national policy against racial discrimination. It is also clear that whites' beliefs and sentiments about black people are substantially more favorable today than they were in the past. Nonetheless, certain antiblack stereotypes and an aversion to close interracial contacts are still prevalent among the majority. It seems that whites' racial attitudes generally have become increasingly complex and differentiated, with positive and negative components often existing side by side within the individual. The present chapter examines the phenomenon of ambivalence and its effect on black–white interactions. We review empirical findings that document its existence and then suggest how it might be rooted in core American values. Following this, we outline a theory of ambivalence-induced behavioral amplification, presenting some experimental results and plans for future research.

* The preparation of this chapter was supported in part by a grant from the National Science Foundation (BNS-8316303) to Irwin Katz and Glen Hass.

PREJUDICE, DISCRIMINATION, AND RACISM

EVIDENCE OF BOTH PROBLACK AND
ANTIBLACK ATTITUDES

There can be no doubt that since the 1950s the position of blacks in this country has greatly improved. Although serious racial inequalities still exist, blacks now have voting rights and equal access to public accommodations; discrimination in housing, employment, and education is illegal. "Indeed, the entire elaborate panoply of legalized discrimination has been swept away" (Rist, 1980). The successful assault on ingrained institutional barriers to civil rights legislation could not have come about without massive pressures for congressional action from outside (Davidson, 1983). In all instances where opinion poll data are available, it can be shown that antidiscrimination legislation was enacted by Congress when the proportion of the public favoring it was over half—usually two-thirds or more—and increasing (Burstein, 1979). During the 1960s and 1970s, whites continued to become more accepting of other groups, as evidenced by a marked decrease in negative racial stereotyping (reviewed by Ashmore & Del Boca, 1976; also see Chapter 1), and increasingly pronounced endorsement of the idea of racial integration and equality (Lipset & Schneider, 1978; Taylor, Sheatsley, & Greeley, 1978). After examining a large number of opinion surveys, Lipset and Schneider concluded that most Americans not only were aware of past discrimination against blacks and other minorities, but also were persuaded that further progress toward complete equality was necessary.

However, the prevailing opinions of whites are by no means always problack. Attitudes about residential integration, for example, tend to be ambiguous: Laws prohibiting racial discrimination in housing are generally accepted as fair and desirable, but proposals that local governments or private groups encourage black people to buy homes in the suburbs receive little support (Lipset & Schneider, 1978). Surveys also show that whites tend to be critical of black people's motives and intentions. Thus, in studies reported by Kinder and Sears (1981) and McConahay (1982) a large percentage of the respondents stated that blacks were getting more economic assistance than they needed or deserved and were demanding too much too quickly in their push for equality.

Antiblack attitudes are revealed in recent experiments involving hidden manipulations of the situation and such unobtrusive measures of intergroup affect and preference as (1) helping behavior, (2) direct and indirect aggression, and (3) nonverbal behavior (e.g., tone of voice and physical distancing). The data generally suggest that, at least at an unconscious level, some amount of racial bias is still commonplace among white Americans (reviewed by Crosby, Bromley, & Saxe, 1980).

THE LIP-SERVICE ARGUMENT

The mixed pattern of findings just reviewed has been taken by some analysts to mean that whites have learned to pay lip service to a norm of equality, but remain fundamentally racist in their feelings (e.g., Feagin, 1980; Hsu, 1972; Jones, 1972; Kovel, 1970). These writers point out that despite Americans' almost unanimous endorsement of the principle of integration, concrete applications like mandatory busing to desegregate schools and racial quotas in hiring are strongly opposed. According to one recent formulation, this apparent inconsistency reflects a new, relatively sophisticated form of prejudice— called "symbolic racism" by Sears and associates (e.g., Kinder & Sears, 1981; Sears, Hensler, & Speer, 1979), "modern racism" by Mc-Conahay (Chapter 4), and "aversive racism" by Gaertner and Dovidio (1981, also Chapter 3). Supposedly, the new type of racist avoids expressing opinions that are blatantly antiblack or segregationist, preferring ones that are relatively ambiguous and amenable to being defended on nonracial grounds. Thus the majority's opposition to busing and quotas is said to be, in fact, opposition to the principle of integration, disguised as adherence to seemingly reasonable values and concepts (e.g., "neighborhood schools," "academic quality," and "a system of rewards based on individual merit"). Another version of the lip-service interpretation is presented by Bobo (1983). He ascribes resistance to school busing and job quotas not to prejudice per se, but rather to whites' interest in preserving the competitive advantages and way of life that they presumably enjoy as a consequence of segregation.

The lip-service argument, then, states that if whites were really interested in racial reform, they would support mandatory busing and job quotas, two of the most promising policies that have been proposed for changing the status quo; presumably these measures are strongly rejected *because* they are seen as effective. Thus antibusing and antiquota attitudes are supposed to be based on racism. If so, they should be closely related to psychological measures of prejudice. We turn now to a consideration of what is actually known about the causes of opposition to busing and quotas.

ARE WHITES AGAINST SCHOOL DESEGREGATION?

Throughout the 1970s, national surveys showed that between 70 and 85% of whites were opposed to the mandatory cross-busing of white and nonwhite pupils, depending on the survey (Armor, 1980). Nor have blacks been clearly in favor of this policy: Gallup found 32% of blacks in favor of forced busing in 1974, Harris 49% in 1976 (reported in Rist, 1980), and NORC 53% in 1977 (reported in Greeley, 1980). But forced busing is only one of several devices that have been employed to desegregate public schools. Since the 1960s, hundreds of school districts in the United States have undergone smooth desegregation by a variety of methods, including voluntary busing, open enrollment, magnet schools in black areas, and changes in school boundaries with minimal busing. As a result, segregation of black students has declined substantially. From 1968 to 1980 the proportion of blacks in 90–100% minority schools decreased by almost half (U.S. Comission on Civil Rights, 1982). (But segregation is still a reality; according to Arrington, 1981, most black students nationally were still attending majority–nonwhite schools at the end of the 1970s.)

National surveys show that most white parents would accept various alternatives to mandatory busing (Rist, 1980; Stinchcombe & Taylor, 1980) and would not object to having their children attend schools where blacks constitute half the enrollment (Rist, 1980). The poll findings are consistent with behavioral evidence. For example, many school districts such as San Diego have implemented desegregation programs that caused nearly all-white schools to enroll large fractions of minority students, and this has occurred without appreciable white flight (Armor, 1980; Rossell, 1976).

When studies have employed traditional psychological measures of racial prejudice and stereotyping, these variables have usually been only weakly related to busing opposition (e.g., Armor, 1980; Casterline, 1977; Kelley, 1974; McClendon & Pestello, 1982; Stinchcombe & Taylor, 1980). A stronger linkage is reported when the new concept of "symbolic" (or modern) racism is employed (e.g., McConahay, 1982; Sears, Hensler, & Speer, 1979). *Symbolic racism* is defined by McConahay and Hough (1976) as "the expression in terms of abstract, ideological symbols and symbolic behaviors of the feeling that blacks are violating cherished values or making illegitimate demands for changes in the racial status quo" (p. 38). But as Armor (1980) has observed, the problem with this approach is that symbolic racism is not clearly distinct from the busing issue itself. "In fact," he writes, "given white opposition to mandatory busing in a community where the courts have ordered busing following a lawsuit brought by the NAACP, it may be logical to expect that whites feel the government is being overly responsive to black demands while ignoring white opinion" (p. 215). That is, antibusing sentiments may be a cause of symbolic racism, as it is measured by Sears, McConahay, and others, rather than the other way around.

Furthermore, despite the conceptualization of symbolic racism as "the feeling that blacks are violating cherished values or making illegitimate demands for change" (McConahay & Hough, 1976, p. 38), Bobo (1983) has shown that when the items of the symbolic racism scale are analyzed separately, the two items most likely to be associated with busing opposition are about the pace of blacks' civil rights push and dislike of black militants. The aspect of symbolic racism that appears to be most closely related to busing attitudes is the perception of blacks as demanding change too quickly, rather than of blacks as threatening the American system in general.

Opposition to busing appears to rest on the belief that it has too many costs and not enough benefits. This has shown up in local studies, whenever information has been gathered on the perceived effects of implementing a busing program—e.g., in Boston (Stinchcombe & Taylor, 1980), Los Angeles (Armor, 1980), and Akron (McClendon & Pestello, 1982). The Boston study tapped whites' (1) acceptance of racial integration, and (2) belief that blacks are still discriminated against in jobs, education, and housing. Neither scale correlated consistently or highly with people's positions on the busing issue. However, the belief that white test scores would decline under a court-ordered exchange of pupils between ghetto and non-ghetto schools was consistently correlated with opposition, as was support for the principle of neighborhood schools. The pattern of relationships among these variables did not support the thesis that "declining test scores" and "neighborhood schools" were mere codewords for racism. The basic problem seemed to be that the average non-ghetto parent perceived ghetto schools as academically deficient and physically dangerous, and feared that these bad qualities might be communicated to their schools under the busing program. Similar findings were obtained in Los Angeles and Akron.

Unfortunately, existing demographic patterns in most large cities dictate that busing is the only effective means of school desegregation. Hence, the impression is created that the American public's opposition to mandatory busing belies its professed commitment to the principle of integration. We have tried to show that this conclusion is not warranted by the evidence at hand. Although racial prejudice is undoubtedly involved in whites' reactions to busing proposals, it apparently is not the main cause of resistance. On the contrary, desegregation seems to be acceptable to most white parents when the means employed are perceived as equitable, legitimate, and likely to produce the intended outcome. That is, the majority's rejection of forced busing for desegregation is not necessarily incompatible with a genuine allegiance to integrationist, pro–civil-rights principles.

ARE WHITES AGAINST AFFIRMATIVE ACTION?

Another civil rights policy that has been highly controversial involves the use of fixed numerical quotas to remedy the effects of past discrimination. Most Americans favor laws which guarantee to members of all groups equal access to employment and higher education. But every major national study has shown strong opposition to quotas. Percentages of adults disapproving of this measure in recent surveys have ranged from 51 to 84% for whites and from 24 to 55% for blacks, depending on the specific questions asked (Lipset & Schneider, 1978).

However, affirmative action is more than just a matter of quotas. It can be limited to programs that help disadvantaged groups win jobs or gain access to education through special training, head start efforts, financial aid, community development funds, and the like. Several sources can be cited (see Kluegel & Smith, 1983; Lipset & Schneider, 1978) to demonstrate that most white Americans support the expenditure of public funds for this purpose. Moreover, Kluegel and Smith found that even proposals for hiring and admission of minority members that fall just short of fixed numerical quotas were endorsed by majorities. Fifty nine percent agreed that places should be set aside for admission of qualified blacks and other minorities to colleges and universities, and 51% felt that places should be held for the hiring of qualified members of these groups by employers. Yet 64% of whites rejected as unfair the suggestion that minorities be given "preferential treatment." It would seem that reserving positions for qualified minority applicants is not necessarily perceived as preferential treatment.

The opinion data just reviewed indicate that Americans make a critical distinction between compensatory action and preferential treatment. The former, according to Lipset and Schneider (1978), is seen to involve helping people in certain categories "catch up to the standards set by the larger society. Preferential treatment involves suspending those standards and admitting or hiring members of disadvantaged groups who do not meet the same standards as white males" (p. 41). There is some evidence (Kluegel & Smith, 1983) that fixed racial quotas are perceived by Americans as going beyond providing equal opportunity in the direction of guaranteeing equal outcomes, and therefore as violating the principle of equity. But the preceding findings refute the claim that when whites reject quotas they are rejecting all forms of affirmative action for blacks and other minorities.

An interesting perspective on the future of affirmative action policy in business and industry is provided by Daniel Seligman (1982) in an article that appeared in *Fortune* magazine. Seligman, an opponent of the federal Equal Employment Opportunity (EEO) program, interviewed a sampling of government policy makers, lawyers, and corporation executives specializing in EEO matters. He came away convinced that the present system of numerical goals and timetables for hiring and promotions (which proponents argue is less rigid than quotas and does not result in reverse discrimination) is here to stay. "The system," he wrote, "will clearly survive the Reaganites, which presumably means that it can survive anything" (p. 143). The reason, according to Seligman, is that big business wants the present system to continue. Assuming that he is correct, the commitment to affirmative action suggests something about how the corporate world assesses the national mood. It seems unlikely that the nation's largest companies would embrace a civil rights policy they had reason to believe was unacceptable to the public.

CONCLUSION ABOUT RACIAL ATTITUDES

Racism and prejudice are no doubt involved in opposition to mandatory busing and quotas. However, we have argued that the public's dislike of these programs does not preclude a genuine commitment of the majority to many important racial equality goals. Both the main trend of government actions over the past quarter-century and the findings of hundreds of attitude and opinion studies are consistent with the notion of such a commitment. As Lipset and Schneider (1978) have put it, most Americans "view race as a categorical disability deserving of special aid, much like physical handicap and impoverishment in old age. Blacks should be helped because they have been down so long" (p. 41). But many of these same white Americans are ready to say that the economic plight of blacks is worsened by blacks' own "lack of ambition, laziness, failure to take advantage of opportunities" (Campbell, 1971, p. 14). Apparently, blacks tend to be seen as both *disadvantaged* (by the system) and *deviant* (in the sense of having psychological qualities that go counter to the main society's values and norms). We believe that this dual perspective engenders in the white perceiver an uneasy equation of conflicting sentiments, consisting of friendliness and sympathy on one side and disdain and aversion on the other.

RACIAL ATTITUDES AND GENERAL VALUES

Probably much can be learned about American racial attitudes by studying their relationship to the values that are held in common by members of the society. Our assumption is that *values*—conceived as generalized standards of the goals and goal-directed behaviors of human existence—are more central and fundamental components of a person's makeup than attitudes and, moreover, are determinants of attitudes as well as behavior. This conception of values is held by many theorists, including Allport (1954), Lipset (1963), and Rokeach (1973). Allport, for example, wrote, "The most important categories a man has are his personal set of values. He lives by and for his values." For Allport, racial attitudes consisted largely of prejudgments stemming from these values.

A common theme in sociological descriptions of the American system is that there are two core value-orientations: *egalitarianism*, which embraces democratic and humanitarian precepts; and *individualism*, with its emphasis on personal freedom, self-reliance, devotion to work, and achievement (cf. reviews of this literature by Hsu, 1972; and Lipset, 1963). Lipset has shown that the history of American social change reflects a shifting back and forth between the two core values, as a period of obsessive concern with equality and social reform is typically followed by a period emphasizing individual achievement and upward mobility.

Although direct evidence on the distribution of these two value orientations in the population is hard to find, the results of recent opinion surveys are suggestive. An overwhelming majority of working Americans express the individualistic, Protestant ethic (Weber, 1904–1905/1976) beliefs that work has intrinsic moral worth, that everyone has an obligation to do his or her best job, and that financial rewards should be based on personal merit (Yankelovich, 1982). Apparently there are fewer data available on the prevalence of egalitarian convictions, although Yankelovich and others (Keller, 1983) report that a major theme in the public's social thinking during the 1960s and 1970s was a concern with *standards of fairness*—not just in the treatment of racial minorities, but more broadly with respect to safeguarding the rights of all people against the operations of powerful interests, such as large corporations, the medical establishment, and the mass media and advertising industries. This notion of *fairness* would seem to be a component of the egalitarian ideal.

Assuming that our culture does indeed foster two core values, how do they affect racial attitudes and behavior? Gunner Myrdal (1944) proposed that the contradiction between racist sentiments and the egalitarianism of the American creed created a strain in the minds of white people. Writing some years before the advent of the civil rights movement, Myrdal concluded that Americans suppressed this moral dilemma by putting their prejudicial feelings about blacks and their often inconsistent beliefs about "equality, justice and fair opportunity for everybody" into separate mental compartments.

Lipset and Schneider (1978) saw many of the inconsistencies in the white majority's reactions to civil rights issues as rooted in a deeper contradiction between individualism and egalitarianism, two values in which it believes strongly. On every issue they examined, they found a positive, pro-civil rights consensus in public opinion when only egalitarian questions (such as discriminatory laws) were at stake; but when an issue also challenged basic notions of individualism (e.g., compulsory integration) the consensus often broke down. On issues that pitted one core value against the other, the public often became polarized into liberal and conservative camps, liberals stressing "the primacy of egalitarianism and the social injustice that flows from un-fettered individualism," and conservatives tending to "enshrine individual freedom and the social need for mobility and achievement as values 'endangered' by the collectivism inherent in liberal nostrums" (p. 43). Thus the Lipset and Schneider analysis deals with the impact of value conflict on processes (political alignments) *at the societal level.*

In contrast, our immediate concern is with value–attitude relationships *within the person*—specifically, with the effect of value conflict on one's feelings and beliefs about blacks. Our earlier review of research on whites' racial attitudes revealed that both pro- and antiblack sentiments were prevalent, suggesting that a large proportion of people were ambivalent. We propose that this duality of attitudes emerges in some degree from a corresponding value duality. This means that in present-day America, to embrace the egalitarian precepts of equality of opportunity, social justice, and the worth of all human beings is to be disposed to identify with the needs and aspirations of minority underdogs, to feel sympathy for them, and to support efforts to improve their lot. Furthermore, there should be a tendency to see the disadvantaged group in a favorable light, perhaps emphasizing stereotypic positive traits like "warmth," "spontaneity," "group pride," and the "will to overcome."

On the other hand, a commitment to the individualistic, Protestant ethic ideal of freedom, self-reliance, devotion to work, and achievement should sensitize the observer to minority behavior patterns that deviate from and thereby threaten these cherished values. It is well known that black rates of unemployment, welfare dependency, school failure, illegitimate birth, crime, and drug addiction are much higher than white rates. Moreover, given the element of Puritanism in the Protestant ethic, its adherents should be inclined to attribute these deviant patterns to personality shortcomings in blacks themselves, rather than to situational factors such as lack of job opportunities. Consistent with this line of reasoning, Feather (1984) found a strong positive relationship between college students' scores on Mirels and Garrett's (1971) Protestant Ethic Scale and their scores on Wilson and Patterson's (1968) Conservatism Scale, which taps beliefs about a range of familiar topics, including race.

Thus it can be seen that value duality may be an important source of ambivalent attitudes about blacks and other minority groups. How those conflicted attitudes are related to behavior is an obvious and important question to which we next address our attention.

RESEARCH ON AMBIVALENCE AND BEHAVIOR

Clinical observation suggests that conflicted attitudes, or ambivalence, about a given object—for example, a person, group, or inanimate thing—will tend to generate unstable behavior with regard to the object, in which extreme responses may occur, either positive or negative depending on factors in the situation. This phenomenon has been discussed by a number of theorists (cf. Katz, 1981). Thus Freud (1923/1961), who used the term *ambivalence* in reference to loving and hating the same person, believed that the conflict could be resolved by a "reactive displacement of cathexis," energy being withdrawn from one impulse and added to the opposite impulse. Gergen and Jones (1963) studied this phenomenon experimentally by having subjects interact with a person who either was or was not supposed to be "mentally ill"—a social category that presumably is regarded ambivalently by people in general. The behavior of the stimulus person was varied to have either positive or negative consequences for the subject. As expected, subjects' responses to the "mentally ill" other were *amplified*—that is, they responded more favorably to the ill person than to the normal counterpart in the positive condition and more unfavorably in the negative condition.

Another suggestive early study, involving race, was done by Dienstbier (1970). He compared the amount of verbal liking and acceptance shown by white subjects toward white and black stimulus persons who were described as having either socially desirable or socially undesirable beliefs and values. When both stimulus persons were described favorably, the black person was rated more positively than the white person. But when unfavorable beliefs were ascribed to both, the opposite outcome occurred. Thus, subjects made more extreme responses, either positive or negative, to blacks than to whites, as a function of certain nonracial features of the situation. Dienstbier interpreted these results as reflecting positive prejudice and negative prejudice, but did not employ the concept of ambivalence.

Although Freud and others have called attention to the ambivalence-amplification phenomenon, no one has specified the psychological mediators or the conditions under which it is likely to occur. Elsewhere, the senior author (Katz, 1981) has proposed a theory of the process underlying ambivalent reactions to a broad range of socially stigmatized others. Ambivalence is assumed to create in the person a high vulnerability to emotional tension in situations of contact with socially stigmatized individuals or cues associated with such persons. Specifically with respect to a black stimulus person, a white actor may perceive himself or herself (consciously or unconsciously) as having friendly feelings for a more-or-less discredited, unworthy other, or as having aversive feelings about someone less fortunate than himself. Either type of self-referent cognition should pose a threat to the white actor's self-image as one who is humane yet discerning in his or her evaluations and treatment of others. It is also proposed that this sense of threat tends to give rise to threat-reductive efforts which are often manifested as extreme behavior toward the attitudinal object, either positive or negative, depending on the structure of the situation.

Further, in a given contact situation, initially occurring stimulus events might accord with one component of an ambivalent disposition but contradict the other, opposite component. For example, the white actor might unintentionally harm the black person, or he or she might unintentionally help the black person; in other situations, the black other might reveal unfavorable traits, or she or he might reveal favorable traits.

Such stimulus events should tend to increase the salience of the attitudinal conflict, hence the threat to self-regard, resulting in heightened efforts at threat reduction. These efforts could take the form of either defense or denial of the discredited attitude. For example, the actor might reinterpret the stimulus events so that they no longer contradicted the attitude or he or she might engage in overt actions that compensated for the attitude. Which of the alternative means of threat reduction was used in a particular instance would largely be determined by relative cost and availability, and (as mentioned earlier) would often be observable as response amplification—that is, as behavior toward the black person that was more extreme than behavior toward a similar white person in the same type of situation.[1]

What is being suggested is a threefold dichotomization of interaction situations involving a white actor–subject and a black other, in which ambivalence-amplification effects will occur: (1) the process would begin with an input of relevant information to the actor from *self* or *other;* (2) the input would discredit either the *positive* or the *negative* component of an ambivalent disposition; and (3) a prepotent coping strategy would be either to defend or deny the discredited attitude. These dichotomies provide a framework for an ongoing research program. Some of the findings of that program are now reviewed. Then, there is a description of work in progress and other studies being planned.

EFFECT OF ACTOR'S NEGATIVE INPUT (HARM-DOING)

The foregoing considerations suggest that extreme behavior toward a black person should be likely to occur after a white actor has unintentionally injured the person. In previous, nonracial, studies of unintentional harm-doing, people who were required to evaluate someone they had just hurt tended to denigrate him or her, apparently as a means of justifying the harmful act (Davidson, 1964; Davis & Jones, 1960; Glass, 1964). In this type of situation, we would expect that if the victim were black, the white subject's conflicted attitudes about the minority person should cause the subject to question whether the behavior was wholly unintentional, and perhaps to suspect the self of having enjoyed hurting the other. (This process need not be wholly

---

[1] In the studies described here, we have not attempted to vary systematically the relative cost and/or availability of alternative threat-reductive behaviors. Our usual strategy for inducing a particular mode of threat reduction has been to structure the experimental situation so that the behavior of interest is made highly available to the subject, whereas little opportunity is provided for engaging in alternative types of threat-reductive actions.

conscious.) Hence, the impulse to denigrate the victim as a means of justifying the harm-doing should be especially strong.

Katz, Glass, and Cohen (1973) required northern white male college students to give what they thought was a series of either painful or mild electric shocks as feedback for errors made by a white or black male confederate working at a learning task. Before and after doing this, subjects had to evaluate the stimulus person by means of an impression rating questionnaire. There were no differences found among the various experimental groups in preshock ratings of the confederate. But as predicted, postshock ratings were more derogatory in the black-confederate–strong-shock condition than in any other condition.

A follow-up experiment was done to test the assumption that the extreme denigration of the black victim was related to ambivalence. A new group of subjects were run in the black-confederate–strong-shock condition only. One month prior to this session, the subjects had filled out a racial attitude questionnaire, ostensibly as part of another, unrelated project. The questionnaire consisted of *prejudice* items from Woodmansee and Cook's (1967) scale and *sympathy* items adapted from Schuman and Harding (1963). The correlation between these scales was known to be low. Subjects' prejudice and sympathy scores, respectively, were split at the median into high and low. The specific prediction was that derogation of a black victim would be more extreme among subjects who were relatively high on both prejudice and sympathy (i.e., relatively high on ambivalence) than among subjects with any other combination of high or low scores. This in fact was what the data showed.

Another study was done to test the theoretical expectation that if, after unintentionally harming another, white subjects are given an opportunity to do a favor for the victim (instead of being required, as in the prior experiment, to evaluate the victim), they will give more aid to a black person than to a white counterpart. This expectation follows from the same assumptions as the denigration prediction, inasmuch as helping and denigration are assumed to be functionally equivalent behaviors in the post-harm-doing situation—that is, alternative means of reducing moral discomfort.

Subjects in this experiment by Katz, Glass, Lucido, and Farber (1979) were northern white male college students who were tested individually. They were induced by an experimenter to make either insulting, critical remarks or neutral remarks to a black or white male stranger. Men in the criticism condition were led to believe that their harsh words had upset the other person, who, unfortunately, had to leave before the experimenter could fully convince him of the bogus nature of the criticism. Those in the neutral condition were merely told that the partner had to leave to get to a job.

In all conditions, the subject at this point thought that the experiment was over. He was sent to an office where he was paid and signed out by a secretary, who handed him a note, supposedly left for him by the confederate. The note stated that the confederate was doing a research project (on how repetition affects motor coordination) for a psychology course and needed "one more subject to complete the sample." The subject was requested to write a brief sentence as many times as possible in a booklet attached to the note, and to leave the booklet to be picked up later. The number of times the subject wrote the specimen sentence constituted the measure of helping behavior.

As predicted, more help was given in the black victim condition than in any other condition. Indeed, almost three times as many sentences were written when the previously insulted help-seeker was black as compared with white (36.1 vs. 12.2 sentences); whereas in the neutral condition the black confederate received slightly less help than the white one (18.1 vs. 20.5 sentences). So, as the theory predicts, harming a stigmatized person can lead to exaggerated denigration or exaggerated helping, depending on the situation.

Effect of Other's Positive or Negative Input

According to our theoretical model, extreme responses to a black person should be likely to occur when the person displays (1) socially desirable or undesirable traits, or (2) behavior that is either beneficial or detrimental to the actor. As described earlier, Dienstbier (1970) showed that white high school boys gave more extreme impression ratings to black than to white fictitious age peers who were described experimentally as having the same positive or negative traits. An unsuccessful attempt at replication was carried out by Carver, Glass, Snyder, and Katz (1977), using white male college students as subjects. Their ratings of blacks were consistently more favorable than their ratings of whites, regardless whether the hypothetical individual was described as having socially desirable or undesirable characteristics. However, Linville and Jones (1980), using a more involving procedure, were able to demonstrate the polarization phenomenon first obtained by Dienstbier. Linville and Jones had white college undergraduates read and evaluate applications for law school from black and white candidates. The applications were academically weak or strong. To maximize subjects' candor and to enhance their involvement, they were told that the data would be informative for revising the procedures used in selecting applicants. It was found that blacks were rated more favorably than whites when both had strong credentials, whereas the opposite relationship was observed when both types of applicant were relatively weak.

Katz, Cohen, and Glass (1975) carried out a field study in which the response measure was willingness to help another. Black and white callers requested the participation of white northern urban residents in a telephone interview about a consumer product. When both were courteous and relatively nonassertive, black callers elicited more willingness to help than white callers. When help-seekers were more demanding in manner, the racial difference in compliance disappeared, although a predicted reversal of racial preference as a function of the social desirability of the caller's self-presentation did not occur. However, in accord with the ambivalence-amplification formulation, negative self-presentation caused twice as much decrease in willingness to help a black, as compared with a white, help-seeker.

ASSUMPTIONS TO BE TESTED

Thus, it has been demonstrated for a number of situations involving a white subject and a black stimulus person—prior harm-doing by the subject, and positive or negative self-presentation by the other person—that reactions to blacks tend to be more extreme than reactions to white counterparts. However, only one of the experiments reviewed—denigration of a black victim of harm-doing—actually showed a relationship between individual differences in ambivalence and response extremity. Additional research on the attitude–behavior linkage is needed.[2]

Another assumption still to be confirmed empirically states that the ambivalence-amplification effect is mediated by threat to positive self-regard. Studies by Dutton and Lake (1973) and by Rokeach (1973) have provided some support for this notion. Consider Rokeach's self-confrontation technique for modifying behavior toward minority groups. He argues that for cognitive inconsistency to influence behavior, it must implicate self-cognitions, and be experienced as a state of

[2] The ambivalence-amplification theory is applicable to reactions not only to blacks but also to a range of other socially marginal groups that are seen as both deviant and disadvantaged (e.g., the physically handicapped, the elderly, and former mental patients). Additional evidence of amplification effects is provided by several experiments involving physically handicapped stimulus persons. These studies are reviewed by Katz (1981). He also compares ambivalence amplification with other theories, such as dissonance and arousal.

self-dissatisfaction. (Aronson, 1969, makes a similar point with regard to dissonance theory.) In Rokeach's investigation, a procedure was designed to make white college students consciously aware of inconsistencies between their ratings of the two values, freedom and equality, and between ratings of these values and attitudes toward civil rights issues. Subjects also rated how satisfied or dissatisfied they were with what they had found out about their values and attitudes. Posttests revealed long-range behavioral effects as well as long-range value and attitude changes as a result of the self-confrontation treatment. For example, several months later, more than twice as many experimental as control subjects responded favorably to a mail solicitation from the NAACP. The effects were related to the self-dissatisfaction scores obtained during the experimental session.

With respect to the ambivalence model, Rokeach's findings are suggestive. First, they support the basic ambivalence assumption by showing that white college students tend to have cognitive systems that are inconsistent as regards minority group referents. Further, they demonstrate that the cognitive inconsistency involves the person's core values, that making the contradiction salient results in self-dissatisfaction, and that the self-dissatisfaction is predictive of behavioral change.

CURRENT AND FUTURE RESEARCH

CONSTRUCTION OF PRO- AND ANTIBLACK SCALES

In accordance with our conceptions about the nature of white Americans' conflicted sentiments and beliefs about black people, we are presently constructing new scales to measure positive and negative racial attitudes. We take the position that blacks tend to be seen both as (1) a group whose life chances have been, and to some extent continue to be, reduced by discrimination and are, therefore, deserving of sympathy and support; and also as (2) a group whose faulty traits and behavior patterns contribute to its plight. Furthermore, we assume both sets of beliefs exist simultaneously in many whites.

As a first step in developing attitude items, we administered 30 sentence stubs to a large sample of college students. Content analysis of the sentence completions led to the construction of 15 problack and 15 antiblack statements. The following are examples of problack items: "Racial discrimination is still the biggest problem for most Blacks," "Most big corporations in America are not really interested in

TABLE 1   Intercorrelations of Preliminary
Racial Attitude Scales and General Values

	PE	Egal	Pro-B	Anti-B
PE	—	.09	.09	.49**
Egal		—	.58**	−.11
Pro-B			—	−.24*
Anti-B				—

Note. N = 75 in all cells.
 * $p < .10$.
** $p < .01$ (two tailed).

moving their Black employees to positions of real importance," and
"This country would be better off if it were willing to assimilate the
good things in Black culture." Examples of negative items are "Black
unemployment would not be so much higher than White unemployment if Blacks were willing to take the jobs that are available and then
work their way up to better jobs," "Black children would do better in
school if their parents had better attitudes about learning," and "A lot
of Black people on public welfare are just taking advantage of the
system."

We were also interested in whether the positive and negative attitude items were related, respectively, to the egalitarian–humanitarian
and Protestant ethic value orientations. Therefore, we took 11 items
from Mirels and Garrett's (1971) Protestant Ethic Scale and culled 11
egalitarianism items from the social attitudes literature.[3] A questionnaire consisting of the 30 racial attitude items and the 22 value
items—all with a six-point response format ranging from strongly
agree to strongly disagree—was administered to 75 white college students.

All scales proved to have adequate internal consistency, as shown
by the following alpha coefficients: Protestant ethic (PE) = .74, Egalitarianism (Egal) = .83, Problack (Pro-B) = .80, and Antiblack (Anti-B)
= .85. The scales' intercorrelations are presented in Table 1.

It can be seen that the obtained correlations fit the model of atti-

[3] The following are examples of Protestant ethic items: "Anyone who is willing and
able to work hard has a good chance of succeeding," "The person who can approach an
unpleasant task with enthusiasm is the person who gets ahead," and "I feel uneasy
when there is little work for me to do." Examples of egalitarianism items are: "There
should be equality for everyone—because we are all human beings," "People should
have what they need; the important things we have belong to all of us," and "Everyone
should have an equal chance and an equal say in most things."

TABLE 2   Intercorrelations of Revised Racial Scales with Other Scales

	PE	Egal	JW	Pro-B	Anti-B
PE	—	.19 (37)	.24 (48)*	.08 (82)	.40 (82)***
Egal		—	.16 (30)	.59 (65)***	−.26 (82)**
JW			—	.08 (75)	.05 (75)
Pro-B				—	−.27 (145)***
Anti-B					—

Note. Numbers in parentheses are Ns.
  * $p < .10$.
 ** $p < .05$.
*** $p < .01$ (all tests are two-tailed).

tude–value relationships that was suggested earlier: (1) at the value level, Protestant ethic and egalitarianism are unrelated to each other; (2) at the attitude level, pro and anti are only weakly (negatively) related, (3) each value scale is a strong predictor of the conceptually corresponding attitude scale but is apparently unrelated to the opposite attitude scale.

Next, we eliminated a few inconsistent items from the racial attitude scales, leaving two scales of 12 items each. These were administered to another sample of white undergraduates, along with the two value scales and Rubin and Peplau's (1975) Just World (JW) Scale. The intercorrelations are shown in Table 2. It can be seen that the general pattern of relationships is similar to that in Table 1, though somewhat less sharply drawn (i.e., egalitarianism and antiblack now have a small but significant negative correlation, and the negative relationship between problack and antiblack is now slightly higher, despite item revisions intended to reduce its magnitude). The Protestant Ethic and Just World Scales were significantly correlated. However, Just World scores were not related to racial attitudes, suggesting that it was not the need to believe in a just world that was responsible for the ability of the Protestant Ethic Scale to predict antiblack scores.

PILOT EXPERIMENT ON AMPLIFICATION OF RESPONSES

A preliminary attempt was made to demonstrate that scores on the new Problack and Antiblack scales would predict extremity of responses to a black stimulus person. Ambivalence was defined as the product of the subject's pro and anti scores (converted to standard scores and with a constant added to make all component scores positive). This multiplicative index takes account of both the *level*, and the *similarity*, of the subject's pro and anti scores, so that subjects who are relatively high on both tend to have higher ambivalence scores than subjects who are high on only one, and subjects who are low on both have the lowest ambivalence scores. This index has the advantage of yielding a single distribution of scores that can be correlated with other measures. However, the ambivalence scores it generates are somewhat ambiguous conceptually in the middle range of the distribution. (For example, a person with a moderate pro score and a moderate anti score could have the same multiplicative score as someone who is high on one and low on the other.)[4]

The main hypothesis was that individual differences in ambivalence would be positively related to favorability of impression ratings of a black person who displayed socially desirable behavior, and negatively related to evaluations of a black whose behavior was undesirable, but would have no relation to ratings of white stimulus persons who showed the same behavior.

The procedure was as follows. First, 100 white undergraduates filled out the revised racial attitude questionnaire. About a month later the same students were given copies of a booklet containing two vignettes; after each vignette there were 12 evaluative trait rating scales. The first sketch, a filler, was identical for all subjects. It described a moderately likeable and interesting female "character" who ran a motel and filling station in the middle of the Nevada desert. The second sketch had four versions: a white or black college student was depicted as behaving with either brave altruism or timid indecision in an emergency situation—a fire in a chemistry lab in which a female student was dangerously entrapped. The four versions of the story were randomly distributed to subjects. Thus, there were four experimental conditions, representing the various combinations of race of actor and desirability of behavior.

Two composite scores were used as response variables. One was the sum of the subject's ratings on all 12 trait dimensions, and the other was the sum of ratings on five trait dimensions, each of which had been designated by a panel of judges as relevant for differentiating between the positive and negative protagonists. The five relevant scores were trustworthy–untrustworthy, considerate–inconsiderate, self-assured–insecure, brave–timid, and likeable–unlikeable. When

[4] There is another procedure for defining ambivalence that will be employed along with the multiplicative measure in future research. It consists of splitting pro and anti score distributions, respectively, at the median, and assigning subjects to categories that represent the four combinations of high and low pro and anti scores. The high-pro–high-anti subjects would be the most ambivalent group.

the four experimental conditions were compared on each type of evaluative score, there were no differences due to the race of the stimulus
person or the interaction of race and social desirability. This outcome
was not unexpected, given the relatively noninvolving nature of the
task. However, the within-treatment correlations between ambivalence scores and the composite rating scores for traits judged to be
relevant tended to support the hypothesis. When the black person
behaved positively, ambivalence was positively related to favorability
of ratings ($r = .48$, $p < .05$ for $N = 22$, two-tailed); when the black
person behaved negatively, ambivalence was negatively related to
favorability of ratings ($r = -.34$, $p < .10$ for $N = 26$, two-tailed);
correlations in the white actor conditions, and all correlations between impression ratings and problack scores alone or antiblack
scores alone were close to zero.

Is Threat to Self-Esteem a Mediator?

A key assumption in the foregoing study was that exposure to a
black person who appears in a very favorable or unfavorable light can
threaten the self-esteem of an ambivalent white observer by discrediting one component of the attitudinal equation regarding blacks in
general. The ambivalent subject's extreme evaluations of the black are
viewed theoretically as an attempt to disavow the contradicted attitude and thereby restore positive self-regard. This threat assumption
is not intuitively obvious and requires empirical testing. This will be
done by using a variant of Rokeach's (1973) self-confrontation technique, whereby inconsistencies between elements of an individual's
cognitive structure are made salient to the person in order to induce
self-dissatisfaction. Subjects will be administered the racial attitude
scales, after which they will be confronted unobtrusively with information about the consistency–inconsistency of their responses to pro
and anti items. Then they will fill out a questionnaire that taps their
perception of attitudinal inconsistencies, level of satisfaction with
their expressed attitudes, self-esteem, and mood self-report. We expect that subjects with relatively high scores on both the pro and the
anti scales will report more inconsistency, less satisfaction, and more
negative affect than other subjects.

Cognitive Complexity versus Ambivalence

An alternative to the ambivalence interpretation of response polarization is Linville's cognitive complexity formulation (see Chapter 6).

Linville has shown that people's cognitive schemas for dealing with outgroup members tend to be relatively simplified and undifferentiated, as compared with their schemas for dealing with ingroup members. Therefore, she states, information about a stranger should have more influence on one's overall evaluation of the person when he or she is a member of an outgroup than when the person belongs to the ingroup.

An experiment will be conducted to compare the two theories. White subjects will be given both the Linville test of cognitive complexity regarding black people and our pro- and antiblack scales. At a later time, the subjects will be placed in a situation of social interaction with a black or a white confederate whose behavior will be beneficial or harmful to the subject. Afterwards, subjects will evaluate the other person's personality. These data should reveal the relative power of cognitive complexity and ambivalence scores to predict the extremity of subjects' favorable and unfavorable evaluations of the black person. The results are expected to clarify the relationship between these individual-difference variables and to indicate their respective roles as mediators of evaluative reactions to blacks in a situation where the behavior of the black person has pleasant or unpleasant consequences for the white evaluator. Our expectation is that in this type of affectively charged encounter, ambivalence will be a more important determinant of response extremity than cognitive complexity. But conceivably the opposite outcome might occur in a different type of contact situation—for example, one in which (1) the other person's behavior did not have hedonic consequences for the subject, and (2) a task was presented that fostered a mental set to appraise the interaction partner objectively. Thus, each type of mediator, ambivalence and cognitive complexity, may prove to have its own domain of dominant influence.

Do Values Determine Attitudes?

Our conditional findings thus far are consistent with the notion that problack and antiblack attitudes are determined by egalitarian and individualistic value orientations. However, a causal linkage has not yet been established. Therefore, we are planning to do an experiment in which the salience of values will be manipulated by means of appropriate stimulus materials and effects on racial attitudes measured. If our theory is correct, making the egalitarian value orientation salient should have the effect of elevating problack attitude scores but should not influence antiblack scores. Making salient the Protestant ethic orientation should tend to raise antiblack attitude scores while having no effect on problack scores.

CONCLUDING COMMENTS

A central feature of the ambivalence-amplification formulation is the notion that a substantial number of whites hold two opposing and contradictory racial attitudes, one friendly and the other hostile. It is assumed that these attitudes tend to be rooted in two central value orientations of American society: humanitarianism and the Protestant ethic. The humanitarian outlook creates sympathy for groups, such as blacks, that have experienced discrimination, whereas the Protestant ethic, with its emphasis on self-reliance and discipline, gives rise to critical perceptions and beliefs. The proposed theory states that this ambivalence can cause behavior toward minority persons to be unstable and extreme—in either a positive or a negative direction, depending on the situation. It should be noted that the positive attitude is assumed to be more than just an adaptive mechanism for controlling the overt expression of prejudice in situations where it is socially inappropriate. It is not merely a presentational strategy employed to cover one's "true" inner feelings. On the contrary, it is construed as a genuinely sympathetic disposition toward blacks, grounded in empathic identification with the minority underdog and internalized democratic values.

This approach is concerned with specifying the conditions that (1) cause arousal of psychic conflict vis-à-vis a black, and (2) determine whether the conflict will lead to extremely positive or negative behavior. The theory asserts that inner conflict may arise as readily from the discrediting of friendly racial attitudes as from the discrediting of hostile racial attitudes.

In addition to its theoretical implications, ambivalence theory also has practical ramifications. For example, this approach implies that the white community's expressions of problack feeling or concern about the social costs of imposed change measures are often authentic and sincere. Therefore, to dismiss these sentiments and opinions as false or superficial not only rules out the possibility of making use of these favorable attitudes in efforts to improve racial relationships, but also could have the effect of alienating many members of the majority group, who would feel misunderstood and maligned. By the same token, to label as spurious people's deep-felt concerns about the dis-

advantageous effects of mandatory programs could be equally coun-
terproductive.

ACKNOWLEDGMENTS

The authors wish to thank John Dovidio, Samuel Gaertner, Patricia Gurin, Suzanne Ouellette, and Herbert Saltzstein for their helpful comments on an earlier draft.

REFERENCES

Allport, G. W. (1954). *The nature of prejudice*. Menlo Park, Calif.: Addison-Wesley.
Armor, D. J. (1980). White flight and the future of school desegregation. In W. S. Stephan & J. R. Feagin (Eds.), *School desegregation: Past, present, and future* (pp. 187–226). New York: Plenum.
Arrington, K. M. (1981). *With all deliberate speed: 1954–19??* Washington, D.C.: U.S. Commission on Civil Rights Clearinghouse Publication 69.
Aronson, E. (1969). The Theory of cognitive dissonance. In L. Berkowitz (Ed.), *Advances in Experimental Social Psychology* (Vol. 4, pp. 2–34). New York: Academic Press.
Ashmore, R. D., & Del Boca, F. K. (1976). Psychological approaches to understanding intergroup conflicts. In P. A. Katz (Ed.), *Towards the elimination of racism* (pp. 73–123). New York: Pergamon Press.
Bobo, L. D. (1983). Whites' opposition to busing: Symbolic racism or realistic group conflict? *Journal of Personality and Social Psychology, 45,* 1196–1210.
Burstein, P. (1979). Public opinion, demonstrations, and the passage of anti-discrimination legislation. *Public Opinion Quarterly, 43,* 157–171.
Campbell, A. (1971). *White attitudes toward black people*. Ann Arbor, Mich.: Institute for Social Research.
Carver, C. S., Glass, D. C., Snyder, M. L., and Katz, I. (1977). Favorable evaluations of stigmatized others. *Personality and Social Psychology Bulletin, 3,* 232–235.
Caterline, J. B. (1977). Demographic correlates of attitudes towards busing and school desegregation: Detroit, 1976. *Proceedings of the American Statistical Association,* 448–453.
Crosby, F., Bromley, S., & Saxe, L. (1980). Recent unobtrusive studies of black and white discrimination and prejudice: A literature review. *Psychological Bulletin, 87,* 546–563.
Davidson, J. (1964). Cognitive familiarity and dissonance reduction. In L. Festinger (Ed.), *Conflict, decision and dissonance* (pp. 45–60). Stanford, Calif.: Stanford University Press.
Davidson, R. (1983). Civil rights and the changing Congress. *Perspectives, 15* (3), 16–25.
Davis, K. E., & Jones, E. E. (1960). Changes in interpersonal perception as a means of reducing cognitive dissonance. *Journal of Abnormal and Social Psychology, 61,* 402–410.
Dienstbier, R. A. (1970). Positive and negative prejudice: Interactions of prejudice with race and social desirability. *Journal of Personality, 38,* 198–215.

58   IRWIN KATZ, JOYCE WACKENHUT, AND R. GLEN HASS

Dutton, D. G., & Lake, R. A. (1973). Threat of own prejudice and reverse discrimination in interracial situations. *Journal of Personality and Social Psychology, 28*, 94–100.

Feagin, J. R. (1980). School desegregation: A political–economic perspective. In W. S. Stephan & J. R. Feagin (Eds.) *School desegregation: Past, present, and future* (pp. 25–50). New York: Plenum.

Feather, N. T. (1984). Protestant ethic, conservatism, and values. *Journal of Personality and Social Psychology, 46*, 1132–1141.

Freud, S. (1961; originally published, 1923). *The Ego and the Id.* In J. Strachey, (Trans. and Ed.), *The standard edition of the complete psychological works of Sigmund Freud* (Vol. 19), London: Hogarth Press.

Gaertner, S. L. & Dovidio J. F. (1981). Racism among the well-intentioned. In E. G. Clausen & J. Berminghan (Eds.), *Pluralism, racism, and public policy: The search for equality* (pp. 208–222). Boston: G. K. Hall.

Gergen, K. J., & Jones, E. E. (1963). Mental illness, predictability, and affective consequences as stimulus factors in person perception. *Journal of Abnormal and Social Psychology, 67*, 95–105.

Glass, D. C. (1964). Changes in liking as a means of reducing cognitive discrepancies between self-esteem and agression. *Journal of Personality, 32*, 531–549.

Greeley, A. M. (1980). School desegregation and ethnicity. In W. S. Stephan & J. R. Feagin (Eds.), *School desegregation: past, present, and future* (pp. 133–155). New York: Plenum.

Hsu, F. L. K. (1972). American core values and national character. In F. L. K. Hsu (Ed.), *Psychological anthropology* (pp. 241–262). Cambridge, Mass.: Schenkman.

Jones, J. M. (1972). *Prejudice and racism.* Menlo Park, Calif.: Addison-Wesley.

Katz, I. (1981). *Stigma: A social psychological analysis.* Hillsdale, New Jersey: Erlbaum.

Katz, I., Cohen, S., & Glass, D. (1975). Some determinants of cross-racial helping behavior. *Journal of Personality and Social Psychology, 32*, 964–970.

Katz, I., Glass, D. C., & Cohen, S. (1973). Ambivalence, guilt, and the scapegoating of minority group victims. *Journal of Experimental Social Psychology, 9*, 423–436.

Katz, I., Glass, D. C., Lucido, D. J., & Farber, J. (1979). Harm-doing and victim's racial or orthopedic stigma as determinants of helping behavior. *Journal of Personality, 47*, 430–364.

Keller, E. B. (1983). A changing climate for civil rights. *Perspectives, 15*, (3), 10–15.

Kelley, J. (1974). The politics of school busing. *Public Opinion Quarterly, 38*, 23–38.

Kinder, D. R., & Sears, D. O. (1981). Symbolic racism versus racial threats to the good life. *Journal of Personality and Social Psychology, 40*, 414–431.

Kluegel, J. R. & Smith, E. R. (1983). Affirmative action attitudes: Effects of self-interest, racial affect, and stratification beliefs on whites' views. *Social Forces, 61*, 797–824.

Kovel, J. (1970). *White racism: A psychological history.* New York: Pantheon.

Linville, P. W., & Jones, E. E. (1980). Polarized appraisals of out-group members. *Journal of Personality and Social Psychology, 38*, 689–703.

Lipset, S. M. (1963). *The first new nation.* New York: Basic Books.

Lipset, S. M., & Schneider, W. (1978). The Bakke case: How would it be decided at the bar of public opinion. *Public Opinion, 1*, 38–44.

McClendon, M. J. & Pestello, F. P. (1982). White opposition: To busing or to desegregation? *Social Science Quarterly, 63*, 70–81.

McConahay, J. B. (1982). Self-interest versus racial attitudes as correlates of anti-busing attitudes in Louisville: Is it the buses or the blacks? *Journal of Politics, 44*, 692–720.

McConahay, J. R., & Hough, J. C. (1976). Symbolic racism. *Journal of Social Issues, 32,* 23–45.

Mirels, H. L., & Garrett, J. B. (1971). The Protestant ethic as a personality variable. *Journal of Consulting and Clinical Psychology, 36,* 40–44.

Myrdal, G. (1944). *An American dilemma,* New York: Harper & Row.

Rist, R. C. (1980). On the future of school desegregation: A new American dilemma? In W. S. Stephan & J. R. Feagin (Eds.), *School desegregation: Past, present, and future* (pp. 117–131). New York: Plenum.

Rokeach, M. (1973). *The nature of human values.* New York: Free Press.

Rossell, C. H. (1976). School desegregation and white flight. *Political Science Quarterly,* 90, 675–695.

Rubin, Z. & Peplau, L. A. (1975). Who believes in a just world? *Journal of Social Issues, 31* (3), 65–89.

Schuman, H. & Harding, J. (1963). Sympathetic identification with the underdog. *Public Opinion Quarterly, 27,* 230–241.

Sears, D. O., Hensler, C. P., & Speer, L. K. (1979). Whites' opposition to busing: Self-interest or symbolic politics? *American Political Science Review, 73,* 369–384.

Seligman, D. (1982). Affirmative action is here to stay. *Fortune, 105* (4), 143–162.

Stinchcombe, A. L. & Taylor, D. G. (1980). On democracy and school integration. In W. S. Stephan & J. R. Feagin (Eds.), *School desegregation: Past, present, and future* (pp. 157–186). New York: Plenum.

Taylor, D. G., Sheatsley, P. B., & Greeley, A. M. (1978). Attitudes toward racial integration. *Scientific American, 238* (6), 42–49.

United States Commission on Civil Rights (1982). *Statement on school desegregation.* Washington, D.C.: U.S. Commission on Civil Rights Clearinghouse Publication 76.

Weber, M. (1976, originally published 1904–1905). *The Protestant ethic and the spirit of capitalism* (T. Parsons, Trans.). London: George Allen & Unwin.

Wilson, G. D., & Patterson, J. R. (1968). A new measure of conservatism. *British Journal of Social and Clinical Psychology, 7,* 264–269.

Woodmansee, J., & Cook, S. W. (1967). Dimensions of verbal racial attitudes: Their identification and measurement. *Journal of Personality and Social Psychology, 7,* 240–250.

Yankelovich, D. (1982). The work ethic is underemployed. *Psychology Today, 15* (12), 5–8.

_____ 3

THE AVERSIVE FORM OF RACISM*

Samuel L. Gaertner

Department of Psychology
University of Delaware
Newark, Delaware 19711

John F. Dovidio

Department of Psychology
Colgate University
Hamilton, New York 13346

INTRODUCTION

The results of several recent surveys indicate that white America's racial attitudes have become substantially more tolerant and liberal over the past few decades (Campbell, 1971; Greeley & Sheatsley, 1971; *Newsweek*, 1979, Taylor, Sheatsley, & Greeley, 1978). Other evidence, however, suggests that although the old-fashioned, "rednecked" form of bigotry is less prevalent, prejudice continues to exist in more subtle, more indirect, and less overtly negative forms (Crosby, Bromley, & Saxe, 1980; Gaertner, 1976; Gaertner & Dovidio, 1981; Katz, 1981; McConahay & Hough, 1976; Sears & Allen, 1984). The present chapter, like that of Katz, Wackenhut, and Hass (see Chapter 2), proposes that the fundamental nature of white America's current attitudes toward blacks is complex and conflicted. Consistent with this assumption, Katz and his colleagues have accumulated evidence supporting Myrdal's (1944) conclusions that the attitudes of many whites toward blacks and other minorities are neither uniformly negative nor totally favorable, but rather are ambivalent.

The aversive racism perspective assumes that given the historically racist American culture and human cognitive mechanisms for processing categorical information, racist feelings and beliefs among white Americans are generally the rule rather than the exception. We use the term *aversive racism* (also see Kovel, 1970) to describe the type of racial attitude that we believe characterizes many white Americans who possess strong egalitarian values. In contrast to aversive racism is

* This essay was awarded the 1985 Gordon Allport Intergroup Relations Prize by the Society for the Psychological Study of Social Issues, Division 9 of the American Psychological Association. The research reported in this chapter was supported, in part, by the Office of Naval Research, Organizational Effectiveness Research Programs (under contract numbers N00014-70-A-003 and N00014-76-C-0062) and by the Colgate University Research Council.

61

the more traditional, dominative form of racism (Kovel, 1970). The *dominative racist*, who exhibits the more "red-necked" form of discrimination, is the "type who acts out bigoted beliefs—he represents the open flame of racial hatred" (Kovel, 1970, p. 54). Aversive racists, in comparison, sympathize with the victims of past injustice; support public policies that, in principle, promote racial equality and ameliorate the consequences of racism; identify more generally with a liberal political agenda; regard themselves as nonprejudiced and nondiscriminatory; but, almost unavoidably, possess negative feelings and beliefs about blacks. Because of the importance of the egalitarian value system to aversive racists' self-concept, these negative feelings and associated beliefs are typically excluded from awareness. When a situation or event threatens to make the negative portion of their attitude salient, aversive racists are motivated to repudiate or dissociate these feelings from their self-image, and they vigorously try to avoid acting wrongly on the basis of these feelings. In these situations, aversive racists may overreact and amplify their positive behavior in ways that would reaffirm their egalitarian convictions and their apparently nonracist attitudes. In other situations, however, the underlying negative portions of their attitudes are expressed, but in subtle, rationalizable ways.

In our view, aversive racism represents a particular type of ambivalence in which the conflict is between feelings and beliefs associated with a sincerely egalitarian value system and unacknowledged negative feelings and beliefs about blacks. Although our position is very much aligned with that of Katz and his colleagues (Chapter 2), we do not assume the widespread existence of genuinely problack, favorable components of whites' racial attitudes that are independent of egalitarian values. Sympathy without additional feelings of friendship or respect does not in our view represent a truly positive racial attitude. Nevertheless, aversive racists' inability to acknowledge their negative racial feelings and their apparent rejection of negative racial stereotypes, together with their sympathetic feelings toward victims of injustice, convince them that their racial attitudes are largely positive, and certainly not prejudiced.

In terms of etiology, aversive racism is conceived to be an adaptation resulting from an assimilation of an egalitarian value system with (1) feelings and beliefs derived from historical and contemporary culturally racist contexts, and (2) impressions derived from human cognitive mechanisms that contribute to the development of stereotypes and prejudice (see Hamilton, 1981, and Chapter 5 of this volume). The aversive racism perspective assumes that cognitive biases in information processing and the historically racist culture of the United States lead most white Americans to develop beliefs and feelings that result in antipathy toward blacks and other minorities. Because of traditional cultural values, however, most whites also have convictions concerning fairness, justice, and racial equality. The existence both of almost unavoidable racial biases and the desire to be egalitarian forms the basis of the ambivalence that aversive racists experience. While we believe that the prevalence of the old-fashioned red-neck form of racism may have declined since the 1930s, we also believe that it would be a mistake to assume that this old-fashioned form is no longer a significant social force in the United States. Indeed, not all racists are ambivalent.

The negative affect that aversive racists have for blacks is not hostility or hate. Instead, this negativity involves discomfort, uneasiness, disgust, and sometimes fear, which tend to motivate avoidance rather than intentionally destructive behaviors. There are a variety of different sources that we believe contribute to the negative content of the aversive racist's attitude. This negativity may be partially due to the affective connotations of blackness and whiteness per se. *White* is considered good and active, whereas *black* is considered bad and passive (Williams, 1964; Williams, Tucker, & Dunham, 1971). Differences in the physical appearance of blacks and whites may also provide bases for differential responses. From an anthropological perspective, Margaret Mead proposes that although people must "be taught to hate, the appreciation and fear of difference is everywhere," (Mead & Baldwin, 1971, p. 28). From a psychological perspective, biasing effects of mere categorization into an ingroup and an outgroup have been empirically demonstrated and are thoroughly reviewed by Brewer (1979) and more recently by Stephan (1985). People behave more positively toward ingroup than toward outgroup members (e.g., Billig & Tajfel, 1973); they also evaluate ingroup members more favorably and associate more desirable personal and physical characteristics to ingroup than to outgroup members (e.g., Doise, Csepeli, Dann, Gouge, Larsen, & Ostell, 1972). Furthermore, greater belief similarity is attributed to members of the ingroup than to members of the outgroup (Stein, Hardyck, & Smith, 1965). Assumptions of belief similarity or dissimilarity can, in turn, mediate interracial attraction (Rokeach & Mezei, 1966). Also, because our society provides greater opportunity for intraracial than interracial contact, the "mere exposure effect" (Zajonc, 1968)—that familiarity promotes liking—could contribute to whites' more positive attitudes toward whites than toward blacks.

In addition, motivational factors can operate on these and other bases to promote and maintain racial biases. At the individual level, needs for self-esteem and superior status are frequently hypothesized to be among the major causes and perpetuators of prejudice and racial discrimination (Allport, 1954; Ashmore & Del Boca, 1976; Harding, Proshansky, Kutner, & Chein, 1969; Tajfel & Turner, 1979). At the societal level, economic competition that threatens to alter the traditionally subordinate status of blacks relative to whites fosters discrimination of whites against blacks (Wilson, 1980). The theory of internal colonization (Hechter, 1975), for example, proposes that the powerful majority group is motivated to ensure its advantages by initiating policies that perpetuate the existing stratification system. Given that traditional social structures have given privileges to whites, practices that threaten deprivation of that advantaged status, particularly when they involve the preferential treatment of blacks, may create negative affect even among people who in principle support ameliorative programs such as affirmative action.

The attempt to maintain a nonprejudiced self-image can, in itself, also increase disaffection for blacks because interracial interactions become characterized by anxiety or uneasiness. Rather than being relaxed and spontaneous, aversive racists may have to guard vigilantly against even an unwitting transgression that could be attributed by themselves or by others to racial antipathy. Thus interracial interactions may arouse negative affect that can become associated directly with blacks.

Social and cultural factors also contribute to aversive racists' negative feelings toward blacks. Black culture in the United States emphasizes values that are not always consistent with the tenets of white culture's Protestant ethic (see Jones & Block, 1984). Thus, belief or value dissimilarity also fosters disaffection. Furthermore, the context of socialization directly influences feelings and beliefs about racial differences. In the United States, traditional cultural stereotypes characterize blacks as lazy, ignorant, and superstitious; they portray whites, in contrast, as ambitious, intelligent, and industrious (Karlins, Coffman, & Walters, 1969). In our culture, blacks are frequently associated with poverty, crime, illegitimacy, and welfare. For example, in the 1950s and 1960s blacks on television "had minor roles and were rarely portrayed as powerful or prestigious" (Liebert, Sprafkin, & Davidson, 1982, p. 161). Even in the 1970s, when blacks were no longer generally characterized less favorably in the media than were whites, blacks were more likely to appear on television as poor, employed in service occupations, and involved in murders and other criminal activities (U.S. Commission on Civil Rights, 1977, 1979). These portrayals of blacks in the media and the culture more generally which associate blacks with roles and values that have negative connotations for whites may contribute to the development of negative affect toward blacks.

From a sociological perspective, the structure of society tends to perpetuate prejudice and discrimination. Specifically, the institutional racism framework proposes that, through the process of internal colonization, beliefs about relative status and power become embedded in social roles and norms (see Feagin & Feagin, 1978). These beliefs, in turn, help to maintain the social, educational, political, and economic advantages that whites have over blacks. Whites currently have advantages relative to blacks in most important aspects of American life: infant mortality, standard of living, educational achievement, socioeconomic status, and life expectancy (see Chapters 1 and 10). Thus, even if people genuinely attempt to reject the socially less desirable stereotypes and characterizations of blacks, it may be difficult for even the most well-intentioned white persons to escape the development of negative beliefs concerning blacks and to avoid feelings of superiority and relative good fortune over the fact that they are white rather than black and are culturally advantaged rather than disadvantaged (also see Ryan, 1971). These impressions, however, are not rooted in the traditional, old-fashioned bigoted belief that white superiority results from innate racial differences. Instead, these impressions of superiority, and accompanying feelings of sympathy, reflect historical and contemporary realities, which aversive racists believe result from racist traditions and practices. Nevertheless, the issue of white superiority characterizes whites' perceptions of the relationship between blacks and whites and may continue to play a role in the forces of oppression.

While we have identified many cognitive, motivational, and sociocultural factors that can contribute to the formation and maintenance of prejudice, the list is by no means exhaustive. Many other processes (e.g., illusory correlation, polarization and schema complexity) are discussed in other chapters in the present volume and are well documented in the literature. Nevertheless, in a nation founded on the principle that "all men [sic] are created equal," there are strong forces that promote racial equality. Norms of fairness and equality have had great social, political, and moral impact on the history of the United States. The prevalence of these egalitarian norms has been clearly documented in experimental (e.g., Sigall & Page, 1971) and survey (e.g., Schuman & Harding, 1964) research. And, of course, because of

the civil rights legislation of the 1960s, it is no longer merely immoral
to discriminate against blacks; it is also illegal. Thus, due to contradictory influences that operate on the levels of both the individual and
the culture, most whites in the United States experience an "American dilemma" (Myrdal, 1944). This chapter, then, is about people who
have developed a value system that maintains it is wrong to discriminate against a person because of his or her race, who reject the content
of racial stereotypes, who attempt to dissociate negative feelings and
beliefs about blacks from their self-concepts, but who nonetheless
cannot entirely escape cultural and cognitive forces.

AVERSIVE RACISM: DERIVATION OF HYPOTHESES AND EMPIRICAL TESTS

Our formulation of aversive racism enables the derivation of predictions concerning when egalitarian values and negative racial attitudes
will each be observable. Because aversive racists are very concerned
about their egalitarian self-images, they are strongly motivated in interracial contexts to avoid acting in recognizably unfavorable or normatively inappropriate ways. Indeed, if the fear of acting inappropriately in interracial contexts is a salient concern of many whites, then
racial discrimination would be most likely to occur when normative
structure within the situation is weak, ambiguous, or conflicting. Under these conditions, the concepts of right and wrong are less applicable, and the more negative components of aversive racists' attitudes
may be more clearly observable. Here, blacks may be treated unfavorably or in a manner that disadvantages them, yet whites can be spared
the recognition that they behaved inappropriately. When the normative structure of a situation is salient, however, racial discrimination
would not then be expected. That is, in situations in which norms
prescribing appropriate behavior are clear and unambiguous, blacks
would not be treated less favorably than would whites because wrong-
doing would be obvious and would more clearly challenge the nonprejudiced self-image. Nevertheless, even when normative guidelines are clear, aversive racists may unwittingly search for ostensibly
nonracial factors that could justify a negative response to blacks.
These nonracial factors, and not race, are then used to rationalize
unfavorable actions. Negative racial attitudes can therefore be expressed indirectly, while whites perceive themselves as nondiscriminating and nonprejudiced.

INTERRACIAL BEHAVIOR: THE INFLUENCE OF NORMATIVE STRUCTURE

Because of the conflict and ambivalence that aversive racists experience, we hypothesize that negative racial affect is expressed subtly and indirectly in interactions involving blacks. Thus racial discrimination among aversive racists may typically go unrecognized because it usually occurs in situations in which there is a lack of normative structure defining appropriate action or under circumstances that allow an unfavorable response to be rationalized by attributing its cause to some factor other than race. When norms indicating appropriate behavior are clear, and rationalization is not possible, deviations from these guidelines during interactions with blacks could readily be attributed to racial bias; here, we hypothesize that aversive racists would be unlikely to discriminate against blacks. Given the high salience of race and racially symbolic issues on questionnaires designed to measure racial prejudice, as well as aversive racists' vigilance and sensitivity to these issues, effective questionnaire measures of aversive racism, in our opinion, would be difficult if not impossible to develop. (See, however, McConahay's work on the Modern Racism Scale in Chapter 4.) Instead, our strategy for assessing the usefulness of including aversive racism within a typology of racial attitudes relies heavily on the degree of discriminatory behavior observed in specially constructed situations of varying normative structure. In some of this research, we preselected subjects from among the highest and lowest prejudice-scoring undergraduates, based on an 11-item scale, which was composed of traditional and modern racism items and correlated highly with portions of Woodmansee and Cook's (1967) inventory.[1] Because even the highest prejudice-scoring students on a uni-

---

[1] Respondents to the 11-item prejudice questionnaire were asked to indicate their agreement or disagreement (on 5-point scales) to the following statements: (1) Busing elementary school children to schools in other parts of the city actually helps their education; (2) Negroes shouldn't push themselves where they are not wanted; (3) Most blacks on welfare could get along without it if they really tried; (4) These days it seems as though government officials pay more attention to requests from black citizens than from white citizens; (5) Manual labor and menial jobs seem to fit the Negro mentality and ability more than skilled or responsible work; (6) Generally, blacks are not overbearing and disagreeable when they are in positions of responsibility and power; (7) Innately, blacks are as intelligent as whites; (8) I consider the present social system to be fundamentally unjust to the black person; (9) A hotel owner ought to have the right to decide for himself whether he is going to rent rooms to Negro guests; (10) Even though we will all adopt racial integration sooner or later, the people of each community should be allowed to decide when they are ready for it; (11) I would probably feel somewhat self-conscious dancing with a black person in a public place. This scale correlates highly ($r = .83$) with three subscales of the Woodmansee and Cook (1967) Inventory of Verbal Racial Attitudes: (a) Ease of Interracial Contacts, (b) Derogatory Beliefs, and (c) Private Rights.

versity campus are usually not dominative racists, we did not expect to obtain main effects or interactions involving prejudice scores.

The evidence that we have accumulated in support of the aversive racism framework draws heavily from experiments addressing the willingness of whites to act prosocially toward black and white people in need of assistance. We have used prosocial behavior as a dependent measure in our work for both practical and theoretical reasons. Pragmatically, helping behavior provides an index that is sensitive to both race (e.g., Crosby et al., 1980) and attraction (see Piliavin, Dovidio, Gaertner, & Clark, 1981). Theoretically, the Kerner Commission's investigation of the causes of civil disorders suggests that white America's responsibility for racial unrest may reside largely in its inability to recognize and understand institutional racism and in its lack of positive response to the needs of minorities. Thus, the culpability of whites may currently lie primarily in their reluctance to help those who are oppressed by institutional racism. Resistance to affirmative action, for example, may partially be attributable to an unwillingness to personally bear the costs associated with helping blacks and other historically disadvantaged minorities.

The first study, which initiated our interest in aversive racism, was a field experiment that examined the likelihood of black and white persons eliciting prosocial behavior from Liberal and Conservative Party members residing in Brooklyn, New York (Gaertner, 1973). Using a method devised earlier by Gaertner and Bickman (1971), Liberal and Conservative households received apparent wrong-number telephone calls that quickly developed into requests for assistance. The callers, who were clearly identifiable from their dialects as being black or white, explained that their car was disabled and that they were attempting to reach a service garage from a public phone along the parkway. The callers further claimed that they had no more change to make another call and asked the subject to help by calling the garage. If the subject refused to help or hung up after the caller explained that he or she had no more change, a "not helping" response was recorded. If the subject hung up prior to learning that the motorist had no more change, the response was considered to be a "premature hang-up." Based on previous findings relating political ideology to authoritarianism, ethnocentrism, and racial prejudice, the major prediction was easily and directly derived: The extent to which black callers would be helped less frequently than white callers would be greater among Conservative than among Liberal Party members.

The results, excluding consideration of premature hang-up responses, indicated that Conservatives were significantly less helpful to blacks than to whites (65% vs. 92%), whereas Liberals helped blacks and whites about equally (75% vs. 85%). In terms of helping, therefore, Liberals seemed relatively well-intentioned. Surprisingly, though, Liberals hung up prematurely more frequently on blacks than on whites (19% vs. 3%), whereas Conservatives did not discriminate in this way (8% vs. 5%). Liberals discriminated against the black male in particular in this regard. That is, Liberals hung up prematurely on black and white male callers 28% and 10% of the time, respectively.

While this study was in progress, other Liberal and Conservative Party members were interviewed about what they believed that they would do if they received a wrong-number call from a black or a white motorist. In virtually every case, participants indicated that they would help and that they would do so without regard to the person's race. These people genuinely seemed to believe that race would not influence their behavior under such circumstances. Nevertheless, the finding that Liberals did not discriminate against blacks once they recognized that help was needed but hung up prematurely more frequently on blacks than on whites suggested the importance of normative structure on the interracial behavior of liberal, well-intentioned people.

Specifically, when social responsibility norms, norms that people should help others who are in need (Berkowitz & Daniels, 1963), were made salient by the plight of the victim or by a full description of the motorist's need, Liberals did not discriminate against blacks. Failure to offer assistance to a black person once the necessity for help has been recognized would violate prescriptions for appropriate behavior and could be attributed to racial antipathy. Discrimination did occur, though, before the motorist's need became clear and when it was not inappropriate to terminate the conversation with a wrong-number caller. That is, at the point where the caller simply explained that he or she reached the wrong number, there were no guidelines for appropriate action; after explaining that the caller reached the wrong number, the question of hanging up or continuing the conversation has no prescribed answer. Because we did not have control over whether or not subjects heard the entire plea for help from the motorist or hung up prematurely, it is of course possible that there were other reasons besides normative structure that could explain the pattern of results. In subsequent research, therefore, we systematically manipulated the salience of normative guidelines.

As a further test of the role of normative structure on the interracial behavior of whites, another experiment (Frey & Gaertner, 1986) varied the clarity of normative structure regarding the appropriateness of delivering assistance to black and white partners on an experimental anagram task. As suggested by the results of the Liberal–Conservative study, we expected that whites would be less helpful to blacks than to whites only in situations in which the failure to help would not violate normative guidelines. When normative guidelines indicate that the failure to help would be clearly inappropriate, it was predicted that discrimination against blacks would be unlikely to occur because not helping a black person would be less rationalizable and would more likely be attributed to bigoted intent.

Normative appropriateness for helping was varied by manipulating the causal locus (internal vs. external) of the recipient's need and the source of the request for help (recipient vs. observer). With respect to the locus of need, Schopler and Matthews (1965) suggest that someone who is dependent because of moral weakness or personal choice does not raise the salience of social responsibility norms relative to victims of unavoidable circumstances. Considering the source of the request for aid, Enzle and Harvey (1977) concluded that, because a request for help from a third party influences a potential benefactor's normative beliefs about the appropriateness of helping, more help is given when a request for assistance is issued by a disinterested third party than by the potential recipient.

In our experiment, the need of the potential recipient, who was a black or a white fellow student working on an experimental task, was either self-induced by a failure to work hard (internal cause) or due to the unusual difficulty of the assignment (external cause). Female subjects subsequently received a request for aid that originated either from the potential recipient or from a third-party observer. They then had an opportunity to help by providing the other student with Scrabble letters to complete a task and bonus points to earn a prize. The dependent measures were whether or not the subject helped, the number of letters given, the utility value of these letters, and the number of bonus points awarded. Because either the external locus of need or the third-party request for assistance could increase the salience of social responsibility norms, the aversive racism framework expected that black recipients would be helped less than whites only in the condition in which the recipient did not work hard and personally made the request for assistance.

The results supported our prediction (see Table 1). They indicated that subjects helped blacks significantly less than they helped whites only in the internal need–recipient request condition. When the locus of need was external (i.e., due to task difficulty), or the request origi-

TABLE 1   Helping Behavior toward Blacks and Whites as a Function of Locus of Need and Source of Request

| | Internal locus | | | | External locus | | | |
| | Recipient asks | | Third-party asks | | Recipient asks | | Third-party asks | |
	Black recipient	White recipient	Black recipient	White recipient	Black recipient	White recipient	Black recipient	White recipient
Help	33%	73.3%	73.3%	60%	93.3%	100%	93%	66.7%
Number of letters	1.47	4.67	4.60	4.20	9.87	7.67	10.60	7.20
Mean utility value	1.25	3.81	3.10	3.27	9.24	7.35	9.21	6.06
Bonus credit	27.80	37.13	30.07	30.60	43.27	43.40	40.80	38.47
Appropriateness of helping	3.60	4.73	4.80	4.27	6.22	6.40	6.33	5.87

Note. From Frey & Gaertner, 1986. Copyright 1986 by the American Psychological Association. Reprinted by permission of the publisher.

nated from a third party, or both, there was no significant effect of race on helping. Thus when social responsibility norms were salient, racial bias in helping did not exist. Only when the deservingness of the victim was questionable, rendering the failure to help more justifiable and rationalizable, were blacks disadvantaged relative to whites. Consistent with our framework, the normative structure of the situation played a critical role in determining the prosocial behavior of whites toward blacks.

In another experiment, we examined interracial help-seeking rather than help-giving (Dovidio & Gaertner, 1983a). Help-seeking is of particular interest because obtaining help involves acknowledging the relative superiority of the potential donor (Wills, 1983). Given the traditional role relationship in which blacks have been subordinate to and dependent on whites, it was assumed that whites would experience discomfort at the possibility of being subordinated to a black person (Dovidio & Gaertner, 1981) and, therefore, they would be motivated to avoid reversals of the traditional status relationship. If, however, the avoidance of subordinate status and dependency involves violating normative guidelines, we hypothesized that whites would be forced to accept such a reversal so as to avoid acting inappropriately.

In this study, high- or low-prejudice-scoring white males were presented with one of two situations in which they could continue to work alone on a task described as involving abstract cognitive ability or they could obtain aid from a black or white partner whom they knew was available to help. In one condition, the partner volunteered assistance and the subject had to choose whether to *accept* or *refuse* the unsolicited offer. Our assumption that refusing assistance that is spontaneously offered would be regarded as normatively inappropriate was supported in two separate pilot surveys of student opinion. Therefore, in this condition we expected generally that subjects would accept spontaneously offered assistance at least as frequently from a black partner as from a white partner. In the other situation, subjects were aware that the partner was available to help, but they had to decide whether or not to *ask* for assistance. Our surveys indicated that the appropriateness of soliciting aid in this situation is unclear. Thus, here we predicted that subjects would *solicit* help less frequently from a black partner than from a white partner, given that the reversal of the traditional role relationship with blacks could be avoided without clearly violating normative guidelines.

The obtained interaction between race of the partner and the type of offer supported our hypotheses. Regardless of the prejudice score of the subject, white college students who received the spontaneous offer of assistance accepted help more often from a black partner than from a white partner (80% vs. 55%). In the conditions in which assistance had to be actively solicited, however, subjects asked for help less frequently from black than from white partners (40% vs. 60%)— even though they reported that blacks were equally capable and equally willing to help as were whites. Thus, whites avoided subordinate status and dependency with blacks, but only when they could avoid the relationship without violating normative guidelines.

In summary, the results of these experiments involving diverse experimental manipulations provide consistent support for a basic proposition of the aversive racism framework. When norms for appropriate behavior are well-defined, white subjects do not discriminate against blacks; when norms are ambiguous or conflicting, rendering the concepts of right and wrong less applicable, both low- and high-prejudice-scoring subjects exhibit racial bias. It is possible, however, that even when normative guidelines are clear, other nonracial factors lead even well-intentioned people to discriminate against blacks. In the following section, we consider this implication of the aversive racism perspective.

INTERRACIAL BEHAVIOR: THE SALIENCE OF NONRACIAL FACTORS

Another proposition of the aversive racist perspective is that even when normative guidelines are relatively clear, aversive racists are sensitive to nonracial factors that can justify, rationalize, or legitimize behavior that more generally disadvantages blacks relative to whites. In particular, we propose an indirect attitudinal process that operates differentially as a function of another person's race to enhance the salience and potency of *non-race-related* elements in a situation that would justify or rationalize a negative response even if a white person were involved (Gaertner & Dovidio, 1977).

Because of the increased salience of these nonracial factors in interracial situations, whites may discriminate against blacks and still perceive themselves as being nonprejudiced and egalitarian: They can attribute the reasons for their behavior to factors other than race. For example, children have been bused for a variety of reasons to public and private schools for many years without substantial vocal opposition from parents. When busing became a tool to implement desegregation, however, there was strong opposition. This protest often was not about desegregation per se but about the nonracial element—

busing. Thus, people may discriminate against blacks while maintaining a nondiscriminating self-concept.

To examine the proposed indirect attitudinal process, we conducted a study (Dovidio & Gaertner, 1981) that examined factors that potentially contribute to resistance to affirmative action. Even though whites may try to avoid circumstances in which they are subordinate to or dependent on minorities (as in our previously described study), affirmative action increases the likelihood that whites will be involved in situations in which they are subordinate to black supervisors or in which whites may perceive that they are disadvantaged relative to black candidates for hiring, advanced training, or promotion. Although recent protests by whites regarding affirmative action seem to express mainly the concern that *qualified* whites will be disadvantaged relative to *less qualified* blacks (Regents of the University of California v. Bakke, 1978), it is possible that the reversal of the traditional role relationship, in which whites occupied positions of superior status, represents the primary threat to whites. Here, beliefs about the superior status of whites may continue to play a role in the forces of oppression. The purpose of this study was to investigate the possibility that the generally articulated issue of relative competence is a rationalization in which a nonracial factor, competence, is used by whites to object to affirmative action programs that increase the likelihood that they will be subordinated to blacks. Specifically, the experiment investigated the manner in which racial attitudes affect the prosocial orientation of whites as they enter supervisory and subordinate role relationships with blacks and whites of high and low ability.

High- and low-prejudice-scoring male college students were introduced to a black or white male confederate who was presented as either the subject's supervisor or subordinate. In addition, the confederate was described as being either higher or lower than the subject in an intellectual ability that was relevant to their dyad's task. After these manipulations of status and ability, but before the experimental task began, the confederate accidentally knocked a container of pencils to the floor. This situation provided the subject with an opportunity to offer assistance which was not absolutely necessary but which could connote affiliative and friendly feelings. If it is relative ability and not a reversal of the traditional status relationship that underlies resistance to affirmative action, then subjects would be expected to be more helpful to higher- than to lower-ability black supervisors. If, however, subordinate status is the major factor, then whites would be expected to respond in a less helpful manner toward black supervisors than toward black subordinates, regardless of ability.

The results indicate that relative status, rather than relative ability, was the primary determinant of both high- and low-prejudice-scoring subjects' helping behavior toward blacks. A Race × Role interaction was obtained: Black supervisors were helped less than black subordinates (58% vs. 83%), whereas white supervisors were helped somewhat more than white subordinates (54% vs. 41%). Relative ability, in contrast, did not affect prosocial behavior toward blacks. Regardless of status, high- and low-ability blacks were helped equally often (70% each); whereas high-ability white partners were helped more frequently than were low-ability white partners (67% vs. 29%). Thus, ability, not status, was instrumental in determining helping toward whites, but status, not ability, was the major factor influencing prosocial behavior toward blacks. Given that there were no significant effects involving subjects' degree of prejudice, it seems that even well-intentioned whites will respond relatively negatively to a black supervisor compared to a black subordinate, *regardless* of apparent qualifications.

How could people in this experiment rationalize responding negatively to a competent black supervisor? Subjects' postexperimental evaluations of their partners revealed that their behaviors may have been mediated by perceptions of *relative* intelligence (competence). Specifically, although subjects' ratings indicated that they accepted high-ability white partners as being somewhat more intelligent than themselves, the ratings revealed that they described even high-ability black partners as significantly less intelligent than themselves. It therefore appears that although whites may accept that a black person is intelligent on an absolute dimension, they are reluctant or unable to recognize that a black person is higher or equal in intelligence compared to themselves. If subjects believed that black partners were relatively less intelligent than themselves, irrespective of their introduced ability, it is not surprising that their prosocial behavior was not affected by the competence of black partners. Furthermore, if whites misperceive the competence of blacks relative to their own ability, then resistance to being subordinated to blacks may appear quite legitimate to the protestors. Insufficient competence, not race, becomes the apparent rationale for resisting the reversal of the traditional role relationship. Similarly, deficiencies in prerequisite qualifications (relative to one's own), not racial antipathy, become the dominant articulated theme for protesting special admissions policies for minorities. Thus, although racist traditions may have initially produced social inequities, many whites, truly believing that they are nonprejudiced and nondiscriminating, may presently be participating in the continued restriction of opportunities for blacks and other minorities by opposing programs that threaten their own advantaged status and by misperceiving the relative competence of those who have traditionally occupied lower-status positions. Although not the specific focus of this chapter, this last experiment was replicated (Dovidio & Gaertner, 1983b) using gender rather than race as a social category with traditionally demarcated role relationships. An identical pattern of results was obtained in response to women as was obtained in response to blacks.

In another experiment, we investigated the influence of the hypothesized indirect attitudinal process in a situation in which an individual's decision to help or not to help could have significant, immediate consequences for a person in need of emergency assistance. In this experiment (Gaertner & Dovidio, 1977), high- and low-prejudice-scoring college women heard an unambiguous emergency involving a black or a white female victim. Subjects were led to believe that they were participating in an extrasensory perception (ESP) experiment in which they would try to receive telepathic messages from a sender who was located in a cubicle across the hallway and whom they could hear through an intercom system. Ostensibly to determine the relationship between physiological reactions and ESP receptivity, subjects were wired with biotelemetry equipment that monitored their heartrates. The race of the sender, who would later become the victim of the emergency, was manipulated by her dialect and also by the picture on her ID card, which was exchanged with the subject at the beginning of the study. Half of the participants in the experiment were informed that they would be the only receiver, whereas the others were told that there were two other receivers, each located in a separate cubicle across the hallway from the sender. Additional ID cards indicated that the other receivers (who were not actually present) were white and female. After several trials of the ESP task passed uneventfully, the sender interrupted the procedure and explained that a stack of chairs piled up to the ceiling of her cubicle looked as if they were about to fall. In a few moments the emergency occurred. The sound of chairs crashing to the floor was accompanied by the victim's screams: "They're falling on me!"

The presence of other bystanders was introduced in this study to provide a non-race-related factor that could allow a bystander to justify or rationalize a failure to intervene. In Darley and Latané's (1968) classic experiment, it was discovered that the mere belief that other bystanders are capable of helping affects the likelihood that a bystander will intervene. When a person is alone, all of the responsibility for helping is focused on this one bystander. Under these conditions, the probability of this bystander intervening is quite high. As the number of bystanders is increased, though, each bystander becomes more likely to believe that one of the other bystanders will intervene or already has intervened, and each bystander's share of the responsibility for helping is decreased. Consequently, the likelihood that each person will intervene is reduced.

We predicted that the belief that other bystanders are present would have a greater inhibiting effect on the subject's response when the emergency involved a black victim than when it involved a white victim. Failure to help a black person in this situation could be justified or rationalized by the belief that the victim is being helped by someone else. Bystanders believing themselves to be the sole witness, however, were not expected to discriminate against black victims relative to white victims because any search for non-race-related factors to rationalize a failure to intervene would not be as successful as when subjects believed that other people were available to help. When alone, the failure to help a black victim could be more readily attributed to bigoted intent. Even relatively high-prejudice-scoring college students were expected to help without regard for the victim's race when they were the sole bystander. Although many of these relatively high-prejudice-scoring people (compared to other college students) may have awareness of their negative racial feelings, we believe that they would not regard themselves as particularly bigoted, and certainly not bigoted enough to be unresponsive to an emergency solely because of the victim's race.

As predicted, the results revealed a significant interaction involving the victim's race and whether or not bystanders thought that other people were available to intervene. Bystanders who thought that they were the only witness helped black victims somewhat more often than they helped white victims (94% vs. 81%). Subjects aware of the presence of other bystanders, however, helped black victims much less frequently than they helped white victims (38% vs. 75%). No main effects or interactions involving subjects' prejudice scores were obtained. Thus, the opportunity to diffuse responsibility for intervening, an apparently nonracial factor, had greater salience and potency among both low- and high-prejudice-scoring subjects when the victim was black than when she was white.

An added feature of this experiment was the monitoring of subjects' heartrates (using biotelemetry equipment) before and just after the emergency occurred. Paralleling the helping behavior findings, subjects who believed that they were the only witness to the emergency showed slightly more heartrate escalation when the accident occurred to a black victim than when it occurred to a white victim (Means = +14.52 vs. +11.39 beats per minute). Bystanders who believed that they were alone appeared equally concerned, both behaviorally and psychophysiologically, about the black and white victims. Subjects who thought that other bystanders were capable of intervening, however, showed lower levels of arousal with black than with white victims (Means = +2.40 vs. +10.84 beats per minute). These subjects thus showed much less evidence of personal concern, in terms of both physiological response and helping behavior, for black victims than for white victims.

As predicted, the results of this experiment indicated that the presence of other bystanders—a nonracial element in an emergency involving a black or white victim—differentially influenced the reactions of both low- and high-prejudice-scoring subjects. This pattern of results supports the hypothesis that when a racially biased response can be rationalized or attributed to factors other than race even well-intentioned people will discriminate, probably unintentionally, against blacks in a situation of deep consequence to the victim. Yet, the subtlety by which motivational factors alter the cognitive and emotional experience of the situation permits the continued maintenance of a nondiscriminating image among these people.

In other research on emergency helping behavior, we found that the face-to-face presence of other bystanders (actually confederates) who uniformly remained inactive and did not intervene had a greater inhibiting effect on white bystanders when the victim was black than when the victim was white (Gaertner, 1975; Gaertner, Dovidio, & Johnson, 1982). Bystanders who believed that they were the only witness, however, again helped black victims somewhat more frequently than white victims. We hypothesize that subjects who were with the inactive bystanders were concerned about deviate status in the group. This normative pressure not to intervene had greater salience and potency when the victim was black than when the victim was white.

It is possible that bystanders' differential responsiveness to the race of the victim represents a prowhite rather than an antiblack bias. That is, favorable feelings toward a person of one's own race may motivate a person to resist forces to diffuse responsibility or to conform to the uniform behavior of a group. On the basis of a review of research in the minimal intergroup situation, Brewer (1979) concludes that intergroup bias, which may provide a general foundation for interracial bias to develop, often reflects a pro-ingroup rather than an anti-outgroup orientation. Some additional research addressed this issue of separate ingroup and outgroup biases.

An experiment by Faranda and Gaertner (1979) investigated the extent to which high- and low-authoritarian-scoring white college students playing the role of jurors would follow a judge's instruction to ignore inadmissible prosecution testimony that was damaging to a black or white defendant. Participants in this study were presented with a court transcript of a fictitious criminal case in which the defendant was accused of murdering a storekeeper and the storekeeper's grandchild while committing a robbery. Subjects receiving a description of the trial in one condition were presented with the prosecution's evidence, which pilot research had indicated was weak. Subjects in a second condition were presented with the same weak prosecution case plus an extremely damaging statement introduced by the prosecution that indicated that the defendant confessed about the crimes to a third party. The defense attorney objected to this statement as hearsay because the prosecution was not able to produce the third party in court. Sustaining the motion by the defense, the judge instructed the jurors to ignore this inadmissible evidence.

Both high- and low-authoritarian subjects discriminated against black defendants relative to white defendants in their handling of the inadmissible testimony, but they did so in different ways. In their ratings of certainty of guilt (see Figure 1), high authoritarian subjects did not ignore the inadmissible testimony when the victim was black. As indicated in Figure 1, they were more certain of the black defendant's guilt when they were exposed to the inadmissible evidence than when they were not presented with this testimony. For the white defendant, however, high authoritarian subjects followed the judge's instructions perfectly: Ratings of the certainty of the white defendant's guilt were equal across the two conditions. High authoritarian subjects thus showed an anti-outgroup bias. Low authoritarian subjects, in contrast, followed the judge's instructions about ignoring the inadmissible testimony when the victim was black. They were equally uncertain of his guilt in both conditions. Low authoritarians, however, were biased *in favor* of white defendants when inadmissible evidence was presented. That is, low authoritarian subjects were less certain of the white defendant's guilt when the inadmissible evidence was presented than when it was omitted. These subjects later reported that they were angry with the prosecution for trying unfairly to introduce this hearsay testimony. They did not express this anger, however, when the defendant was black. Thus, low authoritarian subjects demonstrated a pro-ingroup bias. It is important to note that both

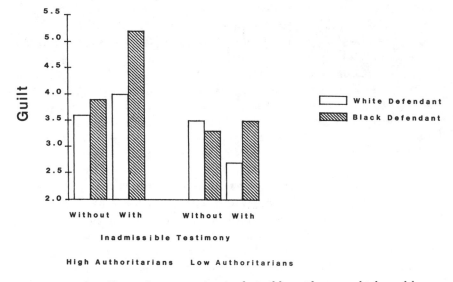

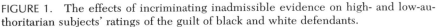

FIGURE 1. The effects of incriminating inadmissible evidence on high- and low-authoritarian subjects' ratings of the guilt of black and white defendants.

the anti-outgroup bias of high authoritarian subjects and the pro-ingroup orientation of low authoritarians disadvantage blacks relative to whites. The question we examine in the next section is how the relative bias is reflected in expressions of racial attitudes.

BELIEF SYSTEMS WITHIN CONTEMPORARY RACIAL ATTITUDES: ATTRIBUTIONS AND ASSOCIATIONS

The implication of aversive racism for contemporary racial attitudes is rather straightforward. We hypothesize that because most whites want to see themselves as fair, just, and egalitarian, they will not directly express their prejudice against blacks. Expressing negative attitudes or endorsing overtly prejudiced statements would obviously challenge a person's egalitarian self-image. Thus, we propose that prejudice and stereotyped belief systems, like discrimination, still exist but that the contemporary forms are more subtle and less overtly negative than their more traditional ancestors.

On the basis of our assumptions about the type of ambivalence that aversive racists experience, we have conducted several experiments to determine the content of contemporary stereotypes among college students. In contrast to previous research (e.g., Woodmansee & Cook,

1967) that directly assessed attitudes toward blacks and assumed a favorable–unfavorable continuum of feelings, we have attempted to measure independently both negative *and* positive beliefs and feelings about blacks *relative* to whites.

With the assumption that a stereotype is a collection of associations that link a target group to a set of descriptive characteristics, Gaertner and McLaughlin (1983, Studies 1 and 2) engaged high- and low-prejudice-scoring white subjects in a task patterned after Meyer and Schvaneveldt's (1971, 1976) lexical decision procedure. This procedure yields a measure of associative strength between two words, based on the time that it takes subjects to decide if two strings of letters are both words. Meyer and Schvaneveldt (1971, 1976) report that highly associated word pairs (e.g., Doctor–Nurse) produce faster reaction times than do unassociated word pairs (e.g., Doctor–Butter).

In our research, the words "blacks" and "whites" were paired with negative (lazy, stupid, welfare) and positive (ambitious, smart, clean) words. It was hypothesized that if white people's characterizations of whites are more positive than are their characterizations of blacks, then subjects would be expected to make more rapid decisions about positive characteristics when they are paired with *whites* than when they are paired with *blacks*. Furthermore, if contemporary stereotypes are actually antiblack, then *blacks* paired with negative attributes would yield faster reaction times than would *whites* paired with these same words. This lexical decision task offers a less reactive approach than do adjective checklists to the study of stereotyping. Subjects are not directly asked to endorse the appropriateness of a specific word-pair combination, but only to indicate whether or not members of the pair are both words.

The results, which are shown in Figure 2, demonstrate the predicted interaction between the evaluative nature of the stereotype-related word and the racial category word. White subjects responded reliably faster when positive traits were paired with *whites* than when they were paired with *blacks*. Both high- and low-prejudice-scoring subjects, however, responded as quickly to *whites* paired with negative attributes as to *blacks* paired with negative attributes. A second experiment that substituted the word *negroes* for *blacks* replicated this pattern of results. These findings, then, are quite consistent with the results of our rating scale studies (discussed later). Specifically, the data indicate that white college students, irrespective of prejudice score, differentially associate positive, but not negative, stereotypic characteristics to whites and blacks.

Another reaction time experiment (Dovidio, Evans, & Tyler, 1984)

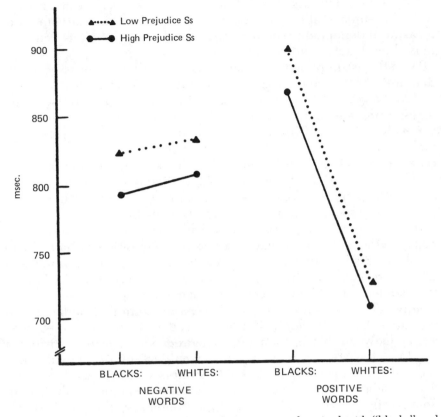

FIGURE 2.   Reaction times to positive and negative words paired with "blacks" and "whites." (From Gaertner & McLaughlin, 1983.)

was conducted to broaden our sample of evaluative words and subject populations and to provide a conceptual replication of our previous work. Specifically, we used words that have been demonstrated to be evaluatively positive or negative (Dovidio & Gaertner, 1981, 1983a), but which are not part of traditional racial stereotypes. In this study, we used a modification of Rosch's (1975a, b) priming technique. In Rosch's method, a cue, or "prime" (e.g., fruit), is presented and provides some information about an upcoming test stimulus (e.g., orange, apricot). Rosch's (1975a, b) results indicate that reaction times to typical instances (e.g., orange, apricot) are significantly facilitated after the category name prime, whereas decisions about atypical instances (e.g., date, prune) are facilitated much less.

In this study, the racial categories black and white were presented as primes, and positive and negative evaluative words were presented as test stimuli. The positive traits were good, responsible, trustworthy, kind, and important; the negative traits were bad, irresponsible, untrustworthy, cruel, and unimportant. Subjects were asked to indicate (by pressing a response key) whether the test word characteristic could "ever be true" of the prime category or was "always false." Despite the differences in stimuli and procedure from those used in our previous reaction time experiment, the results were remarkably similar. In particular, a Prime Type × Trait Type interaction was obtained: Subjects responded more quickly to positive evaluative traits following a prime of *white* than following a prime of *black* (Ms = 767 vs. 908 msec), but for negative traits there was no significant difference (Ms = 891 vs. 885 msec). Thus, racial category labels influence information processing in systematic ways.

Our reaction-time experiments provide consistent evidence across two different experimental procedures, subject populations, and sets of characteristics that contemporary stereotypes involve differential association of positively valued characteristics to whites but not negatively valued traits to blacks. How does this pattern translate into expressed racial attitudes? We performed additional self-report studies that addressed this question.

One of our rating scale experiments (Gaertner & McLaughlin, 1983, Study 3) provided separate groups of white subjects with six-point semantic differential-type rating scales in which either two positive (e.g., Smart–Not Stupid) or two negative (e.g., Unambitious–Lazy) traditionally stereotypic items were presented as anchors. Each of the negative scales represented a negative-to-less-negative dimension, and each of the positive scales reflected a positive-to-less-positive dimension. Using either the positive or the negative rating scales, subjects were asked to complete the phrase, "Blacks relative to whites are _____ ." Then subjects, using the same scales, were asked to complete the phrase, "Whites relative to blacks are _____ ." It was expected that if negative attributes are not differentially ascribed to blacks and whites, then ratings on the scales with negative traits as anchors would be quite similar when subjects responded to "blacks relative to whites" as when they responded to "whites relative to blacks." Furthermore, if positive traits are differentially ascribed to the racial groups, then the ratings of "whites relative to blacks" should be closer to the more positive end of the scale than with the ratings of "blacks relative to whites." This pattern is precisely what occurred. Blacks were not evaluated as more lazy, stupid, or dirty than were whites on the negative trait scales. Whites, however, were regarded as more ambitious, smart, and clean relative to blacks on the positive trait scales.

In a subsequent study (Dovidio, 1984), we broadened our sample of evaluative words. We used the words from our priming experiment that were evaluatively positive or negative, but which were not associated with traditional cultural stereotypes. Subjects were asked to indicate on seven-point scales how well each characteristic describes the typical black (or white) person. Consistent with our previous research, there was no significant difference as a function of race for the mean negative ratings, but there was a significant effect for the mean positive responses. Although the typical black person was not rated more negatively than the typical white person (Ms = 3.30 vs. 3.28), the typical white person was rated more positively than the typical black person (Ms = 4.48 vs. 4.23).

The results of our two rating-scale studies and our two reaction-time experiments converge on similar conclusions. White college students, at least those from primarily northern populations, do not readily express antiblack sentiments and do not appear to have strong antiblack associations. They do, however, exhibit a racially based ingroup bias. Our subjects consistently rated whites more favorably than blacks, and they had stronger positive associations with whites than with blacks. Thus, even though our subject samples appear to be quite liberal and egalitarian on traditional prejudice scales (Dovidio, Tannenbaum, & Ellyson, 1984), racial bias is still evident in their responses. Consistent with our assumptions about racism among well-intentioned people, prejudice is expressed indirectly and in a way that is not recognizably antiblack.

DISCUSSION

In general, the results of several different types of experiments conducted since 1970 have produced consistent support for our aversive racism framework. Specifically, the behavioral findings (presented in the first two subsections) and the findings concerning subjects' associations and beliefs (presented in the third subsection) yield similar conclusions: Prejudiced thinking and discrimination still exist, but the contemporary forms are more subtle, more indirect, and less overtly negative than are more traditional forms. Furthermore, the contemporary form of prejudice is expressed in ways that protect and perpetuate a nonprejudiced, nondiscriminating self-image.

In terms of interracial behavior, the presence or absence of norms governing appropriate behavior is a critical factor mediating the expression of prejudice. When norms are clear, bias is unlikely to occur; when norms are ambiguous or conflicting, discrimination is often exhibited. Regarding the expression of racial attitudes and stereotypes, people do not appear to associate negative traits more strongly with blacks than with whites, an act that would likely appear bigoted. Whites do, however, consistently ascribe more positive characteristics to whites than to blacks. In addition, even when norms are clear, whites continue to be more sensitive to ostensibly nonracial factors that could permit them to rationalize a negative response toward blacks. Specifically, we propose that in situations involving blacks, an indirect attitudinal process operates to increase the salience and potency of factors that can substitute for the issue of race in justifying negative behavior. These nonracial factors may be related to characteristics of the situation (e.g., the presence of other bystanders who could share responsibility for helping) or may refer to personal or cultural values (e.g., perceptions of equity or justice). We do not mean, however, that contemporary white Americans are hypocritical; rather, they are victims of cultural forces and cognitive processes that continue to promote prejudice and racism.

We believe that aversive racism, although it represents a subtle form of racism, is a particularly insidious type. One reason that old-fashioned racism has shown a significant decline in recent years may be that, because it is direct and obvious, it may be susceptible to conventional techniques of attitude change and to social and legal pressures. It is unlikely, however, that aversive racism can be alleviated by such direct methods. Attempts to educate people to accept egalitarian ideals would have little impact on aversive racists; aversive racists already believe that they are egalitarian, nonprejudiced, and nondiscriminating. In fact, whenever aversive racists consciously monitor their behavior in interracial situations, they react in ways that consistently reinforce their egalitarian self-images. Techniques directed at revealing the negative components of aversive racists' attitudes would probably only produce reverse discrimination (Dutton & Lake, 1973) or a token reaction (Dutton & Lennox, 1974) that would permit aversive racists to deny their antiblack feelings. Introducing clear, salient norms into interracial situations would be an effective way of controlling discrimination, but it would probably not have long-term, generalizable consequences. Because of the salient external justification for their actions, aversive racists would not necessarily internalize the principles involved in their interracial behavior. Thus, like a virus that mutates into new forms, old-fashioned prejudice seems to have evolved into a new type that is, at least temporarily, resistant to traditional attitude-change remedies that emphasize the evils of prejudice as a means of eliminating racism.

ACKNOWLEDGMENTS

We gratefully acknowledge the helpful comments offered by Kristen Anderson, Jeffrey Mann, and Richard Tyler on an earlier version of the manuscript.

REFERENCES

Allport, G. W. (1954). *The nature of prejudice.* Cambridge, MA: Addison-Wesley.

Ashmore, R. D., & Del Boca, F. K. (1976). Psychological approaches to understanding intergroup conflict. In P. Katz (Ed.), *Toward the elimination of racism* (pp. 73–123). New York: Pergamon Press.

Berkowitz, L., & Daniels, L. R. (1963). Responsibility and dependency. *Journal of Abnormal and Social Psychology, 66,* 429–436.

Billig, M. & Tajfel, H. (1973). Social categorization and similarity in intergroup behavior. *European Journal of Social Psychology, 3,* 27–52.

Brewer, M. B. (1979). In-group bias in the minimal intergroup situation: A cognitive-motivational analysis. *Psychological Bulletin, 76,* 15–38.

Campbell, A. (1971). *White attitudes toward black people.* Ann Arbor: Institute for Social Research.

Crosby, F., Bromley, S., & Saxe, L. (1980). Recent unobtrusive studies of black and white discrimination and prejudice: A literature review. *Psychological Bulletin, 87,* 546–563.

Darley, J. M., & Latané, B. (1968). Bystander intervention in emergencies: Diffusion of responsibility. *Journal of Personality and Social Psychology, 8,* 377–383.

Doise, W., Csepeli, G., Dann, H., Gouge, C., Larsen, K., & Ostell, A. (1972). An experimental investigation into the formation of intergroup relations. *European Journal of Social Psychology, 2,* 202–204.

Dovidio, J. F. (1984). *Attributions of positive and negative characteristics to blacks and whites.* Unpublished manuscript, Colgate University, Department of Psychology, Hamilton, NY.

Dovidio, J. F., Evans, N., & Tyler, R. (1984). *Racial stereotypes as prototypes.* Unpublished manuscript, Colgate University, Department of Psychology, Hamilton, NY.

Dovidio, J. F., & Gaertner, S. L. (1981). The effects of race, status, and ability on helping behavior. *Social Psychology Quarterly, 44,* 192–203.

Dovidio, J. F., & Gaertner, S. L. (1983a). Race, normative structure, and help-seeking. In B. M. DePaulo, A. Nadler, & J. D. Fisher (Eds.), *New directions in helping, Volume 2, Help-seeking* (pp. 285–302). New York: Academic Press.

Dovidio, J. F., & Gaertner, S. L. (1983b). The effects of sex, status, and ability on helping behavior. *Journal of Applied Social Psychology, 13,* 191–205.

Dovidio, J. F., Tannenbaum, S., & Ellyson, S. L. (1984, April). *The irrationality of prejudice: Logical reasoning about blacks and whites.* Paper presented at the annual meeting of the Eastern Psychological Association, Baltimore, MD.

Dutton, D. G., & Lake, R. A. (1973). Threat of own prejudice and reverse discrimination in interracial situations. *Journal of Personality and Social Psychology, 28,* 94–100.

Dutton, D. G., & Lennox, V. L. (1974). Effect of prior "token" compliance on subsequent interracial behavior. *Journal of Personality and Social Psychology, 29,* 65–71.

Enzle, M. E., & Harvey, M. D. (1977). Effects of a third-party requestor's surveillance and recipient awareness of request on helping. *Personality and Social Psychology Bulletin, 3,* 421–424.

Faranda, J. A., & Gaertner, S. L. (1979, April). *The effect of inadmissible evidence introduced by the prosecution and the defense, and the defendant's race on the verdicts of high and low authoritarians.* Paper presented at the annual meeting of the Eastern Psychological Association, New York.

Feagin, J. R., & Feagin, L. B. (1978). *Discrimination American style: Institutional racism and sexism.* Englewood Cliffs, NJ: Prentice-Hall.

Frey, D., & Gaertner, S. L. (1986). Helping and the avoidance of inappropriate interracial behavior: A strategy that can perpetuate a non-prejudiced self-image. *Journal of Personality and Social Psychology, 50,* 1083–1090.

Gaertner, S. L. (1973). Helping behavior and discrimination among liberals and conservatives. *Journal of Personality and Social Psychology, 25,* 335–341.

Gaertner, S. L. (1975). The role of racial attitudes in helping behavior. *Journal of Social Psychology, 97,* 95–101.

Gaertner, S. L. (1976). Nonreactive measures in racial attitude research: A focus on "Liberals." In P. Katz (Ed.), *Toward the elimination of racism* (pp. 183–211). New York: Pergamon Press.

Gaertner, S. L., & Bickman, L. (1971). Effects of race on the elicitation of helping behavior: The wrong number technique. *Journal of Personality and Social Psychology, 20,* 218–222.

Gaertner, S. L., & Dovidio, J. F. (1977). The subtlety of white racism, arousal, and helping behavior. *Journal of Personality and Social Psychology, 35,* 691–707.

Gaertner, S. L., & Dovidio, J. F. (1981). Racism among the well-intentioned. In E. G. Clausen & J. Bermingham (Eds.), *Pluralism, racism, and public policy: The search for equality* (pp. 208–222). Boston: G. K. Hall.

Gaertner, S. L., Dovidio, J. F., & Johnson, G. (1982). Race of victim, non-responsive bystanders, and helping behavior. *Journal of Social Psychology, 117,* 69–77.

Gaertner, S. L., & McLaughlin, J. P. (1983). Racial stereotypes: Associations and ascriptions of positive and negative characteristics. *Social Psychology Quarterly, 46,* 23–30.

Greeley, A. M., & Sheatsley, P. B. (1971). Attitudes toward racial integration. *Scientific American, 225,* 13–19.

Hamilton, D. L. (Ed.). (1981). *Cognitive processes in stereotyping and intergroup behavior.* Hillsdale, NJ: Erlbaum.

Harding, J., Proshansky, H., Kutner, B., & Chein, I. (1969). Prejudice and ethnic relations. In G. Lindzey & E. Aronson (Eds.), *The handbook of social psychology.* Second edition, Volume 5 (pp. 1–76). Reading, MA: Addison-Wesley.

Hechter, M. (1975). *Internal colonialism.* Berkeley: University of California Press.

Jones, J. M., & Block, C. B. (1984). Black cultural perspectives. *The Clinical Psychologist, 37,* 58–62.

Karlins, M., Coffman, T. L., & Walters, G. (1969). On the fading of social stereotypes:

Studies in three generations of college students. *Journal of Personality and Social Psychology, 13,* 1–16.

Katz, I. (1981). *Stigma: A social psychological analysis.* Hillsdale, NJ: Erlbaum.

Kovel, J. (1970). *White racism: A psychohistory.* New York: Pantheon.

Liebert, R. M., Sprafkin, J. N., & Davidson, E. S. (1982). *The early window: Effects of television on children and youth* (2nd ed.). New York: Pergamon Press.

McConahay, J. B., & Hough, J. C. (1976). Symbolic racism. *Journal of Social Issues, 32,* 23–45.

Mead, M., & Baldwin, J. (1971). *A rap on race.* New York: J.B. Lippincott.

Meyer, D. E., & Schvaneveldt, R. W. (1971). Facilitation in recognizing pairs of words: Evidence of dependence between retrieval operations. *Journal of Experimental Psychology, 90,* 227–234.

Meyer, D. E., & Schvaneveldt, R. W. (1976). Meaning, memory structure, and mental processes. *Science, 192,* 27–33.

Myrdal, G. (1944). *An American dilemma.* New York: Harper.

Newsweek, February 26, 1979.

Piliavin, J. A., Dovidio, J. F., Gaertner, S. L., & Clark, R. D. III (1981). *Emergency intervention.* New York: Academic Press.

Regents of the University of California v. Bakke (1978). *U. S. Law Weekly, 46,* 4896.

Rokeach, M., & Mezei, L. (1966). Race and shared belief as factors in social choice. *Science, 151,* 167–172.

Rosch, E. (1975a). Cognitive representations of semantic categories. *Journal of Experimental Psychology: General, 104,* 192–233.

Rosch, E. (1975b). Cognitive reference points. *Cognitive Psychology, 7,* 532–547.

Ryan, W. (1971). *Blaming the victim.* New York: Pantheon.

Schopler, J., & Matthews, M. (1965). The influence of perceived causal locus of partner's dependence on the use of interpersonal power. *Journal of Personality and Social Psychology, 2,* 247–254.

Schuman, H., & Harding, J. (1964). Prejudice and the norm of rationality. *Sociometry, 27,* 353–371.

Sears, D. O., & Allen, H. M., Jr. (1984). The trajectory of local desegregation controversies and whites' opposition to busing. In N. Miller & M. B. Brewer (Eds.), *Groups in contact: The psychology of desegregation* (pp. 123–151). New York: Academic Press.

Sigall, H., & Page, R. (1971). Current stereotypes: A little fading, a little faking. *Journal of Personality and Social Psychology, 18,* 247–255.

Stein, D. D., Hardyck, J. A., & Smith, M. B. (1965). Race *and* belief: An open and shut case. *Journal of Personality and Social Psychology, 1,* 281–299.

Stephan, W. G. (1985). Intergroup relations. In G. Lindzey & E. Aronson (Eds.), *The handbook of social psychology* (3rd ed., pp. 599–658). New York: Random House.

Tajfel, H., & Turner, J. (1979). An integrative theory of intergroup conflict. In W. G. Austin & S. Worchel (Eds.), *The social psychology of intergroup relations* (pp. 33–47). Monterey, CA: Brooks/Cole.

Taylor, D. G., Sheatsley, P. B., & Greeley, A. M. (1978). Attitudes toward racial integration. *Scientific American, 238,* 42–49.

United States Commission on Civil Rights. (1977). *Window dressing on the set: Women and minorities in television.* Washington, D.C.: U.S. Government Printing Office.

United States Commission on Civil Rights. (1979). *Window dressing on the set: An update.* Washington, D.C.: U.S. Government Printing Office.

Williams, J. E. (1964). Connotations of color names among Negroes and Caucasians. *Perceptual and Motor Skills, 18,* 721–731.

Williams, J. E., Tucker, R. D., & Dunham, F. Y. (1971). Changes in the connotations of color names among Negroes and Caucasians. *Journal of Personality and Social Psychology, 19,* 222–228.

Wills, T. A. (1983). Social comparison in coping and help-seeking. In B. M. DePaulo, A. Nadler, & J. D. Fisher (Eds.), *New directions in helping, Volume 2, Help-seeking* (pp. 109–141). New York: Academic Press.

Wilson, W. J. (1980). *The declining significance of race* (2nd ed.). Chicago: University of Chicago Press.

Woodmansee, J. J., & Cook, S. W. (1967). Dimensions of verbal racial attitudes: Their identification and measurement. *Journal of Personality and Social Psychology, 7,* 240–250.

Zajonc, R. B. (1968). Attitudinal effects of mere exposure. *Journal of Personality and Social Psychology, 9,* 1–27.

MODERN RACISM, AMBIVALENCE, AND THE MODERN RACISM SCALE*

John B. McConahay

*Institute of Policy Sciences and
Public Affairs
Duke University
Durham, North Carolina 27706*

INTRODUCTION

The racial climate in America has changed dramatically since Hitler gave racism a bad name. In 1945, the legal codes of many states and localities—North and South—openly discriminated against blacks, denying them the freedom to compete for and enjoy the good things of American life. By 1954, these laws were being eliminated by the courts and by legislative bodies. By 1965, a new set of laws were in place making it illegal to discriminate. The legal situation had been reversed in only 20 years. White public opinion changed along with the laws. Despite William Graham Sumner's dictum that stateways cannot change folkways (Sumner, 1906), the public opinion polls showed a steady decline in belief in the familiar negative stereotypes, support for *de jure* segregation and support for private as well as government discrimination (Campbell, 1971; Greeley & Sheatsley, 1971; Taylor, Sheatsley & Greeley, 1978). The changes were dramatic and the pace was rapid.

Two features of American race relations did not change so dramatically, however. Measures of antiblack feelings or affect showed only modest declines (Campbell, 1971; Capitman, 1980), and racial conflict did not go away. The issues were different, but the feelings lingered. After 1965, the public debates were not concerned with issues of

* Support for this research has come from grants from the Irwin, Sweeney, Miller Foundation, NIMH, The Ford Foundation, the Institution for Social and Policy Studies of Yale University and the Duke University Research Council.

PREJUDICE, DISCRIMINATION, AND RACISM

blacks' freedom from discrimination, but with equality for blacks. The conflict over how to achieve equal opportunity, a core value of the American system of values (Elder & Cobb, 1983), has been very intense to say the least.

The theory of modern racism attempts to account for the intensity of these new conflicts and to measure the attitudes that have both supported the conflict and emerged from it. The theory draws on some well-established findings in the social learning theory of attitudes (Oskamp, 1977) and racial socialization (McConahay & Hough, 1976; Sears & McConahay, 1973), but it emerged as a result of a practical problem. How do we measure racial attitudes in the general public when the issues, the climate and the structure of public opinion has changed? A new measuring instrument for racial attitudes was needed that would enable us to understand voting behavior (Sears & Kinder, 1971) and community conflict (McConahay, 1982), and to choose fair jurors in trials with racial overtones (McConahay, Mullin, & Frederick, 1977). Thus, the theory has developed simultaneously with the instrument used to operationalize aspects of the theory. The new instrument is the Modern Racism Scale. In this chapter, we are primarily concerned with this scale, its psychometric properties, and its relationship to a measure of pre-civil-rights-movement racism: The Old Fashioned Racism Scale.

THE TENETS OF MODERN RACISM

The Modern Racism Scale is intended to measure a dimension of the cognitive component of racial attitudes. It therefore asks subjects or survey respondents to agree or disagree with a set of beliefs that whites may or may not have about blacks. It distinguishes this set of beliefs from another set of beliefs called old-fashioned racism. According to the theory, both cognitive belief systems are influenced by the affective component of attitudes toward black Americans as well as by other beliefs and values and by the historical context specific to the form of racism. The relationships between the affective and cognitive components and the dimensions of the cognitive component measured by the Modern Racism and Old Fashioned Racism Scales are addressed later in this chapter after we have described the basic beliefs of modern racism.

The principal tenets of modern racism are these: (1) Discrimination is a thing of the past because blacks now have the freedom to compete in the marketplace and to enjoy those things they can afford. (2) Blacks are pushing too hard, too fast and into places where they are not wanted. (3) These tactics and demands are unfair. (4) Therefore, recent gains are undeserved and the prestige granting institutions of society are giving blacks more attention and the concomitant status than they deserve. Two other tenets are added to this psychological syllogism: Racism is bad and the other beliefs do not constitute racism because these beliefs are empirical facts. Racism, as defined by modern racists, is consistent only with the tenets and practices of old-fashioned racism: beliefs about black intelligence, ambition, honesty, and other stereotyped characteristics, as well as support for segregation and support for acts of open discrimination. Thus, those endorsing the ideology of modern racism do not define their own beliefs and attitudes as racist.

Some whites endorse this whole ideology of modern racism, some buy none of it, and some whites believe in some tenets and not in others. That is why it is possible to develop a scale of individual differences along this dimension.

These modern, post-civil-rights-movement beliefs are contrasted with old-fashioned racism—the ideology used to justify the limitations on blacks' freedom in the past. These are the beliefs just listed: the familiar stereotypes and support for segregation and for open discrimination. Some form of the items in the Old Fashioned Racism Scale have been used for years and years and years (Taylor, Sheatsley, & Greeley, 1978). These beliefs are called "old-fashioned" because they are. This form of racism is as out of style in trendy circles as are wide ties and spats.

THE MODERN AND OLD-FASHIONED RACISM ITEMS

The standard, face-valid items used to measure racial attitudes after 1965 posed two problems for the survey researcher. They were reactive in that most white Americans knew the socially desirable answers and they did not correlate very well with what should have been racially relevant behavior such as reported voting intentions or behavior in elections where racism should have been a factor (Kinder & Sears, 1981; McConahay & Hough, 1976; Sears & Kinder, 1971). The items' reactivity created the potential for faking (McConahay, Hardee & Batts, 1981; Sigall & Page, 1971), which would limit their reliability and validity, and it also resulted in people refusing to answer the questions—sometimes in a hostile fashion (McConahay & Hough, 1976; Trickett, McConahay, Phillips, & Ginter, 1985). The refusal rate on paper and pencil questionnaires was a nuisance, but for telephone and face-to-face surveys, it posed a major threat to the entire interview. In one pilot study, after a few rebuffs, the interviewers either openly refused to ask many of the old racism questions of anyone or somehow "forgot" to ask them.

The failure to correlate with voting behavior posed a serious problem. When Tom Bradley, a popular black candidate, lost to Sam Yorty, a very unpopular incumbent white mayor, and measures of racial attitudes were very weakly related to white voting, either a whole body of voting behavior theory would have to change or something was wrong with the way racial prejudice was being assessed (McConahay & Hough, 1976; Sears & Kinder, 1971; Sears & McConahay, 1973).

A series of different items were tried, including those incorporating measures of personal relative deprivation ("Over the past few years, blacks have done better economically than *I have*") and fraternal relative deprivation ("Over the past few years, blacks have done better economically than *most whites* have"). These items did not correlate much better with voting than the old-fashioned items. What did relate were items with an abstract, moral tone ("Over the past few years, blacks have gotten more economically *than they deserve*") or items using code words or symbols for blacks ("The streets aren't safe these days without a policeman around"). A scale composed of a subset of these new items correlated significantly with voting preferences for a black candidate running against a white candidate for mayor of Los Angeles (.392) and this correlation was still significant after controlling for political conservatism (partial $r = .318$). (See McConahay & Hough, 1976.)

The set of items was thought to tap a new form of racism in America: "symbolic racism" (Ashmore & McConahay, 1975; Kinder & Sears, 1981; McConahay & Hough, 1976; Sears & Kinder, 1971; Sears & McConahay, 1973). The term was chosen because of the presence of codewords and moral abstractions in many of the items and in order to emphasize that many of the beliefs were a reaction to certain post-civil-rights-era policies, such as busing or affirmative action, that symbolize to many whites the unfair gains or demands of blacks. The term was also chosen to be consistent with the theoretical analysis and empirical data that suggested the new racism was rooted in abstract principles of justice and diffuse negative feelings acquired in early political and racial socialization and *not* in personal experience or personal competition with blacks (McConahay & Hough, 1976; Sears & Kinder, 1971; Sears & McConahay, 1973).

The subjects of these early studies (seminary students, residents of

TABLE 1   Modern or Symbolic Racism Items Used before 1976

Negroes shouldn't push themselves where they're not wanted. (Agree)
Over the past few years, Negroes have gotten more economically than they deserve.
   (Agree)
Do Los Angeles city officials pay more, less, or the same attention to a request from
   a Negro person as from a white person? (More Attention)
Negroes are getting too demanding in their push for equal rights. (Agree)
Whites should support Negroes in their struggle against discrimination and segrega-
   tion. (Disagree)
It is easy to understand the anger of black people in America. (Disagree)
Negroes have it better than they ever had it before. (Agree)
Do you think that Negroes who receive welfare could get along without it if they
   tried or do they really need this help? (Could get along without it.)
Streets aren't safe these days without a policeman around. (Agree)

Note. Responses coded as prejudiced against blacks are in parentheses after the item.

the mostly white San Fernando Valley in Los Angeles and residents in the virtually all white Los Angeles suburb of Claremont) had had little or no daily contact or previous personal experience with Afro-Americans. They did not have occupations or neighborhoods into which blacks were moving and they did not express feelings or perceptions of personal threat (McConahay & Hough, 1976; Sears & Kinder, 1971). They did express moral outrage at what blacks were doing and demanding as a group. And content analyses of the items and multiple regression analyses of the survey data indicated two roots for this anger: negative feelings and conservatism. The conservatism was not classic laissez-faire conservatism (or market liberalism), but the secularized values of the old Protestant ethic (McConahay & Hough, 1976). There may have been some perception that the prerogatives and dominance of the white group was threatened (Ashmore & McConahay, 1975; Bobo, 1983), but our empirical results did not show it.

The items used in modern or symbolic racism research before 1976 are shown in Table 1. By 1976, there had been enough experience with the items to formulate a general literary definition of *symbolic racism* and then generate a new set of items from this definition.

The first concise literary definition of modern racism was "the expression in terms of abstract ideological symbols and symbolic behaviors of the feeling that blacks are violating cherished values and making illegitimate demands for changes in the racial *status quo*" (McConahay & Hough, 1976, p. 38). This definition is still adequate, although it might be amplified to add the belief that discrimination no longer exists and that the cherished values are those associated with "equality" or "equality of opportunity" (e.g., affirmative action laws or policies) rather than values associated with "freedom of opportunity" (e.g., laws of policies prohibiting open discrimination).

The post-1976 versions of the scale used for adults in Louisville, Kentucky, are shown in Tables 2 and 3 (McConahay, 1982, 1984), and the version used frequently in college student samples is shown in Table 4. These combinations of original items and those derived from the 1976 literary definition had good levels of reliability. The alpha coefficient for the 1976 Louisville sample was .75 (McConahay, 1982). It was .79 in the 1977 Louisville sample (McConahay, 1984). In college student samples, the alpha coefficients ranged from .81 to .86 (McConahay, 1983). Measures of test–retest reliability ranged from .72 to .93 across a number of samples. Hence, the modern racism items derived from the literary definition and the tenets of modern racism formed reliable scales.

The items dealing with people on welfare and crime in the streets have changed their relationships to the other scale items over the years. In the pre-1976 research with the scale, these items correlated highly with the rest of the scale and increased its reliability. However, in the two studies in Louisville done in 1976 and 1977, the welfare and safe streets items did not scale with the other Modern Racism items. Though they correlated somewhat with the rest of the scale, deleting these two items substantially increased the alpha coefficients (from .67 to .75 in 1976 and from .61 to .79 in 1977). It may be that welfare and crime in the streets are no longer as closely associated with blacks as they once were in the minds of whites and these terms have now lost much of their significance as code words or symbols of black threats and failings.

About 1978, I had become so dissatisfied with the term *symbolic racism* that I changed the name of the concept in my thinking and writing. The new term is *modern racism* and the collection of items is called the Modern Racism Scale. This change was made in order to emphasize the contemporary, post-civil-rights-movement nature of the tenets constituting the new ideology or belief system. The change also reflected the realization that both the new racism and old-fashioned racism are symbolic in the sense that both are group-level abstractions rooted in early racial socialization and not in personal experience (Allport, 1954; Horowitz, 1936; McConahay & Hough, 1976; Sears & Kinder, 1971).

Sears and his colleagues have kept the term *symbolic racism* because they think it is a better description of the phenomenon. However, I am not the only researcher in this field to have difficulty with the term. Bobo (1983) expressed a preference for the label *sophisticated prejudice* because he was offended by the application of the term *racism* to these beliefs. He is not the first journal editor, colleague, journalist, subject, student, friend, relative or layperson to be offended by the term *racism* in symbolic or modern racism. Any readers who are offended by this term should substitute the phrase "the A scale of racial attitutes" for "Modern Racism Scale" and the phrase "the B scale of racial attitutes" for "Old Fashioned Racism Scale" throughout the remainder of this chapter.

Later in this chapter, evidence is presented on the validity of the Modern Racism Scale and showing that it is less reactive than the Old Fashioned Racism Scale. That was why the new items were developed: to create valid, nonreactive measures of antiblack prejudice. We expected them to be less reactive in part because they tap into current issues about which there is no clear consensus on the prejudiced and nonprejudiced position and in part because for each item, there is a plausible, nonprejudiced explanation for endorsing the position scored as prejudiced on the scale. However, the same nonracial, nonprejudiced explanation cannot be used for the prejudiced response across all of the items. For example, agreement with the item "Negroes [blacks] shouldn't push themselves where they're not wanted" is scored as the racist response. However, no one likes pushy people, so agreement can be justified by invoking norms of courtesy and privacy as Taylor, Sheatsley, and Greeley (1978) have noted. Disagreement with the item "It is easy to understand the anger of black people in America" is scored as the racist response. Though courtesy is not the norm that can be invoked to justify disagreement with this item, disagreement can be justified by denying that discrimination still exists and concluding that blacks do not have anything to be angry about now. The various abstract, moral references that can be invoked to justify the prejudiced responses on most of the Modern Racism Scale items suggested that they were tapping into a belief in a just world, not racial prejudice (Lerner, 1980; Rubin and Peplau, 1973). However, in two samples of Duke University undergraduates, the correlations between the Modern Racism Scale and the Belief in a Just World Scale (Rubin & Peplau, 1973) were not statistically significant (Polin, 1982). Hence, the belief in a just world was not related to the Modern Racism Scale and cannot be used to explain responses across the scale's items. On the other hand, negative racial feeling or prejudice can be used to explain the racist response to each and every item. It is the common thread that holds all of the items together in the scale.

The items used in various versions of the Old Fashioned Racism

Scale are reported in Tables 2, 3, and 4. They deal with the pre-1965 issues of freedom for blacks and the familiar stereotypes. They are presented for comparison with the Modern Racism Scale items, but are not discussed here because they are face valid and noncontroversial as measures of prejudice. They were not so noncontroversial at one time, however, as indicated by the great lengths Allport (1954, Chapters 6 and 12) went to show that stereotypes reflected prejudice and not reality.

WHITE AMBIVALENCE AND THE THEORETICAL RELATIONSHIP OF THE TWO SCALES

The theory of modern racism proposes that antiblack affect has not declined at the same rate as the measures of racism reported in most opinion polls. The best empirical support for this comes from the work of Campbell (1971), who reported that there was a very little decline over time in negative feeling on the University of Michigan's face-valid Feeling Thermometer for whites socialized between 1930 and 1960. (See also Capitman, 1980). The studies of racial socialization summarized in Sears and McConahay (1973) and McConahay and Hough (1976) indicate that the affective component of racial attitudes is acquired early, mostly nonverbally, without direct contact with blacks and is very resistant to change by later experiences. Modern racism theory proposes that this lingering feeling influences the cognitive and conative components of whites' racial attitudes when they are called on to interpret new events or to engage in such activities as voting, giving opinions to survey interviewers, serving on juries, or interacting with blacks on a day-to-day basis (McConahay, Hardee, & Batts, 1981; McConahay & Hough, 1976; McConahay, Mullin & Frederick, 1977).

However, the affective component is not the only factor influencing the cognitive component or behavior. Other factors are the political attitudes of the person, his/her values—particularly the values of equality, freedom, and fair play found in the American Creed (Myrdal, 1944)—and the context or content of the behavior. The role of political attitudes—especially Protestant ethic conservatism—in the emergence of modern racism was discussed elsewhere (McConahay & Hough, 1976). This chapter examines the ambivalence created by the conflict between the values in the American Creed and negative affect toward blacks, as well as the effect of this ambivalence on the cognitive component of racial attitudes.

The analysis of white ambivalence and its influence on the expression of modern and old-fashioned racism as presented in this chapter is deeply indebted to the theoretical and empirical work of Gaertner and Dovidio (1981) and Katz (1981), whose chapters appear elsewhere in this volume (see Chapters 2 and 3). The three formulations are somewhat different. Katz proposes that the conflict creating the ambivalence is between positive and negative cognitions. The present author and Gaertner and Dovidio see the ambivalence arising from a conflict between negative affect toward blacks and the person's values, cognitions, and/or need to maintain a positive/nonprejudiced self-image. In addition, Katz and Gaertner and Dovidio have mainly applied their theories to interpersonal behavior while the present author has concentrated on voting, policy preferences, and hiring behavior (McConahay, 1982, 1983, 1984; McConahay & Hough, 1976). All agree, however, that at this time, most white Americans are not univalently positive or negative in their attitudes toward black Americans. They are ambivalent.

One source of that ambivalence is the conflict between negative feelings toward blacks and the value many Americans place on equality and fair play. Their views on equality are sincere, but generally moderate. Americans believe in equality of opportunity, but not equality of outcome (Elder & Cobb, 1983). For those extremely low in negative affect, there is no conflict because their feelings toward blacks and their beliefs in equality reinforce one another. For those who are extremely negative, there is little conflict as well. For the extremely negative, their negative feelings overpower their values. But for those who are moderately negative, the two forces are in conflict. They are ambivalent, being pulled in opposite directions at once. The chapters in this volume by Katz, Wackenhut, and Hass (Chapter 2) and Gaertner and Dovidio (Chapter 3) discuss the dynamics of this ambivalence and its psychological consequences. Whether one adopts a psychoanalytic or a social learning position on ambivalence, there is agreement that the ambivalent person is not so much neutralized as he/she is marked by sharp alterations in behavior, while the unambivalent person is more consistent. It is even possible that the energy created by the ambivalence will enhance the ambivalent person's responses (Gergen & Jones, 1963; Katz, 1981). Hence, the ambivalent person will be more positive than might be expected in some situations and more negative than might be expected in others. Whether the ambivalent person is overly positive or overly negative depends on the context and the content of the behavior. (See McConahay, 1983.)

It is further proposed that racial prejudice is regarded as a socially undesirable trait or behavior in the present social and racial climate. As a result, negative racial attitudes cannot be exhibited except in a manner that will defend the person from a self- or other-generated attribution of prejudice. The specific contexts necessary for the expression of negative racial attitudes and behaviors are those characterized by racial ambiguity. That is, a context in which there is a plausible, nonprejudiced explanation available for what might be considered prejudiced behavior or intended behavior. For example, a white survey respondent might express the intention to vote for a conservative white candidate running against a liberal or moderate black candidate. In this context, the political ideology of the candidates can be used as a very plausible explanation for the voting intention, and the respondent is protected from having his candidate choice attributed to racism. (See Chapter 3 by Gaertner and Dovidio in this volume for a further elaboration of the role of the availability of a plausible, nonprejudiced explanation for what otherwise might be considered prejudiced attitudes or behaviors.)

Ideology is not the only factor that can create a racially ambiguous behavioral context. The ambiguity may be created by diffusion of responsibility, by actions initiated by or imputed to black actors who are then the target of the negative behavior, by situations without clear norms or guides for behavior, or by situations low in racial salience (Gaertner & Dovidio, 1981; Katz, 1981; McConahay, 1983). These conditions are elaborated next.

Positive or overly positive behavior is likely to be exhibited by ambivalent people under conditions maximizing the likelihood that a negative behavior will bring a self- or other-generated attribution of prejudice. These are situations low in ambiguity, where the norms are clear, social comparisons are possible, responsibility cannot be diffused, race is salient, or nonracial ideological or other attributions are not readily available.

It is thus proposed that the wording of the items in the Modern Racism Scale permit the expression of negative affect because giving the prejudiced response in each instance can be explained by racially neutral ideology or nonprejudiced race-relevant attributions. (See previous paragraphs.) Hence, we would expect the ambivalent person to score high on the Modern Racism Scale (though perhaps not as high as someone with extremely negative feelings). For the highly reactive

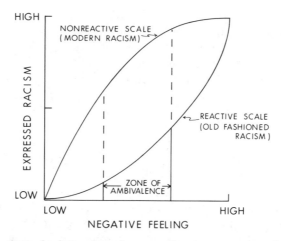

FIGURE 1.   Hypothetical relationship of expressed racism to negative feeling for reactive and nonreactive scales of racism.

Old Fashioned items, a nonprejudiced explanation is harder to give for a prejudiced response. Hence, the ambivalent person should score low on the Old Fashioned Racism Scale.

The dynamics proposed here can be illustrated by reference to Figure 1. The base or X axis is a variable measuring pure negative affect going from zero to maximum.[1] The vertical or Y axis is the amount of racism expressed on a given scale. For a nonreactive scale—one with alternative reasons for giving a prejudiced response—the relationship between negative affect and expressed prejudice is a negatively accelerating curve starting at zero and rising quickly before leveling off near its maximum. For a reactive scale, the relationship is hypothesized to be a positively accelerating curve rising slowly at first and then increasing rapidly at high levels of negative affect. Thus, the persons low and high in negative affect will be consistently low or high on the scales. Those near the middle of the affective dimension will be quite high on the nonreactive scale and quite low on the reactive scale. They will be exhibiting the behaviors associated with ambivalence.

It is *not* proposed that ambivalent persons consciously manipulate

[1] It is theoretically possible that whites could have positive feelings toward blacks as well as neutral or negative affect. However, they should not differ in their behavior from those who are neutral or have zero negative feelings. Therefore, the positives were not discussed in the text for ease and clarity of exposition.

their scores on the two scales. Some may indeed do this. But for most, the process is more unwitting and not under cognitive control. Rather, they truly believe both in integration and that blacks should not push themselves where they are not wanted.

If we assume that the Old Fashioned Racism Scale is reactive and the Modern Racism Scale is relatively nonreactive, then the relationships proposed in Figure 1 allow us to make predictions about the empirical relationship between the two scales. First, they should form distinct dimensions within the cognitive component of racial attitudes. Second, the two scales should be correlated.[2] Though they have different functional forms, both are related to negative affect and tend to increase as it does. Third, the ambivalent person should be high on the Modern Racism Scale and low on the Old Fashioned Racism Scale. That is, the pattern of scores on the two scales should enable us to make predictions about who would exhibit ambivalent behaviors in other situations such as voting, helping, derogating, and the like. Fourth, one should not expect to find many people who exhibit the opposite type of inconsistency across the two scales. That is, high on the Old Fashioned Racism Scale and low on the Modern Racism Scale. Such persons should be few in number, near the middle on both scales and fall in the odd combination mainly due to measurement error.

THE EMPIRICAL RELATIONSHIP BETWEEN THE TWO SCALES

Future research is planned to examine the attitudes and racially relevant behaviors of persons falling into various combinations of the two scales—especially the attitudes and behaviors of those falling into the ambivalent combination of high on the Modern Racism Scale and low on the Old Fashioned Racism Scale. In this chapter, previous work on the relationship between the two scales, their relative reactivity, and the validity of the Modern Racism Scale are summarized. In

[2] McConahay and Hough (1976) reported a nonsignificant correlation between the Scales of Modern and Old Fashioned Racism. This nonrelationship was suspect because of the large number of seminary students who refused to answer one or all of the Old Fashioned Scale items. When these data were reanalyzed for this chapter using a mean substitution whenever possible for those who answered at least two Old Fashioned Racism Scale items, a modest, but significant correlation of .232 was found. Since then, the correlation between the two scales has steadily increased in both student and random samples of adults.

this section, the empirical relationship between these scales is addressed.

Over the years, a number of factor analyses have been performed on various combinations of Modern and Old Fashioned Racism Scale items. Only three of these factor analyses are reported here. The results of the others have been similar, though not identical to these.

In all three of these analyses, the same computer program, extraction procedure, and rotation procedure were used. The initial item pools differed somewhat, and the samples differed as well. In all three studies, the procedure FACTOR from the program SPSS-X (SPSS Inc., 1983) was used. The original factors were extracted by maximum likelihood techniques. The two initial factors with Eigenvalues above 1.0 were rotated obliquely by the oblimin procedure (Kim & Mueller, 1978a, 1978b, SPSS Inc., 1983). An oblique rotation was used in each factor analysis instead of one of the orthogonal rotations because the two scales or factors are theoretically correlated with one another.

FACTOR ANALYSIS 1

The first factor analysis was performed on a sample of 879 white adults (18 years and older) residing in Louisville and Jefferson County, Kentucky, in the spring of 1976. The area probability sampling and the face-to-face interviewing were done by the nationally respected polling firm of Louis Harris and Associates. (See McConahay, 1982, for further details of sampling and interviewing.) The six Modern Racism Scale items, the six Old Fashioned Racism Scale items, and their final factor loadings are shown in Table 2.

The items in Table 2 are arranged in descending order of loading on their respective factors. The factor loadings are the standardized regression coefficients or path coefficients between the item and the factor. For clarity of presentation, those factor loadings below .100 are not shown in the table. The Modern Racism items all loaded together above .300 on the strong first factor and they all loaded below .300 on the second factor. On the other hand, the Old Fashioned Racism Scale items all loaded below .180 on the first factor and loaded at or above .300 on the weaker second factor. The correlation between the two oblique factors was +.68 which was slightly higher than the .58 correlation between the two scales created by simply adding the raw scores for each item (McConahay, 1982).

The two highest loading items on the Modern Racism Factor were the items about the extent to which blacks deserved their economic gains and the government and news media attention they received.

TABLE 2   Factor Loadings for Modern and Old Fashioned Racism Items in 1976
Louisville Sample after Maximum Likelihood Extraction and Oblimin Rotation.

	Factor loadings[a]	
	Factor 1	Factor 2
Modern racism items		
Over the past few years, blacks have gotten more economically than they deserve. (Strongly Agree = 5)	.808	
Over the past few years, the government and news media have shown more respect for blacks than they deserve. (Strongly Agree = 5)	.800	
It is easy to understand the anger of black people in America. (Strongly Disagree = 5)	.553	
How many black people in Louisville and Jefferson County do you think miss out on jobs or promotions because of racial discrimination—many, some, only a few or none? (None = 4)	.398	
Blacks are getting too demanding in their push for equal rights. (Strongly Agree = 5)	.338	.220
How many black people in Louisville and Jefferson County do you think miss out on good housing because white owners won't rent or sell to them—many, some, only a few, or none? (None = 4)	.302	.118
Old fashioned racism items		
If a black family with about the same income and education as you, moved next door, would you mind it a lot, a little or not at all? (A lot = 4)		.695
How strongly would you object if a member of your family had friendship with a black – strongly, somewhat, slightly or not at all? (Strongly Object = 4)		.686
How do you feel about the open housing law in Louisville/Jefferson County which allows more racial integration of neighborhoods? Do you strongly favor, somewhat favor, somewhat oppose or strongly oppose this law? (Strongly Oppose = 5)	.111	.569
Generally speaking, do you favor full racial integration, integration in some areas of life, or full separation of the races? (Full Separation = 3)	.131	.539
In principle, do you think it is a good idea or a bad idea for children to go to schools that have about the same proportion of blacks and whites as generally exists in the Louisville/Jefferson County area? (Bad Idea = 3)	.173	.381
Generally, do you feel blacks are smarter, not as smart or about as smart as whites? (Not As Smart = 3)	.161	.300
Percent of variance	35.3	10.4
Correlation between factors		.68
Sample N		879

[a] Standardized regression coefficients for item and factor from the pattern matrix. Loadings less than .100 are not shown.

The last item to load higher on the Modern Racism (first) Factor than on the Old Fashioned Racism (second) Factor was the modern racism question regarding perceptions of the continued existence of housing discrimination in Louisville and Jefferson County. (See Table 2.) It loaded almost three times as high on the first factor as on the second and loaded higher on the first factor than did any of the Old Fashioned Racism Scale items.

The two highest loading items on the Old Fashioned Racism (second) Factor dealt with social distance and freedom-of-association issues. The highest-loading item involved tolerance for a black family in the respondent's neighborhood. The second-highest-loading item dealt with reactions to a family member having a black person for a close friend. Both of these items loaded below .100 on the Modern Racism (first) Factor. The weakest loading item dealt with the relative intelligence of blacks and whites. This item barely made the cut-off point of .300, but it loaded higher on the Old Fashioned Racism Factor than on the Modern Racism Factor.

Clearly, then, the factor analysis of the two sets of items in this 1976 Louisville random sample, revealed two distinct factors: A Modern Racism Factor and a weaker, correlated, but still distinct Old Fashioned Racism Factor.

FACTOR ANALYSIS 2

The second factor analysis was a replication of the first using an independently drawn random sample of 709 white adults (18 years old or older) residing in Louisville and Jefferson County in the spring of 1977. The area sampling and face-to-face interviews were conducted by Louis Harris and Associates using the same procedures as in 1976. (See McConahay, 1984.)

The results for the 1977 sample were somewhat different in detail from the 1976 sample, but the overall results were very similar. As shown in Table 3, the stronger first factor was the Modern Racism Factor and the weaker second factor was the Old Fashioned Racism Factor. The correlation between the two oblique factors was .70, which was slightly higher than the .59 correlation between the two scales created by summing the items as in a Likert scaling procedure.

The two items loading highest on the Modern Racism (first) Factor were the black economic gains and attention items, which were the top two items in 1976 as well. However, the order of strength of loading was reversed. This time, the attention item loaded highest and the economic gains item was slightly behind it. Only one Modern Racism

TABLE 3 Factor Loadings for Modern and Old Fashioned Racism Items in 1977 Louisville Sample after Maximum Likelihood Extraction and Oblimin Rotation.

	Factor loadings[a]	
	Factor 1	Factor 2
Modern racism items		
Over the past few years, the government and news media have shown more respect for blacks than they deserve. (Strongly Agree = 5)	.801	
Over the past few years, blacks have gotten more economically than they deserve. (Strongly Agree = 5)	.779	
It is easy to understand the anger of black people in America. (Strongly Disagree = 5)	.598	.101
How many black people in Louisville and Jefferson County do you think miss out on jobs or promotions because of racial discrimination—many, some, only a few or none? (None = 4)	.500	
How many black people in Louisville and Jefferson County do you think miss out on good housing because white owners won't rent or sell to them—many, some, only a few, or none? (None = 4)	.455	
Blacks are getting too demanding in their push for equal rights. (Strongly Agree = 5)	.393	
Old fashioned racism items		
How do you feel about the open housing law in Louisville/Jefferson County which allows more racial integration of neighborhoods? Do you strongly favor, somewhat favor, somewhat oppose or strongly oppose this law? (Strongly Oppose = 5)		.829
If a black family with about the same income and education as you moved next door, would you mind it a lot, a little or not at all? (A lot = 4)		.716
How strongly would you object if a member of your family had friendship with a black—strongly, somewhat, slightly or not at all? (Strongly Object = 4)		.654
Generally speaking, do you favor full racial integration, integration in some areas of life, or full separation of the races? (Full Separation = 3)	.165	.580
In principle, do you think it is a good idea or a bad idea for children to go to schools that have about the same proportion of blacks and whites as generally exists in the Louisville/Jefferson County area? (Bad Idea = 3)		.450
Generally, do you feel blacks are smarter, not as smart or about as smart as whites? (Not As Smart = 3)	.110	.313
Percent of variance	38.6	10.8
Correlation between factors	.70	
Sample N	709	

[a] Standardized regression coefficients for item and factor from the pattern matrix. Loadings below .100 not shown.

Scale item loaded above .10 on the second factor: the black anger item. However, its first factor loading (.598) was almost six times its second factor loading (.101). The last item to load higher on the Modern Racism Factor than on the Old Fashioned Racism Factor was the blacks-are-too-demanding Modern Racism item, which loaded almost four times higher on the Modern than on the Old Fashioned Racism Factor, nevertheless.

The second factor was clearly the Old Fashioned Racism Factor. All of the Old Fashioned Racism Scale items loaded higher on it than on the first factor, and none of the Old Fashioned Racism Scale items loaded above .170 on the first factor. The highest-loading item on the second factor was the open-housing-law item. It was followed by the tolerance-for-a-black-family-in-the-neighborhood, which loaded highest on the Old Fashioned Racism (second) factor in the 1976 sample. The weakest loading item on the Old Fashioned Racism Factor was the black intelligence question, which was the weakest in 1976 as well.

Thus, the factor analysis in the 1977 Louisville sample confirmed and replicated the findings of the analysis in the 1976 sample. There were two distinct factors corresponding to the hypothesized distinct scales of modern and old-fashioned racism.

FACTOR ANALYSIS 3

Duke University undergraduates, enrolled in introductory psychology classes, have responded to various paper and pencil versions of the Modern and Old Fashioned Racism Scale items about two times per year over a 10-year period. The filler items have varied, and the order of the scale items within the fillers has varied widely, and the questionnaire administrators have varied. Each of these data sets has been factor analyzed. The results were not identical, but they were similar enough that only one analysis is reported here. These results are from a sample of 167 white students who filled out the questionnaires in the fall of 1984 in the 2-week period before the presidential election of 1984. The items and final factor loadings are shown in Table 4.

In this college student sample, the first factor loaded heavily with Old Fashioned Racism Scale items, while the weaker second factor loaded heavily with Modern Racism Scale items. The correlation between the two oblique factors was .59, which is somewhat lower than the correlation of .66 between the two scales created as Likert-type scales by simply summing the raw scores.

TABLE 4   Factor Loadings for Modern and Old Fashioned Racism Items in 1984
Duke University Student Sample after Maximum Likelihood Extraction and Oblimin
Rotation.

	Factor loadings[a]	
	Factor 1	Factor 2
Old fashioned racism items		
I favor laws that permit black persons to rent or purchase housing even when the person offering the property for sale or rent does not wish to rent or sell it to blacks. (Disagree Strongly = 5)	.784	−.130
Generally speaking, I favor full racial integration. (Disagree Strongly = 5)	.678	
I am opposed to open or fair housing laws. (Agree Strongly = 5)	.578	
It is a bad idea for blacks and whites to marry one another. (Agree Strongly = 5)	.562	
Black people are generally not as smart as whites. (Strongly Agree = 5)	.533	
If a black family with about the same income and education as I have moved next door, I would mind it a great deal. (Strongly Agree = 5)	.503	
It was wrong for the United States Supreme Court to outlaw segregation in its 1954 decision. (Strongly Agree = 5)	.444	.157
Modern racism items		
Over the past few years, the government and news media have shown more respect to blacks than they deserve. (Strongly Agree = 5)	.184	.608
It is easy to understand the anger of black people in America. (Strongly Disagree = 5)		.568
Discrimination against blacks is no longer a problem in the United States. (Strongly Agree = 5)		.548
Over the past few years, blacks have gotten more economically than they deserve. (Strongly Agree = 5)	.224	.514
Blacks have more influence upon school desegregation plans than they ought to have. (Strongly Agree = 5)	.409	.403
Blacks are getting too demanding in their push for equal rights. (Strongly Agree = 5)		.359
Blacks should not push themselves where they are not wanted. (Strongly Agree = 5)		.342
Percent of variance	39.0	9.2
Correlation betweeen factors	.59	
Sample *N*	167	

[a] Standardized regression coefficients for item and factor from the pattern matrix. Loadings below .100 are not shown.

The highest-loading item on the Old Fashioned Racism (first) Factor was a variant of the open or fair housing law question asked in Louisville, but with a more general reference than just Louisville. (See Table 4 for the exact wording of the item.) This item loaded weakly but negatively on the second factor. The Old Fashioned Racism item loading weakest on this factor was the one referring to the 1954 Supreme Court decision outlawing segregation. This *de jure* segregation item was the only item in addition to the open housing question to have a factor loading on the second factor with an absolute value above .100.

Six of the seven Modern Racism Scale items loaded higher on the second factor than on the first, and all of these second factor loadings were above .300. The item loading highest on the second factor was the government and news media attention item. The weakest loading question was the blacks-should-not-push-themselves item. It loaded below .100 on the first factor, however,

One Modern Racism Scale item loaded about the same on both factors, but slightly higher on the Old Fashioned Racism Factor than on the Modern Racism Factor. This was an item referring to the amount of influence blacks have or ought to have on school desegregation plans. (See Table 4 for the exact wording of the item.) A similar version of this item failed to scale with the other Modern Racism Scale items in the two Louisville samples and was dropped from the Modern Racism Scales used in research on antibusing attitudes in those samples (McConahay, 1982, 1984). In this 1984 sample, the item does scale with the rest of the Modern Racism Scale items in the sense that it increases the alpha coefficient from .77 for a six-item scale to .82 for the seven-item scale. The reason the item loads on both factors is probably that the "school desegregation" part of the item taps into the *de jure* discrimination aspect of old fashioned beliefs, and the proper-level-of-influence part of the item taps into the blacks-are-not-playing-fair tenet of modern racism. In the two published studies in which the item was used as part of the Modern Racism Scale (McConahay, Hardee, & Batts, 1981; McConahay, 1983), it did not load so heavily on the Old Fashioned Racism factor. If the 1984 pattern continues, the item should be refined or dropped from research using both scales.

With the exception of the influence item, the results of the factor analysis in the homogeneous student sample were very similar to those in the two more heterogeneous 1976 and 1977 Louisville samples. As in those samples, the empirical relationship between the two scales was what the theory predicted: two distinct but correlated belief dimensions of modern and old fashioned beliefs.

GUTTMAN SCALE ANALYSIS

The items used in these three data sets to measure degrees of endorsement of modern and old-fashioned racial beliefs were also subjected to Guttman or Scalogram analysis. This is because some journal referees and others (e.g., Erbe, 1977) have suggested that the modern and old-fashioned beliefs might be related like a unidimensional Guttman scale with the old-fashioned racism items constituting "easy items to pass" and the modern racism items representing "hard" items. The results of these Guttman analyses were disappointing. The coefficients of reproducibility did not exceed .75 in any of the three datasets and the coefficients of scalability did not exceed .40. Hence, it appears that we have two distinct but correlated empirical, cognitive dimensions: modern racism beliefs and old-fashioned racism beliefs.

THE RELATIVE REACTIVITY OF THE TWO SCALES

In this section, research into the relative reactivity of these two distinct scales of racial prejudice is summarized. Reactivity in this context means the extent to which the items are generally recognized by subjects or survey respondents as measuring racial prejudice, and their response behavior is altered in order to appear to self and others as being less racist than might be the case on another, less reactive type of measuring instrument.

It was proposed that the Old Fashioned Racism Scale was highly reactive, and the Modern Racism Scale was relatively nonreactive (though probably not unreactive). In fact, the Modern Racism Scale was developed to be as nonreactive as possible. The results of three laboratory experiments examining the relative reactivity of the two scales are summarized in this section.

EXPERIMENT 1

In the first experiment, white male undergraduates responded to a questionnaire entitled "Student Opinions" under conditions designed to maximize or minimize the pressures to give nonprejudiced answers to the Old Fashioned and Modern Racism scales. For half of the subjects, the person distributing and collecting the questionnaire was a white female. For the other half, the experimenter was a black female. The subjects were randomly assigned so that a given individual was as likely to encounter a black experimenter as to encounter a white experimenter. The experimenters worked from a memorized script so that each subject was told the same thing. (See McConahay, Hardee, & Batts, 1981, for the published version of this study. See McConahay, Hardee & Batts, 1980, for the exact working of the script, the questionnaire, and other details of procedure.)

When the subject arrived at the small laboratory room, he was handed two forms in a manilla envelope and asked to fill out both forms. He was assured that his answers would be anonymous. The experimenter then said she would return in 20 minutes to collect the forms, which were to be replaced in the envelope before her return. One of the forms was the "Student Opinions" questionnaire, which contained 23 Likert-type opinion statements—six Old Fashioned Racism items, six Modern Racism items and 11 nonracial, but controversial filler items (e.g., "Sex education should be taught in the public school systems of the United States"). The other form had nothing in it that was race related. The experimenter left the subject in the room alone for 20 minutes and then returned to collect the envelope with the two forms.

It was thought that in the condition where the scales were administered by a black experimenter, subjects would be especially motivated to appear not to be racist in order to avoid offending her. In this condition, even though the questionnaires were anonymous, it was hypothesized that subjects would modify the racism they might normally express and score less prejudiced on those items they recognized as tapping racism. Specifically, it was predicted that subjects' Old Fashioned Racism Scale scores would be lower for the black experimenter than for the white and that scores on the Modern Racism Scale would be unaffected by the race of the experimenter.

The results supported the hypotheses. The scale items were summed to form two Likert scales. (The details of the scale construction are given in McConahay, Hardee, & Batts, 1980, 1981.) For the Old Fashioned Racism Scale, subjects scored significantly lower for the black experimenter than for the white. But for the Modern Racism Scale, race of experimenter did not have a significant effect.

EXPERIMENT 2

The results of the first experiment was consistent with the idea that whites are more likely to recognize the Old Fashioned Racism items than they are the Modern Racism items as measures of antiblack prejudice. However, the results were subject to other interpretations as well. Because only one white experimenter and only one black experimenter were involved, it was possible that something unique to these two women other than their race was responsible for the effects on the two scales. It was also possible that the effect of race on the Old Fashioned Racism scale was not a reduction in expressed prejudice when the experimenter was black, but an increase when the experimenter was white. Noel (1972) has demonstrated that whites generally perceive other whites to be racially prejudiced. Hence, it was possible that the white males expressed more Old Fashioned Racism with the white female than with the black in order to please the white experimenter. While this latter possibility was not inconsistent with the hypothesis of different levels of reactivity in the two scales, it was not consistent with the reasoning that guided the predictions in the first experiment. Hence, the second experiment, sought to replicate the essential features of the first, but with different experimenters and with a design permitting us to assess the direction of change as a function of the race of the experimenter.

In the second study, 82 students in an undergraduate introductory statistics class took several questionnaires during the second class of the semester. The data from some of these questionnaires, but not the one used in this study, were used in homework and examination assignments during the semester. All students in the course were required to participate as subjects in some sort of statistical research project. The 34 white male students who had responded to all of the questions participated as subjects in this study.

About 6 weeks after the first administration of the questionnaire, the 34 subjects were blindly and randomly assigned by the flip of a coin to a black female experimenter or a white female experimenter. Neither experimenter had participated in Experiment 1.

When an individual subject arrived at the laboratory, he was greeted by the white or black experimenter and was asked to fill in a questionnaire identical to the one (among several) he had completed previously in class. This second exposure to the questionnaire is referred to as Time 2. The statistics class had heard a lecture on measures of reliability earlier in the semester and the experimenter explained that this was for the purpose of getting a test–retest reliability estimate on this questionnaire. The questionnaire used in this second experiment was very similar to the one used in the first. It was entitled "Personal Opinions," had the same instructions as in the first experiment and had virtually the same Modern, Old Fashioned and filler items as in the first study. (See McConahay, Hardee, & Batts, 1980, for the entire questionnaire, and Table 4 for the Modern and Old Fashioned Racism Scale items.) Consistent with the findings of the first experiment, it was predicted that when the experimenter was black, average scores on the Old Fashioned Racism Scale would decline from Time 1 to Time 2 but they would not change when she was white. It was also expected that the race of the experimenter would have no effect on the mean Modern Racism Scale scores.

The Modern Racism items were summed for Time 1 and Time 2 to create Likert Scales. The Time 1 and Time 2 old-fashioned items were combined to form a similar Likert scale. For Time 2, the correlation between the Modern and Old Fashioned Racism Scales was a statistically significant $+.58$. (See McConahay, Hardee, & Batts, 1980, 1981, for details of scale construction and reliabilities.) The Time 1 scale score was subtracted from Time 2 scale score for each subject and these difference scores were analyzed by means of analysis of variance. (See McConahay, Hardee, & Batts, 1980, for alternative statistical analyses.)

The results were consistent with the findings of Experiment 1. When the experimenter at Time 2 was black, Old Fashioned Racism Scale scores declined over three points from Time 1 on the average. This decline was statistically significant. When the Time 2 experimenter was white, the Old Fashioned Racism Scale scores increased less than a point on the average. For the Modern Racism Scale, there were decreases of less than a point for both the white and black experimenters. These last three changes were not statistically significant.

EXPERIMENT 3

In the first two studies, the white subjects behaved as though they did not perceive the Modern Racism Scale items as revealing possible negative attitudes toward blacks. However, there was not a direct measure of their perceptions. In addition, it was possible that the presence of the old-fashioned items on the questionnaire created the conditions of a contrast effect. The old-fashioned racism items were so blatantly racist that by comparison the modern items might not have appeared to have been offensive to a black person. If only modern items were on a questionnaire administered by a black experimenter, the subjects might have modified their positions on all or some of the modern items as well.

To examine this potential contrast effect on the item context and to examine the extent to which the old-fashioned and modern racism items would be perceived (or at least reported) as tapping negative racial attitudes, a third experiment was performed. In this study, subjects were administered a questionnaire and instructed to rate the extent to which agreement (or disagreement) with a given item indicated a negative attitude toward blacks. Three forms of the question-naire were created so that on one form both sets of items were present among filler items (as in Experiments 1 and 2), on a second form only the old-fashioned items were present among fillers and on a third form only the modern items were present among fillers. If the modern racism items were seen as more racist by themselves than in the context of the old-fashioned items, there would be grounds for inferring a context effect.

At the start of the semester following Experiment 2, students enrolled in two undergraduate introductory statistics classes were given the aforementioned three forms of the questionnaire. The forms were randomly distributed throughout the classes. The questionnaire was entitled "Perceptions of Racial Opinions" and the instructions explicitly told the subjects to disregard their own opinions on each item while concentrating on rating the extent to which the item reflected a negative attitude toward black people. A three-point rating scale was used to rate each item, ranging from clearly reflects a negative attitude (2 points) through tends to reflect a "negative attitude" (1 point) to "unrelated to racial attitudes" (0 points). Of the 56 white students who responded to the questionnaire, 28 received the form with both items present, 14 recieved the form with only old-fashioned items and 14 received the form with only modern racism items. Those receiving the first version were randomly divided into 14 whose old-fashioned items were analyzed and 14 whose modern items were analyzed. The items were summed to form a seven-item, 0- to 14-point rating of perceptions of Old Fashioned Racism Scale items and a similar 14-point scale of rating of Modern Racism Scale items.

The results showed that there was not a context effect. Neither the main effect for context nor the interaction between context and type of racism were statistically significant. On the other hand, the main effect for type of racism was highly significant ($p < .01$). Regardless of context, the Modern Racism Scale had a lower perceived racism mean (5.68) than the Old Fashioned Racism Scale mean (7.68).

However, it should also be noted that the racial implications of the Modern Racism Scale items were not completely lost on the subjects. The Modern Racism Scale differed significantly from the mean perceived racism score of all of the filler items. On the average, then, it is possible that the subjects in the first two experiments may have recognized that the modern racism items had some relevance to a negative racial attitude, but they varied their behavior only on the old fashioned items where the ideological and racial implications were clear.

THE VALIDITY OF THE MODERN RACISM SCALE

The Modern Racism Scale is relatively nonreactive or is at least less reactive than the Old Fashioned Racism Scale, but does it measure racism? Because the scale is not obviously face valid, it is worth reviewing the evidence for its validity.

The original items in the scale were designed to relate to voter preferences in the 1969 and 1973 Los Angeles mayorial contest between Tom Bradley, the black challenger, and Sam Yorty, the white incumbent. Yorty won the first election and Bradley won the second. The Modern Racism scale correlated with voter preferences in both contests. Those whites scoring high on the scale were more likely than low scorers to vote for the white candidate. These correlations were .392 in a sample of white Claremont, California, voters in 1969 (McConahay & Hough, 1976), .365 in a sample of white Los Angeles voters in 1969 (Kinder & Sears, 1981) and .338 in a sample of white Los Angeles voters in 1973 (Kinder & Sears, 1981). Furthermore, the partial correlations after controls for Republican Party identification and political conservatism were .318, .309, and .300 respectively. All were statistically significant. However, many of the whites indicating a preference for Yorty said they were voting for the unpopular incumbent not because they liked Yorty, but because Bradley was too liberal or too soft on crime or too something else. Thus, while this suggested that the scale was valid, the evidence was not unambiguous.

The scale also correlated with strength of opposition to busing in Louisville in surveys done during the conflict there in 1976 and 1977. These correlations were .511 in 1976 and .391 in 1977. In addition, these correlations remained statistically significant in both years, even after controls for being a parent of school-age children, having a child in the public schools, having a child bused for desegregation purposes, education, occupation, union membership, income, region of socialization, gender, political efficacy, authoritarianism, and lifestyle conservatism (McConahay, 1982, 1984). However, the direction of causality here is ambiguous. (See Armor, 1980, and Chapter 2 by Katz et al. in this volume.) Furthermore, opposition to busing is not viewed as being an indicator of racism by some experts and many whites in the general public. Hence, this evidence is also suggestive, but not conclusive.

The Modern Racism Scale correlated −.299 with the Schuman and Harding (1963) scale of Sympathetic Identification with the Underdog (McConahay & Hough, 1976), and it correlated .383 with antiblack feeling as measured by the Feeling Thermometer (Campbell, 1971) in

Louisville (McConahay, 1982). And in Yale and Duke University student samples, the correlation with the Feeling Thermometer has averaged .441 over the past 16 years. The scale also correlated significantly with the Old Fashioned Racism Scale (.581) in Louisville (McConahay, 1982) and from .35 to .66 in college student samples. It *did not* correlate with the Just World Scale in repeated college student samples. Because the Feeling Thermometer and the Old Fashioned Racism Scales are accepted as face valid measures of racism and the belief in a just world might be an alternative explanation for high scores on the moralistic items in the scale, this is stronger evidence for the Modern Racism Scale's validity than the voting and busing studies.

The strongest evidence for the construct validity of the Modern Racism Scale was developed in an experimental study of simulated hiring decisions using white college student subjects. In this study, both the criterion for validation (hiring discrimination) and the direction of causality were clearer than in the field studies. In this experiment, subjects pretested on the Modern Racism Scale rated their preference for hiring simulated black or white job candidates with identical credentials under conditions predicted to encourage the expression of either the negative or positive side of the ambivalence that prejudiced persons feel toward blacks. Because this study is so important for establishing the validity of the scale as a measure of racial prejudice, it is reviewed in detail here.

EXPERIMENT 4

Earlier in this chapter, it was proposed that a necessary condition for the expression of the negative side of the ambivalence by the ambivalent white person was a behavioral context of ambiguity. Previous work with the concepts of racial ambivalence and ambiguity by Katz (1981 and Chapter 2 in this volume) and Gaertner and Dovidio (1981 and Chapter 3 in this volume) had demonstrated that ambivalent subjects acted more negatively toward blacks that unambivalent subjects under conditions fostering negative behavior and more positively than the unambivalent under conditions fostering positive behavior.

Though different factors have been emphasized in the various empirical studies, it is hypothesized that the elements of a context likely to elicit negative behaviors are (1) Ideological ambiguity in which one or more nonracial values or political beliefs can be readily invoked to explain the negative behavior (e.g., a respondent tells an interviewer that he or she is voting against a black candidate because the candidate is too liberal). (2) Situational ambiguity in which one or more nonracial attributions are available to explain the behavior (e.g., a bystander intervention situation involving a black victim under conditions where more than one person could go to her or his aid). (3) Situations making it necessary to derogate a person harmed by the subject. (4) Unstructured or normless situations in which there are no clear anchor points for evaluation or guides for appropriate behavior. (5) Situations in which race is not a particularly salient feature of the context. In general, ambivalent persons will be likely to express the negative side of their conflict to the extent that the situation minimizes the likelihood that a self- or other-generated attribution of racial prejudice will be made for their negative actions (also see Chapter 3).

Positive behavior is likely to be exhibited under conditions maximizing the likelihood that a negative behavior will bring a self- or other-generated atribution of bigotry. Situations in which the norms are clear, social comparisons are possible, race is salient, and nonracial ideological or other attributions are not readily available.

This study assumes that, in a college population, the more prejudiced subjects will feel the greatest ambivalence and therefore show the greatest inconsistency of behavior between contexts fostering negative and positive behavior toward blacks. Hence, if the Modern Racism Scale is a valid measure of prejudice, high scorers should evaluate the black candidate more negatively than low scorers in the negative context and evaluate the black candidate more positively than low scorers in the positive context. The low scorers should feel less ambivalence and thus be more consistent in their behavior across contexts. (For other work examining behavioral extremity across contexts, see Chapters 2 and 6 in this volume.)

In this study a resume was created presenting a graduating senior who was a very ordinary candidate for a job in the private sector (some, but not much work experience; grades slightly below the actual all-school average, but above the all-school average as perceived by the subject population). The race of the job candidate was manipulated by attaching a picture of a black or white recent graduate to the stimulus resume. Hence, the credentials on the resume were identical; only the pictures were different.

The context designed to foster negative behavior toward blacks was created by reducing the salience of the confederate's race by having the subjects rate the stimulus resume at the outset of the experiment before rating the resumes of other confederates. Subjects in this decision context would encounter an undistinguished job candidate (grades near the all-school average, little work experience) in a situation where they had few anchor points for comparison and few explicit norms for behavior. Though race might have been somewhat salient in the black stimulus condition, an elaborate cover story (see below) and lack of other (presumably white) candidates would make race less salient than in the positive behavior enhancing context. It was predicted that prejudiced whites, in this normless, unanchored situation, would reveal their bigotry in this condition. Hence, the hypothesis was that Modern Racism Scale scores would be negatively correlated with evaluations of the black candidate and unrelated to evaluations of the white candidate.

The positive behavior context was created by having subjects rate the undistinguished candidate last after evaluating the credentials of two white students, each of whom was superior in terms of scholastic record or business experience. Hence, the evaluation of two whites prior to the evaluation of a black candidate should have provided a context that would increase the salience of race (Taylor & Fiske, 1978). Salience should have put ambivalent subjects on guard against revealing their prejudices and the experience with evaluating other (presumably white) candidates should enable the ambivalent to protect themselves by inflating their ratings of the black candidate relative to the others. During the first week of the semester, all introductory psychology students were pretested on the seven-item version of the Modern Racism Scale (see Table 4) embedded in a number of political and other racial filler items. The students also filled out a number of other questionnaires given by other experimenters. Approximately 2 weeks later, subjects who had signed up for a study of "Job Placement Resumes" were ushered individually into small laboratory rooms by the experimenter and told that he was an applied psychologist, working for the university's Placement Center, seeking to improve the quality of the resumes shown to prospective employers. According to the experimenter, he and the Placement Center wanted to know how the format, style of type, information included and even color of the paper would affect the impressions formed by potential employers.

The subjects were then asked to play the role of a personnel director working for a large corporation that hired a few bachelors-degree-level people every year for its management training program. The last question asked for each resume was "Would you hire this candidate?" followed by a seven-point, semantic differential type scale running from "Would definitely hire" to "Would definitely *not* hire." After making sure that the subject understood the instructions, the experimenter handed her or him the first resume and left the room. When the subject finished evaluating the first resume and candidate, the experimenter collected both the resume and the rating booklet and gave the subject a new set of materials. This was repeated until all

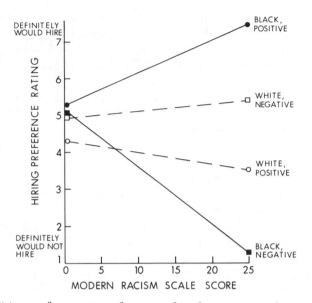

FIGURE 2. Hiring preferences as a function of modern racism scale scores, race of candidate and decision context.

three resumes and candidates had been evaluated. Half of the subjects were randomly assigned to rate the stimulus resume first (the negative behavior context) and half were assigned to rate it last (the positive behavior context). Half of the time the stimulus resume was associated with a white male, and half of the time it was associated with a black male. (See McConahay, 1983, for methodological details.)

The final sample consisted of 81 white subjects (37 males and 44 females). The dependent variable for this study was the bottom line in any job seeking or hiring situation: the question regarding the subjects' degree of preference for hiring the candidate described on the resume with a picture on it. This was converted to a seven-point scale on which seven indicated maximum willingness to hire.

Because the Modern Racism Scale can be considered an interval-level measure, a multiple regression was performed on the hiring preference dependent variable (Cronbach, 1968; Kerlinger & Pedhazur, 1973). The results were that for the saturated model (all main and interaction effects), only the three-way interaction was significant. The regression lines for this triple interaction are plotted in Figure 2. (See McConahay, 1983, for details of the regression equations.)

As shown in Figure 2, when the job candidate was white, making race irrevelant, the independent variables had no effect. The slopes of the regression lines (as well as the Modern Racism Scale correlations with hiring preference) did not differ significantly from zero in either behavior context and they did not differ from each other across decision contexts. Furthermore, the order of rating had no effect on the hiring preference for the white candidate.

When the job candidate was black, quite a different picture emerged. As shown in Figure 2, in the context intended to foster negative behavior among the ambivalent, the slope and correlation were significantly negative as predicted. In the positive context, the slope and correlation were significantly positive, again as predicted. When the modern-racism–hiring-preference slopes were compared across the two decision contexts, the slopes and correlations differed significantly from one another.

The higher Modern Racism Scale scorers not only changed their behavior relative to the low scorers when race was relevant, but also engaged in different forms of discrimination, depending on race of job candidate and decision context. That is, the higher scorers expressed less willingness to hire a black than a white candidate with identical credentials in the negative context and expressed greater preference for the black over the white in the positive context.

The results of this experiment provided strong additional support for the validity of the Modern Racism Scale as a measure of racial prejudice. It was hypothesized that the more prejudiced college student subjects would feel more ambivalent and hence display greater inconsistency in behavior across contexts designed to elicit positive or negative racial behavior. The Modern Racism Scale was related to hiring preferences for black and white candidates with identical credentials in a manner predicted by this hypothesis. As Modern Racism Scale scores increased, there was an increasing tendency to rate the black candidate higher than the white in the positive decision context and to rate the black candidate lower than the white in the negative context. Those low on the scale, having less prejudice, should have felt less ambivalence and, indeed, the lower scores were more consistent in their behavior across the race and context conditions. When race was not relevant because the candidate was white, decision context and Modern Racism Scale scores did not affect hiring evaluations.

FUTURE RESEARCH

After the initial research to develop the Modern Racism Scale, most of the research on the scale concentrated on its reactivity (McConahay, Hardee & Batts, 1981) and its construct validity (McConahay, 1982, 1983). Now that its relative nonreactivity and its validity have been established (to the satisfaction of the present author), future research with the Modern and Old Fashioned Racism Scales will be focussed in four areas. Each of these are discussed briefly here.

THE ROOTS OF MODERN RACISM

Originally, it was proposed that modern racism had at least two roots: negative feeling or affect toward black people and moralistic, Protestant ethic conservatism (McConahay & Hough, 1976; Sears & Kinder, 1971; Sears & McConahay, 1973). These feelings and values/ attitudes have been present in America throughout its history. Two external historical changes combined with these psychological predispositions to create the need for a new form of racial ideology: modern racism. The first historical change resulted from Hitler giving racism a bad name. This has probably inhibited its open expression. The second resulted from the success of the civil rights movement. This changed the racial agenda and policy debate from issues of freedom to issues of equality (or equality of opportunity). This latter change reduced the guilt that many Americans felt and added a tone or moral indignation to the arguments (or ideology) of those opposed to change in the racial status quo (Ashmore & McConahay, 1975; McConahay & Hough, 1976).

One line of research, then, will examine the predictors of Modern and Old Fashioned Racism Scale scores and of those in the high and low combination of the two scales predicted to be the ambivalent Americans. If the theoretical analysis is correct, measures of antiblack affect ought to be curvilinearly related to the two scales in the manner illustrated in Figure 1, and the best multiple correlates of Modern Racism Scale scores ought to be (1) negative feeling, (2) Protestant ethic conservatism, and (3) demographic variables related to prior socialization (education, age cohort) rather than current experience (occupation, contact with blacks). The early research on the psychological and demographic roots of modern racism was based on data collected in 1968 and 1969. Hence, it is entirely possible that the predictors have changed or the interaction between feeling and ideology is not as powerful in its effect on Modern Racism Scale scores as it once was because more and more liberals appear to be joining with conservatives in adopting the tenets of modern racism. (See the chapter by Gaertner and Dovidio in this volume for an examination of the ambivalence of white liberals.)

THE ROLE OF SELF- AND GROUP-INTEREST

The early research found little evidence that modern racism was the product of personal impact, personal threat, or personal self-interest. The Modern Racism Scale scorers were no more likely than the low to be objectively threatened by blacks or to perceive a personal threat. Bobo (1983) and others have argued that the measures of self interest used in this research were too narrow and needed to be broadened to include self-interest in one's group or reference group.

There are two questions raised by this critique of modern or symbolic racism research. First, is it useful to include group threat and personal threat under the same label of "self-interest"? Second, is group conflict a factor in producing modern racism? The answers are no and yes. It is not useful to treat both threats to the individual and threats to his/her reference groups as if they were the same thing. The two types of threats can be distinguished analytically and empirically. The distinction adds analytical rigor and it makes it possible to test the effects of the two factors empirically. (See McConahay, 1982, for an elaboration of this argument.) An individual may have a personal self-interest in the outcome of a political or policy conflict and he/she may belong to or identify with a social group (class, race, profession) that has an interest in the outcome as well. The personal and group interests may coincide or they may conflict, or the interests of one reference group may conflict with those of another. Therefore, it is more useful to call direct threats or benefits to the self "self-interest" and threats or benefits mediated by the many reference groups the individual may have "group-interest."

That group conflict is a factor in producing modern racism is obvious. McConahay and Hough (1976) discussed the resentment whites high on the Modern Racism Scale feel toward the group demands and actions of blacks. McConahay (1982) discussed the symbolic status conflicts involved in the busing controversy in Louisville. To emphasize the psychological roots of modern racism (as was done in this chapter) is not to deny that there are sociological and economic factors. If there had been no civil rights movement, there would not be an ideology of modern racism.

The interesting research question, then, is "What are the relative strengths of self-interest, group-interest, affect, and ambivalence in producing high or low Modern Racism Scale scorers?" Future research will address this question.

THE EFFECTS OF AMBIVALENCE

The first two future research areas are closely related and involve using the Modern and Old Fashioned Racism Scales as dependent variables. In this third area, the two scales and their combination will be treated as independent variables and the main and interaction effects on other variables will be examined. How to combine the two scales to identify the ambivalent will be particularly challenging. They could be treated as nonorthogonal independent variables in a multiple-regression equation or converted to a standard metric and added. (See the chapter by Katz, Wackenhut, and Hass in this volume for a discussion of the similar problem of combining cognitive attitudinal measures.) The work in this area is in a very preliminary stage. The dependent variables of interest are hiring preferences, interpersonal distance perception, voting preferences, and jury decisions.

ULTRAMODERN RACISM

It is expected that new items will have to be generated for the Modern Racism Scale as new issues emerge in American race relations and some of the current scale items become more reactive while the ambivalence lingers. Though that may sound cynical or pessimistic, it is based on an optimistic assumption. The pressures for new, less reactive items will continue because of the changed value attached to racism. This change in the intellectual and social climate that makes it hard to maintain a positive self-image and proper standing with the important reference groups in American national society is perhaps the most important of all the changes in law and custom to take place since World War II. It has meant that much racism must be hidden or covert, but it has also created a dynamic for future change in a positive, less prejudiced direction. The negative feelings are still there to some extent, but when people must behave as if they are not prejudiced, it sets cognitive consistency pressures in motion to change the residual feelings (McConahay, 1981). I do not expect to run out of either theoretical or applied work to do in American race relations in the near future, but I think there are grounds for limited optimism about the long-range future so long as the norm that "nice people can't be racists and racists can't be nice people" establishes the climate for a creative ambivalence.

ACKNOWLEDGMENTS

I want to thank Jack Dovidio and Sam Gaertner for helpful suggestions on early drafts of this chapter and Sonja Hollowy and Roz Kaplin for typing multiple drafts of the manuscript.

REFERENCES

Allport, G. W. (1954). *The nature of prejudice*. Reading, MA: Addison-Wesley.

Armor, D. J. (1980). White flight and the future of school desegregation. In W. S. Stephan & J. R. Feagin (Eds.), *School desegregation: Past, present and future*. (pp. 187–226). New York: Plenum.

Ashmore, R. D., & McConahay, J. B. (1975). *Psychology and America's urban dilemmas*. New York: McGraw-Hill.

Bobo, L. (1983). White's opposition to busing: Symbolic racism or realistic group conflict? *Journal of Personality and Social Psychology, 45*, 1196–1210.

Campbell, A. (1971). *White attitudes toward black people*. Ann Arbor: Institute for Social Research.

Capitman, J. A. (1980). *Symbolic racism theory criteria for individual differences measures of prejudice and the validity of the Feeling Thermometer*. Unpublished doctoral dissertation, Duke University, Durham, NC.

Cronbach, L. J. (1968). Intelligence? Creativity? A parsimonious reinterpretation of the Wallach–Kogan data. *American Educational Research Journal, 5*, 491–511.

Elder, C. D., & Cobb, R. W. (1983). *The political uses of symbols*. New York: Longman.

Erbe, B. M. (1977). On "The politics of school busing." *Public Opinion Quarterly, 41*, 113–117.

Gaertner, S. L. & Dovidio, J. F. (1981). Racism among the well intentioned. In E. Clausen and J. Bermingham (Eds.) *Pluralism, racism and public policy: The search for equality*. (pp. 208–222). Boston: G. K. Hall.

Gergen, K. J., & Jones, E. E. (1963). Mental illness, predictability, and affective consequences as stimulus factors in person perception. *Journal of Abnormal and Social Psychology, 67*, 95–105.

Greeley, A. M., & Sheatsley, P. B. (1971). Attitudes toward racial integration. *Scientific American, 225*, 13–19.

Horowitz, E. L. (1936). The development of attitudes toward Negroes. *Archives of Psychology, 194*.

Katz, I. (1981). *Stigma: A social psychological analysis*. Hillsdale, NJ: Erlbaum.

Kerlinger, F. N., & Pedhazur, E. J. (1973). *Multiple regression in behavioral research*. New York: Holt, Rinehart and Winston.

Kim, J. O., & Mueller, C. W. (1978a). *Introduction to factor analysis: What it is and how to do it*. Beverly Hills: Sage.

Kim, J. O. & Mueller, C. W. (1978b). *Factor analysis: Statistical methods and practical issues*. Beverly Hills: Sage.

Kinder, D. R., & Sears, D. O. (1981). Symbolic racism versus racial threats to "the good life." *Journal of Personality and Social Psychology, 40*, 414–431.

Lerner, M. J. (1980). *The belief in a just world: A fundamental delusion*. New York: Plenum.

McConahay, J. B. (1981). Reducing racial prejudice in desegregated schools. In W. D.

Hawley (Ed.) *Effective school desegregation: Equity quality and feasibility* (pp. 35–53). Beverly Hills: Sage.

McConahay, J. B. (1982). Self-interest versus racial attitudes as correlates of anti-busing attitudes in Louisville: Is it the buses or the blacks? *Journal of Politics, 44,* 692–720.

McConahay, J. B. (1983). Modern racism and modern discrimination: The effects of race, racial attitudes, and context on simulated hiring decisions. *Personality and Social Psychology Bulletin, 9,* 551–558.

McConahay, J. B. (1984). *It's still the blacks and not the buses.* Unpublished paper, Duke University.

McConahay, J. B., Hardee, B. B., & Batts, V. (1980). *Has racism declined? It depends upon who's asking and what is asked.* Working paper no. 8012. Durham, N.C.: Duke University Institute of Policy Sciences and Public Affairs.

McConahay, J. B., Hardee, B. B., & Batts, V. (1981). Has racism declined in America? It depends upon who is asking and what is asked. *Journal of Conflict Resolution, 25,* 563–579.

McConahay, J. B., & Hough, J. C. Jr. (1976). Symbolic racism. *Journal of Social Issues, 32,* 23–45.

McConahay, J. B., Mullin, C. J., & Frederick, J. (1977). The uses of social science in trials with political and racial overtones: The trial of Joan Little. *Law and Contemporary Problems, 41,* 205–229.

Myrdal, G. (1944). *An American dilemma.* New York: Harper and Row.

Noel, J. R. (1972). The norm of white anti-black prejudice in the United States. *International Journal of Group Tensions, 2,* 51–62.

Oskamp, S. (1977). *Attitudes and opinions.* Englewood Cliffs, NJ: Prentice-Hall.

Polin, J. (1982). The Just World Scale and the Modern Racism Scale. Unpublished paper, Duke University, Durham, NC.

Rubin, Z., & Peplau, A. (1973). Belief in a just world and reactions to another's lot: A study of participation in the national draft lottery. *Journal of Social Issues, 29,* 73–93.

Schuman, H., & Harding, J. (1963). Sympathetic identification with the underdog. *Public Opinion Quarterly, 27,* 230–241.

Sears, D. O., & Kinder, D. R. (1971). Racial tensions and voting in Los Angeles. In W. Z. Hirsch (Ed.), *Los Angeles: Viability and prospects for metropolitan leadership* (pp. 51–88). New York: Praeger.

Sears, D. O., & McConahay, J. B. (1973). *The politics of violence: The new urban blacks and the Watts riot.* Boston: Houghton Mifflin.

Sigall, H., & Page, R. (1971). Current stereotypes: A little fading, a little faking. *Journal of Personality and Social Psychology, 18,* 247–255.

SPSS Inc. (1983). *SPSSX User's Guide.* New York: McGraw Hill.

Sumner, W. G. (1906). *Folkways.* Boston: Ginn.

Taylor, S. E., & Fiske, S. T. (1978). Salience, attention, and attribution: Top of the head phenomenon. In L. Berkowitz (Ed.), *Advances in experimental social psychology, Vol. 11* (pp. 249–288). New York: Academic Press.

Taylor, D. G., Sheatsley, P. B., & Greeley, A. M. (1978). Attitudes toward racial integration. *Scientific American, 238,* 42–49.

Trickett, E. J., McConahay, J. B., Phillips, D. & Ginter, M. A. (1985). Natural experiments and the educational context: The environment and effects of an alternative inner city public school on adolescents. *American Journal of Community Psychology, 13,* 617–643.

STEREOTYPES AND STEREOTYPING: AN OVERVIEW OF THE COGNITIVE APPROACH*

David L. Hamilton
and Tina K. Trolier

Department of Psychology
University of California,
   Santa Barbara
Santa Barbara, California 93106

INTRODUCTION

Social scientists who have studied prejudice, stereotypes, and inter-group relations have approached their subject matter from a variety of theoretical perspectives, as the collection of chapters comprising this book well illustrates. Indeed, one of the purposes of this volume is to bring together contributions by authors with differing conceptual orientations as a means of demonstrating the usefulness of recognizing diverse approaches to a related set of topics.

The focus of this chapter is stereotypes. Historically, the development and perpetuation of stereotypes has been viewed as a consequence of three classes of processes (Ashmore & Del Boca, 1981). One approach has emphasized the role of *motivational* processes, in which stereotypes are viewed as serving the intrapsychic needs of the perceiver. From this perspective, perceiving members of minority groups in stereotypic, and often disparaging, terms is functional in maintaining one's self-esteem and in coping with feelings of self-inadequacy. A second, *sociocultural* orientation has focused on the role of social learning processes by which stereotypic beliefs are acquired through socialization, media influences, and the like, and are maintained by social reinforcements obtained from significant others and important reference groups. The third approach, of primary concern in this chap-

* Preparation of this chapter was supported in part by NSF Grant BNS-8216813 and NIMH Grant MH 40058 to the first author.

ter, has sought to understand the role of *cognitive* structures and processes in the development of our conceptions of social groups and their effects on information processing and interpersonal behavior.

This chapter presents an overview of the cognitive analysis of stereotypes and stereotyping. Specifically, we view stereotypes as cognitive categories that are used by the social perceiver in processing information about people. In our analysis, we develop the implications of this relatively simple statement for a number of issues of both theoretical and practical significance. Specifically, we address, from a cognitive perspective, the questions of why people develop stereotypes, the role of cognitive mechanisms in their development, and how cognitive processes can contribute to the perpetuation of stereotypic beliefs. In a final section, we consider the relationship of the cognitive approach to other conceptual orientations.

THE CATEGORIZATION PROCESS IN SOCIAL PERCEPTION

Each person we encounter in our social world is an individual. No two persons are entirely alike. Because of this obvious fact, our social world is extremely rich in variety and diversity. This variation among the persons we meet and interact with conveys an immense amount of information about these persons as individuals. If we, as social perceivers, were to perceive each individual as an individual, we would be confronted with an enormous amount of information that would quickly overload our cognitive processing and storage capacities. Faced, then, with too much information, there is a need to simplify things. One of the ways we do so is by seeking the commonalities among the individuals we encounter in our social world, and we use those commonalities as a basis for grouping those individuals that share common properties or attributes. Thus, we categorize individuals into groups as a means of reducing the amount of information we must contend with, thereby establishing categories of persons whose members are considered to be equivalent in functionally important respects.

This process of categorization is, of course, pervasive in both object and social perception and is of crucial importance in the perceiver's ability to comprehend and adapt to a complex stimulus world. An important component of this process is the perceiver's ability to recognize easily identifiable features of the perceived objects that will constitute the basis for effective categorization. In the case of social perception the identification of such features is not a difficult problem, for numerous cues are readily available that can be used to classify people into categories whose members thereby share some common property. A person's gender, race, and age group are almost immediately obvious to any perceiver. A person's occupation, wealth, or station in life is often communicated by one's dress or other cues. An accent or speech dialect will often reveal one's nationality or the region of the country where one lives. And the list could go on and on. As a result of this process, then, we establish in our minds categories of persons that correspond to a variety of types of people.

What happens when we categorize persons into groups? In part, we are recognizing the real and legitimate similarities and differences that exist among us. There are, in fact, ways that men and women, blacks and whites, old and young people, et cetera, differ from each other. To the extent that the categories we establish, and our use of those categories, reflect those *actual* similarities and differences, the categorization process represents a useful and appropriate means of adapting to the complex social stimulus world with which we interact. However, recent research has demonstrated a variety of consequences that follow from this very act of categorization—consequences that extend beyond any actual differences between the categorized groups. We can summarize the findings of research on the cognitive consequences of the categorization process in terms of two situations: first, the case in which others are perceived according to their membership in some group, and second, the case in which the perceiver differentiates between members of his or her own group and members of some other group.

In the first instance, the question concerns what effects follow from viewing persons as members of groups rather than as individuals. Several consequences of such categorization are well documented in the literature.

1. When others are categorized into groups, we tend to perceive members of the same category as being more similar to each other, and members of different categories as being more dissimilar, than when those persons are viewed as an aggregate of individuals (Tajfel, Sheikh, & Gardner, 1964; Tajfel & Wilkes, 1963; Wilder, 1978a, 1981). That is, persons belonging to the same group are perceived as or assumed to be more alike, and persons belonging to different groups are perceived as being more different from one another than when those same persons are perceived in the absence of group identification. These results are obtained even when (a) assignment of individuals to groups is arbitrary and (b) the group identification itself is

uninformative (e.g., identifying individuals as belonging to "Group J").

2. Categorization of others into groups influences the perceiver's causal attributions about their behavior. For example, in one experiment (Wilder, 1978b), subjects observed a target person who expressed either the same or a different opinion from that stated by several other persons. These persons were either an aggregate of individuals or were identified as members of a group (including the target person). When the target person was identified as being a group member, his agreement with the others was perceived as having been situationally caused, as influenced by the presence of the other group members, whereas his disagreement was attributed more to internal causes. In contrast, if the stimulus persons were not identified as a group but simply as an aggregate of individuals, the target person's agreement or disagreement with the others did not influence subjects' attributions for this behavior. Groupness, then, creates expectations that can influence the perceiver's interpretation of the group member's behavior.

3. The social categories we establish are used in the way we process information about others in our social world. That is, as we process information from a complex social situation, that information may be encoded and stored in terms of relevant social categories as a means of simplifying the information processing task. For example, Taylor and her colleagues (Taylor, 1981; Taylor & Falcone, 1982; Taylor, Fiske, Etcoff, & Ruderman, 1978) had subjects observe a discussion group consisting of three whites and three blacks. Later, subjects were asked to identify which person made various comments by matching the face to the statement. The consistent finding in these experiments has been that subjects made more within-group than between-group errors in their recall of who said what during the discussion. That is, when subjects erred, they were more likely to assign the statement to a different member of the same racial group than to a member of the other race. In effect, subjects could remember the race of the person who made a comment, but they were less accurate in recalling which person in that subgroup had made the statement. Thus, the information the subjects received was organized and stored in terms of the prominent social categories evident to them, rather than in terms of the individual stimulus persons they observed.

These effects are further influenced when the perceiver is a member of one of the groups in question, that is, when the categorization is between an *ingroup* and an *outgroup*. Based on research using the "minimal intergroup situation" paradigm (Tajfel, 1970), the effects of such intergroup differentiation on behavioral discrimination are well known: when subjects are categorized into ingroup and outgroup, even on a relatively arbitrary basis, their behavior (typically the allocation of resources) reveals a clear preferential treatment in favor of ingroup members, even when direct self-interest is not a factor in subjects' decisions. Similarly, evaluative judgments of members of own and other group typically reveal a strong ingroup bias. Because this literature has been well reviewed elsewhere (Brewer, 1979; Brewer & Kramer, 1985; Hamilton, 1976; Tajfel, 1978, 1982), our discussion focuses on cognitive–perceptual concomitants of ingroup–outgroup categorization.

1. The formation of naturally occurring groups (clubs, political parties, professional groups) is often based on some shared interest, belief system, or goal that the members have in common. Differentiation between ingroup and outgroup, however, even when established on an arbitrary basis, leads group members to *assume* that other ingroup members are similar to themselves in other respects as well. For example, Allen and Wilder (1979) created two groups of subjects, ostensibly on the basis of artistic preferences, and then had subjects complete an opinion survey in the manner they thought another member of their own (or the other) group would respond to the items. They found that subjects assumed that another ingroup member would express beliefs more similar to their own (previously assessed) opinions than would an outgroup member. This difference occurred even for belief items irrelevant to art (the presumed basis for intergroup differentiation). This finding obviously parallels the previously reported results of perceived within-group similarity and between-group differences.

2. Although the ingroup members assume some similarity with other ingroup members, the outgroup is perceived as being even more homogeneous. In effect, the social perceiver subscribes to the belief that "they are all alike, whereas we are quite diverse" (Jones, Wood, & Quattrone, 1981; Linville, 1982; Linville & Jones, 1980; Park & Rothbart, 1982; Quattrone & Jones, 1980; Rothbart, Dawes, & Park, 1984; Wilder, 1981). The research evidence related to this point is discussed in detail in Chapter 6 by Linville, Salovey, and Fischer.

3. Related to the perception of outgroup homogeneity is another characteristic of ingroup–outgroup perceptions. Specifically, perceivers evaluate members of the outgroup as more extreme on various psychological characteristics than members of the ingroup. That is, when asked to rate a person on various trait-rating scales, subjects make more extreme ratings if that person belongs to the outgroup than

the ingroup. (Linville, 1982; Linville & Jones, 1980). Evidence indicates that this is a true polarization effect. That is, a positively described stimulus person will be evaluated more favorably, and a negatively described person less favorably, if that person is a member of the outgroup than the ingroup. (The finding of more favorable evaluations of a positive outgroup member suggests a qualification of the ingroup bias effect noted earlier. The conditions under which this qualification will occur need to be clarified in future research. See also Chapter 2.)

4. Studies have also shown differential processing and retention of information about ingroup and outgroup members. For example, Howard and Rothbart (1980) conducted a series of experiments in which intergroup differentiation was presumably established on the basis of a dot estimation task (Tajfel, 1970). They showed that defining ingroup and outgroup in this way was sufficient to create favorable expectations about ingroup members and unfavorable expectations for outgroup members. These differential expectancies then influenced subjects' retention of behavioral information about members of the two groups. Specifically, after subjects had read a number of behavior statements descriptive of ingroup and outgroup members, they had significantly better memory for negative outgroup behaviors than for negative ingroup behaviors. Similarly, Wilder (1981) has reported an experiment in which subjects had better memory for information about ways that other ingroup members were similar and outgroup members were dissimilar to themselves. These memory findings indicate that, once the ingroup–outgroup distinction is established, even in an arbitrary manner, subsequent information processing can be biased in such a way that the intergroup differentiation will be maintained, and indeed, will come to seem justified.

5. Consistent with this conclusion, several studies provide evidence that perceivers make differing attributions for ingroup and outgroup members. Generally, perceivers make more favorable attributions about ingroup than about outgroup members. This tendency has been demonstrated in several ways. For example, for an ingroup member, positive behaviors are much more likely to be attributed to internal causes than are negative behaviors, whereas the opposite is true of one's attributions for an outgroup member's behaviors (Taylor & Jaggi, 1974). The successes and failures of ingroup members are attributed to different causes than are those of outgroup members (Deaux, 1976; Hewstone, Jaspers, & Lalljee, 1982). Responsibility for an accident is more likely to be attributed to the dispositional characteristics of the driver if the driver is a member of a different ethnic

group than of one's own ethnic group (Wang & McKillip, 1978). Similarly, black teenagers blame the white authority system for racial discrimination more than do white teenagers (Hewstone & Jaspars, 1982). And perceivers ascribe to different interpretations of the reasons for favorable and unfavorable facts about ingroup and outgroup (Hewstone, Bond, & Wan, 1983). Hence, these attributional concomitants of the ingroup–outgroup differentiation are pervasive (for further discussion, see Hewstone & Jaspars, 1984; Pettigrew, 1979).

We mentioned earlier that our conceptions of social groups to some extent reflect the real and meaningful differences among those groups. We can see from the accumulated evidence, however, that the social categories we develop are more than convenient groupings of individuals that simplify the actual diversities among the people we observe and encounter. They are also categories that can bias the way we process information, organize and store it in memory, and make judgments about members of those social categories.

There is another way in which these social categories are more than mere groupings of persons, for in this process we also come to associate certain *beliefs* with these categories. We believe that people who belong to a particular group possess certain psychological characteristics in common. And it is those beliefs that constitute the essence of stereotypes.

From a cognitive perspective, then, a *stereotype* can be defined as a *cognitive structure that contains the perceiver's knowledge, beliefs, and expectancies about some human group*. In defining a stereotype this way, we have in essence equated our conception of a stereotype with the terms others (e.g., Rumelhart, 1984; Hamilton, 1981b; Taylor & Crocker, 1981) have used to define a *schema*. This was intentional, for much of the recent literature reflecting the cognitive approach is consistent, at least in its general characteristics, with this view. In subsequent sections of this chapter we hope to demonstrate that adopting this orientation has been fruitful.

COGNITIVE ORIGINS OF SOCIAL CATEGORIES

As we noted earlier, a basic tenet of the sociocultural orientation is that stereotypes develop and are acquired through a process of social learning. That is, stereotypes can have their origins in the socialization process through which we learn the current beliefs, prominent in our subculture, about what psychological attributes are associated with particular subgroups in our society.

This is undoubtedly an important process shaping the development of our stereotypes. In addition to these sociocultural processes, research in social cognition has demonstrated that there are cognitive mechanisms which, in and of themselves, can lay the foundation for the development of stereotypic belief system. In this section, we summarize these recent findings on the cognitive origins of social categories.

At the outset of this analysis, it is important to recognize that the basis for all stereotyping is the differential perception of groups. Without such differentiation between groups, stereotyping cannot occur. As we noted earlier, stereotypes can be said to exist when differential beliefs and values become associated with the differentiated social categories developed by the perceiver. It follows, then, that any psychological process that contributes to or results in the observer perceiving some persons as different from others would qualify as constituting a potential basis for the development of stereotypic concepts.

Some of the research on the categorization process discussed earlier provides evidence of this nature. For example, studies using the minimal-intergroup-situation paradigm (see Tajfel, 1982) demonstrate that the arbitrary categorization of persons into groups can, by itself, result in differential perceptions and evaluations of members of those groups. While in many of these studies the distinction is between ingroup and outgroup, in which self-interest and identification processes may be involved, Wilder's research (Wilder, 1981) shows similar effects due to the arbitrary categorization of a group of individuals into subgroups. Thus, the act of categorization can create for the perceiver an apparent differentiation between groups that would not be perceived were those persons to be considered as a collection of individuals. As we shall see in a later section, Tajfel's social identity theory (Tajfel, 1978; Tajfel & Turner, 1979) of intergroup differentiation has its starting point in this act of categorization.

Other research has shown that the distinctiveness of certain informational cues can result in the differential perception of group members. The distinctiveness of a stimulus can, of course, be based on several different factors. The novelty or unusualness of certain stimuli make them distinctive, in which case the distinctiveness may be inherent in the stimulus itself. Stimulus salience can also have its roots in the value system of the perceiver. For example, for the racially prejudiced individual, a black person's race may always constitute a salient stimulus and hence become the focus of the perceiver's attention. Finally, and of particular interest here, stimulus distinctiveness may be determined by the social context. In any case, distinctive stimuli will receive differential attention from the perceiver (McArthur, 1981), and hence can lead to differential perceptions. Two instances of this effect that have particular implications for stereotyping are considered here.

One consequence of stimulus distinctiveness is that it draws the perceiver's attention. Taylor (1981) has described a series of studies in which one person is visually distinctive or salient in a social group, as when one black person interacts with several whites, and has investigated how this salience influences the perception of that individual. In one study, subjects listened to a tape-recorded discussion among six men, and as each of them spoke, a slide presumably showing that person was projected on a screen. By using the same tape but varying the race of the persons shown in the slides, it was possible to manipulate the racial composition of the group while holding all other aspects of the discussion constant. In one condition (the integrated condition) three white and three black males were portrayed, while in the other case the group was composed of five whites and one black (the solo condition). The black solo in the latter case was one of three blacks— same voice, same face—in the integrated condition, but the situational context presumably would make him much more salient in the solo condition. The question was whether this context-based distinctiveness would have an influence on subjects' perceptions of him. Compared to the integrated condition, the same person in the solo condition was perceived as more active and talkative during the discussion, as having had more influence on the group discussion, and was rated more extremely on personality characteristics. In addition, subjects remembered more of what the black had said when he was the solo than when he was one of the three blacks in an integrated group, a finding consistent with the view that these results were mediated by subjects' closer attention to that person in the solo condition.

These results demonstrate the importance of basic attentional processes for social perception. Stimulus salience, through its effect on attention, resulted in the same person being perceived differently in a context in which his (racial) group membership was made salient.

Distinctiveness can also stem from the infrequency of occurrence of a stimulus. For example, most white people have relatively infrequent exposure to and interaction with blacks. Aside from any other bases for the distinctiveness of blacks, this relative novelty of experience would make the black person salient for the white perceiver. Certain forms of behavior, such as undesirable behaviors, also occur with relative infrequency, thereby affording them a distinctive quality for the same reason. It seems reasonable, then, that the co-occurrence of distinctive stimulus events—in this example, a black performing an undesirable behavior—would be particularly salient to the observer. If so, then such distinctiveness might result in differential processing of that information, with consequent biases in the way that information is represented in memory and subsequently used in making judgments.

Hamilton and Gifford (1976; see also Hamilton, 1981c) have reported evidence in support of this notion. Subjects were shown a series of sentences, each of which described a person as belonging to one of two groups and as having performed either a desirable or an undesirable behavior. To test the distinctiveness hypothesis in the absence of effects due to pre-existing attitudes towards specific societal groups, the two groups were identified only as Group A and Group B. In the set of stimulus sentences, there were twice as many members of Group A than of Group B, and desirable behaviors occurred more frequently than undesirable behaviors. However, the ratio of desirable to undesirable behaviors was the same for both groups. Because of this property, there was no relation between group membership and behavior desirability in the information presented to the subjects. In spite of this fact, subjects provided evidence of bias in the conceptions they developed of these groups. When given a list of the behaviors described in the sentences and asked to indicate the group membership of the person who had performed each one, subjects overassigned the undesirable behaviors to Group B, the smaller group. When asked to estimate the number of undesirable behaviors performed by members of the two groups, subjects overestimated the frequency for Group B. Finally, when asked to rate their impressions of the two groups on some evaluative trait scales, subjects made less favorable ratings of Group B. Thus an illusory correlation between group membership and behavior desirability had been formed and influenced subjects' perceptions and evaluations of the two groups.

Subsequent studies have replicated and extended these findings. Specifically, it has been shown: (1) that these effects are not confined to the case where undesirable behaviors are distinctive, but that when *desirable* behaviors occur infrequently, subjects form more *favorable* impressions of the smaller group (Hamilton & Gifford, 1976); (2) that the effects are due to biases in the encoding of the stimulus information, and not to errors in the judgment process (Hamilton, Dugan, & Trolier, 1985); (3) that subjects recall a higher proportion of those sentences representing the most distinctive category of stimulus sentences (Hamilton et al., 1985); (4) that the evaluative differences do not reflect an overevaluation of the larger group, but rather a lowered evaluation of the smaller group (Hamilton et al., 1985; Regan & Craw-ley, 1984); and (5) that the evaluative difference can generalize to influence judgments on dimensions other than those on which the illusory correlation was based (Acorn, Hamilton, & Sherman, 1986). These additional findings provide important support for the hypothesis that these effects have their basis in the differential processing of the distinctive stimulus events.

In sum, these findings demonstrate that a cognitive bias in the way distinctive information is processed produced differential perceptions of the two stimulus groups, despite the fact that the information provided about these groups was evaluatively equivalent. Since, as we noted earlier, all stereotyping rests on the differential perceptions of groups, these results indicate that the development of stereotypes can have its foundation in cognitive, information-processing biases.

THE NATURE OF SOCIAL CATEGORIES

In the preceding section we summarized research indicating ways in which basic cognitive processes can contribute to the initial establishment of social categories through information-processing biases that produce differential conceptions of groups. These processes undoubtedly converge with the consequences of social learning processes by which the perceiver develops richly articulated patterns of associations and beliefs about significant social groups. The combined effect of these processes, of course, is that by the time we are adults (and undoubtedly well before then), we all have well-established stereotypic conceptions of numerous social groups. Some of these stereotypes may be quite benign (e.g., the typical conception of a rabbi), some may be largely humorous (e.g., the stereotypic New York cab driver), but others—such as traditional stereotypes of blacks, Hispanics, homosexuals, women—are negative in their characterizations and potentially destructive to members of the victimized groups.

The Structure of Social Categories

Earlier, we defined stereotype as a knowledge structure containing a perceiver's beliefs about the characteristics and behaviors of a particular social group. An important question concerns how the knowledge, beliefs, and expectancies that compose a stereotype are organized and represented in memory structures.

There has been surprisingly little research addressed specifically to investigating the nature of these cognitive structures. However, some model of cognitive representation is at least implicit in much of the research on stereotypes. For example, when Katz and Braly (1933) conducted their now-classic study of the stereotypes then held by Princeton undergraduates, they had their subjects indicate, on an adjective checklist, those attributes they felt characterized each of several national, racial, and religious groups. Two assumptions about the nature of stereotypes are implicit in this methodology. First, it is assumed that the content of stereotypes consists largely, or at least primarily, of traits. Although other kinds of content might also be considered using this procedure, it is clear that Katz and Braly felt that the essence of the stereotypes being assessed would be captured in the trait attributes they included in their measure. Second, the cognitive structure implicitly assumed by this methodology is one in which various attributes are connected by association with the subject's group concept. No other form of organization in the cognitive representation is suggested by this procedure. Given that the Katz–Braly method became the predominant means for studying stereotypes for the next several decades (Brigham, 1971; Hamilton, 1976), this simplistic model continued to represent the assumed nature and structure of stereotypic concepts implicit in research on stereotypes.

In the 1970s, research on the nature of stereotypes was influenced by methodological advances developed in the study of implicit personality theories. Several researchers (e.g., Ashmore, 1981; Jones & Ashmore, 1973) applied sophisticated statistical techniques such as multidimensional scaling and hierarchical clustering analysis to the task of investigating the structure of stereotypes. This work continued to rely on trait terminology as the primary units of analysis, but it specifically sought to determine the structural complexities of stereotypic concepts. Thus, the model underlying this research explicitly recognized the multicomponential nature of stereotypes.

More recent work on the nature of stereotypic concepts has been influenced by developments in cognitive psychology concerned with the hierarchical structure of cognitive categories, and in particular this research has been guided by the theorizing of Rosch (1978). According to this viewpoint, objects in the perceiver's stimulus world are classified into broad categories, each of which can have several subcategories, each of which in turn can have subcategories, and so on. Thus, for example, an initial classification of persons into broad racial categories, such as blacks, whites, Asians, etc., might be useful for gross differentiations, but with increasing experience, the perceiver will develop more distinct subordinate categories corresponding to subgroups. For the superordinate category, *blacks*, for example, the perceiver might develop subtypes representing urban ghetto blacks, middle-class blacks, black athletes, blacks on welfare, etc. And each of these subordinate categories may be further differentiated into more specific subtypes. Each of these categories is represented by a *prototype*, which reflects the characteristic features of the members of that category. In Rosch's view, objects encountered in the world are classified into that category whose prototype most closely resembles the features of the stimulus object. Thus, upon seeing a black male dressed in a business suit, the perceiver would categorize him as a middle-class black rather than a ghetto black. Once an object has been so classified, all of the consequences of the categorization process, discussed earlier, are assumed to follow (e.g., the black businessman will be perceived as being similar to, that is, having the same features as, other middle-class blacks represented by this categorical concept). Finally, although object classification can occur at any level, Rosch argues that there is a basic level at which this categorization process typically occurs. The basic level is defined as being that level at which the categories individually are well articulated and also are well differentiated from each other. Typically, the superordinate category would be considered too broad to provide an optimal basis for categorization, and consequently the argument is that more subordinate levels are commonly used in processing information about stimulus objects.

Although this line of thinking was developed in work on object classification, its application to social perception has been quite useful and informative (Brewer, Dull, & Lui, 1981; Cantor & Mischel, 1979; Deaux & Lewis, 1984; Deaux, Winton, Crowley, & Lewis, 1985). The research of Brewer et al. (1981) most clearly illustrates the potential of this approach for expanding our conception of stereotypes. In a series of studies, these experimenters investigated subjects' stereotypic categories for the elderly. By instructing subjects to sort a large number of photographs of elderly individuals into meaningful piles, and subsequently examining the hierarchical structure of these sortings, it was found that subjects' conceptions of the elderly were well differentiated into consistent and meaningful subcategories (for example, "grandmothers" and "senior citizens"). In addition, these subcategories appeared to be reliably associated with distinctive physical features, traits, and behaviors. These researchers have also shown that these subcategories are utilized in processing and categorizing information about elderly individuals (Brewer et al., 1981; Brewer & Lui, 1984; Lui & Brewer, 1983).

Although this approach has not been applied to understanding the structure of racial stereotypes, it seems evident that white perceivers have and use well-differentiated subtypes in their thinking about blacks (e.g., ghetto blacks, black businessmen, black athletes, welfare blacks). Indeed, some contemporary slang terms refer explicitly to such subtypes ("oreo cookies," "streetwise blacks," "Uncle Toms," etc.). This view has important implications for understanding racial stereotypes. It suggests, for example, that although the category *blacks* may be used for some purposes, as a superordinate category, it is too broad and inclusive to be useful for the perceiver in many contexts. This approach implies, then, that most stereotyping occurs at a more subordinate level, and that processing information about and perceptions of blacks are guided by these more specific conceptions. It also suggests that one's interpersonal interactions with blacks will differ depending on the particular subgroup that they are perceived as belonging to. Finally, this view has important implications for research strategies in studying racial stereotypes, for it becomes important to understand not only the perceiver's beliefs about the superordinate category, but also to determine (1) the nature of the subcategories composing the cognitive structure, (2) the beliefs associated with each one, (3) the degree of differentiation among them, and (4) the conditions under which each categorical level, as well as each subtype, are most likely to be employed (see Hamilton, 1981d).

THE CONTENT OF RACE STEREOTYPES

The work we have discussed to this point has focused on the *structure* of social categories. An equally important concern for the study of stereotypes is the *content* associated with those categories. The Katz–Braly adjective checklist method was devised specifically to assess the content of stereotypes and has been widely used for this purpose. However, as others have noted (Brigham, 1971; Sigall & Page, 1971), this procedure is highly reactive and susceptible to distortion due to social desirability and impression management effects, the consequence being that the data obtained may not accurately reflect the belief systems being assessed. Because of these problems, investigators have adopted other research strategies for studying the impact of racial concepts, including the development of alternative, less obvious measures of racial beliefs and attitudes (e.g., Kinder & Sears, 1981; McConahay, this volume) and the use of nonreactive methods (Crosby, Bromley, & Saxe, 1980; Gaertner, 1976). As useful as these alternatives may be for some purposes, they generally provide only indirect means of tapping the content of stereotypes.

More recent research has begun to explore this issue more directly by applying techniques of cognitive psychology to the problem of determining the content associated with racial categories. The rationale underlying this research is as follows. If race stereotypes consist of beliefs associated with specific racial groups, then the content of those stereotypes can be studied by methods that measure the associative strength between race concepts and various beliefs or attributes. Attributes that are strongly associated with a particular racial concept, then, would compose the content of the stereotype about that group. In contrast, content that is less strongly associated with the concept presumably is less central to the stereotype.

Two recent studies based on this rationale provide useful illustrations of this approach. In one, Gaertner and McLaughlin (1983) used a variant of the lexical decision task (Meyer & Schvaneveldt, 1971) to investigate the traits most strongly associated with racial categories. Pairs of stimulus terms were presented to subjects, whose task it was to respond "yes" if both stimuli were words or "no" if one of them was not a word. In all stimulus pairs, one term was a race concept (blacks or whites) and was paired with either a negatively valued trait stereotypic of blacks (e.g., lazy), a positively valued trait (e.g., smart), or a nonsense term (e.g., zumap). Subjects' response latencies were measured as an index of associative strength. Gaertner and McLaughlin (1983) found that positively valued traits were more strongly associated with whites than with blacks, but that negative attributes were not differentially associated with the racial groups. In another study, Dovidio, Evans, and Tyler (1986) used a priming paradigm to investigate the content of race stereotypes. Subjects were first shown a word that primed a racial category (black or white), which was then followed by an adjective. The adjectives included positive and negative traits that were stereotypic of blacks or of whites. Again, subjects' response latencies were used to assess associative strength. Dovidio et al. (1986) found that, following a white prime, subjects responded faster both to white stereotypic traits and to positively valued attributes. (For a more detailed discussion of these experiments, see the Gaertner and Dovidio chapter in this volume.)

These studies are cited as illustrations of the use of cognitive methodologies for the purpose of understanding an issue of fundamental social psychological importance—namely, the content of race stereotypes. As for any new technique, these initial findings must be viewed with caution until the usefulness of the methodologies can be clarified as further research has accumulated. These techniques do, however, offer a potentially informative means of investigating questions of stereotype content that circumvent many of the problems associated with the more transparent questionnaire methods.

In concluding this section on the nature of social categories, a final comment is in order. For a long time, research on stereotypes consisted primarily of attempts to measure the content of stereotypic beliefs (Hamilton, 1976). That is, the Katz–Braly adjective checklist method, and later developments of it, provided a useful first step toward determining the specific beliefs that were associated with various racial, religious, and ethnic groups. While informative in this regard, this approach was limited by the constraints of what was essentially an assessment technique. As such, it was unable to address a variety of questions of central importance to understanding the consequences of stereotypes, such as how stereotypes influence the way we process information about group members, how they affect our perceptions of group members, and how they guide our interpersonal behavior. More recent developments in social cognition, both theoretical and methodological, have provided the means of systematically pursuing those questions. We now turn to a consideration of that research.

THE USE OF SOCIAL CATEGORIES: COGNITIVE CONSEQUENCES OF STEREOTYPES

Earlier, we defined *stereotype* as a cognitive structure containing the perceiver's knowledge, beliefs, and expectancies about a social group. This conception essentially views stereotypes as schemas. Thus, the activation of a group stereotype should have the same general effects of the activation of any schema. Guided by this assumption, much of the recent literature on stereotyping has been concerned with how stereotypes influence information processing and interpersonal behavior. A thorough discussion of this literature, which is now quite extensive, is beyond the scope of this chapter (for recent reviews, see Hamilton, 1979, 1981a; Jones, 1982; Tajfel, 1982). In this section, we present an overview of the implications of this cognitive orientation, illustrating the major points with representative examples of research.

At the outset of this chapter, we indicated that the social world continuously presents a rich, varied, and complex stimulus environment that can easily tax the attentional and information-processing capacities at the perceiver's disposal. As a consequence, the perceiver's attention to the stimulus field is often, of necessity, selective. We have already seen, in Taylor's (1981) research on solo members of small groups, that a salient stimulus can draw the perceiver's attention. In addition to such external, stimulus-based determinants of selective attention (see also McArthur, 1981; Taylor & Fiske, 1978), variables specific to the perceiver can guide his or her attention to certain aspects of the stimulus field. According to schema theory (Rumelhart, 1984; Taylor & Crocker, 1981), information is processed within the framework of the particular schema operative at the particular moment. Thus, activation of a schema, such as a stereotype, can influence what aspects of the available information are attended to, how that information is interpreted as it is encoded, and hence what information will be available for later retrieval.

Findings from several studies provide support for this contention. Zadny and Gerard (1974) have shown that the use of different cognitive frameworks for understanding a behavior sequence can result in different aspects of a constant stimulus sequence being encoded and stored in memory. Priming different schemas through recent experience can also influence both the interpretation and the retention of specific aspects of the information available (Higgins, Rholes, & Jones, 1977; Srull & Wyer, 1980).

The effects of racial stereotypes on the encoding of information was demonstrated by Sagar and Schofield (1980). School children were shown cartoon-like stick figure drawings of children, along with a verbal description read by the experimenter. Each sketch portrayed an actor whose behavior toward another child was ambiguous and open to interpretation. For example, one sketch showed two students sitting in class, one behind the other. The verbal description was, "Mark was sitting at his desk, working on his social studies assignment, when David started poking him in the back with the eraser end of his pencil. Mark just kept on working. David kept poking him for a while, and then he finally stopped." Subjects rated the actor's behavior on four rating scales, evaluating the extent to which it was playful, friendly, mean, and threatening. The primary manipulation of the study was the race of the actor. If the actor was black, his behavior was judged to be more mean and threatening, and less playful and friendly, than if the actor was white. Thus the same behavioral act was interpreted differently depending on the race of the person who performed it. These results replicate and extend findings previously reported by Duncan (1976). Thus, stereotypes can not only have a directive effect on our attentional processes, influencing *what* we perceive, but can also guide our interpretation of what we do observe, thereby influencing *how* we perceive (see also Bodenhausen & Wyer, 1985).

Because schemas influence our attention and encoding processes, information that fits our stereotypic expectations would seemingly be more likely to enter into the information-processing system. Moreover, once this has occurred, a stereotypic schema can provide an organized structure within which that information can be stored and represented in memory. As a consequence, we might expect that information consistent with stereotypic expectancies would be better retained than information that conforms less well with those expectations. In fact, there is considerable evidence in support of this general proposition, although the picture is somewhat more complex than it might seem at first glance.

Several research strategies have been used to investigate perceivers' retention of information that does or does not fit with prior expectations. One approach has been to determine whether subjects' frequency estimates, based on retrieval of previously presented information, are biased by stereotypic expectancies (Hamilton & Rose, 1980; Rothbart, Evans, & Fulero, 1979). For example, Hamilton and Rose's (1980) subjects read a series of sentences, each of which described a person by first name, occupation, and two trait-descriptive adjectives. In the set of 24 sentences, there were eight persons belonging to each of three occupational groups (e.g., accountants, doctors, salesmen). Eight trait adjectives occurred repeatedly throughout these descriptions in such a way that each adjective described a member of each occupation exactly twice. Thus, in the stimulus information, there was no relationship between occupational group and any of the descriptive terms. Some of the traits were stereotypically associated with one or another of the occupations (accountant–timid; salesman–talkative), while other traits were not associated with any of the groups. Subjects were then asked to judge, for each occupation, how often each trait had described a member of that group. Although each attribute described each group with equal frequency, subjects' judgments indicated that they believed that the groups had been described by the stereotypic traits with higher frequency. Thus, subjects' stereotypic beliefs systematically influenced their judgments on this task. In a second study, Hamilton and Rose (1980) extended these findings to the situation where some attributes were in fact more descriptive of some groups than others. That is, each attribute—stereotypic and nonstereotypic—described members of one occupational group more frequently than the other groups. When asked to judge how often each trait had described members of each group, subjects again estimated higher frequencies for traits stereotypic of that group. Together, these studies demonstrate two consequences of stereotypic expectancies for subjects' judgments: (1) The first study showed that, in the absence of any actual relation between group membership and descriptive information, subjects perceived such a relationship consistent with their stereotypic beliefs. (2) The second study showed that when group membership and descriptive information were in fact associated, subjects were more likely to detect that association if it involved stereotypic, rather than nonstereotypic, traits.

An alternative strategy to investigating this question has been to examine subjects' ability to recall information that is consistent or inconsistent with prior expectancies. Experiments of this type have typically followed the same general paradigm: through experimental instructions, subjects develop an initial expectation regarding a person (or group of persons) about whom they then read a series of behavior-descriptive sentences. These stimulus sentences include some behavior descriptions that are consistent with the expectation, some that are inconsistent with it, and some that are irrelevant to that expectancy. Subsequently subjects are asked to recall as many of those behaviors as they can.

In discussing the findings from these studies, it is important to differentiate the effects of prior expectancies on recall of consistent and inconsistent information. When subjects' recall of consistent information is compared to that for information irrelevant to the activated schema, it has been found that expectancy-consistent information is more likely to be retrieved (Cohen, 1981; Hastie & Kumar, 1979; Rothbart et al., 1979; Srull, 1981). This is well illustrated in the research of Rothbart et al. (1979). Subjects were presented with 50 behavior descriptions, each one describing a different member of a group of 50 men. Some of the sentences described friendly behaviors, some described behaviors reflecting intelligence. Before reading the sentences, half of the subjects were led to believe that the members of the group were very friendly; the other half were told that the group was quite intellectual. On a subsequent recall task, subjects were able to remember more of the behaviors consistent with their expectation about the group. That is, more friendly behaviors were recalled by subjects given the friendly expectancy than by subjects in the intelligent expectancy condition, whereas the latter group recalled more of the intelligent behaviors. Thus, information that confirmed a stereotypic expectancy was more effectively processed and retained than information unrelated to the stereotype.

What about information that clearly contradicts a stereotype? What impact does such expectancy violation have on information processing? This question is of considerable importance, for presumably one way to change stereotypic beliefs would be to present information indicating that those beliefs are wrong. The results of several experiments indicate that items of information that are inconsistent with schematic expectancies are more likely to be retained than are items of information consistent with those expectancies (Crocker, Hannah, & Weber, 1983; Hastie, 1984; Hastie & Kumar, 1979; Srull, 1981). Why would this be so? Presumably, information that violates or contradicts a schematic expectancy is surprising—it doesn't fit with what we either know or believe to be true. As a consequence, we spend more time processing this inconsistent information and relating it to other facts known about the stimulus person(s) (Brewer et al. 1981; Hemsley & Marmurek, 1982; Srull, 1981). This additional processing may include the perceiver's attempting to explain the inconsistency (Clary & Tesser, 1983; Hastie, 1984). Moreover, Lui and Brewer (1983) suggest the interesting possibility that, when those expectancies derive from stereotypic categories, information that fits with one's group conception will be processed categorically, whereas information inconsistent with the stereotype will be processed in an individuated manner.

Several of the studies that have reported a higher probability of recall for inconsistent than consistent information have investigated this issue in the context of processing information about an individual person. An important question for the purposes of this chapter concerns whether the same findings obtain for processing information about members of groups. Earlier, we referred to the distinction made by Wilder (1981) between perceiving others as a group or as an aggregate of individuals. It appears that this distinction is important in this domain as well. Experiments have shown that the advantaged recall of inconsistent information occurs when individuals are perceived as being members of a meaningful group, but that congruent information is more likely to be recalled when they are perceived as a collection of individuals who do not share meaningful group membership (Rothbart et al., 1979; Srull, 1981; Srull, Lichtenstein, & Rothbart, 1985; Stern, Marrs, Millar, & Cole, 1984).

In sum, there are several mechanisms that may contribute to the differential retention of consistent and inconsistent information, the relative influence of which may determine the results in any particular experimental context. The issues, both theoretical and empirical, are complex, and any brief summary of this literature (including the foregoing account) will necessarily suffer from oversimplification. For more extensive reviews of this research, the reader is referred to Hastie, Park, and Weber (1984) and Wyer and Gordon (1984).

The differential impact of stereotypically consistent and inconsistent information is important for another reason as well, for information that contradicts a stereotypic expectancy might lead the perceiver to question the validity of that belief. Inconsistent information, then, might lead to belief change. The processes by which such change might come about is at present an unresolved issue. Several possible processes have been discussed in the literature (Crocker, Fiske, & Taylor, 1984; Hamilton, 1981d; Rothbart, 1981). According to a "book-keeping" model (Rothbart, 1981), as information incongruent with a stereotype is acquired, the perceiver would adjust and revise the stereotypic belief in light of the accumulated evidence. If enough disconfirming information is acquired, it would produce a change in one's belief about the group in question. In a second process, that Rothbart called a "conversion" model, change occurs suddenly rather than gradually, due to the compelling impact of highly salient and/or convincing information that contradicts a stereotypic belief. Finally, in a "subtyping" process (Crocker et al., 1984), stereotype change takes a different form. As one encounters instances of group members who do not fit the stereotype, the perceiver's conception of the stereotyped group becomes differentiated into subtypes, with one subtype maintaining the existing stereotype and another subtype representing the disconfirming instances (Hamilton, 1981d). These are three quite different processes by which stereotype-inconsistent information might bring about belief change, and the nature of the change differs in each case. And each process probably occurs under appropriate circumstances. The conditions that promote each process, and when disconfirming information will produce each type of change, remain unknown, and the little evidence available is mixed (Gurwitz & Dodge, 1977; Weber & Crocker, 1984). Specifying these conditions remains an important task for further research.

To this point, our discussion has concentrated on the effects of preexisting stereotypic beliefs on subsequent information processing—that is, on how stereotypic expectancies influence the perceiver's attention to, interpretation of, and retention of information about members of the stereotyped group. The evidence we have reviewed clearly indicates that the cognitive consequences of stereotypes are both widespread and substantial. An important issue then becomes what influence these cognitive structures have on interpersonal behavior. In considering this issue, our discussion again consists of an overview of this topic, providing illustrations of research investigating the impact of stereotypes in the interpersonal domain.

Stereotypes can be conceptualized as expectations or hypotheses that an individual holds concerning members of a particular social group. Given this perspective, an important question concerns how perceivers go about testing these stereotype-based hypotheses in their interactions with others. In one study addressing this issue (Snyder & Swann, 1978), subjects were told they would interview another individual to determine if his or her personality was consistent with personality information provided by the experimenter. Specifically, some subjects were told to determine whether the interviewee was an extravert; others were told to determine whether the person was an introvert. Subjects were given a list of possible interview questions and were instructed to indicate 12 questions they would ask the interviewee. Examination of the questions subjects selected showed that individuals searched for information that would confirm their stereotypic expectations rather than disconfirm their expectations. For example, when the target individual was hypothesized to be an extravert, subjects would preferentially select questions that would elicit answers consistent with their expectations (e.g., "What would you do to liven things up at a party?"), instead of questions that would elicit more introvert-like responses (e.g., "What factors make it hard for you to open up to people?"). Snyder and Swann concluded that individuals tend to seek out information which confirms their hypotheses, rather than to solicit evidence that would effectively disconfirm their hypotheses.

More recently, Darley and Gross (1983) have proposed a two-stage process to explain biased hypothesis-testing and its influence on subjective judgments. Initially, a stereotypic expectation may not be perceived as necessarily true, but rather, may function as a tentative hypothesis that may or may not be true about any particular member of the group. In this initial phase, then, individuals' judgments concerning some target should not reveal substantial stereotype-consistent biases. However, when perceivers later observe the behavior of an individual group member, and thus can test their hypothesis through observation, they will tend to utilize a hypothesis-confirming strategy, much as Snyder and Swann (1978) observed. This biased testing strategy can then result in an apparent confirmation of the initially tentative expectancy.

To test this model, Darley and Gross (1983) first had two groups of subjects make judgments of a child's academic abilities based solely on information concerning the child's socioeconomic status (either high or low). The resulting performance judgments were found to be essentially the same for children of both socioeconomic levels. Thus, activation of the stereotype alone did not result in biased judgments. Two additional groups of subjects were given one or the other type of socioeconomic information and then shown a videotape of the child taking an academic test. For these subjects, judgments of the child's ability were found to be biased. Those subjects who believed the child was from a high socioeconomic background perceived the child to have greater ability than those who believed the child was from a low socioeconomic background. Additionally, subjects in both groups recalled information concerning the test difficulty, the number of problems the child answered correctly, and ability-relevant behaviors in a manner consistent with stereotypic expectations. Darley and Gross concluded that stereotypes do not always result in biased judgments of individuals, but rather serve as a basis for hypotheses about target individuals. However, due to the tendency to use a confirmatory strategy when processing expectancy-relevant information, the perceiver ultimately finds those expectancies confirmed in the target person's behavior.

The impact of stereotypes in interpersonal behavior is also evident in research on self-fulfilling prophecies. This phenomenon occurs when one's stereotypic expectations guide one's behavior when interacting with a member of some social group, and this expectancy-driven behavior in turn elicits behaviors from the target person that actually confirm the perceiver's initial stereotype. That is, one's behavior toward a member of the stereotyped group constrains the target's behavioral repertoire in such a way as to direct the person to behave in a stereotypic manner.

Research by Word, Zanna, and Cooper (1974) demonstrates the self-fulfilling properties of racial stereotypes. In a first experiment, white undergraduate college students were asked to interview either white or black job applicants. In reality, the job applicants were experimental accomplices who were trained to respond similarly to the interviewers. The experimenters measured a variety of both verbal and nonverbal behaviors of the interviewer during the interaction, and found that the interviewers behaved quite differently with the black and white applicants (though all applicants manifested similar interview behavior). Compared to whites, black applicants were given shorter interviews and were responded to less positively on several nonverbal measures. Also, interviewers tended to make a greater number of speech errors when interacting with black applicants. All of these variables reflect the interviewers' greater discomfort in the presence of the black applicant. In a second study, white experimental confederates were trained to act in either the positive or negative interview styles revealed in the first experiment. These accomplices then interviewed white subjects who were assigned to the role of job applicants. The interview interactions were videotaped, and independent judges evaluated the performance of the job applicants. The results indicated that subjects responded to the negative interview style (i.e., the way interviewers had responded to black job applicants in the first study) by performing in a less effective and more nervous manner than those subjects responding to the positive interview style. Taken together, these two studies not only indicate that the white interviewers interacted differently with white and black job applicants (as might be expected from prevailing stereotypes), but more importantly, these different interaction styles elicited different levels of performance in the interviewees. Specifically, when faced with the less optimal interviewer behavior, applicants manifested less effective interview behaviors.

The phenomenon of self-fulfilling prophecy reveals two behavioral effects that are driven by the perceiver's stereotypic expectations. The perceiver's stereotype influences how he or she interacts with some member of the stereotyped group. In addition, these stereotype-driven behaviors influence the responses of the target person in such a way as to elicit behaviors that fit, or confirm, the perceiver's initial expectancies. The perceiver's behavior actually draws out behavioral confirmation of the pre-existing stereotype. In this way, then, stereotypes not only can influence the perceiver's own behavior directly, but also can have a profound impact on the behavior of those who are categorized as belonging to the stereotyped group.

Finally, two additional points about self-fulfilling prophecies deserve comment. First, it seems highly unlikely that perceivers are aware of their own contribution to this process—that is, that their prior beliefs are influencing their own behavior, which in turn influences the target person's behavior. In contrast, perceivers may very well recognize that the other's behavior is "just what one would have expected." Given the perceiver's awareness of the confirmatory nature of the target's behavior and lack of awareness of his or her own role in producing it, it would seem particularly difficult to convince the perceiver that his or her stereotypic beliefs are wrong. Second, although numerous studies have demonstrated the self-fulfilling nature of prior beliefs in a broad range of contexts (see Darley & Fazio, 1980; Snyder, 1981), there undoubtedly are boundary conditions on these effects. For example, Hilton and Darley (1985) have shown that when the target person is aware of the perceiver's expectancy, expectancy confirmation does not occur. Other limiting conditions probably exist as well. Research on this topic needs to proceed beyond demonstrations of self-fulfilling outcomes to an investigation of the conditions under which these effects are and are not likely to occur.

Our review of the consequences of stereotypes, as schematic structures, for information processing and interpersonal behavior has been selective in the interest of highlighting the implications of a cognitive approach to understanding how stereotypes function. But even this cursory overview makes it clear that stereotypes bias information processing in a variety of ways. Moreover, for most of these biases, the effect is the same: They serve to maintain and preserve the existing belief system. The implications for stereotypes are both clear and important: "The perceiver 'sees' or creates evidence which seemingly indicates that the stereotypic schema employed is indeed useful and appropriate. Thus, use of the stereotype serves to reinforce its apparent usefulness. A stereotype's persistence, then, is a natural consequence of the biases inherent in its employment" (Hamilton, 1979, p. 80).

THE COGNITIVE APPROACH: IMPLICATIONS AND EXTENSIONS

Even our brief overview of research stimulated by the cognitive perspective demonstrates that this has been an active and productive area of experimentation during the last decade. As a result of this research, we have learned a considerable amount about the nature of stereotypes as cognitive structures representing social categories and about how these structures have impact on both cognitive functioning and interpersonal processes. In closing this chapter, it is appropriate to step back from the specific theoretical concepts and experimental findings that have commanded our attention, and to try to view the place and role of the cognitive approach in the larger task of understanding stereotyping, prejudice, and discrimination.

THE COGNITIVE APPROACH IN PERSPECTIVE

As we indicated in our introduction to this chapter, Ashmore and Del Boca (1981) made the useful differentiation among three conceptual approaches to the study of stereotypes—the motivational, sociocultural, and cognitive orientations. In attempting to understand the

cognitive approach in a broader context, let us consider some of its
metatheoretical implications. Clearly, the emphasis in this approach
is on the central importance of cognitive structures and processes for
understanding stereotypes and stereotyping. Beyond that basic premise, it is useful to point specifically to three "messages" that can be
derived from this approach and the research it has generated.

First, the cognitive approach assumes that the fundamental nature
and functioning of all stereotypes is the same. As cognitive categories,
all stereotypes are assumed to have the same basic structural properties and to influence information processing in the same ways. It is
because of this assumption that, in a volume focusing on American
race relations, we have freely cited studies investigating stereotypes
of such diverse groups as women, the elderly, librarians, British private school students, and the Muslims of India and have not limited
our attention to stereotypes of blacks. The cognitive mechanisms involved in stereotyping are assumed to be general across all stereotypes. Consequently, in any attempt to understand how those processes function, the specific content of the stereotypes used in any
given study is of secondary concern. This is an assumption about basic
structures and basic processes, and as an assumption, it may have its
limits. If so, then those limits need to be identified. Nevertheless,
based on the findings reviewed in this chapter, the principles we have
discussed appear to be quite generalizable across a wide variety of
stereotypes. Idiosyncracies of content do not modify fundamental
mechanisms.

A second message of the cognitive approach is that biases inherent
in our information-processing systems can, in and of themselves, have
profound implications for understanding stereotypes and stereotyping. In many of the experiments we have discussed, the research
strategy has involved a deliberate attempt to demonstrate effects that
are cognitive in origin, independently of the influence of noncognitive factors. This strategy was most clearly seen in the section on the
cognitive origins of social categories. Thus, for example, research on
ingroup–outgroup differentiation demonstrated discriminatory behavior that seemed to parallel phenomena observed in situations of
intergroup conflict, yet these outcomes occurred in the absence of
intergroup conflict. This work emphasized the role of categorization
processes in producing intergroup competition. Similarly, in studies
of illusory correlations, subjects made different evaluative ratings of
two groups described by evaluatively equivalent information, and
they did so under conditions where prior beliefs and motivational
variables could not play a role. The context-based salience of a black

in an otherwise all white group was shown, through its effects on attentional processes, to influence subjects' perceptions of that black person. This same strategy was evident in the section on the cognitive consequences of stereotypes. The myriad of cognitive biases that researchers have shown to emanate from perceivers' beliefs about group members give the appearance that stereotypic judgments may be largely schema-driven phenomena.

In much of this research, then, the strategy has been to push the cognitive analysis as far as it could go—exploring the extent to which cognitive factors *alone* could produce judgmental and behavioral outcomes that parallel real-world manifestations of stereotyping and discrimination. And as we have seen, that effort has progressed with impressive success. However, because of this focus on cognitive mechanisms, some readers of this literature have mistakenly assumed that the cognitive approach argues that contemporary real-world instances of stereotyping and discrimination can be explained *solely* as due to biases in cognitive functioning. This is an inappropriate conclusion. Any particular form of stereotyping or prejudice, such as racism, is in all likelihood multiply determined by cognitive, motivational, and social learning processes, whose effects combine in a given social context to produce specific judgmental and behavioral manifestations. Therefore, any attempt to understand such phenomena as a product of one process alone is probably misguided. The fact that a cognitive mechanism, by itself, can produce stereotype-like perceptions of group members does not mean that contemporary stereotypes are the product only of that mechanism, any more than a finding that high and low prejudiced whites behave differently toward blacks means that discriminatory behaviors derive solely from racist attitudes. In both cases, however, those processes are thereby implicated as important for understanding the mechanisms underlying the everyday manifestations that we seek to explain. Viewed in this perspective, then, it becomes clear that the interest of the cognitive approach is to clarify the nature and consequences of the cognitive component of stereotyping, prejudice, and discrimination, and not to discredit the potential importance of other components of these phenomena.

A third message of the cognitive approach is that, even in understanding how *noncognitive* variables influence stereotyping, it is essential to attend to cognitive processes. There are really two aspects of this argument. The first is simply the obvious point that if stereotypes consist of beliefs about social groups, then the elements of the entity under study are at least partially cognitive in nature. To illustrate, consider some noncognitive processes that might be implicated in the traditional stereotype that blacks are lazy. This belief may have been learned during one's socialization within a particular subcultural context; the negativity of that belief may play a functional role in meeting the perceiver's intrapsychic needs; and the affect associated with that belief may have important and widespread consequences. Thus, for a particular perceiver, noncognitive factors may have been crucial in both the development and utilization of that belief. Still, it is a belief, and in all likelihood, it is but one element in a broader belief system about the characteristics of blacks. So, even when we discuss a stereotype in totally noncognitive terms, we are still referring to an entity that is inherently cognitive in nature. This means that any account of stereotypes must include a cognitive component.

The second aspect of this argument concerns the means by which affective, motivational, and sociocultural variables have their effects on stereotyping. Stereotyping involves perceptions and judgments of group members. Therefore it seems to us that, to a considerable extent, noncognitive factors influence stereotyping through their effects on the cognitive processes that mediate those perceptions and judgments. Consider the following examples. When we talk about the effect of media portrayals of blacks on the nature of race stereotypes, we are in essence referring to a learning process in which beliefs develop from exposure to certain kinds of information. In this example, aspects of the social environment shape stereotype development by influencing the content of the information one processes about a particular group. Similarly, in considering the effect of race prejudice on perceptions of blacks, we are in essence referring to the impact of negative affect on the use of information in making judgments of others. In other words, these situational and motivational variables seem to influence aspects of information processing, which in turn affect perceptions and judgments of group members. If so, then cognitive processes function as crucial mediators between these noncognitive influences and their ultimate manifestations in stereotyping. Yet, we know very little about how motivational and sociocultural variables affect these cognitive mediators, or even which cognitive mechanisms play this mediational role. This analysis, then, has implications for research guided by motivational and sociocultural conceptualizations. It suggests that we can increase our understanding of these noncognitive influences on stereotyping by investigating their effects on cognitive functioning and then determining how those cognitive functions translate these effects into instances of stereotyping and discrimination.

As Pettigrew (1981) has aptly noted, research reflecting this cognitive approach to stereotyping has, for the most part, been conducted by investigators who come from a background in experimental social psychology. Because of their training and disciplinary roots, their work reflects a fundamental interest in basic psychological processes, rather than an emphasis on stereotyping as a macrolevel substantive problem. But as Pettigrew (1981, p. 311) also points out, any such singular approach to a topic that is inherently multifaceted will necessarily encounter its limits. It therefore becomes important to explore the ways in which cognitive processes combine with other processes in their influence on stereotyping.

Compared to the volume of work specifically aimed at testing the implications of one or another of the conceptual orientations we have discussed, there has been relatively little research focused on understanding the intersection or integration of two or more approaches in their effects on stereotyping. Several of the chapters in this volume reflect this more eclectic approach, particularly in their consideration of the mutual influence of cognitive and motivational variables. In this section, we briefly describe two illustrative examples of developments that offer potential for conceptual integration.

Social Identity Theory

Earlier in this chapter, we stressed the importance of the categorization process for understanding stereotyping. We observed that the categorization of persons into groups has a number of consequences for interpersonal perceptions, among them the augmented perception of homogeneity within groups and heterogeneity between groups, and in the case of ingroup—outgroup differentiation, a consistent ingroup bias whereby members of the ingroup are favored over outgroup members. The cognitive act of categorization itself can account for the exaggerated perceptions of similarity within and dissimilarity between groups; comparable effects have been obtained with nonsocial stimuli (Tajfel & Wilkes, 1963). However, categorization alone would not necessarily produce ingroup favoritism. Some additional process must be added to account for this finding.

According to social identity theory (Tajfel & Turner, 1979; see also Tajfel, 1978, 1981; Tajfel & Forgas, 1981), stereotyping and prejudice have their roots in the categorization process, by which the social world is differentiated and organized into social categories or groups. But social categorizations do more than segment and systematize the social world. They also provide an important basis for the individual's self-identification. That is, individuals derive important aspects of their self-concepts from the social groups to which they belong. It is assumed that persons are motivated to achieve and maintain positive self-esteem, and because their self-evaluations depend in part on their evaluations of the groups to which they belong, they are therefore motivated to perceive those groups in positive terms. Group evaluations, however, are inherently comparative, determined with reference to specific other groups through social comparison on relevant attributes. As a consequence, individuals are motivated to perceive their own group as both distinct from and better than other groups (lest their self-esteem be threatened). Hence, there is a pressure to differentiate one's own group from other groups in order to achieve and maintain perceived superiority. This results in ingroup favoritism. In this theoretical framework, then, categorization is a central process in defining the social world, but the process works in the service of basic motivational pressures toward positive self-identity.

Our application of social identity theory to the issue of ingroup bias provides a useful illustration of how this framework integrates basic assumptions and concepts from two of the metatheoretical orientations we cited earlier. Our brief statement of the theory does not do it justice, however, for it is much broader than our summary reveals and has pervasive ramifications for a wide range of topics concerning intergroup conflict (Tajfel, 1978; Tajfel & Turner, 1979). The theory is currently the focus of a considerable amount of research, particularly among European social psychologists. An evaluation of the theory as a whole awaits the results of research testing its implications, particularly in competition with alternative theoretical positions.

Social Roles and the Content of Stereotypic Beliefs

Whereas our first illustration of the intersection of conceptual orientations represented a mixing of cognitive and motivational variables, our second example reflects a combination of the cognitive and sociocultural approaches. Eagly and Steffen (1984) have argued that gender stereotypes—people's beliefs about the characteristics of males and females—have their origins in the distributions of men and women in different social roles. Research on gender stereotypes has clearly documented that men are perceived as possessing *agentic* characteristics (self-assertion, mastery) more than women, whereas women are perceived as possessing *communal* characteristics (selflessness, concern for others) to a greater degree than men. Social roles may also differ in the extent to which agentic or communal qualities are appropriate. Eagly and Steffen (1984) argued that if men and women commonly occupy different social roles in society, and if those roles differ in the agentic and communal properties they confer upon the persons enacting them, then perceivers' stereotypic conceptions of women and men may derive from the differential distribution of the sexes in various social roles.

In an impressive series of experiments, Eagly and Steffen (1984) obtained considerable support for their hypothesis. To illustrate, in one of their studies subjects were asked to rate an average woman or an average man on a series of rating scales. The stimulus person (female or male) was described either as being employed full time or as caring for a home and children and not employed outside the home; or no occupational description was provided. The rating scales included several agentic and communal attributes. Ratings of the average female or male, with no occupational description, were consistent with traditional gender stereotypes: an average woman was perceived as being more communal and less agentic than an average male. However, including information about occupational role substantially altered these perceptions. Homemakers, regardless of sex, were perceived as similar to stereotypic females (low in agency, high in communion), whereas persons employed full-time, regardless of sex, were perceived as similar to stereotypic males (high in agency, low in communion). Moreover, males and females in the same occupational role were generally perceived equivalently. Thus, when information about social roles was equated, differences between males and females disappeared.

Eagly and Steffen's (1984) findings strongly suggest that gender stereotypes are derivatives of the differential frequency with which women and men have been encountered, in everyday experiences, in roles that manifest agentic and communal qualities. The paradox, of course, is that gender stereotypes reflect the perceiver's beliefs—their schematic representations—about women and men as social categories. To quote the authors:

> Our claim that observations of social roles underlie gender stereotypes is not meant to imply that the stimulus person's social role is ordinarily retrieved for perceivers to infer her or his attributes. Instead, perceivers' prototype or schema of a typical woman or man is retrieved, and judgments are made in terms of the personal attributes already associated with it. Because people's activities are determined primarily by their social roles, the prototypes or schemata that perceivers possess of woman and man consist largely of attributes that covary with the role assignments of women and men. (p. 751)

Thus, properties of our social structure, which happen to covary with gender, have a determining influence on the content of gender concepts.

Although Eagly and Steffen's (1984) research focused specifically on gender stereotypes, the same principles may apply to other stereotypes as well. Of particular interest to this volume, it seems plausible that the content of American racial stereotypes may be at least partially a function of the differential social roles predominantly occupied by whites and blacks in this society. Some evidence consistent with this view has been reported (Smedley & Bayton, 1978), and further research exploring this sociocultural influence on the nature of our stereotypic concepts would seem warranted.

In this section, then, we have summarized two examples of theoretical and empirical developments that reflect the integration of different conceptual orientations. As we have seen, these conceptual approaches that have guided thinking about and research on stereotypes are complementary, rather than competing, perspectives (Hamilton, 1981d). The stereotypes whose manifestations we observe in everyday life are multiply determined by processes reflecting each of these perspectives. Given that this is true, progress in understanding the nature and functioning of stereotypes in real-world context will require increased attention to how these approaches intersect and mutually influence our perceptions of groups.

ACKNOWLEDGMENT

The authors are grateful to Diane M. Mackie for her comments on a preliminary version of the manuscript.

REFERENCES

Acorn, D., Hamilton, D. L., & Sherman, S. J. (1986). *Generalization of Biased Perception of Groups Based on Illusory Correlations.* Unpublished manuscript, University of California, Santa Barbara.

Allen, V. L., & Wilder, D. A. (1979). Group categorization and attribution of belief similarity. *Small Group Behavior, 10,* 73–80.

Ashmore, R. D. (1981). Sex stereotypes and implicit personality theory. In D. L. Hamilton (Ed.), *Cognitive processes in stereotyping and intergroup behavior* (pp. 37–81). Hillsdale, N. J.: Erlbaum.

Ashmore, R. D., & Del Boca, F. K. (1981). Conceptual approaches to stereotypes and stereotyping. In D. L. Hamilton (Ed.), *Cognitive processes in stereotyping and intergroup behavior* (pp. 1–35). Hillsdale, N.J.: Erlbaum.

Bodenhausen, G. V., & Wyer, R. S., Jr. (1985). Effects of stereotypes on decision making and information-processing strategies. *Journal of Personality and Social Psychology, 48,* 267–282.

Brewer, M. B. (1979). Ingroup bias in the minimal intergroup situation: A cognitive-motivational analysis. *Psychological Bulletin, 86,* 307–324.

Brewer, M. B., Dull, V., & Lui, L. (1981). Perceptions of the elderly: Stereotypes as prototypes. *Journal of Personality and Social Psychology, 41,* 656–670.

Brewer, M. B., & Kramer, R. M. (1985). The psychology of intergroup attitudes and behavior. *Annual Review of Psychology, 36,* 219–243.

Brewer, M. B., & Lui, L. (1984). Categorization of the elderly by the elderly: Effects of perceiver's category membership. *Personality and Social Psychology Bulletin, 10,* 585–595.

Brigham, J. C. (1971). Ethnic stereotypes. *Psychological Bulletin, 76,* 15–33.

Cantor, N., & Mischel, W. (1979). Prototypes in person perception. In L. Berkowitz (Ed.), *Advances in experimental social psychology* (Vol. 12, pp. 3–52). New York: Academic Press.

Clary, E. G., & Tesser, A. (1983). Reactions to unexpected events: The naive scientist and interpretive activity. *Personality and Social Psychology Bulletin, 9,* 609–620.

Cohen, C. E. (1981). Person categories and social perception: Testing some boundaries of the processing effects of prior knowledge. *Journal of Personality and Social Psychology, 40,* 441–452.

Crocker, J., Fiske, S. T., & Taylor, S. E. (1984). Schematic bases of belief change. In J. R. Eiser (Ed.), *Attitudinal judgment* (pp. 197–226). New York: Springer-Verlag.

Crocker, J., Hannah, D. B., & Weber, R. (1983). Person memory and causal attributions. *Journal of Personality and Social Psychology, 40,* 441–452.

Crosby, F., Bromley, S., & Saxe, L. (1980). Recent unobtrusive studies of black and white discrimination and prejudice: A literature review. *Psychological Bulletin, 87,* 546–563.

Darley, J. M., & Fazio, R. H. (1980). Expectancy confirmation processes arising in the social interaction sequence. *American Psychologist, 35,* 867–881.

Darley, J. M., & Gross, P. H. (1983). A hypothesis-confirming bias in labeling effects. *Journal of Personality and Social Psychology, 44,* 20–33.

Deaux, K. (1976). Sex: A perspective on the attribution process. In J. H. Harvey, W. J. Ickes, & R. F. Kidd (Eds.), *New directions in attribution research* (Vol. 1, pp. 335–352). Hillsdale, N. J.: Erlbaum.

Deaux, K., & Lewis, L. L. (1984). Structure of gender stereotypes: Interrelationships among components and gender label. *Journal of Personality and Social Psychology, 46,* 991–1004.

Deaux, K., Winton, W., Crowley, M., & Lewis, L. L. (1985). Level of categorization and content of gender stereotypes. *Social Cognition, 3,* 145–167.

Dovidio, J. F., Evans, N., & Tyler, R. B. (1986). Racial stereotypes: The contents of their cognitive representations. *Journal of Experimental Social Psychology, 22,* 22–37.

Duncan, B. L. (1976). Differential social perception and attribution of intergroup violence: Testing the lower limits of stereotyping of blacks. *Journal of Personality and Social Psychology, 34,* 590–598.

Eagly, A. H., & Steffen, V. J. (1984). Gender stereotypes stem from the distribution of women and men into social roles. *Journal of Personality and Social Psychology, 46,* 735–754.

Gaertner, S. L. (1976). Nonreactive measures in racial attitude research: A focus on "liberals." In P. A. Katz (Ed.), *Towards the elimination of racism* (pp. 183–211). New York: Pergamon Press.

Gaertner, S. L., & McLaughlin, J. P. (1983). Racial stereotypes: Associations and ascriptions of positive and negative characteristics. *Social Psychology Quarterly, 46*, 23–30.

Gurwitz, S. B., & Dodge, K. A. (1977). Effects of confirmations and disconfirmations on stereotype-based attributions. *Journal of Personality and Social Psychology, 35*, 495–500.

Hamilton, D. L. (1976). Cognitive biases in the perception of social groups. In J. S. Carroll & J. W. Payne (Eds.), *Cognition and social behavior* (pp. 81–93). Hillsdale, N. J.: Erlbaum.

Hamilton, D. L. (1979). A cognitive-attributional analysis of stereotyping. In L. Berkowitz (Ed.), *Advances in experimental social psychology* (Vol. 12, pp. 53–84). New York: Academic Press.

Hamilton, D. L. (Ed.). (1981a). *Cognitive processes in stereotyping and intergroup behavior.* Hillsdale, N. J.: Erlbaum.

Hamilton, D. L. (1981b). Cognitive representations of persons. In E. T. Higgins, C. P. Herman, & M. P. Zanna (Eds.), *Social cognition: The Ontario Symposium* (Vol. 1, pp. 135–159). Hillsdale, N. J.: Erlbaum.

Hamilton, D. L. (1981c). Illusory correlation as a basis for stereotyping. In D. L. Hamilton (Ed.), *Cognitive processes in stereotyping and intergroup behavior* (pp. 115–144). Hillsdale, N. J.: Erlbaum.

Hamilton, D. L. (1981d). Stereotyping and intergroup behavior: Some thoughts on the cognitive approach. In D. L. Hamilton (Ed.), *Cognitive processes in stereotyping and intergroup behavior* (pp. 333–353). Hillsdale, N. J.: Erlbaum.

Hamilton, D. L., Dugan, P. M., & Trolier, T. K. (1985). The formation of stereotypic beliefs: Further evidence for distinctiveness-based illusory correlations. *Journal of Personality and Social Psychology, 48*, 5–17.

Hamilton, D. L., & Gifford, R. K. (1976). Illusory correlation in interpersonal perception: A cognitive basis of stereotypic judgments. *Journal of Experimental Social Psychology, 12*, 392–407.

Hamilton, D. L., & Rose, T. L. (1980). Illusory correlation and the maintenance of stereotypic beliefs. *Journal of Personality and Social Psychology, 39*, 832–845.

Hastie, R. (1984). Causes and effects of causal attribution. *Journal of Personality and Social Psychology, 46*, 44–56.

Hastie, R., & Kumar, P. A. (1979). Person memory: Personality traits as organizing principles in memory for behaviors. *Journal of Personality and Social Psychology, 37*, 25–38.

Hastie, R., Park, B., & Weber, R. (1984). Social memory. In R. S. Wyer, Jr., & T. K. Srull (Eds.), *Handbook of social cognition* (Vol. 2, pp. 151–212). Hillsdale, N. J.: Erlbaum.

Hemsley, G. D., & Marmurek, H. H. (1982). Person memory: The processing of consistent and inconsistent person information. *Personality and Social Psychology Bulletin, 8*, 443–438.

Hewstone, M., Bond, M. H., & Wan, K. (1983). Social facts and social attributions: The explanation of intergroup differences in Hong Kong. *Social Cognition, 2*, 142–157.

Hewstone, M., & Jaspars, J. M. F. (1982). Intergroup relations and attribution processes. In H. Tajfel (Ed.), *Social identity and intergroup relations* (pp. 99–133). Cambridge: Cambridge University Press.

Hewstone, M., & Jaspars, J. M. F. (1984). Social dimensions of attribution. In H. Tajfel (Ed.), *The social dimension: European developments in social psychology* (pp. 379–404). Cambridge: Cambridge University Press.

Hewstone, M., Jaspars, J., & Lalljee, M. (1982). Social representations, social attribution and social identity: The intergroup images of "public" and "comprehensive" schoolboys. *European Journal of Social Psychology, 12*, 241–269.

Higgins, E. T., Rholes, W. S., & Jones, C. R. (1977). Category accessibility and impression formation. *Journal of Experimental Social Psychology, 13*, 141–154.

Hilton, J. L., & Darley, J. M. (1985). Constructing other persons: A limit on the effect. *Journal of Experimental Social Psychology, 21*, 1–18.

Howard, J. W., & Rothbart, M. (1980). Social categorization and memory for in-group and out-group behavior. *Journal of Personality and Social Psychology, 38*, 301–310.

Jones, E. E., Wood, G. C., & Quattrone, G. A. (1981). Perceived variability of personal characteristics in in-groups and out-groups: The role of knowledge and evaluation. *Personality and Social Psychology Bulletin, 7*, 523–528.

Jones, R. A. (1982). Perceiving other people: Stereotyping as a process of social cognition. In A. G. Miller (Ed.), *In the eye of the beholder: Contemporary issues in stereotyping* (pp. 41–91). New York: Praeger.

Jones, R. A., & Ashmore, R. D. (1973). The structure of intergroup perception: Categories and dimensions in views of ethnic groups and adjectives used in stereotype research. *Journal of Personality and Social Psychology, 25*, 428–438.

Katz, D., & Braly, K. (1933). Racial stereotypes in one hundred college students. *Journal of Abnormal and Social Psychology, 28*, 280–290.

Kinder, D. R., & Sears, D. O. (1981). Prejudice and politics: Symbolic racism versus racial threats to the good life. *Journal of Personality and Social Psychology, 40*, 414–431.

Linville, P. W. (1982). The complexity–extremity effect and age-based stereotyping. *Journal of Personality and Social Psychology, 42*, 193–211.

Linville, P. W., & Jones, E. E. (1980). Polarized appraisals of out-group members. *Journal of Personality and Social Psychology, 38*, 689–703.

Lui, L., & Brewer, M. B. (1983). Recognition accuracy as evidence of category-consistency effects in person memory. *Social Cognition, 2*, 89–107.

McArthur, L. Z. (1981). What grabs you? The role of attention in impression formation and causal attribution. In E. T. Higgins, C. P. Herman, & M. P. Zanna (Eds.), *Social cognition: The Ontario Symposium* (Vol. 1, pp. 201–246). Hillsdale, N. J.: Erlbaum.

Meyer, D. E., & Schvaneveldt, R. W. (1971). Facilitation in recognizing pairs of words: Evidence of a dependence between retrieval operations. *Journal of Experimental Psychology, 90*, 227–234.

Park, B., & Rothbart, M. (1982). Perception of out-group homogeneity and levels of social categorization: Memory for the subordinate attributes of in-group and out-group members. *Journal of Personality and Social Psychology, 42*, 1051–1068.

Pettigrew, T. F. (1979). The ultimate attribution error: Extending Allport's cognitive analysis of prejudice. *Personality and Social Psychology Bulletin, 5*, 461–476.

Pettigrew, T. F. (1981). Extending the stereotype concept. In D. L. Hamilton (Ed.), *Cognitive processes in stereotyping and intergroup behavior* (pp. 303–331). Hillsdale, N. J.: Erlbaum.

Quattrone, G. A., & Jones, E. E. (1980). The perception of variability within ingroups and outgroups: Implications for the law of small numbers. *Journal of Personality and Social Psychology, 38*, 141–152.

Regan, D. T., & Crawley, D. M. (1984). *Illusory correlation and stereotype formation: Replication and extension.* Paper presented at American Psychological Association Convention, Toronto.

Rosch, E. (1978). Principles of categorization. In E. Rosch & B. B. Lloyd (Eds.), *Cognition and categorization* (pp. 27–48). Hillsdale, N. J.: Erlbaum.

Rothbart, M. (1981). Memory processes and social beliefs. In D. L. Hamilton (Ed.), *Cognitive processes in stereotyping and intergroup behavior* (pp. 145–181). Hillsdale, N. J.: Erlbaum.

Rothbart, M., Dawes, R., & Park, B. (1984). Stereotyping and sampling biases in intergroup perception. In J. R. Eiser (Ed.), *Attitudinal judgment* (pp. 109–134). New York: Springer-Verlag.

Rothbart, M., Evans, M., & Fulero, S. (1979). Recall for confirming events: Memory processes and the maintenance of social stereotypes. *Journal of Experimental Social Psychology, 15,* 343–355.

Rumelhart, D. E. (1984). Schemata and the cognitive system. In R. S. Wyer, Jr., & T. K. Srull (Eds.), *Handbook of social cognition* (Vol. 1, pp. 161–188). Hillsdale, N. J.: Erlbaum.

Sagar, H. A., & Schofield, J. W. (1980). Racial and behavioral cues in black and white children's perceptions of ambiguously aggressive acts. *Journal of Personality and Social Psychology, 39,* 590–598.

Sigall, H., & Page, R. (1971). Current stereotypes: A little fading, a little faking. *Journal of Personality and Social Psychology, 18,* 247–255.

Smedley, J. W., & Bayton, J. A. (1978). Evaluative race-class stereotypes by race and perceived class of subjects. *Journal of Personality and Social Psychology, 36,* 530–535.

Snyder, M. (1981). On the self-perpetuating nature of social stereotypes. In D. L. Hamilton (Ed.), *Cognitive processes in stereotyping and intergroup behavior* (pp. 183–212). Hillsdale, N. J.: Erlbaum.

Snyder, M., & Swann, W. B., Jr. (1978). Hypothesis-testing processes in social interaction. *Journal of Personality and Social Psychology, 36,* 1202–1212.

Srull, T. K. (1981). Person memory: Some tests of associative storage and retrieval models. *Journal of Experimental Psychology: Human Learning and Memory, 7,* 440–463.

Srull, T. K., Lichtenstein, M. & Rothbart, M. (1985). Associative storage and retrieval processes in person memory. *Journal of Experimental Psychology: Learning, Memory and Cognition, 11,* 316–345.

Srull, T. K., & Wyer, R. S., Jr. (1980). Category accessibility and social perception: Some implications for the study of person memory and interpersonal judgment. *Journal of Personality and Social Psychology, 38,* 841–856.

Stern, L. D., Marrs, S., Millar, M. G., & Cole, E. (1984). Processing time and the recall of inconsistent and consistent behaviors of individuals and groups. *Journal of Personality and Social Psychology, 47,* 253–262.

Tajfel, H. (1970). Experiments in intergroup discrimination. *Scientific American, 223,* 96–102.

Tajfel, H. (Ed.). (1978). *Differentiation between social groups.* London: Academic Press.

Tajfel, H. (1981). *Human groups and social categories.* Cambridge: Cambridge University Press.

Tajfel, H. (1982). Social psychology of intergroup relations. *Annual Review of Psychology, 33,* 1–39.

Tajfel, H., & Forgas, J. P. (1981). Social categorization: Cognitions, values, and groups. In J. P. Forgas (Ed.), *Social Cognition: Perspectives on everyday understanding* (pp. 113–140). New York: Academic Press.

Tajfel, H., Sheikh, A. A., & Gardner, R. C. (1964). Content of stereotypes and the inference of similarity between members of stereotyped groups. *Acta Psychologica, 22,* 191–201.

Tajfel, H., & Turner, J. C. (1979). An integrative theory of intergroup conflict. In W. Austin & S. Worchel (Eds.), *The social psychology of intergroup relations* (pp. 33–47). Monterey, California: Brooks/Cole.

Tajfel, H., & Wilkes, A. L. (1963). Classification and quantitative judgment. *British Journal of Psychology, 54,* 101–114.

Taylor, D. M., & Jaggi, V. (1974). Ethnocentrism and causal attribution in a South Indian context. *Journal of Cross-Cultural Psychology, 5,* 162–171.

Taylor, S. E. (1981). A categorization approach to stereotyping. In D. L. Hamilton (Ed.), *Cognitive processes in stereotyping and intergroup behavior* (pp. 83–114). Hillsdale, N. J.: Erlbaum.

Taylor, S. E., & Crocker, J. (1981). Schematic bases of social information processing. In E. T. Higgins, C. P. Herman, & M. P. Zanna (Eds.), *Social cognition: The Ontario symposium* (Vol. 1, pp. 89–134). Hillsdale, N. J.: Erlbaum.

Taylor, S. E., & Falcone, H. (1982). Cognitive bases of stereotyping: The relationship between categorization and prejudice. *Personality and Social Psychology Bulletin, 8,* 426–432.

Taylor, S. E., & Fiske, S. T. (1978). Salience, attention, and attribution: Top of the head phenomena. In L. Berkowitz (Ed.), *Advances in experimental social psychology* (Vol. 11, pp. 249–288). New York: Academic Press.

Taylor, S. E., Fiske, S. T., Etcoff, N. L., & Ruderman, A. J. (1978). Categorical bases of person memory and stereotyping. *Journal of Personality and Social Psychology, 36,* 778–793.

Wang, G. & McKillip, J. (1978). Ethnic identification and judgements of an accident. *Personality and Social Psychology Bulletin, 4,* 296–299.

Weber, R., & Crocker, J. (1983). Cognitive processes in the revision of stereotypic beliefs. *Journal of Personality and Social Psychology, 45,* 961–977.

Wilder, D. A. (1978a). Homogeneity of jurors: The majority's influence depends upon their perceived independence. *Law and Human Behavior, 2,* 363–376.

Wilder, D. A. (1978b). Perceiving persons as a group: Effects on attributions of causality and beliefs. *Social Psychology, 1,* 13–23.

Wilder, D. A. (1981). Perceiving persons as a group: Categorization and intergroup relations. In D. L. Hamilton (Ed.), *Cognitive processes in stereotyping and intergroup behavior* (pp. 213–257). Hillsdale, N. J.: Erlbaum.

Word, C. O., Zanna, M. P., & Cooper, J. (1974). The nonverbal mediation of self-fulfilling prophecies in interracial interaction. *Journal of Experimental Social Psychology, 10,* 109–120.

Wyer, R. S., Jr., & Gordon, S. E. (1984). The cognitive representation of social information. In R. S. Wyer, Jr., & T. K. Srull (Eds.), *Handbook of Social Cognition* (Vol. 2, pp. 73–150). Hillsdale, N. J.: Erlbaum.

Zadny, J., & Gerard, H. B. (1974). Attributed intentions and informational selectivity. *Journal of Experimental Social Psychology, 10,* 34–52.

STEREOTYPING AND PERCEIVED DISTRIBUTIONS OF SOCIAL CHARACTERISTICS: AN APPLICATION TO INGROUP–OUTGROUP PERCEPTION*

Patricia W. Linville
Peter Salovey

Department of Psychology
Yale University
New Haven, Connecticut 06520

Gregory W. Fischer

Department of Social and
Decision Sciences
Carnegie-Mellon University
Pittsburgh, Pennsylvania 15213

INTRODUCTION

How do people form stereotypes, use them to infer features of individual members, and revise them in light of new knowledge? One common assumption has been that people think about broad social categories such as blacks, females, or the elderly in terms of a single list of most typical traits—the stereotype (e.g., Katz & Braly, 1933; Karlins, Coffman, & Walters, 1969). This single trait list is then used to make inferences about the behavior of individual category members. Category instances that do not fit the stereotype are either ignored, rationalized, or eventually used to revise the trait list or the values given to specific traits.

In contrast, the central argument of the present chapter is that *category differentiation* is at the heart of the stereotype concept. By greater category differentiation, we mean a tendency to perceive many types within a given category, and to be highly likely to distinguish among category members. In this paper, we propose a formal

* Preparation of this chapter was facilitated by a Yale University Junior Faculty Fellowship Award to the first author. Portions of this chapter are based on a paper presented at the Conference on Social Cognition, Nags Head, North Carolina, May 1983.

statistical measure that reflects these properties of category differentiation. Our analysis of stereotyping rests on three assumptions concerning category differentiation.

First, we assume that general social categories are represented in terms of multiple feature sets. These feature sets are then used to classify and to draw inferences about category members. For example, in describing members of the category "black," one perceiver created seven subtypes described by the following feature sets: "young, strong, athletic male"; "young, bright, hard-working, professional"; "young, illiterate, male, criminal"; "middle-aged, blue collar worker"; "middle-aged, male, unemployed, discouraged"; "single, welfare mother"; "middle-aged, articulate, civil rights activist." (Also see Chapter 5.)

Second, we assume that the feature sets associated with a category differ in degree of perceived likelihood. For example, the preceding perceiver believed that "welfare mothers" and "blue collar males" are the most common types; that "young athletes" and "unemployed men" are also quite common; that "professionals" and "juvenile criminals" are less common, and that "civil rights activists" are very rare.

Third, we assume that category differentiation is embedded in basic learning processes involving both generalization and discrimination. Thus, our approach is compatible with the recently developing cognitive approach to stereotyping and intergroup processes (see Hamilton, 1981a; Chapter 5 by Hamilton & Trolier, in this volume). We assume that social categories evolve from relatively general, undifferentiated structures to more highly differentiated ones. Thus, new instances that do not fit the category are dealt with in part through increasing category differentiation. We assume that category differentiation tends to occur when the perceiver encounters numerous and varied instances of the category, and experiences incentives to distinguish among category members. This leads us to our basic hypothesis that *greater category familiarity leads to greater category differentiation.*

In the context of stereotyping, this implies that to the extent that people are more familiar with groups to which they belong, perceivers will tend to be more differentiated in their thinking about their own groups than about other groups. This prediction is the well known *outgroup homogeneity hypothesis.* While the outgroup homogeneity hypothesis is widely cited and accepted, the evidence from studies testing the hypothesis is somewhat mixed. We argue in this chapter that these mixed findings result in part from the varied and often imprecise measures and definitions of the homogeneity concept. These problems, in turn, are related to the fact that the homogeneity concept is rarely embedded in a clear theoretical framework that makes explicit structure and process assumptions. In this chapter, we attempt to develop both an explicit model of the categorization processes surrounding stereotyping, and a precise measure of the homogeneity concept.

This chapter consists of four sections following this introduction. The first section reviews current evidence for perceived outgroup homogeneity. The second presents a general framework for thinking about social categories, one in which stereotyping is conceived of in terms of degree of perceived category differentiation. Then we propose a specific measure of category differentiation. The third and fourth sections describe our empirical results supporting this framework. The third describes work on perceived differentiation for ingroups and outgroups, and the fourth on perceived differentiation for a group over time.

INGROUP–OUTGROUP PERCEPTION: THE EVIDENCE FOR OUTGROUP HOMOGENEITY

Two hypotheses have dominated the attention of those studying the impact of group membership on social perception. The first is the *ingroup favoritism* hypothesis; that people tend to be more favorable toward members of groups to which they belong (the "ingroup") than toward members of other groups (the "outgroup") (Brewer, 1979; Wilder, 1981). The second is the *outgroup homogeneity* hypothesis; that people tend to perceive outgroup members as being more homogeneous in their traits and behavior than ingroup members. For example, the belief that "all blacks look alike" or that "all Arabs are alike" reflects this homogeneity perception. This section critically reviews the literature regarding the outgroup homogeneity hypothesis. While the outgroup homogeneity hypothesis is almost a truism, a review of the literature shows that slightly more than 20% of the published tests of the hypothesis have failed to support it. One possible reason for these mixed results is that the concept of homogeneity has been operationalized in multiple ways. Here, we organize our discussion of previous studies in terms of how researchers have conceptualized and measured homogeneity. These include five approaches: direct measures of intragroup similarity; single attribute, multiple attribute, and organizational properties of representations of groups; and consequences of perceived homogeneity. (See also Quattrone, 1986, for an excellent review based on the concepts of general, dimensional, and taxonomic variability.)

DIRECT MEASURES OF INTRAGROUP SIMILARITY

Several studies have asked subjects to directly rate the extent to which members of a group resemble one another without reference to any particular dimensions. Park and Rothbart (1982, Experiment 3) asked members of three sororities to rate the intragroup similarity within each sorority by responding to the question "how similar or dissimilar are the [members of sorority "X"] to one another?" As predicted by the outgroup homogeneity hypothesis, members of each sorority rated their own members as more dissimilar to one another than did members of other sororities.

As part of a study on group inferences, Quattrone and Jones (1980) had subjects from Princeton and Rutgers rate the variability of either Princeton or Rutgers students on a scale ranging from "They're pretty much alike" to "They're all completely different from one another." Subjects showed absolutely no tendency to rate the ingroup as more variable. Quattrone and Jones report two additional studies using this same type of direct measure of perceived variability. Premedical and nursing students did not rate the ingroup as more variable; but college students did rate their own political group as more variable.

Assuming that one's "opinion group" is in some sense an ingroup, Goethals, Allison, and Frost (1979) found support for outgroup homogeneity in three studies. Subjects first checked their own opinion on an issue such as whether President Carter's performance was good, fair, or poor. Later they rated the "diversity" of students in each of the three "opinion groups" (i.e., those rating Carter's performance as good, those rating it fair, and those rating it poor). They made their diversity ratings on a scale ranging from "similar to each other, sharing the same values and outlook" to "a diverse group of people with different values and outlooks." Subjects viewed members of their own opinion group as more diverse than members of other opinion groups.

In summary, direct ratings of intragroup similarity have produced mixed results, with five of the seven studies favoring the outgroup homogeneity hypothesis.

MEASURES OF PROPERTIES OF REPRESENTATION

Other researchers have employed measures that were more directly tied to the assumed knowledge structure or representation regarding a social group. We organize these studies into three groupings: those measuring perceived homogeneity with respect to single attributes, those that measure it with respect to the relationship among multiple attributes, and those that measure it in terms of organizational properties of the representation of a social group.

Single-Attribute Properties

Several research programs have examined perceived homogeneity of ingroups and outgroups with respect to single attributes.

Range across Dimensions. Two studies measuring the perceived range of beliefs and traits of ingroups and outgroups show support for outgroup homogeneity. Jones, Wood, and Quattrone (1981) had members of four undergraduate clubs mark the range on various trait scales (e.g., introverted–extroverted) within which members of a particular club fell. The perceived range was greater for the ingroup club than the outgroup clubs, and range was not correlated with either number of acquaintances known in a club or favorability rating of the club. Wilder (1980) divided subjects into an ingroup and an outgroup on the basis of their painting preference, then asked them to estimate the range of beliefs on several topics that would be endorsed by each group. Subjects were presented with a range of possible positions on each topic (e.g., political beliefs from reactionary to radical). Subjects checked a wider range of belief positions for the ingroup than for the outgroup on two of three topics.

Ascribing Stereotypic Traits. Park and Rothbart (1982) related homogeneity to perceiving most group members as having stereotypic traits and few as having counterstereotypic traits; and they related heterogeneity to perceiving a more equal balance of stereotypic and counterstereotypic traits. In two studies, male and female subjects estimated the proportion of males and females who would endorse each of 54 attitude and behavioral items. The 54 items varied in their favorability and their relevance to male or female stereotypes. As predicted, outgroup subjects (males and females estimating opposite-sex endorsements) estimated that a higher proportion of group members would endorse stereotypic items, and that a lower proportion would endorse counterstereotypic items than did ingroup subjects. Subjects ascribed more stereotypic traits to the opposite-sex than to their same-sex whether the traits were favorable or not.

Quattrone and Jones (1980) report results consistent with this finding. Princeton and Rutgers subjects rated the average male student at either Princeton or Rutgers along 10 dimensions that discriminate between the Princeton and Rutgers stereotypes (e.g., upperclass versus lowerclass). While the ratings of subjects from both schools supported the stereotypes, the average male at each school was rated more in line with his school's stereotype by outgroup than by ingroup subjects (e.g., Rutgers subjects rated the average Princeton male as more upperclass than did Princeton subjects).

Multiple Attribute Properties

Several research programs have examined the perceived homogeneity of ingroups and outgroups in terms of the relationships among the attributes of group members. This research differs from that described above in that it focuses on relationships between the attributes of group members rather than on a single attribute.

Intercorrelations among Attribute Judgments. Linville and Jones (1980) asked white college subjects to rate a set of black and white law school applicants on a variety of attributes (trait scales). Linville and Jones then correlated the ratings assigned to applicants on various attributes (e.g., intelligence and motivation). They found that the average correlations between pairs of attributes were higher for black (outgroup) than for white applicants, even though the black and white applications were identical apart from race. A similar pattern was found for male and female subjects rating male and female applicants. The average intercorrelations were higher for opposite-sex than for same-sex applicants. Similarly, in separate factor analyses of attribute ratings for black and white as well as male and female applicants, fewer independent factors emerged for opposite-race and opposite-sex ratings. Thus when rating group members on a variety of characteristics, people appear to perceive less correlation among the attributes of ingroup members than among the attributes of outgroup members.

Dimensional Complexity. Linville and Jones (1980; Linville, 1982) proposed that in areas of life where people have greater experience or familiarity, they develop more complex knowledge structures. Assuming that people are more familiar with ingroups than outgroups, they should have a more complex representation for ingroups. Complexity was operationalized in terms of the number and distinctiveness of dimensions used to represent members of a social group and was measured using a trait-sorting task. Subjects sorted traits into piles according to which traits they thought belonged together. Complexity scores were calculated from these trait sorts. White subjects demonstrated higher complexity when thinking about whites than blacks

(Linville & Jones, 1980); young subjects demonstrated higher complexity when thinking about young than elderly persons (Linville, 1980, 1982); and elderly subjects demonstrated higher complexity when thinking about elderly than young persons (Brewer & Lui, 1984; Linville & Salovey, 1982). Because both young and elderly subjects demonstrated greater complexity for their respective age-related ingroups, differential perceptions of complexity cannot simply be due to actual differences in the diversity of these two populations.

Prototypicality. Using the framework of Rosch's (1978) theory of natural categories, Brewer and her colleagues demonstrated that perceivers' conceptions of the elderly were differentiated into distinctive subcategories (grandmother, elder stateman, senior citizen) (Brewer, Dull, & Lui, 1981). Brewer and Lui (1984) found that elderly subjects demonstrated greater differentiation for the category "elderly" than did college students. For example, in a picture-sorting task, elderly subjects created more categories, demonstrated higher complexity, and clustered the photos less consistently into a priori elderly subcategories than did college-age subjects. Results from a behavior-sorting task suggest that elderly subjects made more complex attribute associations to representative members of the subcategory "grandmother," the one perceived most similar to themselves.

Number of Subtypes of Persons. If we think of subtypes of individuals as being characterized by a whole list of features (or attribute values), then research on the number of subtypes within a social category can be viewed as an instance of research focusing on multiple attributes. Two studies looking at a simple count of perceived subtypes within a group showed support for outgroup homogeneity. Supporters of the women's movement checked a greater number of subtypes of students (e.g., artistic, athletic, religious) as supporting the movement than did nonsupportive subjects (Goethals et al., 1979). Unfortunately, subjects were not asked also to check subtypes of nonsupporters. Another study found that both premedical and nursing students listed more subtypes of people within their own group (cited in Quattrone & Jones, 1980).

Organizational Properties

Several research programs have examined perceived homogeneity by using recall measures to tap the organization of information regarding ingroup and outgroup members. This research focuses on organizational properties that reflect greater individuation of ingroup members. These studies differ from those described previously in that they focus on the encoding and organization of new information about group members rather than on previously stored schemas for the group.

Memory for Superordinate and Subordinate Categories. Park and Rothbart (1982) suggest that perceivers use different levels of social categorization to encode behavior of ingroup versus outgroup members, a process they believe accounts for perceptions of outgroup homogeneity. More specifically, outgroup behaviors are encoded primarily at the superordinate level, whereas ingroup behaviors are encoded at the superordinate and subordinate level. Men and women read news stories which included the sex and occupation of the main character. Two days later subjects were equally likely to recall the sex (superordinate attribute) of ingroup and outgroup members, yet they were more likely to recall the occupation (subordinate attribute) of ingroup members than of outgroup members. This interesting research suggests that memory structures encode more information about ingroups.

Within-Category Recall Errors. Taylor, Fiske, Etcoff, and Ruderman (1978) tested the outgroup homogeneity hypothesis as part of a series of studies on social categorization. Subjects viewed a tape of a group of interacting individuals. These groups were composed of blacks and whites in one study and of males and females in two others. After viewing the tape, subjects recalled which individuals within a group made specific comments. Outgroup homogeneity was conceptualized in terms of intraracial and intragender recall errors. That is, white subjects should confuse black speakers with each other more than they confuse white speakers with each other. Likewise, male subjects should confuse female speakers with each other and female subjects should confuse male speakers with each other more than they confuse speakers of their own sex. Recall errors showed no support for outgroup homogeneity in any of the studies.

Person versus Category Organization. Carpenter and Ostrom (1985) suggest that perceivers encode and organize information about ingroup members in terms of individual persons and outgroup members in terms of category information. Male and female subjects viewed items of information about four male and four female target persons. For each target person, they viewed four items of information representing four different categories (e.g., favorite sport, major). Subjects later recalled information about target persons. The order in which items are listed in free recall reflects their organization in memory. Thus strong person organization should be reflected in more person clustering in free recall. As predicted, perceivers organized information about same-sex targets (ingroup members) in terms of persons and information about opposite-sex targets (outgroup members) in terms of categories. Their finding is consistent with prior findings that person organization is prevalent in processing information about familiar persons and category organization is prevalent in processing information about strangers (Ostrom, Pryor, & Simpson, 1981).

In summary, studies using more direct measures of properties of representation have produced mixed results, but a high proportion, 14 of 17 studies, favor the outgroup homogeneity hypothesis. All of the twelve reported studies on single and multiple attribute homogeneity favored outgroup homogeneity. The three studies that did not all involved memory measures (i.e., within-group recall errors).

CONSEQUENCES OF HOMOGENEITY

Several researchers have proposed consequences of perceived homogeneity. Because it is useful to separate measures of a construct from their implications, we suggest that tests of the hypothesized consequences of perceived homogeneity be considered separately from tests of perceived homogeneity. Also, support for consequences of homogeneity should not be confused with tests of perceived homogeneity.

Evaluative Extremity

Linville and Jones (1980; Linville, 1982) proposed that the less complex a person's representation of a given domain, the more extreme will be the person's judgments regarding stimuli in that domain. Two series of experiments manipulated complexity in terms of ingroup–outgroup status. Assuming that perceivers have a less complex representation of outgroups, then perceivers should rate outgroup members more extremely than ingroup members. (See Chapter 2 by Katz, Wackenhut, and Hass for a motivational interpretation of extremity effects.) In one set of experiments, white subjects read and evaluated several law-school applications from strong and weak applicants that contained incidental information on the race and sex of the applicant (Linville & Jones, 1980). The results supported outgroup extremity. When reading a strong application, white subjects rated a black applicant higher than a comparable white applicant; when reading a weak application, they rated a black applicant lower than a comparable white applicant. Similar results were obtained for cross-sex pairings on one dimension—activeness. Male subjects viewing a female applicant, and female subjects viewing a male applicant, were more extreme in their ratings than when rating an applicant of their same sex. Similar results were found in studies using age as the group variable. When reading a favorable vignette, young subjects rated an older male more positively than a comparable younger one; when reading an unfavorable vignette, they rated an older male more negatively than a comparable younger one (Linville, 1982). Similarly, older subjects evaluated young male targets more extremely than older male targets (Linville & Salovey, 1982). Thus outgroup extremity has been found for both young and old subjects, ruling out alternative explanations idiosyncratic to one age group (e.g., favorable older persons are evaluated more favorably because they are in the minority or are violating negative stereotypic expectations of the old).

A second more powerful prediction of the complexity–extremity relationship involves complexity as an individual difference variable. Those less complex in their thinking about a given group should be more extreme in their evaluations of individual group members. As predicted, young subjects' complexity regarding the category of older males was significantly negatively correlated with the extremity of their ratings of individual older males ($r = -.65$) (Linville, 1982). Those less complex in their thinking about older males were both more favorable toward the positively described older male and more unfavorable toward the negatively described older male compared to those more complex in their thinking about older males. Finally, two studies manipulated complexity by drawing subjects' attention to varying numbers of stimulus features. As predicted, those asked to think about fewer features of stimuli made more extreme evaluations of those stimuli (Linville, 1982; Linville & Jones, 1980).

This research program provided three conceptual replications of the basic complexity–extremity relationship. Lower complexity—assumed in terms of perception of outgroups, measured as an individual difference measure, or manipulated in terms of attention to fewer attributes—resulted in more extreme evaluative ratings.

Member-to-Group Inferences

Quattrone and Jones (1980) proposed that perceived homogeneity of a group facilitates generalization from the behavior of a specific member to the group as a whole. Princeton and Rutgers undergraduates viewed a tape of either a Princeton or a Rutgers student making a choice during a psychology experiment (e.g., to wait alone or with others). After viewing the choice of the one student, subjects then estimated the proportion of students from that same university who would make the same decision as that particular student. The estimated proportions were greater when the student was an outgroup member, but only when subjects had a weak prior expectancy concerning the target's likely choice. While subjects made stronger person-to-group generalizations for the outgroup than the ingroup, there was no direct evidence that perceived homogeneity was the mediator. Direct ratings revealed no difference in the perceived homogeneity of the ingroup and the outgroup, and revealed no significant relationship between perceived homogeneity and the tendency to make person-to-group inferences.

Nisbett and colleagues replicated and extended the Quattrone and Jones study, using University of Michigan subjects viewing the choices of either University of Michigan or Ohio State students (Nisbett, Krantz, Jepson, & Kunda, 1983). In the replication conditions, subjects made stronger person-to-group generalizations for the outgroup. Nisbett et al. reasoned that inducing subjects to contemplate the central tendencies of a population would make the homogeneity of the population more salient, thus increasing the degree of generalization. As expected, subjects contemplating the central tendencies of the group increased their tendency to generalize, especially about the ingroup.

Outgroup Discrimination

Wilder (1978) proposed that deindividuation of the outgroup promoted outgroup discrimination. In conditions that individuated the outgroup, outgroup discrimination was reduced or eliminated. For instance, subjects were informed that the outgroup was either unanimous in their judgments of two legal cases or that one outgroup member dissented. While subjects in the unanimous condition displayed outgroup discrimination, subjects in the dissenter condition showed reduced discrimination both toward the dissenter as well as toward another outgroup member. Thus outgroup members receive poorer treatment when they are seen as an undifferentiated group rather than differing individuals (see also Chapter 7).

CONCLUSIONS REGARDING THE OUTGROUP HOMOGENEITY HYPOTHESIS

While the outgroup homogeneity hypothesis has become almost a truism, empirical evidence regarding the hypothesis is somewhat mixed. Slightly more than 20% of the published tests failed to support the hypothesis. There are several problems with prior approaches to homogeneity. The first problem is the varied and imprecise measures and definitions of the homogeneity concept. Some measures rely heavily on subjects' intuitive judgments of their representations. For instance, the use of direct similarity ratings is somewhat analogous to asking subjects for their own implicit theories of group homogeneity. Work of Nisbett and Wilson (1977) suggests that subjects cannot accurately report the determinants or higher-order processes influencing their behavior. Also, to the degree that perceived homogeneity for the outgroup exists only for certain attributes such as those relevant to the group stereotype, direct similarity ratings which focus the perceiver's attention on the group as a whole may be too global to pick up differential perceptions (see also Quattrone, 1986).

Measures more directly linked with the content and structure of representations of social categories have produced results consistently supportive of outgroup homogeneity. While on firmer theoretical ground, some of these measures are still limited. For example, a sheer count of the number of subtypes of people within a given group does not take into account the degree of perceived redundancy or overlap of subtypes. Measures of the range of values across a dimension are not applicable to nonquantifiable attributes for which there is no natural ordering (e.g., religion, profession). The number of types and range of attributes within a group do not take into consideration the relative likelihood of the various types or various attribute levels. Research tapping perceived homogeneity through recall measures has produced some mixed results. Ingroup–outgroup differences were found for level of categorization and for person clustering but not for intragroup recall errors.

Likewise, the evidence regarding perceived homogeneity as a mediator is mixed. Perceived homogeneity appears to be a mediator of evaluative extremity. But while person-to-group inferences were stronger for the outgroup, perceived homogeneity was not associated with the tendency to make these inferences. It is useful to separate measures of a construct from their implications. We believe that direct measures of perceived homogeneity should be theoretically and methodologically separate from predicted consequences of perceived homogeneity. Support for predicted consequences of outgroup homogeneity should not be taken as evidence for perceived homogeneity. Likewise, failures to confirm predicted consequences may simply reflect incorrect assumptions regarding inference or evaluative processes.

Finally, a more basic problem is that only a few researchers link their measures of homogeneity to assumptions concerning the representation and processing of categorical information. One promising approach is the research showing that perceivers given identical person information encode and organize the information in a more individuating manner when descriptive of an ingroup than an outgroup member. Person clustering in free recall (Carpenter & Ostrom, 1985) and recall of subordinate attributes (Park & Rothbart, 1982) for ingroup members suggests information processing differences in encoding and organization. Given identical person information, the tendency to make more extreme evaluations (Linville & Jones, 1980; Linville, 1982) and to generalize more from the behavior of a specific member (Quattrone & Jones, 1980) for outgroup than ingroup members also suggests differences in information processing.

Taking a different approach in developing the present framework, we attempt to be explicit about representational assumptions regarding the processing of categorical information and to develop a more precise definition of differentiation that is embedded in these representational assumptions. Concepts like homogeneity are inherently ambiguous. They have no concrete meaning until they are formalized. The present framework includes formal definitions of the concepts of differentiation and variability that lead directly to relatively precise measures.

SOCIAL CATEGORIZATION PROCESSES

The central notion underlying the research reported in this chapter is that stereotyping can be conceived of in terms of the degree of differentiation of a perceiver's beliefs regarding the members of a social category. In this section, we describe a general model of social categorization processes, and describe the conditions under which these processes lead to highly differentiated beliefs about the members of a category. The section begins by describing three key assumptions underlying our model regarding the differentiation of beliefs about category members. These assumptions lead to two hypotheses regarding category differentiation. Then it describes and explains two quantitative measures of the differentiation and variability of a perceiver's beliefs regarding a social category.

MAJOR ASSUMPTIONS

Assumption 1. Knowledge about members of a social group is represented in terms of "multiple feature sets."

A *feature* is any encoded property or characteristic of a stimulus; for instance, a person's physical traits (tall, muscular, coarsely-featured), personality characteristics (assertive, arrogant, insensitive), behaviors, or attitudes. Most features may be thought of as specific values of more general *attributes*. For instance, the feature "tall" is a specific value of the attribute "height," the feature "hard-working" is a specific value of the attribute "work motivation," and the feature "prochoice" is a specific value of the attribute "attitude toward abortion." A *feature set* is a list of features describing either a single stimulus or a set of stimuli sharing a particular pattern of features. For instance, one medical student used the feature set "hard-working, bright, serious, but likes to party" to describe one subtype of medical student that he frequently encountered. In social domains, feature sets may describe either single individuals, or groups of individuals sharing common features.

Multiple feature set models of categorization assume that people store frequently occurring feature combinations (i.e., patterns of features) associated with a category (Anderson, 1980; Anderson, Kline, & Beasley, 1979; Elio & Anderson, 1981; Hayes-Roth & Hayes-Roth, 1977; Reitman & Bower, 1973). The central idea behind feature set models is that people attend to and store in memory frequently occurring patterns of features. People classify new instances by matching their features with those of each of the feature sets associated with a category. The better the match, the more likely the instance is to be assigned to the category.

Applying this general model to social categorization, we assume that knowledge of social categories is represented in terms of a variety of feature sets, each describing a different subtype within the category. For example, the medical student mentioned above also described a variety of other subtypes of medical students, each described by a different feature set. These types included "happy-go-lucky, friendly, altruistic" and "intellectual, intense, money-grubbing." Another example comes from a verbal protocol analysis of the thoughts of young subjects as they completed a trait-sorting task describing older males (Linville, 1980). The analysis revealed a variety of subtypes of older males, each described by a different feature set. For example, one young subject mentioned the following subtypes of older males: "grumpy complainer," "wise old man with a twinkle in his eye," and "open-minded, independent fellow with lots of hobbies." The assumption that social categories are represented by multiple feature sets is consistent with recent work suggesting that broad social groups are represented in terms of subtypes (see Ashmore, 1981; Brewer et al., 1981; Linville, 1982; Taylor, 1981; Weber & Crocker, 1983).

The multiple feature set model may be contrasted with *prototype* models that assume that people learn a single list of features reflecting the "central tendency" of a category (Bransford & Frank, 1971; Posner & Keele, 1970; Reed, 1972; Rosch & Mervis, 1975). The prototype for a category is usually assumed to be based on the average or most frequently encountered features of a category. Similarly, traditional approaches to stereotyping have often implicitly assumed that social categories are represented in terms of a list of "most typical" traits (e.g., Katz & Braly, 1933). Multiple feature set models differ from prototype models in that they assume that each category is represented by multiple feature patterns rather than by a single ideal type or prototype. Thus, the multiple feature set model represents variability among category members, whereas the prototype model does not.

Categories might also be represented by *multiple prototypes*, each representing a different type or subtype within the category. Because each of these multiple prototypes for the category is described by a list of features, this representation of categorical knowledge closely resembles the multiple feature set model. However, Anderson (1980) discusses two important differences between the models and concludes that the feature set formulation is superior. First, feature-set models include partially described types—that is, types for which only a subset of features is specified. By contrast, prototype models usually specify or fill in all of the features of each prototype. Second, the two models assume different classification processes. In prototype models, similarity to prototypes provides the basis for classifying new instances. In multiple feature set models, the relative frequencies with which different feature sets have occurred in the past provides the basis for forming generalizations and classifying new instances.

Finally, multiple feature set models may be contrasted with *multiple instance models*, which assume that people retain in memory the features of specific past instances of a category (Medin & Schaffer, 1978). Thus, multiple instance models assume a more concrete, less abstracted knowledge structure than do multiple feature set models. (See Anderson, 1980; Anderson et al., 1979; and Elio & Anderson, 1981, for comparisons between prototype, instance, and feature set models.)

Assumption 2. Each feature set has a "strength of association" to the category label. This provides a basis for judgments regarding the relative likelihoods of features and feature combinations within the category.

Abstracted category information is based on the frequency with which features and feature combinations occur across instances of a category. Thus, patterns of frequently co-occurring features comprise the category representation. The frequency with which a feature set occurs determines in part its associative strength to the category. (See assumptions of frequency or strength models of schema abstraction; e.g., Elio & Anderson, 1981; Hayes-Roth & Hayes-Roth, 1977; Reitman & Bower, 1973). Each time a pattern of features successfully classifies an instance, the specific feature pattern as well as generalizations consistent with the pattern are strengthed (Anderson, 1980).

Strength of association may be thought of as akin to availability in memory. Associative strength implies that a feature set may be quickly and easily retrieved when one thinks about the category. Thus, the strength of association may be influenced by factors such as the frequency, recency, and vividness of the types of people one thinks about in regard to the category. The key notion for the present framework is that we have some basis in memory for making judgments about the relative likelihood of various features sets linked with a category. The greater the strength of association between a feature set and a category, the greater the perceived likelihood that a member of the category will be characterized by this feature set. Thus, our model implies that those whites whose views of blacks are based mainly on watching television are likely to overestimate the proportion of blacks who are entertainers or athletes, and to underestimate the proportion in white collar jobs.

Social categories may be thought of in either deterministic or probabilistic terms. In a deterministic model, category membership determines features with certainty. A strong or literal interpretation of such a model would imply that all members of a category share a common set of features. In a probabilistic model, the likelihood of features varies with category membership, but members of a given category do not all share the same features. Rather, the probabilistic view assumes a distribution of features or attribute values across members of a given category, with different distributions of attribute values being associated with different categories.

Feature set models lead to a probabilistic view of categorization. Because social categories generally include many possible feature sets, knowledge of an individual's category membership does not allow a perceiver to uniquely predict the features of a particular individual in a category. Similarly, many feature sets may be associated with more than one category. Thus, knowing that a particular feature set characterizes a given individual (e.g., blond hair and blue eyes) is not sufficient in many cases to permit a unique determination of the individual's category membership (e.g., U.S. versus Swedish citizen).

One direct approach for getting at the probabilistic nature of categorical knowledge is to ask people to assess the relative likelihood of different features (i.e., values of a given attribute) for members of a particular social category. For instance, we might ask a perceiver to estimate the proportion of young blacks that are "very good," "good," "fair," "poor," or "very poor" students, say by distributing 100 young blacks across these five levels of the attribute "academic ability." We assume that in responding to this task, the subject retrieves those feature sets associated with the category "black" that include information concerning academic ability. If the perceiver's experiences with blacks have been varied, we expect the perceiver to distribute the hypothetical sample of blacks across several ability levels, rather than lumping them all together into only one most typical level. The belief that the members of a given social category are distributed across a variety of different levels of any given attribute is one direct manifestation of the probabilistic nature of social categorization processes.

Assumption 3. The feature sets associated with a particular social category are acquired and modified through basic learning processes of "generalization" and "discrimination."

The tendency to generalize lies at the heart of categorization processes (Anderson, 1980). *Generalization* occurs when a person notes that a certain pattern of features characterizes two or more instances of the same category, then (often implicitly) forms a mental association between this pattern of features and the category in question. Abstracting out common feature patterns is the essence of generalization and is closely related to traditional notions of stereotyping. For example, exposed to a few nightly television news reports about crime, a viewer might form the generalization, "If a person is young, black, and male, he is likely to be a criminal." Like most generalizations, this one is clearly false. It is an "overgeneralization" from a few instances. As Anderson et al. (1979) have argued, however, people have been shown to overgeneralize in language acquisition, and may well overgeneralize in other contexts as well.

Nonetheless, the human cognitive system does correct some false generalizations, especially when relying on them results in negative feedback. For instance, a bank teller who automatically hit the robbery alarm button every time a young black male entered the bank would soon be out of a job. So given negative feedback, people learn to correct past overgeneralizations by developing more "discriminating" feature sets for characterizing category members. The process of discrimination involves adding additional features to past generalizations to distinguish between appropriate and inappropriate applications of the generalization (Anderson et al., 1979). For instance, most bank tellers quickly learn that the only young black males who can be classified confidently as bank robbers are those who display weapons but are not wearing police uniforms, or those who announce that they are robbing the bank.

HYPOTHESES REGARDING CATEGORY DIFFERENTIATION

The three preceding assumptions lead us to the following hypotheses.

Hypothesis 1. The more experience a perceiver has with
the members of a given social group, the more differentiated
the perceiver's representation of the group will tend to be.

The more experience a perceiver has with members of a social category, the more likely he is to encounter a wide variety of types of individuals from the category. As a consequence, the perceiver is likely to form a variety of generalizations. Moreover, the more contact a perceiver has with members of a category, the more likely he is to receive negative feedback regarding false generalizations, and thus to develop more differentiated feature sets that distinguish among various types within the category.

Hypothesis 2. People will tend to have more highly
differentiated representations of members of "ingroups" than
"outgroups."

In most cases, perceivers have had a greater amount and variety of experiences with "ingroup" members (e.g., people of the same age, race, social class, occupation, or interests) than with "outgroup" members. So we expect them to form a greater variety of generalizations about ingroup members. Further, perceivers are likely to receive more *feedback* regarding the accuracy of the generalizations they have formed about members of groups with which they have extensive contact. Such feedback leads to greater elaboration through discrimination processes. As a result, people should tend to form more highly differentiated representations of groups of which they are members. The principle exceptions to this hypothesis should arise when people have more extensive experience with members of groups other than their own.

FORMAL MEASURES OF DIFFERENTIATION AND VARIABILITY

Up to this point, our treatment of the concept of differentiation has been intuitive and informal. Here, we provide a precise, quantitative definition that also serves as a measure of differentiation across attributes. We propose that the concept and measurement of differentiation is close to our concept of stereotyping. We also formally define what we refer to as the "variability" of a perceiver's representation of a category. While many researchers have treated the concepts of differentiation and variability as if they were interchangeable, we show that the concepts are conceptually distinct.

In the discussion that follows, we focus on differentiation and variability with respect to one attribute, rather than across a set of attributes. While both the single and multiple attribute cases are important, in this paper we restrict our attention to the single attribute case.

Differentiation

As we use the term, *differentiation* refers to the likelihood of distinguishing among group members in terms of various characteristics. For instance, consider the following example: Smith and Jones are professors in the psychology department of a large university who have been asked by their department chairman to estimate the percentages of their department's graduating class who fall into each of the following five levels of intellectual ability: Very Good, Good, Fair, Poor, and Very Poor. We can think of each ability level as being a specific *feature* relating to the *attribute* "intellectual ability." That is, we view each level of an attribute as a specific feature. According to our model, Smith and Jones will perform this task by retrieving feature sets that include information regarding the intellectual ability of this year's seniors. This process might be viewed as a special case of the availability heuristic (Tversky & Kahneman, 1973) in which information is retrieved regarding feature sets rather than specific past instances.

Suppose that Smith and Jones produce the subjective probability distributions displayed in Table 1. One simple approach to measuring the extent to which a perceiver differentiates among different levels of a given attribute is to equate differentiation with the *number of levels*

TABLE 1   Mean, Probability of Differentiation, and Standard Deviation of Probability Distributions of "Intellectual Ability" Ratings

Professor	Ability level					Measure		
	Very good	Good	Fair	Poor	Very poor	M	P_d	SD
Smith	5	10	70	10	5	3	.485	.77
Jones	15	20	30	20	15	3	.785	1.27

Note. Higher numbers indicate higher mean (M), probability of differentiation (P_d), and standard deviation (SD).

of the attribute that are assigned nonzero probabilities. Because each level of an attribute may be conceived of as a distinct feature, this measure equates differentiation with the number of features used by the perceiver. But as the Smith and Jones example in Table 1 reveals, this is a crude measure that fails to capture important differences in degree of differentiation. Though both Smith and Jones use five ability levels to characterize students, it is apparent that Smith is less differentiating than Jones. Smith views the graduating seniors as being highly homogeneous, lumping 70% together at the average level. Jones views the students as more heterogeneous, distributing them more uniformly across the five ability levels.

To measure differentiation with respect to a particular attribute, we need a measure that reflects the likelihood that a perceiver will distinguish among stimuli in terms of that attribute. Here we define a new measure, which we refer to as the *probability of differentiation* (P_d), that has this property. It is defined by

$$P_d = 1 - \sum_{i=1,n} P_i^2 \tag{1}$$

where i denotes the level of the attribute in question, and P_i denotes the probability for the ith level of the attribute. It follows from the basic laws of probability theory that P_d reflects the *probability that a perceiver will differentiate between two randomly chosen instances of the category in terms of the attribute in question;* i.e., assign them to different levels of the attribute. For example, Jones is more likely than Smith to perceive a difference between the ability levels of two randomly chosen students. Thus, while the P_d measure has not previously been used in the stereotyping literature, it provides the most direct measure possible of differentiation with respect to a single attribute.

Applying the P_d measure to the probability distribution assessed by Professor Smith (see Table 1), we obtain

$$P_d = 1 - [.05^2 + .10^2 + .70^2 + .10^2 + .05^2] = .485$$

For Jones we obtain

$$P_d = 1 - [.15^2 + .20^2 + .30^2 + .20^2 + .15^2] = .785$$

So there is a 79% chance that Jones will discriminate between two randomly chosen students, but only a 49% chance that Smith will, thus confirming our earlier observation that Jones is more discriminating than Smith.

For our purposes, the P_d measure has two critical properties. First, P_d is an increasing function of the number of levels of the attribute in question. Thus, P_d reflects the common sense intuition that the more levels of an attribute the perceiver uses, the more differentiated the perceiver is. Second, for any given number of levels of an attribute, P_d is maximized when each level is perceived to be equally likely. For instance, with only two levels of an attribute, the greatest probability of differentiating between a pair of stimuli occurs when each level has a probability of 1/2. Here $P_d = 1 - [(1/2)^2 + (1/2)^2] = 1/2$. With three levels, the greatest degree of differentiation occurs when each level has a likelihood of 1/3. Here, $P_d = 1 - [(1/3)^2 + (1/3)^2 + (1/3)^2] = 2/3$. And so forth. Thus, P_d is greatest when there are many levels of an attribute, each with an equal but low probability of occurrence.[1]

Variability

The term *variability* connotes *range* or *spread* with respect to naturally ordered attributes such as income, height, or intelligence. Intuitively, this notion seems closely related to that of differentiation, though we show here that the two concepts are distinct and can conflict with one another.

If the attribute in question is measured on at least an interval scale, *the standard deviation of the perceiver's subjective probability distribution* over the levels of the attribute in question provides a natural measure of variability. For instance, consider the preceding Smith and Jones example. From inspection, it is clear that Jones' distribution reflects a greater degree of perceived variability than Smith's. Jones perceives many more students as falling far from the mean than does

[1] Readers familiar with Shannon and Weaver's (1949) information theory will recognize that the *entropy* statistic for a probability distribution has these same properties. In fact, P_d and entropy were so highly correlated in our studies that results for the two measures were essentially identical. We restrict our discussion to P_d in this chapter because this measure is easier to understand and more directly related to the concept of differentiation.

Smith. To apply the standard deviation measure to this example, we must assume that Smith and Jones both view the five intellectual ability levels as being "equally spaced." Thus we can assign numerical *scale values* of 5, 4, 3, 2 and 1 to the Very Good, Good, Fair, Poor, and Very Poor levels of the perceived ability attribute. Then the *mean* or *expected value* of a perceiver's subjective probability distribution for a given attribute is given by:

$$M = \sum_{i=1,n} P_i X_i \tag{2}$$

and the *standard deviation* by

$$SD = \sqrt{\Sigma_i P_i (X_i - M)^2} \tag{3}$$

where P_i denotes the probability for the ith level, and X_i is the scale value for this ith level. For instance, referring to Smith's distribution in Table 1, $i = 1$ denotes the "Very Good" ability level, so $X_1 = 5$ and $P_1 = .05$. Applying these equations to the data in Table 1, we obtain $SD = .77$ for Smith and $SD = 1.27$ for Jones, which confirms what is visually apparent. Jones displays much greater variability than Smith.

Variability and Probability of Differentiation Compared

The P_d and SD measures defined above reveal that differentiation and variability are conceptually distinct concepts with fundamentally different properties. In general, the SD measure reflects a tendency to use attribute levels far from the mean, whereas P_d reflects a tendency to use many attribute levels and to perceive them to be roughly equal in likelihood. For instance, P_d is maximized when every level of an attribute is equally likely (see Figure 1c) whereas SD is maximized by assigning a .50 probability to the two most extreme levels of the attribute (see Figure 1d). Further, the two measures may be positively correlated under certain circumstances; negatively correlated under others. For example, if a perceiver's distribution over levels of the attribute in question is "bell-shaped," then both P_d and SD increase as the distribution gets "flatter" (see Figures 1a through 1c). On the other hand, if the distribution is "U-shaped," flattening the distribution increases P_d but reduces SD (see Figures 1d through 1f). So, depending on the form of the distributions in question, P_d and SD can be either positively or negatively correlated. Further, as Figures 2a and 2b reveal, two distributions of equal P_d may differ in terms of SD. And, as Figures 2c and 2d reveal, two distributions of equal SD may differ in terms of P_d.

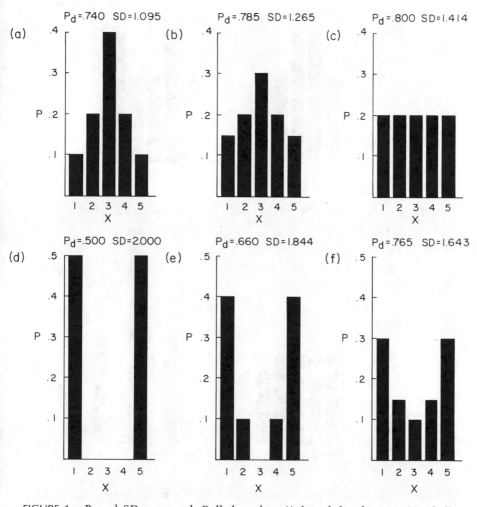

FIGURE 1. P_d and SD compared: Bell-shaped vs. U-shaped distributions. (For bell-shaped distributions, both P_d and SD increase as the distribution becomes flatter. For U-shaped distributions, P_d increases but SD decreases as the distribution becomes flatter. 1c reflects maximum P_d and 1d reflects maximum SD.)

The SD and probability of differentiation measures also differ substantially in the assumptions required to justify their use. Assuming that the attribute levels are mutually exclusive and exhaustive, the P_d measure requires only that subjective probabilities assigned to different levels of an attribute sum to 1.0. The SD measure requires the additional assumption that it be possible to assign numerical "scale

188   PATRICIA W. LINVILLE, PETER SALOVEY, AND GREGORY W. FISCHER

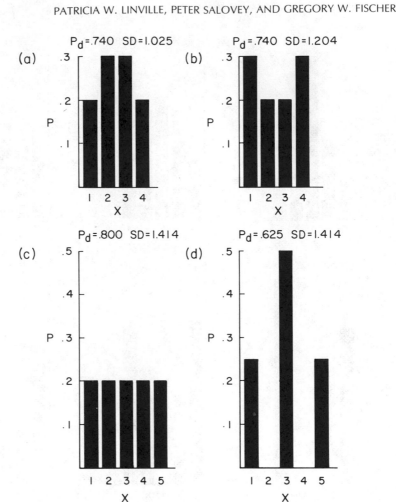

FIGURE 2.   Distributions of equal P_d can have different SD (2a and 2b); and distributions of equal SD can have different P_d (2c and 2d).

values" to different levels of the attribute in a manner that satisfies the formal properties of an "interval scale" (see Torgerson, 1958). Many social attributes (hair color, religion, favorite form of music) do not satisfy this property. Thus, use of the P_d measure is theoretically justified in a much wider range of contexts than is use of the SD measure.

If P_d and SD have different properties, why not merely pick the measure with superior properties? The difficulty with this approach is that no single measure can completely summarize everything that is important about a perceiver's subjective probability distribution over the possible levels of an attribute. Different measures capture different properties. Measures of central tendency, such as the mean or median, are useful because they reveal systematic bias for or against the members of a given group. Such measures are usually used when the goal of research is to examine prejudice per se.

The P_d and SD measures are more relevant to questions regarding the extent to which people perceive the members of various groups to be heterogeneous or homogeneous with respect to various attributes. But they reflect different aspects of perceived heterogeneity. The SD measure reflects perceived degree of variability of dispersion over the levels of a given feature. According to this measure, a high degree of perceived heterogeneity entails perceiving large differences between the members of a social group. By contrast, the P_d measure reflects the probability that a person will distinguish among the members of a group in terms of a given attribute. According to this measure, a high degree of perceived heterogeneity entails having a high probability of making distinctions. Superficially, the two concepts seem very similar, but they are conceptually distinct. You can get a high SD score and a low P_d score by making relatively few distinctions, but seeing the distinctions you make as being very large. You can get a high P_d score but a low SD score by making many distinctions, but seeing each of these distinctions as involving a small difference with respect to the attribute in question. Because the two measures reflect different notions of degree of perceived heterogeneity, it is useful to use both.

If forced to choose, we believe that P_d is a purer measure of perceived heterogeneity. Recall that SD is maximized when the perceiver uses only the two most extreme categories. In our view, distributions that maximize the SD measure actually manifest a form of stereotypic thinking—to see all members of a group as lying at polar extremes; either very good or very bad. By contrast, P_d is maximized when the perceiver uses many levels of the attribute, each with equal likelihood. Such distributions clearly reflect nonstereotypic thinking. Thus, P_d appears to be a purer measure of stereotypic thinking and perceived degree of heterogeneity.

EMPIRICAL EVIDENCE: INGROUP–OUTGROUP DIFFERENTIATION

Recall that our basic hypothesis is that perceivers tend to be more differentiated in their thinking regarding more familiar domains. In the context of social categorization and stereotyping, this implies that perceivers will tend to be more differentiated in their thinking about their own groups than about other groups. Two experiments tested this hypothesis. (A more complete presentation of these studies is reported in Linville, Fischer, & Salovey, 1985).

THE DISTRIBUTION TASK

The studies reported here use a distribution task designed primarily to tap perceived differentiation with respect to single attributes for a given social group. For instance, in one study we asked young and old subjects to make judgments about young and old people, whereas in a second study we asked American and Irish college students to make judgments about American and Irish students. The instructions and response scale in the nationality study were as follows:

> Each of the following items lists different degrees of a specific personal characteristic. Your task is to estimate the percent of *American college students* who fall into each of the levels of each characteristic. In other words, among 100 students, please indicate how many fall into each level. For instance, consider the characteristic "friendliness." What percent of American college students are "very friendly"? What percent are "friendly"? What percent are "moderately friendly"? And so forth. Assume that any given student falls into one and only one level of a characteristic. Please write your estimates above each level on the scale, and be sure that the percentages you assign to the different levels of a characteristic add up to 100.

Friendliness

very unfriendly	moderately unfriendly	slightly unfriendly	slightly friendly	moderately friendly	very friendly

Subjects typically completed six to ten attribute scales for a given target group.[2]

MEASURES AND HYPOTHESES TESTED

For each subject's distribution for each item, we calculate three scores: the mean of the distribution (as a measure of central tendency); the P_d of the distribution (as a measure of differentiation); and the SD of the distribution (as a measure of variability). These scores are calculated in the manner described in the prior section.

The primary hypothesis tested by the experiments reported in this section is Hypothesis 2 of our theoretical framework; namely that *people should tend to be more differentiated with respect to ingroup*

---

[2] Some studies used attributes with six levels and others used seven levels with a middle "neutral" level.

members than outgroup members. Because our framework focuses on the likelihood of making distinctions between stimuli as a function of experience with the domain, the P_d measure of differentiation provides an appropriate measure for testing this hypothesis.

We also examine two hypotheses that do *not* follow from the preceding model, but that have been suggested by other research. The first is the ingroup favoritism hypothesis: *People will be more favorable toward ingroup members than outgroup members* (Brewer, 1979; Wilder, 1981). Although the hypothesis is *not* a logical consequence of our Assumptions 1 through 3, it is not inconsistent with them. Favorability and differentiation are distinct notions, and the theory developed here has implications regarding only differentiation. This hypothesis regarding central tendency will be tested using the *means* of perceivers' distributions.

The final hypothesis to be tested is that *people should perceive greater variability among ingroup members than outgroup members.* This final hypothesis can be directly tested using the *SD* measure. Although this hypothesis closely resembles Hypothesis 2 of our model, they are conceptually distinct because, as we have argued throughout this chapter, differentiation and variability are conceptually distinct. Moreover, because our theoretical framework focuses on differentiating among group members, not on perceiving large differences, it does not necessarily predict that people will perceive greater variability among ingroup members. In particular, if a perceiver uses bimodal distributions in which the modes are widely separated, our theory makes exactly the opposite prediction; namely, that the person will perceive greater variability among outgroup members. On the other hand, if the perceiver's probability distributions for attributes are roughly bell-shaped, then our theory predicts greater perceived variability as well as greater differentiation among ingroup members.

AGE AS INGROUP–OUTGROUP VARIABLE

The first study presented here focused on how young and old subjects perceive variation with respect to individual attributes among the young and among the old. A group of elderly persons living in a retirement community and a group of college students were asked to imagine either 100 random "persons 65 years or older" or "persons of college age." Subjects then "distributed" these 100 people across seven levels of a given attribute (e.g., friendliness, motivation, interesting, typical mood, irritability) according to the proportion of members who fall within each level.

TABLE 2   Mean, Probability of Differentiation, and Standard Deviation of Probability Distributions of Trait Index: Young and Old Subjects Perceive the Young and the Old Target Populations (TP)

Measure	Old subjects		Young subjects		Interaction F
	Ingroup (old TP)	Outgroup (young TP)	Ingroup (young TP)	Outgroup (old TP)	
M	4.20	3.80	4.24	4.13	6.78**
P_d	.832	.797	.822	.762	10.65***
SD	1.85	1.76	1.84	1.50	14.89***

Note. Higher numbers indicate higher mean (M), probability of differentiation (P_d), and standard deviation (SD). The possible range for M is 1 to 7; for P_d, 0 to .857; and for SD, 0 to 3.

* $p < .05$.
** $p < .01$.
*** $p < .005$.

Our dependent measures were derived from subjects' responses on this distribution task. From each subject's distribution for each item, we calculated three scores: the mean of the distribution (as a measure of "central tendency"), the SD of the distribution (as a measure of "variability"), and the P_d score of the distribution (as a measure of "differentiation"). For each dependent variable (i.e., mean, SD, and P_d), an index was formed averaging scores over the eight trait items.[3]

Central Tendency

Analysis of the means measure revealed only partial support for ingroup favoritism. Old subjects were significantly more favorable toward the old than toward the young; but young subjects were essentially equally favorable toward both groups (see Table 2).

Differentiation and Variability

As predicted, both young and old subjects were more differentiated with respect to their own age group. Older subjects had significantly higher P_d scores for the old than for the young. Likewise, young subjects had significantly higher P_d scores for the young than for the old

[3] In forming these trait index scores, the subject's score for the dependent variable in question (e.g., P_d) was separately calculated for each trait item. These P_d scores for individual items were then averaged over the eight traits to obtain the subject's trait index P_d score. An analogous procedure was used in calculating the mean and SD scores for the trait index items.

(see Table 2). A closer look at the individual trait items revealed that the tendency toward greater ingroup differentiation occurred both for trait items that are relatively stereotypic as well as for those that are not.[4]

While our model predicts greater ingroup differentiation (P_d), it yields no clear prediction for variability (SD). If the distribution is unimodal (e.g., bell-shaped), we expect there to be more variability as well as greater differentiation for the ingroup. If the distribution is bimodal (or multimodal), we still expect greater differentiation but not necessarily greater SD for the ingroup. Young subjects clearly perceived more variability among the young than the old; but old subjects displayed only a weak and nonsignificant tendency to perceive more variability among the old than the young (see Table 2).

In short, both young and old perceivers were more differentiated in their perceptions of their own age group than of the other; but old subjects were not significantly more variable in their perceptions of old persons.[5] From the perspective of our theory, which deals with category differentiation, the P_d score results are what is critical, and these results supported our prediction.

How could old subjects be more differentiated but not more variable for members of their own group? This can occur if old subjects constructed multimodal distributions. A count of the number of modes in each subject's distribution for each item revealed that old subjects indeed constructed distributions with more modes than those constructed by young subjects. The difference occurred almost exclusively in distributions describing outgroup members. Young subjects thinking about the old tended to construct unimodal distributions that were low in both P_d (because the mode had high probability) and SD (because there was little spread around the mode). By contrast, old

---

[4] One might define a stereotypic feature in the present study as one showing a significant mean difference between old and young target groups (i.e., friendliness, overall reaction, mood) and a nonstereotypic feature as one showing no mean difference (i.e., attractiveness, interesting, irritability, purposeful, motivation). Because greater differentiation for the ingroup occurred for all attributes, the hypothesis appears to hold for both stereotypic and nonstereotypic attributes. We qualify this conclusion by noting that the measure used here is but one measure of stereotypicality.

[5] One possible confound needs to be addressed. The question arises as to whether differences in ingroup–outgroup means can account for differences in ingroup–outgroup differentiation and variability. The intuition here is that highly skewed distributions have less room for variability. A close examination of the shapes of the distributions for ingroups and outgroups revealed that differences in central tendency cannot account for our observed differences in ingroup–outgroup differentiation and variability.

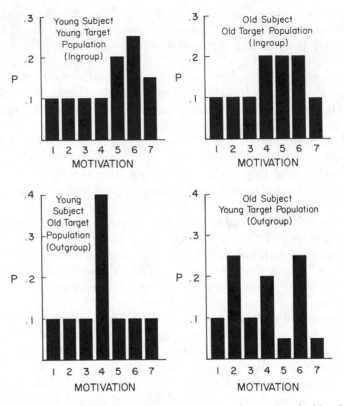

FIGURE 3. Most typical "motivation" distributions of young and old subjects and young and old target populations.

subjects thinking about the young tended to construct multimodal distributions that were low in P_d (because the modes had high probabilities) but relatively high in SD (because the modes were widely spaced over the scale range).

To illustrate this point, we selected the "most typical" distribution for each of the four conditions for each attribute; i.e., the distribution which was closest to the average distribution for the condition in terms of the mean (M), probability of differentiation (P_d), and standard deviation (SD).[6] We focused on the most typical, rather than the "aver-

---

[6] The "typicality" measure used to select a distribution was $FIT = Z_M^2 + Z_P^2 + Z_S^2$, where Z_M is the (within-cell) standardized score for the distribution's mean, Z_P the standardized score for the distributions's P_d, and Z_s the standardized score for the distribution's standard deviation. The distribution with the lowest fit score was chosen as the "most typical" for that condition.

age distribution," because averaging over a set of probability distributions produces a result that is much "smoother and flatter" than the individual distributions. The "most typical" distributions for the attribute "motivation" illustrate that while the most typical young subject constructed unimodal distributions for both the young and the old, the most typical old subject constructed a trimodal distribution for the young (see Figure 3). Because these three modes contained 70% of the probability mass, this distribution was relatively low in P_d; but because these three modes covered most of the feature levels, this distribution was not low in SD. Note also that the most typical young subject put the greatest probability in the central attribute level (i.e., level 4), whereas the most typical old subject put the greatest probabilities in two of the relatively extreme attribute levels (i.e., levels 2 and 6). The tendency of old subjects to place substantial probability in widely separated attribute levels apparently accounts for their pattern of relatively low P_d but relatively high SD toward the young.[7]

Age is a unique ingroup–outgroup variable in that the elderly were once young. In light of that, it is interesting to note that while young and old subjects demonstrated approximately equal differentiation for their respective ingroups, they differed in their degree of differentiation for their respective outgroups. Specifically, older subjects were more differentiated toward the young than young subjects were toward the old. A similar difference occurred for the SD measure (see Table 2). These differences are consistent with the hypothesis that greater familiarity leads to greater differentiation.

NATIONALITY AS INGROUP–OUTGROUP VARIABLE

A second experiment focused on how Irish and American students perceive variation with respect to attributes among the Irish and among Americans. College students in Ireland and in America were asked to imagine either 100 random "students in Ireland" or "students in America." They then distributed these 100 people across six levels of seven attributes (e.g., friendliness, academic motivation, pace of life, typical mood, intelligence).

[7] A detailed analysis of the probabilities assigned to various attribute levels supported this general observation. Averaging over subjects and items, young subjects tended to assign greatest probabilities to central attribute levels (i.e., 3, 4, 5) when constructing distributions for the old than for the young, whereas old subjects tended to assign greater probabilities to the extreme attribute levels (i.e., 1, 2, 6, 7) when constructing distributions for the young than for the old.

TABLE 3   Mean, Probability of Differentiation, and Standard Deviation of Probability Distributions of Trait Index: Irish and American Subjects Perceive Irish and Americans

Measure	Irish subjects		American subjects		
	Ingroup (Irish TP)	Outgroup (American TP)	Ingroup (American TP)	Outgroup (Irish TP)	Interaction F
M	4.22	4.14	3.98	4.09	.03
P_d	.690	.628	.746	.704	7.49**
SD	1.20	1.16	1.29	1.26	.49

Note. Higher numbers indicate higher mean (M), probability of differentiation (P_d), and standard deviation (SD). The possible range for M is 1 to 6; for P_d, 0 to .833; and for SD, 0 to 2.5.
 * $p < .05$.
** $p < .01$.

Central Tendency

An analysis of the means measure found no support for ingroup favoritism. Both Irish and American students were essentially equally favorable toward both groups (see Table 3).

Differentiation and Variability

Here again the group differentiation prediction was clearly supported. Irish students had significantly higher P_d scores for the Irish than for the Americans; likewise, American students had significantly higher P_d scores for Americans than for the Irish (see Table 3). Interestingly, no differences were observed in perceived variability. This discrepancy underscores the theoretical significance of the distinction made here between variability and differentiation, and further reinforces our model, which predicts ingroup–outgroup differences in differentiation but not necessarily in variability.

EMPIRICAL EVIDENCE: INCREASING DIFFERENTIATION OVER TIME

According to our model, familiarity, not ingroup–outgroup status per se, is the key to category differentiation. With greater exposure to multiple instances of a category, the processes of generalization and discrimination lead to the formation of a greater number of feature sets. Hence, greater category differentiation occurs with greater expo-

TABLE 4 Mean, Probability of Differentiation, and Standard Deviation of Probability Distributions over Time

Measure	Time			Trend F
	1	2	3	
M	4.42	4.36	4.31	9.53***
P_d	.725	.745	.752	3.64*
SD	1.31	1.34	1.37	3.92*

Note. Higher numbers indicate higher mean (M), probability of differentiation (P_d), and standard deviation (SD). The possible range for M is 1 to 7; for P_d, 0 to .857; and for SD, 0 to 3.
* $p < .05$.
** $p < .01$.
*** $p < .005$.

sure to members in a group. This assumes, of course, that one is actually encountering a greater variety of individuals in the group. Rarely is familiarity per se studied in the homogeneity literature. Here, we do so by studying the evolution of attribute differentiation in a newly formed group. The longitudinal nature of this study allows us to more directly test the idea that exposure or familiarity, rather than simple ingroup–outgroup status per se, leads perceivers to be more differentiated about members of a group.

Yale undergraduates in an introductory psychology class considered their classmates and estimated the proportion who fell within the various levels of a given attribute. Students completed the task three times during the semester: once near the beginning when they had had minimal opportunity for interactions with classmates, again at the midpoint of the semester, and finally near the end of the semester. Students distributed their classmates along seven levels of five attributes: likeability, number of hours spent studying per week, SAT scores, typical mood, and friendliness.

Central Tendency

A trend analysis of the means measure indicated that students became *less* favorable toward their classmates over time (see Table 4). This trend contradicts what one expects from the mere exposure literature (Zajonc, 1968) and seems to contradict the idea that familiarity accounts for ingroup favoritism. Perhaps freshmen come to schools like Yale with inflated expectations concerning the quality of their peers.

Differentiation and Variability

Our model predicts that as students have more contact with their classmates, they will become more differentiated in their thinking about them. As predicted, a trend analysis revealed that the students' distributions displayed increasing P_d scores over time (see Table 4). Students' distributions also displayed increasing variability over time (see Table 4). This is what we would expect if the distributions tend to be unimodal (e.g., bell-shaped).

In summary, with greater exposure, students become more differentiated in their view of their classmates. Several features of this study are noteworthy. First, most of the students were freshmen, and all were taking their first psychology course, so they were learning about a group of people with whom they had had relatively little prior contact. Second, the course was quite interactive, providing an opportunity for them to learn about each other. We would not necessarily expect to observe increased differentiation over time when there has been a great deal of prior contact or when there is very little interaction among group members. These results also suggest that familiarity rather than ingroup–outgroup status per se may be a critical key to differentiation. The present study is not decisive on this point, however, because it is possible that as students become more familiar with class members, their perspective shifted from that of an outgroup member to that of an ingroup member.

CONCLUSION

Most theories of stereotyping have proceeded from the assumption that stereotypes regarding social groups consist of a single most typical kind of person for the group in question. This chapter proceeds from a different conception. Our approach rests on the assumption that people use multiple feature sets—not a single list of features—to represent the members of a given social group. With this approach, it is natural to define stereotypic thinking as having a relatively undifferentiated representation of the members of the group. Thus, stereotyping is a matter of degree. The more differentiated a perceiver's cognitive representation of the members of a given group, the less stereotypic the perceiver's thinking about that group.

Given this general formulation, one critical task is to define what one means by the term *differentiation*. In this chapter, we introduce a new way of thinking about this concept, one that rests on perceivers' subjective probability distributions regarding the characteristics or features of members of different social groups. Thus, our research relies on a new task that is useful for studying stereotyping.[8] We ask subjects to distribute 100 randomly chosen members of a social group over a number of features or levels of a particular attribute such as motivation, intelligence, honesty, or friendliness. We assume that subjects complete this task by drawing on two types of knowledge: first, their metaknowledge regarding the distribution of social characteristics in general, or regarding the distribution of a particular trait (e.g., that it is bell-shaped); and second, on specific knowledge about a given social group that is encoded in terms of feature sets about members of that group. By sampling from the feature sets associated with a group, subjects can make judgments about the relative likelihood (or frequency) of different levels of different attributes. This latter basis thus might be viewed as an instance of the availability heuristic (Tversky & Kahneman, 1973).

In this chapter, we also introduce a new measure of stereotyping, the *probability of differentiation statistic*, P_d, that reflects the likelihood that a perceiver will distinguish between two randomly chosen members of a given group in terms of a given attribute. The more likely the perceiver is to make a distinction, the higher P_d. Thus, low P_d scores reflect stereotypic thinking. The distribution task and P_d statistic provide the basis for the empirical studies reported here.

In addition, we suggest a general theoretical framework which leads to the prediction that people are likely to be more differentiated in their perceptions of ingroup members than outgroup members. This framework rests on three assumptions: first, that social categories are represented in terms of multiple feature sets; second, that the various feature sets associated with a social category differ in their degrees of perceived likelihood; and third, that these feature sets result from basic learning processes involving generalization and discrimination. As a result, the tendency to form highly differentiated representations of social groups depends in part on having encoun-

---

[8] Since the completion of this chapter, Nisbett and Kunda (1985) reported results of a study in which they compared subjective distributions of attitudes and behaviors with the actual distribution of these attitudes and behaviors. This important work indicates that these perceived distributions tend to correspond relatively closely to actual distributions. While Nisbett and Kunda used a methodology similar to ours, their focus is on the accuracy of perceived distributions, whereas ours is on intergroup stereotyping.

tered numerous and varied instances of the group and in part on having an incentive to make distinctions among group members. Variety of experience provides the feedback that results in the formation of more differentiated representations of group members. If we make the additional assumption that people generally tend to have more as well as more varied experience with members of ingroups than outgroups, and further that they are more likely to have an incentive to distinguish among ingroup members (because of interaction with them), then our general theoretical framework leads to the prediction that people will tend to be more differentiated in their thinking about ingroup members.

Two experiments supported this prediction. In the first, we found that young perceivers were more differentiated in their thinking about young than old people, while exactly the opposite was the case for old perceivers. In the second, we found that American subjects were more differentiated in their thinking about American than Irish students, while Irish subjects displayed exactly the opposite pattern. A third study tested a related hypothesis; namely, that greater familiarity with the members of a group leads to greater differentiation. This prediction was supported in a study of how students perceived other members of a large class as they became more familiar with them over the course of a semester.

IMPLICATIONS FOR PERCEIVED HOMOGENEITY

The results of these initial studies support several points regarding probability distributions as measures of perceived homogeneity. First, it allows us to add precision to the concept of perceived homogeneity. Concepts like perceived homogeneity or variability are inherently ambiguous and have no concrete meaning until formalized. Second, the disparity between current results for variability and differentiation underscores the importance of this distinction. Third, ingroup–outgroup differences in differentiation generalized across several types of groups (young and elderly persons, Irish and Americans, and classmates over the period of a semester). Thus, the effect is not idiosyncratic to specific group factors such as minority or stigmatized status. The effect also generalized across several variations of scales as well as across a variety of traits (e.g., friendliness) and numerical (e.g.,

SAT scores) items.[9] Thus alternative explanations concerning specific types of scales or items are unlikely.

WHY INGROUP–OUTGROUP DIFFERENCES IN DIFFERENTIATION?

We predict that people tend to be more differentiated regarding ingroup members in part because they usually have more frequent contact with ingroup members, and are likely to encounter a wider variety of types of ingroup members under more varied circumstances. For example, an elderly person is more likely to know many more elderly persons and is more aware of variation of dispositions, abilities, interests, attitudes, and problems of the elderly than is a young person. With an increase in the number and range of experiences with a social group, one has the opportunity as well as the incentive to abstract more features and feature combinations and to develop more articulated features. Thus, greater differentiation is likely to be linked in part with greater familiarity rather than with ingroup–outgroup status per se. The results of the class study are consistent with this.

There appears, however, to be no simple relationship between the sheer number of members known in a group and perceptions of differentiation. For example, Jones, Wood, and Quattrone (1981) found no relationship between the number of outgroup members known in a club and the perceived range of traits for the club. Likewise, Linville found no relationship between the numbers of elderly persons known and dimensional complexity regarding elderly persons. And the fact that males and females perceive greater homogeneity for the opposite sex (Carpenter & Ostrom, 1985; Park & Rothbart, 1982) suggests that factors other than sheer number of members with whom one has contact influence these perceptions. Such factors include information-processing differences in the encoding and organization of information (Carpenter & Ostrom, 1985; Park & Rothbart, 1982), the nature of the interaction one has with group members (Quattrone, 1986; Wilder, 1981), and the incentives to discriminate among group members.

---

[9] Experiment 1, focusing on age, used trait items with seven levels (e.g., very friendly, friendly, somewhat friendly, neutral, somewhat unfriendly, unfriendly, very unfriendly). Experiment 2, focusing on nationality, used items with six levels (e.g., very intelligent, moderately intelligent, slightly intelligent, slightly unintelligent, moderately unintelligent, very unintelligent). Experiment 3 focusing on differentiation overtime in a classroom used a combination of trait (e.g., likeability) and numerical items (e.g., average number of hours per day spent studying) with seven levels (e.g., 0–1, 2–3, 4–5, 6–7, 8–9, 10–11, 12–13).

The mechanism of familiarity raises a possible exception to ingroup–outgroup differences in category differentiation. Members of some groups, particularly minorities, may actually have more familiarity with the majority outgroup than with their own ingroup. For instance, blacks raised in a nonblack environment may not be more differentiated for blacks than for whites.

IMPLICATIONS FOR THE STEREOTYPE CONCEPT

The present framework views stereotyping in terms of the statistical properties of beliefs about the members of social categories (e.g., central tendency, differentiation, and variability). This approach has several implications for the concept of stereotyping. First, it puts us squarely in the camp of those who view stereotyping as arising in part from basic cognitive categorization processes. Category differentiation arises from basic learning processes involving generalization and discrimination. This approach is consistent with approaches that do not necessarily assume faulty reasoning processes for stereotyping, but view the development, organization, and maintenance of stereotypes as similar to those of other semantic categories (see Hamilton, 1981a).

Second, this approach supports and extends the work suggesting that broad social categories are represented in terms of subtypes. For example, Ashmore (1981) used a spatial model to study multiple trait clusters representing subtypes of males and females (e.g., tough guy, businessman); and Brewer used a prototype model to study subtypes of elderly persons (grandmother, elder statesman, senior citizen) (Brewer et al., 1981). Taylor (1981) found that racial and gender stereotyping occurred in terms of role subtypes (e.g., oreo cookie or streetwise black, motherly type or bitch). Research by Weber and Crocker (1983) suggests that a subtyping model may be the best description of how stereotypes change in the face of disconfirming evidence, especially when the disconfirming information is concentrated within a few members of the group. What form do these subtypes take? Taylor suggests that increasing familiarity with a group leads to subtyping in the form of social roles rather than traits. Pettigrew (1981) observes that the recent rapid growth of the black middle class and the resulting class stratification among blacks have led many whites to distinguish among black people. He suggests that the dominant feature of these new forms of black subtypes is class position and its related attributes, and observes that blacks have learned to emit visual class cues when dealing with whites. A central argument of this chapter has been that categories of persons are represented in terms of multiple feature sets, a notion that is closely related to that of multiple subtypes. In addition, though, we add the notion that not all feature sets or subtypes are perceived to be equally likely. Subjective probability estimates are an important key to our conceptual and methodological basis for understanding differentiation and stereotyping.

Third, the current assumption that people perceive multiple feature sets for a given group suggests an interesting link to Katz's ambivalence-amplification theory (Katz, 1981; Katz, Wackenhut, & Hass in this volume). Both approaches, one coming from a cognitive perspective and the other from a motivational perspective, predict that whites will be more extreme in their reactions to blacks. Katz proposes that whites tend to hold two contradictory racial attitudes toward blacks: one friendly and the other hostile. These ambivalent feelings have their roots in two conflicting attitudes: a humanitarian outlook creating sympathy for blacks as the underdog; and the Protestant ethic, with its emphasis on self-reliance and self-discipline, which creates critical perceptions of blacks. According to Katz, having friendly feelings toward an unworthy black, or having hostile feelings toward a less fortunate black, threaten one's self-image as a humane yet discerning perceiver. Perceivers reduce the psychic tension due to their conflicting beliefs about blacks by engaging in extreme behavior toward blacks and other stigmatized persons. By contrast, the current approach suggests that whites hold multiple perceptions of blacks, some favorable and some less favorable, each represented in terms of different feature sets and associated feelings. Activation of one feature set may evoke positive feelings toward blacks, whereas activation of another may evoke negative feelings. Interpreted from a more cognitive perspective, Katz's theory implies that whites have a very simple cognitive representation of blacks involving one positive and one negative stereotype. Because of this simple and polarized cognitive representation, whites make extreme evaluations of blacks, depending on which of the two feature sets is evoked. Viewed from this perspective, Katz's ambivalence model and the complexity–extremity model proposed by Linville and Jones are more similar than they initially appear. Thus, the two theories, one focusing on a simple cognitive representation of blacks with few feature sets and the other focusing on ambivalent feelings for blacks, may be one example of how cognitive and motivational/affective theories may complement one another.

IMPLICATIONS FOR STEREOTYPING MEASUREMENT

The present research suggests that different measures of a perceiver's probability distribution over the levels of an attribute capture different aspects of the stereotyping concept. Measures of central tendency, such as the mean or median, capture systematic bias for or against the members of a group, and thus are useful for studying prejudice per se. By contrast, the P_d measure reflects the likelihood that a perceiver will distinguish between two group members in terms of a given attribute. Thus, it provides a direct measure of the extent to which a perceiver holds a differentiated view of the group. Moreover, because stereotypic thinking involves overgeneralization and a failure to make distinctions, P_d may be viewed as a direct measure of stereotyping per se. Finally, the SD measure reflects perceived variability in a quantitative sense; i.e., perceiving group members as being widely dispersed about the mean of an attribute. Thus, use of a variety of measures provides a richer impression of the "pictures in our heads" (Lippmann, 1922) than can any single measure.

Our methodology differs from traditional measures of stereotyping in several respects. With the adjective checklist, subjects check the traits most typical of a particular group (Karlins et al., 1969; Katz & Braly, 1933). The group stereotype is defined as the set of traits most frequently ascribed to the group. This approach assumes that all attributes are binary (e.g., lazy or not lazy) and fails to acknowledge the probabilistic nature of stereotypes. Several recent approaches have moved beyond this traditional measure by explicitly incorporating probability estimates in measures of stereotyping. For example, Brigham (1971) asked subjects to indicate the percentage of group members thought to have a given trait. McCauley and Stitt's (1978) Bayesian approach defined a stereotype as a diagnostic ratio of the percentage of group members having a trait divided by the percentage of "all the world's people" having the trait. Stereotypic traits are those seen as more probable for the group than for people in general. Finally, Park and Rothbart (1982) asked subjects to estimate the proportion of group members who would endorse various stereotypic and counterstereotypic attitude and behavioral items. They found that subjects ascribed a higher proportion of stereotypic items and a lower proportion of counterstereotypic items to the outgroup than the ingroup. These innovative approaches to the probabilistic nature of stereotyping retain one important feature of the traditional approach. They implicitly assume that the attributes of interest are binary. We build on and extend these approaches in three ways: first, by incorporating the notion of a multiple feature set representation of group members; second, by generalizing the notion of attributes to include multiple levels (e.g., extremely motivated, moderately motivated, moderately lazy, extremely lazy), each of which may be thought of as a feature; and third, by distinguishing between perceived differentiation, as measured by P_d, and perceived variability, as measured by SD.

STEREOTYPE PERSISTENCE AND MODIFICATION

Viewing group perceptions in probabilistic terms helps explain in part why stereotypes are so persistent even in the light of disconfirming data. Consider how disconfirming instances might be dealt with in the current probabilistic model. If even the strongest stereotypes tend to be probabilistic, then for every stereotype, the perceiver expects that there will be "exceptions to the rule." With disconfirming evidence, perceivers may simply alter their probability distributions across given attributes and over various feature sets or subtypes. With repeated disconfirming evidence, they may create new feature sets. Thus, through subtle differentiation, stereotypes can persist in the face of disconfirming data. (See Hamilton, 1981b; Rothbart, 1981; Taylor, 1981; Weber & Crocker, 1983, for related discussions of stereotype revision.) Incorporating measures of probability estimates with respect to single attributes and to attribute clusters may help capture the complex nature of modern stereotypes and subtle shifts in these stereotypes.

Our approach also has implications for the twin problems of stereotyping and prejudice. We propose that prejudice reduction involves not only more favorable judgments about group members, but also increased differentiation among members of the group. Thus, experiments and social programs designed to reduce prejudice through intergroup contact should be evaluated not only in terms of their effectiveness in fostering more favorable beliefs, but also in terms of whether they foster more differentiated perceptions. The properties of intergroup contact that encourage differentiated perceptions may include contact with a wide variety of group members across a variety of situations, as well as incentives that reward making distinctions among group members.

This view of prejudice does not deny the existence of knee-jerk prejudice or the need to combat it. But the affective, evaluative, and inferential aspects of intergroup relations are tied to the lack of differentiated categories for processing information about individual group members. For example, undifferentiated thinking about a group results in more extreme evaluations of individual group members (Linville, 1982; Linville & Jones, 1980). Undifferentiated thinking about a group leads people to draw stronger inferences from the behavior of one member to the group as a whole (Quattrone & Jones, 1980). And perceiving outgroup members as individuals rather than as an undifferentiated group reduces outgroup discrimination (Wilder, 1978; Miller & Brewer, Chapter 7). Thus, promoting differentiated thinking about outgroup members may be a useful strategy for combating prejudice, discrimination, and racism.

ACKNOWLEDGMENTS

The authors would like to thank Jack Dovidio, Sam Gaertner, Jay Kadane, and Tom Ostrom for their helpful comments and suggestions.

REFERENCES

Anderson, J. R. (1980). *Cognitive psychology and its implications*. San Francisco: W.H. Freeman.

Anderson, J. R., Kline, P. J., & Beasley, C. M. (1979). A general learning theory and its application to schema abstraction. In G. H. Bower (Ed.), *The psychology of learning and motivation* (Vol. 13, pp. 277–318). New York: Academic Press.

Ashmore, R. D. (1981). Sex stereotypes and implicit personality theory. In D. L. Hamilton (Ed.), *Cognitive processes in stereotyping and intergroup behavior* (pp. 37–81). Hillsdale, NJ: Erlbaum.

Bransford, J. D., & Frank, J. J. (1971). The abstraction of linguistic ideas. *Cognitive Psychology, 2*, 717–726.

Brewer, M. B. (1979). Ingroup bias in the minimal intergroup situation: A cognitive-motivational analysis. *Psychological Bulletin, 86*, 307–324.

Brewer, M. B., Dull, V., & Lui, L. (1981). Perceptions of the elderly: Stereotypes as prototypes. *Journal of Personality and Social Psychology, 41*, 656–670.

Brewer, M. B., & Lui, L. (1984). Categorization of the elderly by the elderly: Effects of perceiver's category membership. *Personality and Social Psychology Bulletin, 10*, 585–595.

Brigham, J. C. (1971). Ethnic stereotypes. *Psychological Bulletin, 76*, 15–33.

Carpenter, S. L., & Ostrom, T. M. (1985). The perception of outgroup homogeneity: Differential information organization. Unpublished manuscript, Ohio State University, Department of Psychology, Columbus.

Elio, R., & Anderson, J. R. (1981). Effects of category generalizations and instance similarity on schema abstraction. *Journal of Experimental Psychology: Human Learning and Memory, 7*, 397–417.

Goethals, G. R., Allison, S. J., & Frost, M. (1979). Perceptions of the magnitude and diversity of social support. *Journal of Experimental Social Psychology, 15*, 570–581.

Hamilton, D. L. (Ed.). (1981a). *Cognitive processes in stereotyping and intergroup behavior.* Hillsdale, NJ: Erlbaum.
Hamilton, D. L. (1981b). Stereotyping and intergroup behavior: Some thoughts on the cognitive approach. In D. L. (Ed.), *Cognitive processes in stereotyping and intergroup behavior* (pp. 333–353). Hillsdale, NJ: Erlbaum.
Hayes-Roth, B., & Hayes-Roth, F. (1977). Concept learning and the recognition and classification of exemplars. *Journal of Verbal Learning and Verbal Behavior, 16,* 321–338.
Jones, E. E., Wood, G. C., & Quattrone, G. A. (1981). Perceived variability of personal characteristics in in-groups and out-groups: The role of knowledge and evaluation. *Personality and Social Psychology Bulletin, 7,* 523–528.
Karlins, M., Coffman, T. L., & Walters, G. (1969). On the fading of social stereotypes: Studies in three generations of college students. *Journal of Personality and Social Psychology, 13,* 1–16.
Katz, D., & Braly, K. W. (1933). Racial stereotypes of one hundred college students. *Journal of Abnormal Psychology, 28,* 280–290.
Katz, I. (1981). *Stigma: A social psychological analysis.* Hillsdale, NJ: Erlbaum.
Linville, P. W. (1980). Stereotypes of the elderly: Verbal protocol analysis of the complexity trait-sorting task. Unpublished manuscript, Yale University, Department of Psychology, New Haven, CT.
Linville, P. W. (1982). The complexity–extremity effect and age-based stereotyping. *Journal of Personality and Social Psychology, 42,* 193–211.
Linville, P. W., Fischer, G. W., & Salovey, P. (1985). Perceived distributions of the characteristics of ingroup and outgroup members. Unpublished manuscript, Yale University, Department of Psychology, New Haven, CT.
Linville, P. W., & Jones, E. E. (1980). Polarized appraisals of outgroup members. *Journal of Personality and Social Psychology, 38,* 689–703.
Linville, P. W., & Salovey, P. (1982). The complexity–extremity effect: Age-based perceptions by the elderly. Unpublished manuscript, Yale University, Department of Psychology, New Haven, CT.
Lippman, W. (1922). *Public opinion.* New York: Harcourt Brace Jovanovich.
McCauley, C., & Stitt, C. L. (1978). An individual and quantitative measure of stereotypes. *Journal of Personality and Social Psychology, 36,* 929–940.
Medin, D. L., & Schaffer, M. M. (1978). Context theory of classification learning. *Psychological Review, 85,* 207–238.
Nisbett, R. E., Krantz, D. H., Jepson, C., & Kunda, Z. (1983). The use of statistical heuristics in everyday intuitive reasoning. *Psychological Review, 90,* 339–363.
Nisbett, R. E., & Kunda, Z. (1985). Perception of social distributions. *Journal of Personality and Social Psychology, 48,* 297–311.
Nisbett, R. E. & Wilson, T. D. (1977). Telling more than we know: Verbal reports on mental processes. *Psychological Review, 84,* 231–259.
Ostrom, T. M., Pryor, J. B., & Simpson, D. D. (1981). The organization of social information. In E. T. Higgins, C. P. Herman, & M. P. Zanna (Eds.), *Social Cognition: The Ontario Symposium* (Vol. 1, pp. 3–38). Hillsdale, NJ: Erlbaum.
Park, B., & Rothbart, M. (1982). Perception of out-group homogeneity and levels of social categorization: Memory for the subordinate attributes of in-group and out-group members. *Journal of Personality and Social Psychology, 42,* 1051–1068.
Pettigrew, T. F. (1981). Extending the stereotype concept. In D. L. Hamilton (Ed.), *Cognitive processes in stereotyping and intergroup behavior* (pp. 303–332). Hillsdale, NJ: Erlbaum.

Posner, M. I., & Keele, S. W. (1970). Retention of abstract ideas. *Journal of Experimental Psychology, 83,* 304–308.

Quattrone, G. A. (1986). On the perception of a group's variability. In S. Worchel & W. Austin (Eds.), *Psychology of intergroup relations* (Vol. 2, pp. 25–48). Nelson Hall.

Quattrone, G. A., & Jones, E. E. (1980). The perception of variability within ingroups and outgroups: Implications for the law of small numbers. *Journal of Personality and Social Psychology, 38,* 141–152.

Reed, S. (1972). Pattern recognition and categorization. *Cognitive Psychology, 3,* 382–407.

Reitman, J. S., & Bower, G. H. (1973). Storage and later recognition of exemplars of concepts. *Cognitive Psychology, 4,* 194–206.

Rosch, E. (1978). Principles of categorization. In E. Rosch & B. B. Lloyd (Eds.), *Cognition and categorization* (pp. 27–48). Hillsdale, NJ: Erlbaum.

Rosch, E., & Mervis, C. B. (1975). Family resemblances: Studies in the internal structure of categories. *Cognitive Psychology, 4,* 573–605.

Rothbart, M. (1981). Memory processes and social beliefs. In D. L. Hamilton (Ed.), *Cognitive processes in stereotyping and intergroup behavior* (pp. 145–182). Hillsdale, NJ: Erlbaum.

Shannon, C. E., & Weaver, W. (1949). *The mathematical theory of communication.* Urbana, Illinois: University of Illinois Press.

Taylor, S. E. (1981). A categorization approach to stereotyping. In D. L. Hamilton (Ed.), *Cognitive processes in stereotyping and intergroup behavior* (pp. 83–114). Hillsdale, NJ: Erlbaum.

Taylor, S. E., Fiske, S. T., Etcoff, N. L., & Ruderman, A. J. (1978). Categorical and contextual bases of person memory stereotyping. *Journal of Personality and Social Psychology, 36,* 778–793.

Torgerson, W. S. (1958). *Theory and method of scaling.* New York: Wiley.

Tversky, A., & Kahneman, D. (1973). Availability: A heuristic for judging frequency and probability. *Cognitive Psychology, 5,* 207–232.

Weber, R. & Crocker, J. (1983). Cognitive processes in the revision of stereotypic beliefs. *Journal of Personality and Social Psychology, 45,* 961–977.

Wilder, D. A. (1978). Reduction of intergroup discrimination through individuation of the out-group. *Journal of Personality and Social Psychology, 36,* 1361–1374.

Wilder, D. A. (1980). Predictions of belief homogeneity and similarity as a function of the salience of an outgroup following social categorization. Unpublished manuscript, Rutgers—The State University, Department of Psychology, New Brunswick, NJ.

Wilder, D. A. (1981). Perceiving persons as a group: Categorization and intergroup relations. In D. L. Hamilton (Ed.), *Cognitive processes in stereotyping and intergroup behavior* (pp. 213–258). Hillsdale, NJ: Erlbaum.

Zajonc, R. B. (1968). Attitudinal effects of mere exposure. *Journal of Personality and Social Psychology, 9,* 1–27.

CATEGORIZATION EFFECTS ON INGROUP AND OUTGROUP PERCEPTION*

Norman Miller

Department of Psychology
University of Southern
 California
Los Angeles, California
 90089-1061

Marilynn B. Brewer

Department of Psychology
University of California,
 Los Angeles
Los Angeles, California 90024

INTRODUCTION

In their attempts to understand and combat prejudice, psychologists have developed a number of distinct theoretical accounts that differ in their specific approaches to its reduction. Elsewhere (Brewer & Miller, 1984), we presented three conceptual models in each of which cooperative intergroup interaction was the starting point of the theoretical analysis (see Figure 1). In the first model, structural features of the environment assume the most critical role. Intergroup competition is seen as the instigating or primary source of prejudiced behavior, and the major approach to its reduction lies in structuring cooperative interdependence between the members of the respective groups. This functionalist view, which can be traced back to William Graham Sumner (1906) and his emphasis on the concept of ethnocentrism and the distinction between the "we group" and "others group," owes much to the magnificent field studies of Muzafer Sherif and colleagues (1961). As seen in the figure (Model 1), it views the cognitive, perceptual, affective, and behavioral dimensions of prejudice as es-

* Preparation of this chapter was supported in part by a grant to the first author from the Graduate School of the University of Southern California, and by Fulbright and Guggenheim Research Fellowships.

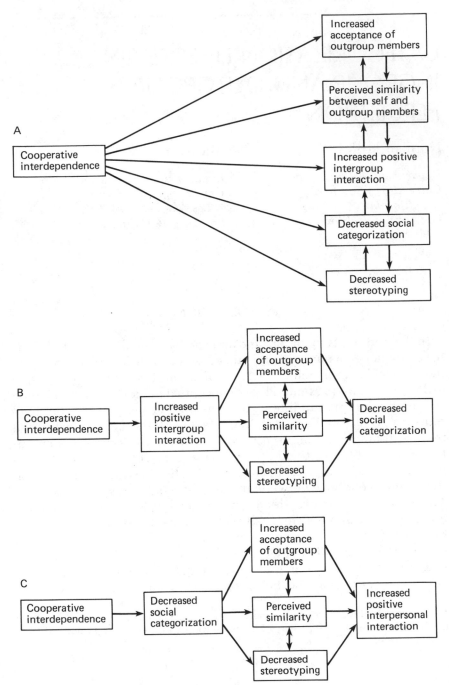

FIGURE 1. Alternative models of the process of intergroup contact effects. (From Brewer & Miller, 1984.)

sentially equivalent, interchangeable aspects, all of which are simultaneously altered by the externally engineered change in the structure of intergroup interaction. The model can be labeled functional not only because of Sumner's view about the role of competition in intergroup relations, but also because successful social engineering relies on making the cooperative interaction instrumental to the achievement of selfish, individual, or ingroup goals.

In his field studies of groups of boys in summer camp, Sherif tried to demonstrate that when two groups have come to view one another as respective outgroups, simply placing them together to participate mutually in activities they might ordinarily find unusually pleasurable does not reduce their antagonism toward one another. Indeed, overt manifestation of their hostility was increased, if not simply maintained at existing levels, as a consequence of the increased contact. Only after the successful arrangement of several contact situations in which the external environment had been manipulated to require the participation of both groups in joint action toward the achievement of superordinate goals did any reduction in intergroup conflict and stereotyping appear. For example, in one of these situations, after a vigorous morning swim at adjacent water holes the two groups of summer camp boys discovered that their truck was stalled because of a dead battery. Only by jointly tugging on ropes could they move the stalled truck to a sufficiently steep and lengthy incline to permit a rolling start and thereby enable the counselors of the two groups to go off for food for the boys' lunch.

The second model is, from a theoretical standpoint, more articulated than the first. It sees changes in cognitive, perceptual, and affective systems as emergent consequences of behavioral action. As was true for the first model, the social engineer might start with attempts to restructure the environment so as to require cooperative interaction. But here, the emphasis is more on the nature and quality of the interaction between members of the two groups than on the means used to achieve it. Indeed, from the standpoint of this model, it is relatively unimportant how the positive interaction is induced. Rather than relying on the creation of cooperative interdependence for the pursuit of some superordinate goal, positive interaction might be induced instead via the observation of high-status social models who behave cooperatively with outgroup members, by the presence and/or increased salience of social norms relevant to positive interaction with outgroup members, by structuring dependence of an outgroup member's survival on help from an ingroup member, etc. In any case, according to this model, once positive behavior toward outgroup members is elicited, it has impact on perceptual, affective, and cognitive systems.

One can trace the theoretical roots of this model to cognitive dissonance (Festinger, 1957) and self-perception (Bem, 1967) theories. The changes toward reduced prejudice are seen as emerging from the need to justify and explain to oneself, and perhaps to others too, the observed positive valence of one's prior action toward outgroup persons. From the standpoint of this model, Sherif's failure to succeed in reducing hostility between the two groups of camp boys in his initial approach—namely, by arranging for their spatial adjacency while they engaged in highly enjoyable activity such as watching an exciting movie or lighting firecrackers—cannot be viewed as disconfirmation of the model.

Adherents to Model 2 can legitimately claim that the model was not even tested because the experimental treatment—spatial adjacency of the outgroup during pleasureful activity—failed to induce positive social interaction between members of the two groups. Similarly, from the standpoint of Model 2, Sherif's successful manipulation—jointly pulling on ropes to move the truck to the crest of the incline—worked not specifically because of the presence of a superordinate goal, but instead, because it induced the boys of the two groups to engage in positive interaction with one another. After the second episode in which the truck had failed to start, instead of maintaining their clear group boundaries by pulling on separate ropes, group boundaries became diffused and boys from each of the two groups pulled on each of the ropes. Had the counselors induced them to retain their group boundaries and thereby avoid opportunity for positive interaction (e.g., by pulling on separate ropes or by having one group push the truck from the back while the other pulled), Model 2 would predict little reduction in ingroup favoritism and outgroup stereotyping despite the fact that these procedures also constitute joint action toward a superordinate goal. Instead, adherents of Model 2 would expect continued bickering and hostile derogation of the other group's contribution to the success of the effort.

Thus, although the external structuring of cooperative behavior can be the starting point for putting both models into action, as indicated, there is an important implicit theoretical distinction between them with respect to cooperation. The first model places emphasis on the nature of the reward structure—a joint goal is achieved only via cooperative interaction. In contrast, the second places emphasis on the qualitative nature of the social interaction that transpires between members of the two groups; it only requires that an observer watching the interaction between ingroup and outgroup persons could describe it as positive or prosocial, though in some instances, it might also appropriately be described as cooperative.

In the third model, perceptual processes are given greater weight and viewed as antecedent to effects observed in cognitive, emotional, and behavioral systems. As seen by inspection, Model 3 reverses the causal direction presented in the second model. Here the impetus to the reduction of prejudice is the abandonment of social categorization as the primary basis for organizing information about others. To reduce prejudice, persons must first adopt a more individuated, personalized approach to processing information about others before changes in their habits of intergroup rejection can occur. Whereas the major assumption of the functional theory of intergroup behavior is that ingroup bias and favoritism are the result of intergroup competition, and, hence, the way to eliminate it is to restructure intergroup relations into cooperative interdependence, proponents of social identity theory maintain that functional competitive interdependence is not a necessary antecedent for such bias (Tajfel, 1978; Tajfel & Turner, 1979). Instead, ingroup favoritism and outgroup hostility are seen as consequences of the unit formation between self and other ingroup members and the linking of one's identity to them. Experiments on the minimal intergroup situation show that the establishment of category membership per se in the presence of those of another social category can be a sufficient basis for such bias (Tajfel, 1970; Turner, 1978).

In terms of Model 3, Sherif's structuring of cooperative interdependence for the achievement of a superordinate goal was successful primarily because it succeeded in breaking down perceptions of group boundaries. Had the boys been induced to maintain their group identity, little or no positive benefit would ensue. Imagine that the counselors said to the boys, "What we need is some team spirit in order to get this heavy truck moving," and then encouraged the two groups of boys to don respectively their Eagles and Rattlers t-shirts (their self-adopted names), gave each group a rope that matched their flag color(s), positioned a group flag bearer at the front of each line with the rope wrapped around his waist, and preceded the rope pulling with brief pep-rallies in which the groups simultaneously shouted out their individual group chants. Once again, Model 1 predicts reduced prejudice because there is cooperative intergroup behavior toward a superordinate goal. Without coordinated pulling, the truck will not move. Model 3 requires the dissolution of sharp group boundaries and interaction with outgroup members that is personalized and attentive to the unique aspects of that person. In contrast to Model 2, which argues that the valence of the interaction must be positive for benefit to occur, Model 3 predicts positive effects from negatively valenced interaction as well, as long as the basis for it is not category-linked. In other words, in Model 3, the critical ingredient is the processing of information that serves to personalize the other person and thereby reduce the tendency to view him or her as merely a representative of a particular social category. In the face of the aforementioned convergent symptoms of group identity and intergroup separation, however, Model 3 argues that even had the counselors succeeded in getting members of each group to shout encouragements to those on the other rope, a procedure that according to Model 2 should effectively reduce prejudice, little positive benefit would ensue.

Models are formulated not only to help organize one's thinking about an issue, but also to draw distinctions among ways to view things. In this latter aspect, they depict extreme and oversimplified positions. The models presented are no exceptions in this regard. Reality may in fact be far better represented by a model that incorporates aspects of each of the three and that is less unidirectional in its causal assumptions than are the preceding three. Nevertheless, it makes sense to try to demonstrate that there is some value in emphasizing these distinctions.

In our own work we have adopted the third model as the basis for an experimental laboratory research program (Brewer & Miller, 1984; Miller, Brewer, & Edwards, 1985) concerned with how to maximize the positive consequences of cooperative intergroup interaction. In doing so, our purpose is not to prove that the other models are wrong, but instead, to draw attention to a particular set of variables that play important roles in the augmentation of prejudice—variables that adherents to the other two models are likely to ignore. Briefly, such variables might include a task rather than an interpersonal focus; team assignment based on attributes linked to category membership rather than unique traits; role assignments within the team that are correlated with category membership as opposed to role assignments that cross-cut category membership; team or category-linked failure in contrast to individual failure or failure that cross-cuts category membership; high versus low threat; and numerical distinctiveness in contrast to nondistinctiveness. The work, though obviously relevant to theory construction, evolves out of first-hand experience and prior field research in desegregated school settings (Gerard & Miller, 1975; Miller, Rogers, & Hennigan, 1983; Rogers, Hennigan, Bowman, & Miller, 1984; Rogers, Miller, & Hennigan, 1981).

At the time of the historic Brown decision in 1954, and throughout the 1950s and 1960s, many researchers assumed school desegregation to be a constructive social policy that would improve the self-concepts and academic performance of minority children and, in addition, improve intergroup relations. Recent reviews of its effects, however, cast doubt on whether desegregation does indeed promote these goals in the absence of additional specific interventions in the desegregated classroom (Gerard, 1983; Miller, 1981; St. John, 1975; Stephan, 1978).

Consequently, in order to improve intergroup relations, a number of researchers for some years now have disseminated various procedures for intrateam cooperative activity among racially or ethnically heterogeneous small groups of children, arguing that their use will produce the positive outcomes initially intended and documenting this with a spate of supporting research findings (Aronson, Blaney, Stephan, Sikes, & Snapp, 1978; DeVries, Slavin, Hennessey, Edwards, & Lombardo, 1980; Johnson, Johnson, & Maruyama, 1984; Rogers et al., 1981; Sharan, 1984; Slavin, 1983). Thus, as is now undoubtedly apparent, it makes sense for us to have used cooperative intergroup interaction as the starting point for each of the models in Figure 1, in that it reflects its widespread adoption as a remedial intervention in educational settings. From detailed inspection of published materials (as well as direct experience conducting workshops on their use and observing how others implement them), it seemed likely to us that some of the standard practices contain features that might detract from the intended effects. Emerging research from field settings provided some suggestive confirmation (Johnson et al., 1984; Kagan, Zahn, Widaman, Schwarzwald, & Tyrrell, 1985; Rogers et al., 1984). Our analysis suggested that Model 3 was the most useful point of departure for assessing the role of implementation factors in the success of cooperative interventions.

LEVELS OF INTRAGROUP DIFFERENTIATION

Behavior toward members of an outgroup can, at one extreme, exemplify thoughtless automatic action driven by the crude perception that they are members of "that" social category, whatever it happens to be. At this extreme, information processing is shallow, highly efficient, and unelaborated. At the other extreme, judgments about another's social category membership are absent or not salient and, instead, one responds to the other person as someone who is unique, complex, characterized by inconsistencies as well as consistencies, and as one with both similarities as well as dissimilarities to self; thus, at this other extreme, depth of processing is great. In our view, this dimension is a continuous one. For the purpose of theoretical analysis and discussion, however, we chose to partition the continuum into three levels: (1) category-based responding; (2) differentiated responding; and (3) personalized responding (Brewer & Miller, 1984). The preceding first extreme typifies category-based responding.

The second level, differentiation, is intermediate between the two extremes. The ingroup member no longer sees the outgroup as a collection of interchangeable units whose qualities are known only in a general sense and are seen as highly similar to one another but quite different from self and other ingroup members. Instead, one notices the distinctiveness of individuals within the outgroup category. In this level of relating to members of an outgroup, although one attends to information that makes outgroup persons distinct from one another, the basic distinction between the ingroup and the outgroup is preserved; the basic dissimilarity of outgroup members to self and other ingroup members is also preserved. In this stage or process of social interaction, the actor's cognitive complexity has been increased from that found in category-based responding; consequently, not only are outgroup persons seen as more distinct from one another, but additionally, ingroup members are also viewed as more differentiated from each other and from self.

In personalized interaction, persons attend to information that replaces category identity as the most useful guide for determining the character of interactions with another. One attends to personal information about the other that is self-relevant and not correlated with category membership. In terms of our practical interests in desegregated settings such as schools, the military, or industrial plants, we assume that the goal of legal remedies, such as termination of segregated schools and military services and the instigation of fair labor practices, is not simply to place members of diverse groups into a common setting. Nor is it merely to place them there and ensure that they interact with minimal conflict or, additionally, with positively toned behavior. Rather, the purpose is to reduce the role that category membership plays in a broad array of behaviors outside the particular setting. The real confirmation of success occurs when, in future occasions involving interactions with new members of the social category, one is less inclined to view and treat them as members of a category. Particularly when one is a member of the dominant, more powerful group—one with higher social status—successful achievement of desegregation goals implies a reduction of behavior that preserves exist-

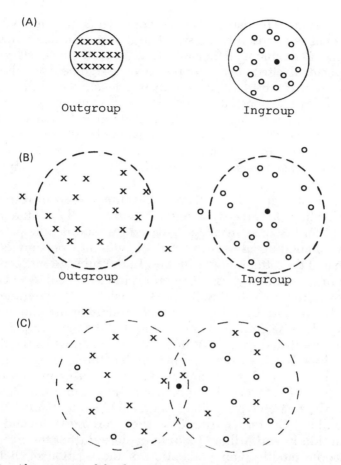

FIGURE 2.   Alternative models of intergroup contact: (a) category-based, (b) differentiated, (c) personalized. (From Brewer & Miller, 1984.)

ing status differences and restricts others' social and economic mobility. We see the latter behavior as the typical consequence of
category-based responding, whereas personalized responding essentially removes impetus to the perpetuation of institutionalized prejudice. Figure 2 presents the three levels of responding in pictorial
form.

On the basis of this analysis, we have initiated a program of experimental laboratory research which tests hypotheses derived from social
categorization theory (Model 3). The research uses an experimental
laboratory paradigm that structurally parallels applied research in
which cooperative team learning interventions are used in desegre-

gated classrooms. The data from two experiments indicate that (1) an interpersonal as opposed to a task orientation toward team members and (2) the assignment of persons to teams on the basis of their unique personal attributes as opposed to assignment on the basis of attributes that explicitly exemplify their category will not only increase the acceptance of outgroup persons on one's own team, but more importantly, will produce a generalized increase in outgroup acceptance. We have reported this work elsewhere (Miller et al., 1985) and, therefore, will not repeat it here. Instead, we report here research that bears on the details of the analysis implicit in Figure 2.

Inspection of Figure 2 reveals that the three levels of responding have implications for process among ingroup as well as outgroup persons. Thus, for instance, in category-based responding, the perceived similarity of ingroup as well as that of outgroup persons is high, though that of the latter group is higher. In the subsequent sections of this chapter we examine these distinctions in the light of recent experimental data from two studies. The first, a laboratory experiment undertaken by Ventura Charlin, a graduate student at the University of Southern California, focuses on perceptions of the outgroup. Based on previously published work by Wilder (1978), it addresses the distinctions we draw between the aforementioned three categories of responding, and it clarifies the impact of a dissenter in an outgroup on the reduction of categorical responding. The second experiment, a field study by Sharon Gross, who is a graduate student at the University of Southern California, extends earlier work by Holtz and Miller (1985) and Marks and Miller (1985) to explore further the manner in which people modify their perception of the relation of their own belief system to that of other ingroup members when an outgroup is made salient. Specifically, it examines the effect of increased outgroup salience on perceptions of belief similarity to other ingroup members on important attitudinal issues, unimportant issues, and issues specifically related to the conflict between the ingroup and outgroup. Taken together, the studies examine perceptions both of ingroup and outgroup persons, assessing the role of salience of intergroup boundaries on both.

INDIVIDUATION OF OUTGROUP MEMBERS

In the first of three experiments concerned with reducing intergroup bias by individuating the outgroup, Wilder (1978) divided eight subjects into two groups allegedly on the basis of the relative similarity and dissimilarity of their preferences among a set of paintings by Kandinsky and Klee, but in fact, via random assignment. After separating the two groups into different rooms they were both told that the other group would be making decisions about legal cases while their own group filled out a questionnaire. When they had completed the questionnaire, the experimenter entered the room to give them the individual verdicts of the members of the jury group (the outgroup). The manipulated verdicts they received either; (1) indicated that all members agreed on both cases; (2) indicated that a particular jury member dissented from the other three on both cases; or (3) only indicated the verdict of one of the four jury members. Among the dependent measures subjects completed after inspecting the verdict information were reward allocation matrices in which subjects divided 15 chips between an ingroup member and the dissenter (or in the case of the unanimous group, the person with the same code number as the dissenter) and between an ingroup member and a nondissenter.

Wilder found that the presence of a dissenter augmented reward allocation, not just to the dissenter but also to the other members of the group. Furthermore, the dissenter did not merely eliminate ingroup favoritism, but instead caused allocations to outgroup members to exceed those to ingroup persons. Wilder viewed these data as indicating that a dissenter is not only individuated from other group members by virtue of his or her act of dissent, but also, that the dissenter's presence in the outgroup individuates the other outgroup members as well.

Although we do not disagree with Wilder's general theoretical orientation, from the standpoint of our earlier discussion, we view his data from the dissenter condition as reflecting only one step on the continuum from category-based responding to personalized responding. Although his analyses show that the presence of a dissenter in the group increased reward allocations not just to the dissenter but also to nondissenters in the outgroup, we have little confidence that the presence of a dissenter goes very far toward making one perceive other outgroup members as unique persons. Given the details of Wilder's experimental procedure, the subjects had no basis for making such differentiation among the nondissenting jury members; other than learning of their unanimous subgroup decision, subjects literally received no information about them. In other words, reality provided no basis for attributions of uniqueness. Thus, we view the dissenter condition at best as decategorizing the jury group to some degree, but perhaps, not even going as far as the differentiation stage depicted in Figure 2.

In a conceptual replication of Wilder's first experiment, Charlin compared four conditions in which, unlike Wilder's procedure, subjects were given unique distinctive information about each of the four jury members. This was achieved by giving each subject a copy of four forms, each completed in a different handwriting and each ostensibly completed by one of the four jury members. Each form indicated three reasons why that jury member reached the decision that he or she did and, in addition, gave some distinctive biographical and personal information about that jury member's characteristics. Thus, the forms provided a basis on which, if they chose to do so, subjects could form distinct impressions about each jury member; that is, they had a basis on which to differentiate among them. In the context of this modification, Charlin included No Dissent and Neutral Dissent conditions in her design, paralleling Wilder, but in addition, added Positive and Negative Dissent conditions. In contrast to the affectively neutral information provided about the dissenter in the Neutral Dissent condition, the latter conditions provided information about the dissenter that was positive or negative, respectively. The information about the nondissenting group members in all conditions was affectively neutral.

The affective quality of the information about the dissenter (as well as that concerning the nondissenters) was conveyed in the forms containing jury members' verdicts that were distributed to the subjects during the study. Negative, positive, and neutral affect was created via the quality of the three reasons the dissenting jury member gave for his or her verdict; answers to questions regarding how carefully the dissenter weighed the evidence in the case; and answers to other questions (e.g., what do you like to do in your free time? Negative dissenter: "I like to take city buses"). The material developed for the forms was generated by other undergraduates who did not serve as subjects and was pilot tested and modified in several stages prior to use in the experiment.

Charlin's results on a reward allocation measure identical to Wilder's essentially confirmed his findings regarding the effect of a dissenter (see Table 1). In the No Dissent condition, the mean reward allocation to the jury group (versus the ingroup) departed from the 7.5 midpoint of no bias in the direction of ingroup favoritism ($M = 6.89$), whereas in the Neutral Dissent condition it deviated from equality in the direction of outgroup favoritism ($M = 7.89$). As seen from inspection of Table 1, as was true in Wilder's data, these pooled results for

TABLE 1   Mean Reward Allocations to Outgroup Persons in
the Dissenter and a Nondissenter Position

Condition	Dissenter	Nondissenter	Pooled
Positive dissent	9.40[a]	8.30[ac]	8.85
Negative dissent	3.36[b]	7.55[cd]	5.45
Neutral dissent	7.47[cd]	8.31[ac]	7.89
No dissent	6.84[d]	6.94[d]	6.89

Note. Lower numbers indicate more ingroup favoritism.
Means that share the same superscript are not significantly
different from one another.

members of the jury group are not solely due to the allocations to the
dissenter; indeed, allocations to a person in the Neutral Dissent condition who did not dissent, though not significantly different in mean
absolute magnitude, did exceed those given to the dissenter. The
effect of a positive dissenter also increased allocations to a nondissenting member of the jury group relative to those allocated in the No
Dissent condition. The results in the Negative Dissent condition,
however, are troublesome for Wilder; the presence of a negative dissenter failed to augment allocations to nondissenting members of the
outgroup compared to those allocated to the No Dissent control group.
Supplementary rating data indicate that this was not due to a generalization of the negative dissenter's undesirable qualities onto other
group members; indeed the general impression of nondissenting persons in the Negative Dissent condition ($M = 1.96$) was the most favorable of those in all four conditions (M Positive = 0.40; M Neutral =
1.48; M No Dissent = 1.01), and was clearly more favorable than those
in the No Dissent condition ($p < .05$). If, as Wilder contends, the
presence of a dissenter functions to break the perceptual unity of the
outgroup and thereby causes the people in it to be individuated and
thus perceived as individuals, why does this fail to occur in the case of
the negative dissenter?

Data from other response measures add further doubt to the view
that a dissenter causes individuation among the nondissenting members of the group. Memory recall and recognition measures disclosed
no differences between any of the dissent conditions and the No Dissent control condition. Trait evaluation measures of liking, trust, and
respect were used to assess whether the experimental manipulations
affected the distinctiveness of nondissenting outgroup members. An
index of distinctiveness among the nondissenting group members was
derived by computing the absolute value of the difference in overall

favorability of evaluation between each of the nondissenting outgroup members. Presumably, if the presence of a dissenter among the outgroup serves to individuate the other outgroup members, this index should be higher in the three dissent conditions than in the No Dissent control condition. Note that unlike Wilder's procedure in which subjects received no information about the jury members other than their vote, in Charlin's replication, subjects received detailed, unique personal information about each outgroup member. Despite the availability of such individuating information, no difference was observed between Dissent and No Dissent conditions in the distinctiveness index. In fact, the direction of effect was opposite to that expected if a dissenter does indeed individuate other group members; the mean of the three dissenter conditions was 1.16, whereas that of the No Dissent control condition was 2.37 (with high scores reflecting greater differentiation among the nondissenting outgroup members). Analyses of the variability among ratings of the outgroup members similarly showed no evidence of greater variability (individuation) when there was a dissenter in the group.

Additional analyses of subjects' perceptions of outgroup members' similarity to self indicated that a positive dissenter was seen as more similar to self than a negative or neutral dissenter (Ms = 6.27, 1.68, 4.40, respectively, $p < .05$). Further, subjects saw nondissenting outgroup members as more similar to themselves when there was a negative dissenter in the group as opposed to no dissenter (M's = 6.02 and 4.87, respectively, $p < .05$). On the other hand, if a dissenter individuates other outgroup members, we should find greater distinctiveness or variability in subjects' perception of similarity to nondissenting outgroup members. No such evidence was found, and again the direction of effect was toward greater distinctiveness in the absence of a dissenter; the mean of the three dissenter conditions was .47, whereas the mean in the No Dissent control condition was .85, with high scores reflecting greater differentiation.

These data basically replicate Wilder's findings in showing that the presence of a dissenter in an outgroup increases reward allocations to nondissenting members of the outgroup in a manner that eliminates ingroup favoritism. They add a qualification, however, in that this outcome only occurs when the dissenter is highly likeable or is of neutral likeability. If, as Wilder originally postulated, the presence of a dissenter individuates the other group members, the dissenter's valence should not matter. Further challenging this initial interpretation is Charlin's failure to find any evidence from memory, perceptual, or evaluative data that subjects differentiated the outgroup members more when there was a dissenter in the outgroup, even though her experimental procedure provided them with information that could be used for this purpose.

If we must reject Wilder's individuation explanation, however, what does account for the reward allocation effects? One possibility is that a dissenter elicits sympathy toward all group members because his or her presence gives the group a harder time in trying to come to a decision. Within the context of this explanation, the failure to find the effect with the negative dissenter might be explained by assuming that he was so negative and undesirable that his position and arguments could be rejected with little further consideration and thus had no impact on difficulty of group decision making. This explanation might seem more reasonable, however, had the jury group been required to reach a unanimous decision.

A second possibility is that the presence of a dissenter suggests to the subjects that the jury group took their task more seriously and, therefore, was more deserving of reward. If correct, this explanation implies that dissenter groups would receive more favorable ratings on the trait competence; they did not.

A third explanation focuses on the effect of making salient the fact that legitimate diverse positions exist with respect to an issue. The existence of diversity between two opposing camps, dissenter and other group members, captures attention, draws focus away from the ephemeral, unimportant original ingroup–outgroup distinction based on paintings most subjects cared little about to begin with, and directs it instead to thoughts about whom the subject would have sided with in the court case(s), thereby replacing painting preference as a basis of ingroup–outgroup boundary with verdict as the basis. Because subjects do not see the case materials, dissent can only draw attention to the new dimension for defining group boundaries, but cannot direct the subjects' loyalties preponderantly in one direction or the other apart from the numerical preponderance on one side of the issue. Although neither Wilder's nor Charlin's study finds a difference between allocations to the dissenter and the other group members, the direction of effect in both is toward the more numerous group, the nondissenters.

In terms of this explanation, the heightened interest in the new group boundary based on verdict reduces attention to old categorized distinctions and thereby generates the more favorable allocations given to the outgroups. The failure to find such an effect in the Negative Dissent condition can be accounted for by assuming that it reflects the absence of any perception by subjects of legitimate conflict of opinion in this condition. The negative dissenter's reasons for his position were so unacceptable that subjects viewed the jury members of this condition as a unanimous group of three plus a jerk.

Of course, we cannot choose among these explanations without additional data. Our discussion and data, however, do not merely challenge Wilder's interpretation of ingroup–outgroup process, but additionally argue that differentiation among outgroup persons may not be achieved as readily as Wilder implies. The next section turns from data concerned with perceptions of outgroup members to the effects of outgroup salience on perceptions of other ingroup members.

GROUP BOUNDARIES AND PROJECTED SIMILARITY

Previous work shows that group membership gives special meaning to the issues that are highly involving to the members of that group (Crano, 1983; Kiesler, Nisbett, & Zanna, 1969). Elsewhere, we have shown that when group identity is high, group members distort perceptions of belief similarity to see ingroup members as closer to themselves on issues they consider important than are outgroup persons (Holtz & Miller, 1985). This distortion occurred with respect to the specific issue content and was not simply a global non-content-related distortion. On the other hand, when ingroup identity and outgroup salience were low, exaggerated perceptions of similarity of ingroup to self were more global and less related to the specific content of meaning of various belief dimensions (Marks & Miller, 1982). Additionally, however, when a conflict between the ingroup and outgroup is salient, such distortions function to increase one's certainty about the correctness of one's beliefs, particularly on issues considered important (Holtz & Miller, 1985), whereas when group-based identity lacks salience, such distortion does not function to augment belief certainty (Marks & Miller, 1985).

Although intriguing, these studies did not examine effects on issues of personal importance separately from those relevant to the specific conflict between the ingroup and the outgroup. In experiments conducted in a field setting, Sharon Gross examined this issue in more detail. Identifying herself as a campus newspaper reporter conducting research for a news article, she first determined whether the male she approached was a commuter student, and, if so, asked him to take about 10 minutes to complete a questionnaire. Four types of questionnaires constituted the experimental conditions of the 2 × 2 between-groups factorial design in which salience of ingroup–outgroup conflict and opportunity to estimate the attitudinal positions of other ingroup members were manipulated. The former variable was viewed conceptually as a manipulation of the salience of group identity. In the high intergroup conflict condition, the experimenter described the contents of a previous campus newspaper article concerned with the many differences between commuter and fraternity row students and ending with information concerning attempts by alumni of the outgroup to restrict admissions of commuters to the University. Subjects in the low salience condition responded to an innocuous set of questions concerning their year in school, major, study habits, educational plans, and living arrangements, designed to take the same length of time in interaction with the experimenter as the high intergroup-conflict condition.

Following this manipulation, both groups indicated their own position on 18 attitudinal issues, their certainty about it, and its importance. For half of the subjects in each of the salience-of-intergroup-conflict conditions, an additional sheet asked them to estimate the attitudinal positions of other ingroup members (social projection), whereas for the other half this task was omitted. When included in the questionnaire packet, ingroup projection was positioned after the own-attitude response sheet but prior to assessments of attitudinal certainty and issue importance. On the basis of previous pilot testing, the 18 attitude questions contained six of low importance, six of high importance, and six that were of intermediate importance but directly related to conflict between fraternity row and commuter students. (The latter set were above the scale midpoint in importance, but of less importance than the high-importance set.)

The opportunity to estimate the attitudinal positions of other ingroup members (i.e., projection) increased certainty of own position only on items concerned with the intergroup conflict (projection $M = 6.90$; no projection $M = 6.35$; $t = 2.13$, $p < .05$). Although subjects were most certain of their position on important issues ($M = 7.23$) and least certain on unimportant issues ($M = 6.30$), the projection manipulation did not affect certainty on these items.

Of greater interest here, however, is the effect of the manipulation of conflict salience on perceived similarity to other ingroup members. As in our previous work, we separated perceptions of self–other similarity into two orthogonal components, one reflecting global perception that is independent of the specific meaning of content of the attitudinal item (viz., elevation similarity) and the other reflecting similarity with respect to the specific meaning of the attitude dimensions (viz., item content similarity) (Holtz & Miller, 1985; Marks &

Miller, 1982; Marks, Miller, & Maruyama, 1981).[1] These analyses showed that the manipulation of the salience of intergroup conflict had a strong effect. Raising the salience of intergroup conflict not only increased general (noncontent) perceptions of similarity between self and other ingroup members on all three types of items—$F(1, 34) = 6.69$, $p < .02$—but also increased perceived content similarity—$F(1, 34) = 9.36$, $p < .01$. Additionally, however, item type interacted with the type of assumed similarity—$F(2, 68) = 3.31$, $p < .05$. Whereas general similarity was greater on the conflict-related items than on the other two sets, content similarity showed an opposite pattern. There, less perceived similarity was found on both conflict-related items and items of high importance than on items of little importance. In other words, despite a general tendency to see oneself as globally similar to other group members on items specifically related to group membership, subjects also differentiated themselves from other group members in terms of their agreement with specific item content on items that were related to the intergroup conflict or were of high personal importance.

Additional analyses of general similarity were performed in order to compare the six conflict-related items to a subset of the three important and three unimportant items that were most intermediate in importance. This created two sets matched in importance to the third decimal and thereby controlled for the confound of item importance and item type that exists in the analyses of Table 2 (i.e., there, the conflict items were of intermediate importance, whereas the other two sets had more extreme polarity). Analysis of these data showed even clearer effects than the preceding. Main effects occurred both for salience of intergroup conflict ($F = 4.32$; $df = 1,32$; $p < .05$) and for Item Type ($F = 4.17$; $df = 1,34$; $p < .05$). The greater assumed similarity found when group conflict was salient was due almost entirely to the conflict-related items: For the conflict-related items, the means under high and low intergroup conflict were .41 and .85, respectively;

[1] The details of these procedures can be found in Marks and Miller (1982) and Holtz and Miller (1985). Basically, global similarity is assessed by the absolute difference between each subject's mean attitudinal position across the attitude items within each of the three sets, and the mean position attributed to others within each set. Of course, whenever necessary, items are first reversed to give the set a common polarity. In contrast, to assess content (meaning) similarity within each set, each subject's own attitudes and attitudes attributed to others are standardized separately; then the mean of the absolute differences between the standardized scores within each set provides a content similarity score for each subject. The use of standardized scores in this second procedure has removed the contribution of average elevation differences between own and attributed attitudes.

TABLE 2 Effects of Salience of Intergroup Conflict on
Perceptions of Attitudinal Similarity to One's Ingroup

Salience of intergroup conflict	Type of attitude dimension	Orthogonal dimensions of perceived similarity	
		General	Item content
High	Conflict-related	.41	.67
	Important	.65	.66
	Unimportant	.66	.56
Low	Conflict-related	.85	1.02
	Important	1.00	.93
	Unimportant	.90	.69

Note. Lower scores indicate greater perceived similarity.

whereas for items unrelated to the conflict, the respective means were
.90 and 1.08.

As indicated, when we turn to examine effects on perceptions of
similarity to ingroup members in terms of the specific beliefs with
respect to the content of each attitude item (i.e., with the effects of
general noncontent similarity removed), a different picture emerges.
Again, when intergroup conflict is salient, subjects exaggerate belief
similarity. However, the crossover nature of the interaction between
the orthogonal components of assumed similarity and the types of
items suggests that one seeks general social support or greater identity
(similarity) with ingroup members with respect to conflict-related
items in particular, but at the same time, one also preserves and exag-
gerates one's perception of uniqueness (and potential contribution to
the ingroup) on two types of important items: those belief dimensions
that are directly related to one's group membership (namely, the conflict-related items that are a subset of items directly concerned with
group identity) and those items that are important in terms of personal
values.

SUMMARY

Compared to the other models depicted in Figure 1, Model 3 is
unique in its emphasis on the need to alter category boundaries *before*
any changes in behavior, perceptions, or affect toward specific group
members can be expected to have any generalized effects. If category
boundaries remain salient, differentiation of individual group mem-

bers, or subgroups, will not affect the tendency to treat other group members as undifferentiated representatives of a social category. Similarly, learning to distinguish among group members on one dimension will not necessarily generalize to other dimensions of potential differentiation.

Though addressing very different aspects of categorization processes, the two studies briefly described here both support the view that category boundaries suppress interpersonal differentiation and limit the generalizability of interventions aimed at individuating group members. Charlin's experiment challenges the conclusion that differentiation of a single outgroup member transfers to other group members. Instead, her findings indicate that making dissenting opinions salient can alter *affective* responses to the outgroup, but that such effects are exhibited in an undifferentiated manner to the outgroup as a whole. Gross's experiment indicates that category boundary salience affects differentiation among ingroup members as well, enhancing perceived global similarity between self and other group members except on dimensions of importance to self identity.

The model of *personalization* depicted in Figure 2 represents the conditions we think are necessary to alter in any fundamental way the nature of intergroup relations. The critical feature of that model is that perceived similarity among group members, including the self, effectively cuts across category boundaries. In our view, such personalization will not occur unless intergroup interaction takes place in an environment where (1) the basis for assignment of roles, status, and social functions is perceived to be category-independent rather than category-related, and (2) the nature of the interaction promotes an interpersonal orientation rather than a task orientation toward others in the situation (Brewer & Miller, 1984). Our current laboratory experiments are designed to assess the success of cooperative interventions under conditions that vary on these two dimensions. Preliminary findings (e.g., Miller et al., 1985) indicate that both significantly affect the effectiveness of cooperative interaction with individual outgroup members in producing a general reduction in one's tendency to rely on category distinctions in intergroup settings.

ACKNOWLEDGMENTS

We wish to acknowledge the excellent secretarial help received from the psychology department of Bar-Ilan University.

REFERENCES

Aronson, E., Blaney, N., Stephan, C., Sikes, J., & Snapp, M. (1978). *The Jigsaw class-room*. Beverly Hills, CA: Sage.

Bem, D. (1967). Self-perception: An alternative interpretation of cognitive dissonance phenomena. *Psychological Review, 74,* 183–200.

Brewer, M. B., & Miller, N. (1984). Beyond the contact hypothesis: Theoretical perspectives on desegregation. In N. Miller & M. B. Brewer (Eds.), *Groups in contact: The psychology of desegregation* (pp. 281–302). Orlando, FL: Academic Press.

Crano, W. D. (1983). Assumed consensus of attitudes: The effect of vested interest. *Personality and Social Psychology Bulletin, 9,* 597–608.

DeVries, D. L., Slavin, R., Hennessey, G., Edwards, K., & Lombardo, M. (1980). *Teams-Games-Tournament: The team learning approach.* Englewood Cliffs, NJ: Educational Technology Publications.

Festinger, L. (1957). *A theory of cognitive dissonance.* Evanston, IL: Row, Peterson.

Gerard, H. (1983). School desegregation: The social science role. *American Psychologist, 38,* 869–877.

Gerard, H., & Miller, N. (1975). *School desegregation.* New York: Plenum Press.

Holtz, R., & Miller, N. (1985). Assumed similarity and opinion certainty. *Journal of Personality and Social Psychology, 48,* 890–898.

Johnson, D. W., Johnson, R., & Maruyama, G. (1984). Goal interdependence and interpersonal attraction in heterogeneous classrooms: A metanalysis. In N. Miller & M. B. Brewer (Eds.), *Groups in contact: The psychology of desegregation* (pp. 187–212). Orlando, FL: Academic Press.

Kagan, S., Zahn, G., Widaman, K., Schwarzwald, J., & Tyrrell, G. (1985). Classroom structural bias. In R. Slavin, S. Sharan, S. Kagan, R. Hertz-Lazarowitz, C. Well & R. Schmuck (Eds.), *Learning to cooperate, cooperating to learn.* New York: Plenum Press.

Kiesler, C., Nisbett, R., & Zanna, M. (1969). On inferring one's beliefs from one's behavior. *Journal of Personality and Social Psychology, 11,* 321–327.

Marks, G., & Miller, N. (1982). Target attractiveness as a moderator of assumed attitude similarity. *Personality and Social Psychology Bulletin, 8,* 728–735.

Marks, G., & Miller, N. (1985). The effect of certainty on consensus judgments. *Personality and Social Psychology Bulletin.*

Marks, G., Miller, N., & Maruyama, G. (1981). Effect of target's physical attractiveness on assumptions of similarity. *Journal of Personality and Social Psychology, 41,* 198–206.

Miller, N. (1981). Changing views about the effects of school desegregation: *Brown* then and now. In M. B. Brewer & B. Collins (Eds.), *Scientific inquiry and the social sciences* (pp. 413–453). San Francisco: Jossey-Bass.

Miller, N., Brewer, M. B., & Edwards, K. (1985). Cooperative interaction in desegregated settings: A laboratory analogue. *Journal of Social Issues.*

Miller, N., Rogers, M., & Hennigan, K. (1983). Cooperative games as an intervention to promote interracial contact. In L. Bickman (Ed.), *Applied social psychology annual* (Vol. 4, pp. 199–216). Beverly Hills, CA: Sage.

Rogers, M., Hennigan, K., Bowman, C., & Miller, N. (1984). Intergroup acceptance in classroom and playground settings. In N. Miller & M. B. Brewer (Eds.), *Groups in contact: The psychology of desegregation* (pp. 213–227). Orlando, FL: Academic Press.

Rogers, M., Miller, N., & Hennigan, K. (1981). Cooperative games as an intervention to promote cross-racial acceptance. *American Educational Research Journal, 18*(4), 513–516.

St. John, N. S. (1975). *School desegregation: Outcomes for children.* New York: Wiley.

Sharan, S. (1984). *Cooperative learning in the classroom: Research in desegregated schools.* Hillsdale, NJ: Erlbaum.

Sherif, M., Harvey, O. J., White, B. J., Hood, W. R., & Sherif, C. W. (1961). *Intergroup conflict and cooperation: The Robber's Cave experiment.* Norman, OK: University of Oklahoma Press.

Slavin, R. E. (1983). *Cooperative learning.* New York: Longman.

Stephan, W. G. (1978). School desegregation: An evaluation of predictions made in *Brown v. the Board of Education. Psychological Bulletin, 35,* 217–238.

Sumner, W. G. (1906). *Folkways.* Boston: Ginn.

Tajfel, H. (1970). Experiments in intergroup discrimination. *Scientific American, 223*(2), 96–102.

Tajfel, H. (1978). Social categorization, social identity and social comparison. In H. Tajfel (Ed.), *Differentiation between social groups* (pp. 61–76). London: Academic Press.

Tajfel, H., & Turner, J. C. (1979). An integrative theory of intergroup conflict. In W. Austin & S. Worchel (Eds.), *The social psychology of intergroup relations* (pp. 33–48). Monterey, CA: Brooks/Cole.

Turner, J. C. (1978). Social categorization and social discrimination in the minimal group paradigm. In H. Tajfel (Ed.), *Differentiation between social groups* (pp. 101–140). London: Academic Press.

Wilder, D. A. (1978). Reduction of intergroup discrimination through individuation of the outgroup. *Journal of Personality and Social Psychology, 36,* 1361–1374.

CAUSES AND CONSEQUENCES OF THE COLORBLIND PERSPECTIVE*

Janet Ward Schofield

Psychology Department
University of Pittsburgh
Pittsburgh, Pennsylvania 15260

INTRODUCTION

Although the motivational and cognitive approaches to understanding intergroup attitudes and behavior as exemplified by Chapters 2 through 7 of this volume come out of rather different research traditions and focus on somewhat different issues, they share an important but often unemphasized assumption—that the context in which intergroup attitudes develop and in which they are expressed in behavior has a very real influence on such attitudes and behavior. For example, Gaertner and Dovidio (1977), who clearly emphasize motivational factors, have demonstrated that many liberal whites discriminate mainly in situations in which their negative response can be justified with a non-race-related rationale. Similarly, McConahay's Chapter 4 finding that less old-fashioned racism is expressed in the presence of a black than of a white experimenter suggests the power of contextual factors, as does his general point that old-fashioned racism is apparently on the wane because in many milieus it is no longer socially acceptable. Cognitive theories about intergroup relations also take account of contextual factors. For example, Hamilton (1979; also see Chapter 5) describes the way in which distinctiveness, which is to some extent a function of context, influences individual's conceptions about the extent to which two factors, such as minority group status and the pro-

* The research on which this paper is based was funded by the author's contract with the National Institute of Education (Contract 400-76-0011). Other expenses relating to the chapter's preparation were covered by the Learning Research and Development Center, which is partly funded by NIE. However, all opinions expressed herein are solely those of the author and no endorsement of the ideas by NIE is implied or intended.

PREJUDICE, DISCRIMINATION, AND RACISM

pensity for aggressive behavior, are perceived as correlated. An even more clear-cut demonstration of the effect of context on cognitive processes occurs in research on the solo effect, which shows how perceptions of an individual are influenced by the mere fact that that person is the only member of a particular social category, such as women or blacks, in a given situation (Taylor & Fiske, 1978).

Although both the motivational and cognitive approaches to intergroup relations touch on the importance of the social context, neither of them typically systematically explores this issue in nonlaboratory contexts. The purpose of this chapter is to utilize an in-depth study of intergroup relations in a desegregated school to discuss the ways in which context can and does influence the course of intergroup relations. Previous work stemming from the cognitive and motivational perspectives has tended to confine itself to assessing the impact of experimentally manipulated context effects on various aspects of intergroup attitudes and behavior. This chapter takes a radically different approach. It examines the development of one specific aspect of context in an ongoing social situation, a desegregated school, and analyzes both its functions in that situation and its consequences. The aspect of context examined is the existence of a belief system which Rist (1974) has characterized as the colorblind perspective. The basis for the analysis presented is a 4-year ethnographic study of peer relations in a desegregated school. Before proceeding to this analysis, I both discuss the main components of colorblind perspective and describe the study on which the analysis is based.

Rist (1974) defines *the colorblind perspective* as a point of view which sees racial and ethnic group membership as irrelevant to the ways individuals are treated. Taking cognizance of such group membership in decision making is perceived as illegitimate and likely to either lead to discrimination against the minority group or reverse-discrimination in its favor. Neither of these is viewed as desirable. From this perspective, school desegregation is an effort to provide all children, regardless of their background, with equal educational opportunities in order to assure that they have a fair chance to compete with others as they make their way in American society. Thus, school desegregation is a mechanism for class assimilation because it functions to facilitate social mobility on the part of blacks who are to be treated exactly like their white peers.

The class assimilation view of school desegregation is very much in tune with a widely held American democratic philosophy: people are to be judged as individuals and not as members of ethnic or racial groups; they should be rewarded on the basis of their behavior rather than of social category membership; and the American economic and social system should be open to all those willing to work hard and strive for advancement. As Rist points out, however, this view does not grant any positive status to lower-class values or modes of behavior. Regardless of whether these values and behaviors reflect pathological reactions to a deprived childhood or creative adaptations to a lower-class environment, they are seen as a problem, standing in the way of the child's success at school and in the larger society (see Chapter 10).

I would argue that two basic factors make study of the implications of the colorblind perspective worthwhile. First, there is evidence that this perspective is widespread in American schools, either as part of official policy or as an informal but nonetheless powerful social norm (Sagar & Schofield, 1984). It is also frequently espoused as a goal to be sought for in many other realms such as employment practices, judicial proceedings, and the like. Second, although in many ways the colorblind perspective is appealing because it is consistent with a long-standing American emphasis on the importance of the individual, it easily leads to a misrepresentation of reality in ways which allow and sometimes even encourage discrimination against minority group members, as later parts of this chapter demonstrate.

THE RESEARCH SITE: WEXLER MIDDLE SCHOOL

In choosing a site for the research, I adopted a strategy that Cook and Campbell (1976) have called generalizing to target instances. The aim was not to study what happens in a typical desegregated school, if such an entity can even be said to exist. Rather, it was to explore peer relations under conditions that theory suggests should be relatively conducive to positive relations between blacks and whites.

Over thirty years ago in his classic book, *The Nature of Prejudice*, Allport (1954) proposed that intergroup contact may reinforce previously held stereotypes and increase intergroup hostility unless the contact situation is structured in a way that (1) provides equal status for minority and majority group members, (2) encourages cooperation toward shared, strongly desired goals, and (3) provides institutional support for positive relations. These ideas, as elaborated and refined by more recent theoretical and empirical work (Amir, 1969, 1976; Cook, 1969, 1985; Pettigrew, 1967, 1969), constitute a useful foundation for understanding the likely outcomes of interracial contact. For example, although equal status may be neither an absolutely necessary prerequisite nor a sufficient condition for change, it does appear to be very helpful (Amir, 1969, 1976; Cohen, 1975; Cohen, Lockheed, & Lohman, 1976; Cook, 1978, 1985; Riordan, 1978). In addition, a rapidly growing body of research suggests that cooperation toward mutually desired goals is indeed generally conducive to improved intergroup relations (Aronson, Blaney, Stephan, Sikes, & Snapp, 1978; Ashmore, 1970; Cook, 1978, 1985; Johnson & Johnson, 1982; Johnson, Johnson, & Maruyama, 1984; Johnson, Maruyama, Johnson, Nelson, & Skon, 1981; Sharan, 1980; Sherif, 1979; Slavin, 1980, 1983a, 1983b, 1985; Worchel, 1979).

Wexler Middle School, which serves 1200 children in sixth through eighth grades, was chosen for study because the decisions made in planning for it suggested that it would come reasonably close to meeting the conditions specified by Allport and the more recent theorists who have built on his work. The school's strong efforts to provide a positive environment for interracial education can be illustrated by examination of its staffing policy. The administration, faculty, and staff of the school are biracial, with about 25% of the faculty being black. The top four administrative positions are filled by two blacks and two whites, clearly symbolizing the school's commitment to providing equal status for members of both groups.

The extent to which Wexler met the conditions specified by Allport and his intellectual heirs as conducive to the development of improved intergroup relations has been discussed at length elsewhere (Schofield, 1982). Here, I merely report the conclusion drawn in that discussion—that Wexler came considerably closer to these criteria than most desegregated public schools. Yet, it fell seriously short of meeting them completely in a number of ways, many of which were the direct result of societal conditions over which Wexler had little or no control. For example, in spite of Wexler's commitment to a staffing pattern which would provide equal formal status for blacks and whites, the proportion of black teachers on its staff was considerably lower than the proportion of black students in the school because the school system did not want to put too high a proportion of its black teachers in one school. In sum, Wexler made stronger than usual efforts to foster positive relations between blacks and whites, but fell markedly short of being a theoretically ideal milieu for the accomplishment of this goal.

Wexler is located in a large industrial northeastern city. Just over 20% of the city's population is black. The school was constructed to serve as a model of high quality integrated education. When it first opened its doors, its student body was almost precisely 50% black and 50% white, mirroring closely the proportion of black and white stu-

dents in the school system of which Wexler was a part. A large majority of Wexler's white students came from middle- or upper-middle-
class homes. Although some of the black children were middle class,
the majority came from either poor or working-class families.

DATA GATHERING

The analysis that follows is based on an intensive 4-year study of
peer relations at Wexler. The basic data-gathering strategy was *intensive* and *extensive* observation in Wexler's classrooms, hallways, playgrounds, and cafeteria. Observers used the full field-note method for
recording the events they witnessed (Olson, 1976). A large number of
events were observed because they were representative of the events
that filled most of the school day at Wexler. However, an important
subgroup of events was oversampled in relation to their frequency of
occurrence because of their direct relevance to the study's focus. This
strategy, which Glaser and Strauss (1967) call theoretical sampling,
led to oversampling certain activities, such as affective education
classes, designed to help students get to know each other, and meetings of Wexler's interracial student advisory group set up to handle
the special problems students may face in a desegregated school.
Over the course of the study, more than 500 hours were devoted to
observation of students and staff at Wexler.

A wide variety of other data-gathering techniques ranging from so-
ciometric questionnaires to experimental work was also used (Sagar
& Schofield, 1980; Schofield, 1979; Schofield & Francis, 1982; Schofield & Sagar, 1977; Schofield & Whitley, 1983; Whitley & Schofield,
1984). Interviews were employed extensively. For example, randomly
selected panels of students participated in open-ended interviews
twice a year. Teachers and administrators were also interviewed repeatedly. In addition, graffiti in the bathrooms and on the school walls
were routinely recorded, school bulletins were collected, and careful
note was taken of such things as wall decorations and public address
system announcements.

Space does not allow full discussion of the many varied techniques
which were employed in collecting and analyzing the data on which
this chapter is based. However, two general principles which guided
the research must be mentioned. First, both data-gathering and analysis were as rigorous and systematic as possible. For example, sampling techniques were employed where appropriate; trained coders,
who were unaware of the race and sex of particular respondents, co-

ded the open-ended interviews using reliable systems developed for
this research; field notes were carefully indexed so that all notes relevant to a given topic could be examined, et cetera. Second, because it
is often impossible to achieve extremely high levels of precision and
control in field research, strong efforts were made to triangulate the
data (Webb, Campbell, Schwartz, & Sechrest, 1966). Great care was
taken to gather many different types of information bearing on the
same issue, to minimize the potential problems with each data source,
and to be sensitive in analyzing and interpreting the data to biases
which could not be completely eliminated. The basic approach used
in the analysis of the qualitative data is outlined in works such as
Becker and Greer (1960), Bogdan and Taylor (1975), Campbell (1975),
and Glaser and Strauss (1967). Fuller details on data-gathering and
analysis are presented elsewhere, as is information on the strategies
used to minimize observer reactivity and bias (Schofield, 1982; Schofield & Sagar, 1979).

THE COLORBLIND PERSPECTIVE AND ITS COROLLARIES

Wexler's faculty clearly tended to subscribe to the colorblind view
of interracial schooling. Interviews with both black and white teachers suggested that the majority of both groups tended to see Wexler as
an institution which could help impart middle-class values and modes
of behavior to lower-class students so that they could break out of the
cycle of poverty and become middle-class persons themselves. Even
though the bulk of these-lower-class students were black, race was
seen as quite incidental to the class assimilation process.

A black administrator, with perhaps more candor than many similarly oriented white administrators and teachers, made her class assimilation goals explicit and, at the same time, made it clear just which
students needed to be so assimilated:

> I really don't address myself to group differences when I am dealing with
> youngsters . . . . I try to treat youngsters, I don't care who they are, as young-
> sters and not as black, white, green or yellow . . . . Many of the black young-
> sters who have difficulty are the ones who . . . have come from communities
> where they had to put up certain defenses and these defenses are the antithe-
> sis of the normal situation . . . like they find in school. It is therefore [diffi-
> cult] getting them to become aware that they have to follow these rules be-
> cause [they] are here . . . not over there in their community. . . . I think that
> many of the youngsters [from the] larger community have a more normal set of
> values that people generally want to see, and therefore do not have [as] much
> difficulty in coping with their school situation. . . . [The black children] do

have difficulty in adjusting because they are just not used to it. Until we can adjustively counsel them into the right types of behavior . . . I think we're going to continue to have these types of problems.

The only thing atypical in the preceeding remarks is the frank acknowledgment that the children perceived as lacking the "normal set of values that people generally want to see" are indeed "our black youngsters." More usually, this was implicit in remarks emphasizing the negative effects of growing up in a poor family or a low-income neighborhood.

As a reaction to the invidious distinctions which have traditionally been made in the United States on the basis of race, the colorblind perspective is understandable and, from a social policy standpoint, it seems laudable. However, this orientation was accompanied at Wexler by a number of other logically related beliefs, which taken together with it had some important though largely unrecognized negative consequences. These beliefs and their basis in the ongoing social reality at Wexler are discussed individually. Then the consequences of such a belief system are discussed in some detail.

RACE AS AN INVISIBLE CHARACTERISTIC

It is not a very great leap from the colorblind perspective, which says that race is a social category of no *relevance* to one's behavior and decisions, to a belief that individuals should not or perhaps even do not *notice* each other's racial group membership. At Wexler, acknowledging that one was aware of another's race was viewed by many as a possible sign of prejudice, as illustrated by the following excerpt from project field notes:

> When I was arranging the student interviews, I mentioned to Mr. Little [white] that I thought there was only one white girl in one of his classes. I asked if I was right about this and he said, "Well, just a minute. Let me check." After looking through the class roster in his roll book he said, "You know, you're right. I never noticed that . . . I guess that's a good thing."

Our data suggest that teachers not only denied that they noticed children's race when the researchers were present, but also did so among themselves. For example, when one white teacher was complying with our request to mark down the race of his students on a class roster to enable the research team to learn students' names more quickly, he remarked, "Did you ever notice those teachers who say, 'I never notice what they are?'"

Although there was less unanimity on the issue of whether students noticed the race of others than of whether teachers did, a substantial proportion of Wexler's faculty asserted that the students rarely noticed race. This point of view is exemplified by the following excerpt from an interview with a black science teacher:

Ms. Monroe: You know, I hear the things the students usually fight about. As I said before, it's stupid things like someone taking a pencil. It's not because [the other person] is black or white . . . . At this age level . . . . I don't think it's black or white.
Interviewer: There's something I'm wondering about. It is hard to believe, given the way our society is, that you can just bring kids together and they won't be very much aware—
Ms. Monroe: They just go about their daily things and don't . . . . I don't think they think about it really . . . . I see them interacting with one another on an adult basis . . . . They are not really aware of color . . . or race or whatever.
Interviewer: You really don't see that as a factor . . . in their relationships?
Ms. Monroe: No.

Although the faculty at Wexler saw themselves and to a lesser extent their students as oblivious to the race of others, there are a wide variety of data suggesting that this view was not accurate. Most removed from the specific situation at Wexler but nonetheless pertinent is a substantial body of data from research on stereotyping and person perception. This work suggests that individuals tend to utilize pre-existing categories in perceiving and responding to others (Taylor, 1981). More specifically, there is research suggesting that individuals spontaneously utilize the physical appearance of others as a basis for categorizing them by race. Further, this categorization has an impact on how individuals are perceived and on how others respond to them (Duncan, 1976; I. Katz, Wackenhut, & Hass, Chapter 2; P. Katz, 1976; Malpass & Kravitz, 1969; Sagar & Schofield, 1980; Taylor, Fiske, Etcoff, & Ruderman, 1978). The teachers and students at Wexler were to some extent self-selected members of an interracial institution and thus might conceivably be less prone to utilize race as a category for processing information about others than the college student populations utilized in most of the studies on person perception. However, given the importance of race as a social category in many aspects of life in the U.S., it seems highly unlikely that the prevailing tendency at Wexler was for individuals not even to notice each other's race.

Interviews with students made it clear that many of them were very conscious of their race or of the race of other students, which is hardly surprising given the fact that interracial schooling was a new and somewhat threatening experience for many of them. The following excerpt from an interview in which the interviewer had not herself previously mentioned race suggests just how salient racial categories were to the children.

> *Interviewer:* Can you tell me who some of your friends are?
> *Beverly (black):* Well, Stacey and Lydia and Amy, even though she's white.

Similarly, students' awareness of racial group membership is illustrated by an excerpt from field notes taken in a seventh-grade class which had a higher-than-average proportion of black students in it because the teachers had decided to put many of the lower-achieving children in a class by themselves.

> Howard, a white male, leaned over to me (*a white female observer*) and said, "You know, it just wasn't fair the way they set up this class. There are 16 black kids and only nine white kids. I can't learn in here." I said, "Why is that?" Howard replied "They copy and they pick on you. It just isn't fair."

RACE AS A TABOO TOPIC

Before proceeding to discuss why the view that they and their students tended not even to notice race gained considerable popularity among Wexler's teachers in spite of everyday indications that this was often not the case, I would like to discuss two other phenomena closely related to the development of the colorblind perspective. The first of these was the development of a norm strong enough to be labeled a virtual taboo against the utilization of the words *white* and *black* in a context in which they referred to racial group membership. Thus, for example, in almost 200 hours of observations in classrooms, hallways, teachers meetings, et cetera during Wexler's first year, fewer than 25 direct references to race were made by school staff or students (Schofield, 1982). Any use of the words *black* and *white* in a context in which they referred to an individual or group was classified as a reference to race, as were racial epithets, and words and phrases used almost exclusively within one group to express solidarity (e.g., "Hey, Brother") or the like.

The extremely infrequent reference to race was all the more surprising when one considers that our observations included a wide variety of formal and informal situations, ranging from workshops funded by the Emergency School Assistance Act, federal legislation which provides funds to desegregating schools to help them handle special problems that may arise as a result of desegregation, to informal student interactions on the playgrounds and in the hallways.

Students' awareness of the taboo is shown clearly in the following field notes, which recount a conversation with a white social worker

whose work at Wexler on the extracurricular program was funded by a
local foundation concerned with race relations. Perhaps not surprisingly under these circumstances, she showed much less reluctance
than most staff to deal in a straightforward manner with the issue of
race.

> Ms. Fowler said that a short while ago she had heard from Martin (*black*) that
> another child had done something wrong. The offense was serious enough so
> that she wanted to track down this individual. She asked Martin to describe
> the child who had committed the offense. Marting said, "He has black hair
> and he's fairly tall," He didn't give the race of the other person even though
> he went on to give a fairly complete description otherwise. 'Finally, Ms.
> Fowler asked, "Is he black or white?" Martin replied, "Is it all right for me to
> say?" Ms. Fowler said that it was all right . . . . Martin then said, "Well, the
> boy was white."

Students were well aware that making references to race displeased
many of their teachers and might also offend peers.

> *Interviewer:* You know the other day I was walking around the school and
> heard a sixth grade student describing a student from the seventh grade to a
> teacher who needed to find this student in order to return something she had
> lost. The sixth grader said the seventh grader was tall and thin. She described
> what the girl had been wearing and said her hair was dark, but she didn't say
> whether the girl was black or white. . . .Why do you think she didn't mention that?
> *Sylvia (black):* The teacher might have got mad if she said whether she was
> white or black.
> *Interviewer:* Do some teachers get mad about things like that?
> *Sylvia:* Some do . . . they holler. . . .
> *Interviewer:* Now when you talk to kids who are black, do you ever mention that someone is white or black?
> *Sylvia:* No.
> *Interviewer:* What about when you're talking with kids who are white?
> *Sylvia:* Nope.
> *Interviewer:* You never mention race? Why not?
> *Sylvia:* They might think I'm prejudiced.

SOCIAL LIFE AS A WEB OF PURELY INTERPERSONAL RELATIONS

Consistent with the view that race is not, or at least should not be, a
salient aspect of other individuals and with the practice of not speaking about race was a tendency to conceptualize social life as a web of
interpersonal rather than intergroup relations and to assume that interpersonal relations are not much influenced by group membership.
As one teacher put it,

> Peer group identity here in middle school . . . has nothing to do with race.
> There's a strong tendency to group that exists independent of . . . racial
> boundaries . . . We started in September with these students letting them

know we weren't going to fool around with that. . . . You're a student and we
don't care what color you are.

This tendency to minimize the potential importance of intergroup
processes was illustrated clearly during an in-service training session,
the stated purpose of which was to help teachers deal effectively with
the racially heterogeneous student body. The facilitator, a white clinical psychologist employed by a local foundation, started the session
off by making some general statements about the importance of understanding cutural differences between students. Although the facilitator kept trying to nudge and finally to push the group to discussing
ways in which the biracial nature of the student body influenced peer
relations, appropriate curricular materials, and the like, the group
ended up discussing issues such as the problems caused by individual
children who acted out aggressively in the classroom, the difficulty
that overweight children have in gaining peer acceptance, and the fact
that handicapped children were sometimes taunted by their classmates.

Contrasting sharply with the teacher's tendency to insist that they
and their students reacted to each other exclusively as individuals and
to de-emphasize the importance of intergroup as opposed to interpersonal processes was the students' willingness to discuss with interviewers the importance race played in Wexler's social life.

> *Interviewer:* I have noticed. . . that [in the cafeteria] very often white kids
> sit with white kids and black kids sit with black kids. Why do you think that
> is?
> *Mary (white):* Cause the white kids have white friends and the black kids
> have black friends . . . . I don't think integration is working . . . . Blacks
> still associate with blacks and whites still associate with whites . . . .
> *Interviewer:* Can you think of any white kids that have quite a few black
> friends or of any black kids who have quite a few white friends?
> *Mary:* Not really.

The tendency for students to group themselves by race in a variety of
settings was very marked. For example, on a fairly typical day at the
end of the school's second year of operation 119 white and 90 black
students attended the seventh grade lunch period. Of these over 200
children, only six sat next to someone of the other race (Schofield &
Sagar, 1977).

Of course, it is possible that it was not race itself which was a factor
in producing such interaction patterns, but something correlated with
race such as socioeconomic status, academic achievement, or the opportunity for previous contact with each other. Such factors did appear
to reinforce the tendency to prefer intragroup interactions, and were

often cited by teachers as the actual cause of the visually apparent tendency of students to cluster with those of their own race. Yet, the results of an experiment conducted at Wexler demonstrate that race itself was a real factor in peer relations. In this study, 80 male sixth-graders were presented with carefully drawn pictures of a number of ambiguously aggressive types of peer interactions which were quite common at Wexler, such as poking another student with a pencil. For each type of interaction, some students were shown pictures in which both students were black, others saw pictures in which both students were white, and still others saw mixed race dyads with the black student shown as either the initiator of the behavior or as the student to whom it was directed. The results suggested that the race of the person initiating the behavior influenced how mean and threatening it was interpreted as being (Sagar & Schofield, 1980) (see Table 1). Such a finding is, of course, inconsistent with the notion that students take no notice of others' race. It is also incompatible with the idea that intergroup processes have no influence on students' reactions to their peers because the data suggest that the perception of an individual's behavior is influenced by the group membership of the person performing it.

THE FUNCTIONS AND CONSEQUENCES OF THE COLORBLIND PERSPECTIVE AND ITS COROLLARIES

Regardless of the fact that the colorblind perspective and its corollaries were not completely accurate views of the social processes occurring at Wexler, they appeared to influence the development of the social fabric at Wexler in ways which had a number of important consequences, some positive and some negative. The following discussion of the functions of this set of beliefs suggests why the colorblind perspective was attractive to teachers and how it affected both the education and social experiences of Wexler's students.

REDUCING THE POTENTIAL FOR OVERT CONFLICT

One concern that typifies many desegregated schools, and which is often especially salient in newly desegregated situations, is a desire to avoid dissension and conflict which are or could appear to be race related (Sagar & Schofield, 1984). The adopting of colorblind policies is often seen as useful in achieving this goal because if such policies are implemented fully they can help protect the institution and those

TABLE 1   Mean Ratings of Both White and Black Actors' Ambiguously Aggressive Behaviors by White and Black Subjects

Subject group	Actor race	Rating scale: mean/threatening
White	White	8.28
	Black	8.99
Black	White	7.38
	Black	8.40

Note. Means are based on sums of paired 7-point scales indicating how well the given adjective described the behaviors, from 1 (not at all) to 7 (exactly). $N = 40$ in each group. Each subject rated two white and two black actors (e.g., the perpetrator of the ambiguously agressive act) and two white and black targets. The 4×4 nature of the Latin square required treating the race permutations as four levels of a single factor. Significant F values on this factor provided justification for testing actor race, target race, and interaction effects with simple contrasts, using the error variance estimate generated by the ANOVA. The significant main effect of race permutations on the summed mean/threatening scales, $F(3,192) = 3.02$, $p < .05$, was found to reflect, as predicted, tendency for subjects to rate the behaviors of black actors more mean/threatening than identical behaviors by white actors, $t(144) = 2.90$, $p < .01$. Means are not broken down by target race because no statistically significant main effects or interactions were found for this variable.
From Sagar, H. A., & Schofield, J. W. (1980). Racial and behavioral cues in black and white children's perceptions of ambiguously agressive acts. *Journal of Personality and Social Psychology, 39*(4), 590–598. Copyright 1980 by the American Psychological Association. Adapted by permission.

in positions of responsibility in it from charges of discrimination. This is not to say that such policies lead to equal outcomes for members of all groups. Indeed, when there are initial group differences on criteria relevant to success in a given institution, such policies are likely to lead to differential outcomes, a situation that some would characterize as institutional racism (Jones, 1972; also see Chapter 10). However, as noted earlier, the colorblind perspective is consistent with notions of fairness which have long held sway in the U. S. and thus can be relatively easily defended. Policies which give obvious preference to either minority or majority group members are much more likely to spark controversy and conflict.

An example from Wexler illustrates the way in which the operation of the colorblind perspective helps to minimize overt conflict in situations where the outcomes for blacks and whites as a whole are extremely different. The suspension rate for black students at Wexler was roughly four times that for white students. The strong correlation between race and socioeconomic background at Wexler made it predictable that the black students' behavior would be less consistent than that of white students with the basically middle-class norms prevailing in the school. However, the colorblind perspective appeared instrumental in helping to keep Wexler's discipline policies from becoming a major focus of contention. To my knowledge, the disparity in suspension rates was never treated as a serious issue which needed attention. When researchers asked faculty and administrators about it, some, perhaps not altogether candidly, denied having noticed it. Others argued that it was not a problem in the sense that individual students were generally treated fairly. In fact, teachers often emphasized strongly the effort they made to treat discipline problems with white and black students in exactly the same way.

On the relatively rare occasions in which charges of discrimination were raised by students unhappy with the way a teacher had dealt with them, teachers tended to discount the complaints by reiterating their commitment to the colorblind perspective.

> Ms. Wilson (white): I try not to let myself listen to it (the charge of discrimination). Maybe once in a while I ask myself "Well, why would he make that statement?" But I know in my mind that I do not discriminate on the basis of race . . . . And I will not have someone create an issue like that when I know I have done my best not to create it.

Only an occasional teacher, more often than not black, suggested that the colorblind perspective actually worked to help create the disparity, an issue which is addressed in a later part of this chapter. Be this as it may, the colorblind perspective clearly fostered an atmosphere which minimized the chances that the disparity itself was likely to become the focus of overt discontent or constructive action.

MINIMIZING OF DISCOMFORT OR EMBARRASSMENT

Many of the faculty and students at Wexler had little prior experience in desegregated schools. Also, most of them lived in neighborhoods which were either heavily white or heavily black. Thus, for many, there was an initial sense of awkwardness and anxiety, like the intergroup anxiety Stephan and Stephan (1985) discuss. Under such circumstances, avoiding mention of race and contending that it rarely influenced relations between individuals seemed to minimize the potential for awkward or embarrassing social situations. This is related to the aforementioned conflict-avoidance function of these beliefs but can be distinguished conceptually because feelings of awkwardness and embarrassment can but do not always lead to conflict. In fact, these beliefs and norms seemed to help to maintain the veneer of politeness which Clement, Eisenhart, and Harding (1979) have argued is part of the etiquette of race relations in some desegregated situations.

One way to illustrate the ways in which the colorblind perspective and the associated beliefs and norms helped to smooth social relations between blacks and whites is to compare the situation at Wexler to another sort of interaction which is often rather strained, at least initially, i.e., interaction between individuals who are visibly handicapped and those who are not. In a fascinating analysis of this latter situation, Davis (1961) argues that the emotion aroused in the nonhandicapped person by the sight of a handicapped one creates tension and an uncertainty about what is appropriate behavior that interferes with normal interaction patterns. There is a tendency for the handicap to become the focus of attention and to foster ambiguity about appropriate behavior. Davis argues that the initial reaction to this situation is often a fictional denial of the handicap and of its potential effect on the relationship—that is, a tendency to pretend to ignore the existence of the handicap, which at least temporarily relieves the interactants of the necessity of dealing with its implications. Analogously, one can think of the racial group membership of individuals in a biracial interaction, be they black or white, as a sort of visually apparent handicap. Like a handicap, one's group membership may well provoke an affective response in others which predisposes them to avoidance or at least raises questions about appropriate behavior. Of course, just as some individuals will feel more awkward than others when interacting with a handicapped person, so some individuals will more likely be more affected by interacting with someone of the other race. However, to the extent that either is a potential threat to a smooth, relaxed, and pleasant interaction, one way of handling that threat is to pretend one is unaware of the attribute which creates it.

Although Davis argues that initial interactions between the handicapped and others are characterized by a fictional denial of the handicap, he also suggests that with time this fiction is discarded because, based on an obvious falsehood, it is inherently unstable and in the long run dysfunctional. Similarly, I would argue that although this colorblind perspective and the accompanying taboo may have made the initial adjustment to Wexler easier, in the long run they tended to inhibit the development of positive relations between black and white students. These students were vividly aware of differences and tensions between them which were related to their group membership. Yet such issues could not be dealt with in a straightforward manner in the colorblind climate. Thus, anger sometimes festered and stereotypes built when fuller discussion of the situation might have made it easier for individuals to see each other's perspectives. This is not to suggest that schools have the responsibility to function as giant T-groups or as therapeutic institutions. Rather, it is to say that the refusal of many of Wexler's faculty to recognize the fundamental role that race played in peer relationships meant that they played a less constructive role than they might have in guiding students through a new and sometimes threatening experience.

INCREASING TEACHERS' FREEDOM OF ACTION

The colorblind perspective and its corollaries undoubtedly gained some of their appeal because they tended to simplify life for Wexler's staff and to increase their freedom of action. An example can illustrate both points. After being asked by one of the research team about the outcome of a closely contested student council election, a white teacher disclosed that she had purposely miscounted votes so that a "responsible child" (a white boy) was declared the winner rather than the "unstable child" (a black girl) who had actually received a few more votes. The teacher seemed ambivalent about and somewhat embarrassed by her action, but the focus of her concern was her subversion of the democratic process. She reported that she had looked at the two children as individuals and decided that one was a more desirable student council representative than the other. As far as I could tell from an extended discussion with her, she did not consciously consider the race of the students involved. Further, she did not appear to consider the fact that her action had changed the racial composition of the student council.

The failure to consider such issues clearly simplified the decision-making process because there was one less item, and an affect-laden one at that, to be factored into it. Related to this, such a colorblind approach increased teachers' freedom of action because actions which appeared acceptable if one were to think about them in a colorblind way often appeared much less acceptable from a perspective which is not colorblind. Indeed, the colorblind perspective and its corollaries fostered an environment which two related lines of work would suggest is conducive to discriminatory behavior, at least on the part of certain types of individuals. First, work by Snyder, Kleck, Strenta and Mentzer (1979) demonstrates that people are more likely to act in accordance with feelings they prefer not to reveal when they can appear to be acting on some other basis than when no other obvious explanation for their behavior is available. Specifically, they found that individuals avoided the physically handicapped when such avoidance could easily be attributed to preference for a certain kind of movie. However, when the situation did not provide this sort of rationale for avoidance behavior, the tendency to avoid handicapped others disappeared. Thus, by analogy, one might expect that an environment which minimizes the importance of race and even forbids overt consideration or discussion of the topic would free individuals whose basic tendency is to discriminate (a normatively unacceptable orientation at Wexler) to do so. The vast majority of Wexler's faculty espoused basically equalitarian racial attitudes and would quite rightly be insulted by the idea that they would intentionally discriminate against their black students. Yet, the work of Gaertner and Dovidio (1981; see also Chapter 3) demonstrates that one need not be an old-fashioned racist to discriminate against blacks when the conditions are conducive to it.

Specifically, Gaertner and Dovidio argue that a great many liberal whites these days are highly motivated to maintain an image of themselves as egalitarian individuals who neither discriminate against others on the basis of race nor are prejudiced. However, the desire to maintain such an image is coupled with some negative affect and with certain beliefs which predispose them to react negatively to blacks. This predisposition is expressed primarily in circumstances in which it does not threaten an egalitarian self-concept. One important relevant circumstance is the availability of non-race-related rationales for the behavior in question (Gaertner & Dovidio, Chapter 3). It is precisely this aspect of the situation which is influenced by the colorblind perspective and its corollaries. To the extent they help to remove awareness of race from conscious consideration, they make other explanations for one's behavior relatively more salient. Thus, they free the aversive racist to act in a discriminatory fashion. Further, to the extent the taboo at Wexler inhibited individuals from challenging others' behaviors as racist in outcome or intent, it removed a potential barrier to racist behavior because it minimized the probability that such behavior would pose a threat to a liberal self-concept.

IGNORING THE REALITY OF SUBJECTIVE CULTURE

Although the colorblind perspective and its corollaries served some useful purposes such as minimizing social awkwardness in certain situations, they also had several unrecognized negative effects, as indicated. One important consequence of this mind set was a predisposition to ignore or deny the possibility of cultural differences between white and black children which influenced the way they functioned in school. For example, the differential suspension rate for black and white children may have stemmed partially from differences between the white and black students in what Triandis, Vassiliou, Vassiliou, Tanaka, and Shanmugam (1972) would call their subjective culture. Specifically, data from the Sagar and Schofield (1980) experiment described earlier suggested that black boys saw certain types of ambiguously aggressive acts as less mean and threatening and more playful and friendly than their white peers. These behaviors were ones which sometimes began conflicts between students which resulted in suspensions. Awareness of the differential meaning of such behaviors to white and black students might at least have suggested ways of trying to reduce the disproportionate suspension of black students. Other research suggests that black–white differences in subjective culture are not limited to this one area (also see Chapter 10). Kochman (1981) has argued convincingly that black and white students utilize widely differing styles in classroom discussion and that misunderstanding of the cultural context from which students come can lead peers and teachers to misinterpret involvement for belligerence. Heath's (1982) research suggests that the type of questions which teachers typically pose in elementary school classrooms are quite similar to those asked in white middle-class homes but differ substantially from those typically addressed to young children in poor black homes. Thus, there is reason to think that in assuming a completely colorblind perspective teachers may rule out awareness of information which would be useful in deciding how best to structure materials for their students as well as in interpreting many aspects of their behavior.

FAILING TO RESPOND TO AND CAPITALIZE ON DIVERSITY

There were numerous less subtle ways in which the colorblind perspective and the accompanying de-emphasis on the biracial nature of the school worked to the disadvantage of Wexler's students, and more often to the disadvantage of black than of white ones. One of the more obvious of these concerned the extent to which efforts were made to provide instructional materials which were likely to reflect the interests and life experiences of Wexler's black students. Wexler operated as part of a school system which made some effort to utilize multicultural texts. In addition, a number of teachers, a disproportionate number of whom were black, took special care to relate class work to the concerns and interests of black students by assigning class projects like essays on the TV movie *Roots*. Yet, the prevailing tendency was to abjure responsibility for making sure instructional materials reflected the biracial nature of the student body. Interviews with teachers suggested that many saw no reason to try to locate or develop instructional materials which reflected black Americans' participation in our society. For example, one math teacher who used a book in which all individuals in the illustrations were white contended that "math was math" and that an interview question about the utilization of biracial or multicultural materials was irrelevant to his subject matter. Similar claims were made by other teachers, including some who taught topics like reading, language arts, and social studies.

The colorblind perspective and its corollaries not only made it more likely that individual faculty members would ignore the challenge of presenting students with materials which related in motivating ways to their own experience, but actually led to a constriction of the education provided to students. For example, in a lesson on the social organization of ancient Rome, one social studies teacher discussed the various classes in Roman society, including the nobles and plebians at length but avoided all reference to slaves. Another teacher included George Washington Carver on a list of great Americans from which students could pick individuals to learn about but specifically decided not to mention he was black for fear of raising racial issues. In the best of all worlds, there would be no need to make such mention, because children would have no preconceptions that famous people are generally white. However, in a school where one white child was surprised to learn from a member of our research team that Martin Luther King was black, not white, it would seem reasonable to argue that highlighting the accomplishments of black Americans and making sure that students do not assume famous figures are white is a reasonable practice. Such constriction based on a desire to avoid racial problems is not unique at Wexler. For example, Scherer and Slawski (1979) report that a desegregated high school they studied eliminated the lunch hour and study halls to minimize the sort of loosely supervised contact between students which seemed to be likely to lead to conflict. However, the nature of the constriction at Wexler was influenced by the colorblind perspective and its corollaries. At Wexler, the tendency was to ignore or avoid certain topics. Such a tendency, while undeniably a low-risk one, failed to take advantage of the diversity of experiences and perspectives of its students as a resource for the educational process.

CONCLUSIONS

Since Supreme Court Justice Harlan first spoke of a colorblind society as a goal to be striven for, such a perspective has often been held up as a needed antidote to the virulent racism in our society which traditionally consigned certain individuals to subordinate positions on the basis of their color and their color alone. However, this chapter takes the position that the colorblind perspective is not without some subtle dangers. It may ease initial tensions and minimize the frequency of overt conflict. Nonetheless, it can also foster phenomena like the taboo against ever mentioning race or connected issues and the refusal to recognize and deal with the existence of intergroup tensions. Thus, it fosters an environment in which aversive racists, who are basically well-intentioned, are prone to act in a discriminatory manner. Further, it makes it unlikely that the opportunities inherent in a pluralistic institution will be fully realized and that the challenges facing such an institution will be dealt with effectively.

ACKNOWLEDGMENTS

The author wishes to express her deep appreciation to the students and staff of Wexler School.

REFERENCES

Allport, G. W. (1954). *The nature of prejudice*. Cambridge, MA: Addison-Wesley.
Amir, Y. (1969). Contact hypothesis in ethnic relations. *Psychological Bulletin, 71*(5), 319–342.
Amir, Y. (1976). The role of intergroup contact in change of prejudice and ethnic relations. In P. A. Katz (Ed.), *Towards the elimination of racism* (pp. 245–308). NY: Pergamon.
Aronson, E., Blaney, N., Stephan, C., Sikes, J., & Snapp, M. (1978). *The jigsaw classroom*. Beverly Hills, CA: Sage Publications.
Ashmore, R. (1970). Solving the problem of prejudice. In Collins (Ed.), *Social psychology* (pp. 246–296). Reading, MA: Addison-Wesley.
Becker, H. S., & Greer, B. (1960). Participant observations: Analysis of qualitative data. In R. N. Adams & J. J. Preiss (Eds.), *Human organization research* (pp. 267–289). Homewood, IL: The Dorsey Press.

Bogdan, R. C., & Taylor, S. J. (1975). *Introduction to qualitative research methods: A phenomenological approach to the social sciences.* NY: Wiley.

Campbell, D. T. (1975). Degrees of freedom and the case study. *Comparative Political Studies, 8*(2), 178–193.

Clement, D. C., Eisenhart, M., & Harding, J. R. (1979). The veneer of harmony: Social–race relations in a southern desegregated school. In R. C. Rist (Ed.), *Desegregated schools* (pp. 15–62). NY: Academic Press.

Cohen, E. G. (1975). The effects of desegregation on race relations. *Law and Contemporary Problems, 39*(2), 271–299.

Cohen, E., Lockheed, M., & Lohman, M. (1976). The center for interracial cooperation: A field experiment. *Sociology of Education, 49,* 47–58.

Cook, S. W. (1969). Motives in the conceptual analysis of attitude-related behavior. In W. J. Arnold & D. Levine (Eds.), *Nebraska Symposium on Motivation* Vol. 17 (pp. 179–235). Lincoln: University of Nebraska Press.

Cook, S. W. (1978). Interpersonal and attitudinal outcomes in cooperating interracial groups. *Journal of Research and Development in Education, 12*(1), 97–113.

Cook, S. W. (1985). Experimenting on social issues: The case of school desegregation. *American Psychologist, 40,* 452–460.

Cook, T., & Campbell, D. (1976). The design and conduct of quasi-experiments and true experiments in field settings. In M. Dunnette (Ed.), *Handbook of organizational psychology* (pp. 223–281). Chicago: Rand McNally.

Davis, F. (1961). Deviance disavowal: The management of strained interaction by the visibly handicapped. In H. S. Becker (Ed.), *The other side: Perspectives on deviance* (pp. 119–137). New York: The Free Press.

Duncan, B. L. (1976). Differential racial perception and attribution of intergroup violence. *Journal of Personality and Social Psychology, 35,* 590–598.

Gaertner, S. L., & Dovidio, J. F. (1977). The subtlety of white racism, arousal and helping behavior. *Journal of Personality and Social Psychology, 34,* 691–707.

Gaertner, S. L., & Dovidio, J. F. (1981). Racism among the well-intentioned. In E. Clausen & J. Bermingham (Eds.), *Pluralism, racism, and public policy: The search for equality* (pp. 208–222). Boston: G. K. Hall.

Glaser, B. G., & Strauss, A. L. (1967). *The discovery of grounded theory: Strategies for qualitative research.* Chicago, IL: Aldine.

Hamilton, D. L. (1979). A cognitive-attributional analysis of stereotyping. In L. Berkowitz (Ed.), *Advances in experimental social psychology, 12,* (pp. 53–84). New York: Academic Press.

Heath, S. B. (1982). Questioning at home and at school: A comparative study. In G. Spindler (Ed.), *Doing the ethnography of schooling: Educational anthropology in action* (pp. 102–131). NY: Holt, Rinehart and Winston.

Johnson, D. W., & Johnson, R. T. (1982). The study of cooperative, competitive, and individualistic situations: State of the area and two recent contributions. *Contemporary Education: A Journal of Reviews, 1*(1), 7–13.

Johnson, D. W., Johnson, R. T., and Maruyama, G. (1984). Goal interdependence and interpersonal attraction in heterogeneous classrooms: A meta-analysis. In N. Miller & M. B. Brewer (Eds.), *Groups in contact: The psychology of desegregation* (pp. 187–212). Orlando, FL: Academic Press.

Johnson, D. W., Maruyama, G., Johnson, R. T., Nelson, D., & Skon, L., (1981). Effects of cooperative, competitive, and individualistic goal structures on achievement: A meta-analysis, *Psychological Bulletin, 89,* 47–62.

Jones, J. M. (1972). *Prejudice and racism.* Reading Mass: Addison-Wesley.

252 JANET WARD SCHOFIELD

Katz, P. A. (1976). The acquisition of racial attitudes. In P. Katz (Ed.), *Toward the elimination of racism* (pp. 125–156). New York: Pergamon Press.

Kochman, T. (1981). *Black and white styles of conflict.* Chicago: University of Chicago Press.

Malpass, R. S., & Kravitz, J. (1969). Recognition for faces of own and other races. *Journal of Personality and Social Psychology, 13,* 330–334.

Olson, S. (1976). *Ideas and data: Process and practice of social research.* Homewood, IL: The Dorsey Press.

Pettigrew, T. (1967). Social evaluation theory: Convergences and applications. In D. Levine (Ed.), *Nebraska symposium on motivation* (Vol. 5, pp. 241–315). Lincoln: University of Nebraska Press.

Pettigrew, T. (1969). Racially separate or together. *Journal of Social Issues, 25*(1), 43–69.

Riordan, C. (1978). Equal-status interracial contact: A review and revision of the concept. *International Journal of Intercultural Relations, 2*(2), 161–185.

Rist, R. C. (1974). Race, policy and schooling. *Society, 12*(1), 59–63.

Sagar, H. A., & Schofield, J. W. (1980). Racial and behavioral cues in black and white children's perceptions of ambiguously aggressive acts. *Journal of Personality and Social Psychology, 39*(4), 590–598.

Sagar, H. A., & Schofield, J. W. (1984). Integrating the desegregated school: Problems and possibilities. In M. Maehr and D. Bartz (Eds.), *Advances in motivation and achievement: A research annual.* Greenwich, Connecticut: JAI Press.

Scherer, J., & Slawski, E. J. (1979). Color, class, and social control in an urban desegregated school. In R. C. Rist (Ed.), *Desegregated schools* (pp. 117–153). NY: Academic Press.

Schofield, J. W. (1979). The impact of positively structured contact on intergroup behavior: Does it last under adverse conditions? *Social Psychology Quarterly, 42*(3), 280–284.

Schofield, J. W. (1982). *Black and white in school: Trust, tension or tolerance?* New York: Praeger.

Schofield, J. W., & Francis, W. D. (1982). An observational study of peer interaction in racially-mixed "accelerated" classrooms. *The Journal of Educational Psychology, 74*(5), 722–732.

Schofield, J. W., & Sagar, H. A. (1977). Peer interaction patterns in an integrated middle school. *Sociometry. 40*(2), 130–138.

Schofield, J. W., & Sagar, H. A. (1979). The social context of learning in an interracial school. In R. Rist (Ed.), *Inside desegregated schools: Appraisals of an American experiment* (pp. 155–199). San Francisco, CA: Academic Press.

Schofield, J. W., & Whitley, B. E. (1983). Peer nomination versus rating scale measurement of children's peer preferences. *Social Psychology Quarterly, 46*(3), 242–251.

Sharan, S. (1980). Cooperative learning in teams: Recent methods and effects on achievement, attitudes and ethnic relations. *Review of Educational Research, 50*(2), 241–272.

Sherif, M. (1979). Superordinate goals in the reduction of intergroup conflict: An experimental evaluation. In W. G. Austin & S. Worchel (Eds.), *The social psychology of intergroup relations* (pp. 257–261), Monterey, CA: Brooks/Cole Publishing Company.

Slavin, R. E. (1980). Cooperative learning. *Review of Educational Research, 50*(2), 315–342.

Slavin, R. E. (1983a). *Cooperative learning.* New York: Longman.

Slavin, R. E. (1983b). When does cooperative learning increase student achievement? *Psychological Bulletin, 94,* 429–445.

Slavin, R. E. (1985). Cooperative learning: Applying contact theory in desegregated schools. *Journal of Social Issues, 41*(3), 45–62.

Snyder, M. L., Kleck, R. E., Strenta, A., & Mentzer, S. J. (1979). Avoidance of the handicapped: An attributional ambiguity analysis, *Journal of Personality and Social Psychology, 12,* 2297–2306.

Stephan, W. G., & Stephan, C. W. (1985). Intergroup anxiety. *Journal of Social Issues, 41*(3), 157–175.

Taylor, S. E. (1981). A categorical approach to stereotyping. In D. Hamilton (Ed.), *Cognitive processes in stereotyping and intergroup behavior* (pp. 83–114). Hillsdale: Erlbaum.

Taylor, S. E. & Fiske, S. T. (1978). Salience, attention and attribution: Top of the head phenomena. In L. Berkowitz (Ed.), *Advances in experimental social psychology* (Vol. 11, pp. 249–288). New York: Academic Press.

Taylor, S., Fiske, S., Etcoff, N., & Ruderman, A. (1978). Categorical and contextual basis of person memory and stereotyping. *Journal of Personality and Social Psychology, 36*(7), 778–793.

Triandis, H. C., Vassiliou, V., Vassiliou, G., Tanaka, Y., & Shanmugam, A. (Eds.). (1972). *The analysis of subjective culture.* NY: Wiley.

Webb, E., J., Campbell, D. T., Schwartz, R. D., & Sechrest, L. (1966). *Unobtrusive measures: Nonreactive research in the social sciences.* Chicago, IL: Rand McNally.

Whitley, B. E., & Schofield, J. W. (1984). Peer preference in desegregated classrooms: A round robin analysis. *Journal of Personality and Social Psychology, 46*(4), 799–810.

Worchel, S. (1979). Cooperation and the reduction of intergroup conflict: Some determining factors. In W. G. Austin & S. Worchel (Eds.), *The social psychology of intergroup relations* (pp. 262–273). Monterey, CA: Brooks/Cole Publishing Company.

RACISM IN THE COURTROOM

Stephanie Nickerson

*Graduate School of Management
and Urban Professions
New School for Social Research
New York, New York 10011*

Clara Mayo*
Althea Smith

*Psychology Department
Boston University
Boston, Massachusetts 02215*

INTRODUCTION

Within the American courtroom, individual, institutional, and cultural forms of racism can produce unjustly severe consequences for minority defendants. Because judges and jurors are in positions of unusual power, their racial biases can have important consequences for people of color. This chapter, therefore, examines the literature pertaining to the role of prejudice, discrimination, and racism in the courtroom. It is based on a view of social psychology in which knowledge building and application are reciprocally linked to improving the quality of life (Mayo & LaFrance, 1980). Our purpose in this chapter is threefold. First, we review the literature on racial bias in verdicts and sentencing. Second, we apply the empirical literature on racial attitudes to procedures used in the courtroom in the selection of juries. Third, we describe a study comparing *voir dire* questions allowed by the court with those disallowed by the court. The purpose of this comparison is to ascertain whether systematic dimensions underlie judges' decisions concerning what is and is not asked of potential jurors with regard to racial prejudice. In addition to being informative in its own right, the outcome of this study may add to social psychological knowledge of racial attitude assessment. Thus, information travels in both directions, from the social psychological literature to the courtroom and from court practices to the field of social psychology.

---

* Clara Mayo died before we completed this chapter. However, the expert witness work on which the paper is based and the idea for the study were hers.

PREJUDICE, DISCRIMINATION, AND RACISM

RACIAL BIAS IN VERDICTS AND SENTENCING

Racial attitudes can affect juridic decisions blatantly or, more likely, in the subtle ways discussed in other chapters of this volume. For example, because whites associate certain crimes with blacks (Sunnafrank & Fontes, 1981), they may process information differently in criminal proceedings depending on racial factors. Also, if whites are generally distrusting of blacks, then for motivational reasons they may be more readily influenced by the prosecution than by the defense in trials involving black defendants. The research on racial discrimination in juridic decision-making falls into two categories: so-called *simulated juror experiments* and *archival research* of court records. We discuss each type separately.

SIMULATED JUROR EXPERIMENTS

Most of the simulation experiments follow a similar format: They are variants of Landy and Aronson's (1969) juridical judgment technique in which subjects, usually undergraduates, read a summary of a trial transcript and then, on a questionnaire, individually make judgments about the guilt or innocence of the defendant, typically without benefit of discussion. Sometimes the jurors also sentence the defendant to a prison term. In the simulation studies we discuss, the defendant's race, usually black or white, is systematically manipulated. Occasionally, participants actually do deliberate with one another about the guilt or innocence of the defendant.

The bulk of the simulation studies in which college student participants did not deliberate with one another found no main effects for race of defendant. Presumably, this indicates that the students treated black and white defendants equally (Barnett & Feild, 1978; Bromley, Saxe, & Crosby, 1977; Faranda & Gaertner, 1979; Foley, Chambin, & Fortenberry, 1979; Gleason & Harris, 1975; Nemeth & Sosis, 1973; Sunnafrank & Fontes, 1981). However, in a simulation study using only blacks as participants (Ugwuegbu, 1976), blacks attributed more negative traits to a white than to a black defendant. In a later extension of that study, Ugwuegbu (1979) used both white and black subjects as mock jurors in a forcible rape case and found that jurors were most lenient when the defendant was the same race as themselves. In addition, some researchers using older, white samples found main effects for race: Blacks received longer sentences than whites (Feild, 1979; Gray & Ashmore, 1976).

Faranda and Gaertner (1979; also see Chapter 3) conducted an interesting experiment varying the usual pattern. They had white high and low authoritarian students judge the guilt of a black or white defendant when incriminating but inadmissible evidence was or was not presented. When the defendant was black, these white high-authoritarian students gave higher ratings of guilt when the inadmissible evidence was presented than when it was omitted, whereas this made no difference to white low-authoritarian students. When the defendant was white, however, the high authoritarians were unaffected, but the low authoritarians rated the white *less* guilty when the inadmissible evidence was presented than when it was not. Faranda and Gaertner suggested that while high-authoritarian whites are more clearly *against* black defendants, low authoritarian whites seem more biased *in favor of* white defendants.

Some studies demonstrate that the victim's race, as well as the defendant's race, can affect the outcome. Feild (1979) found that the mock judges imposed harsher sentences on defendants charged with raping a white woman than on those accused of raping a black woman. Moreover, while mock judges treated black and white rapists no differently when their victim was black, black offenders received more severe sentences than did white offenders when the victim was white. In addition, Miller and Hewitt (1978) found that black and white undergraduates gave harsher sentences to defendants whose victim was the same race as themselves.

Bernard (1979), citing several critiques of the jury simulation research (cf. Gerbasi, Zuckerman, & Reis, 1977; Weiten & Diamond, 1979; Wilson & Donnerstein, 1977), attempted to create a more realistic situation. He presented black and white undergraduates with a videotaped mock trial and asked the students in juries of 12, composed of differenct racial mixtures, to deliberate (after an immediate predeliberation ballot) until they reached a unanimous decision. The videotape showed the defendant as either a black or a white lower-class male. The students deliberated either in racially homogeneous juries, in predominantly black or predominantly white juries, or in juries with equal numbers of blacks and whites. Comparing the votes on the first ballot with the final ballot, Bernard found that individuals generally shifted from a guilty to a not guilty vote as the result of discussion with others. This pattern was true with one exception. Whites who voted guilty on the first ballot almost never shifted their vote to not guilty when the defendant was black. They did shift to not guilty, however, when the defendant was white. Black jurors, in contrast, shifted from about 30% voting guilty on the first ballot to 100%

voting not guilty after deliberation, regardless of the defendant's race. Furthermore, only 1 of the 10 juries reached a guilty verdict—the uniformly white jury judging a black defendant.

In perhaps the most realistic jury simulation study, Lipton (1983) investigated racism among white and Hispanic college students. He created a situation in which six-person juries believed their decisions would actually affect defendants. Under the guise of running an experimental intercampus grievance program, Lipton recruited white and Hispanic students of both sexes, ostensibly to explore alternative means of dealing with disciplinary problems. Participants were asked to act as a jury of peers for other students involved in discipline cases. Each jury read two cases, one involving a white defendant, the other involving a Hispanic defendant. Jurors read the transcript of each case and completed a predeliberation questionnaire, and then, as in Bernard's (1979) study, they attempted to deliberate until a unanimous decision was reached. Juries were formed with either whites or Hispanics predominating or with equal representation of each.

The important results involve the differences between predeliberation and postdeliberation decisions. Before deliberation, the white jurors, compared to Hispanic jurors, attributed more guilt to the Hispanic defendant. After deliberation, however, Hispanic and white judgments became more equivalent: Hispanic jurors became more severe, and white jurors became more lenient in their judgments of the Hispanic defendant. Another significant finding was that whites tended to change their verdict to innocent if they were on a predominantly Hispanic jury, whereas Hispanics changed their verdict to guilty more often if they were on a mostly white jury. It is clear that both Bernard's and Lipton's research is very different from the other simulations, and that the defendant's race as well as the racial composition of the jury can affect juridic decisions.

In summary, the results of the studies without deliberation suggest that white jurors typically do not discriminate against minority defendants. These jurors appear to believe, at least in the abstract, that people of different races should be treated equally in criminal trials. The subjects in the studies by Gray and Ashmore (1976) and by Feild (1979) were older than the jurors in the other studies, and older people, having grown up before the civil rights movement, may not have internalized the principle of racial equality to the same degree.

We can look at these studies in another light, however. With the exceptions of Lipton's and Bernard's research, the simulation experiments can be thought of as somewhat veiled attitude questionnaires about race and crime. Rather than asking directly, "What do you think about blacks (or whites) in general?", researchers present subjects with black or white target persons in courtroom situations and ask indirectly, "What do you think of black (or white) defendants in criminal trials?" If one accepts the premise that the simulation studies are, essentially, legal–racial attitude surveys, the lack of evidence for anti-black sentiment is not surprising. A review of unobtrusive studies of racism (Crosby, Bromley, & Saxe, 1980), as well as the chapters by Gaertner and Dovidio (Chapter 3) and McConahay (Chapter 4), all demonstrate that prejudice, discrimination, and racism still abound but in substantially more subtle forms that often cannot be tapped by direct, traditional forms of questioning. Thus, there were few main effects in the simulation experiments, but the interaction effects and the results of Lipton's and Bernard's studies suggest the presence of antiminority feeling.

As the Bernard (1979) and Lipton (1983) studies show, interaction among jurors was crucial. Deliberation made a difference to student jurors, and the results varied in accordance with the racial composition of the jury. These experiments make it evident that one cannot usefully compare simulations without interaction among jurors with those simulations where there is interaction. Lipton's cover story also created a situation in which students believed their decisions actually had consequences for defendants. None of the other simulation experiments appears to have the same degree of experimental realism.

The research into court records reveals a consistent pattern of racism in the courtroom, indeed, more consistent than that shown by the simulation experiments.

ARCHIVAL RESEARCH

In archival research, records of actual court trials are examined for evidence of racial discrimination. Occasionally such studies are supplemented with interviews of jurors and observations of trials. By their very nature, archival studies are much broader than the simulation experiments reviewed earlier. Moreover, in actual criminal trials, the jury determines the verdict, but typically the judge imposes sentence. Thus, in this section we examine the literature concerning judges' as well as jurors' behavior. As much as possible, we confine our review to that research which compares the verdicts and sentences of minority and white defendants involved in criminal proceedings.

Several researchers have examined records of sentencing in cases involving race and rape. Traditional wisdom suggests that blacks convicted of raping white women are given the most severe sentences, and that intraracial rapes involving black victims carry the least severe sentences. Howard (1975) found the traditional wisdom borne out. His study in Maryland showed that the greatest proportion of death penalties for rape were inflicted on a black defendant convicted of raping a white woman. Howard found that no black was executed for raping a black woman. Similarly, in their study of capital rape convictions from 1945 to 1965, Wolfgang and Riedel (1973) showed that of all persons convicted of rape, all other nonracial factors (such as prior convictions) held constant, the judges sentenced to death a vastly higher proportion of blacks than whites.

Bullock (1961) studied the records of over 3500 inmates in a Texas state prison. He assumed that burglary is an interracial crime for blacks but not for whites, and that rape and murder are intraracial crimes for both blacks and whites. He found that blacks got longer sentences when their victims were white (that is, for burglaries) than when their victims were black (that is, for rape and murder). Similarly, Myrdal (1944) and Kalven and Zeisel (1966) concluded that judges and juries are more lenient on a black defendant if the victim is also black, the notion being that if blacks can confine unruliness and violence to their own race, whites need not be concerned. According to Myrdal, 40 years ago at any rate, this thinking was traditional, particularly in Southern courts.

Other research demonstrates that the courts generally treat black defendants more harshly than whites. According to Gerard and Terry (1970), in state courts in Missouri, many more blacks than whites were convicted, and for most crimes, the judges meted out prison sentences to more blacks than whites. Whites received probation almost twice as often as blacks. Researchers in other states have turned up similar results: Blacks get harsher sentences than whites (Chiricos & Waldo, and Warren, as cited in Bell, 1973).

Using data from Philadelphia's juvenile justice system, Thornberry (1973) examined the cases of black and white boys born in 1945. Holding constant nonracial factors such as seriousness of crime and prior offenses, he found that both race and socioeconomic status affected the severity of treatment. Judges gave blacks and poor people harsher sentences than whites and middle-class people. A larger study conducted for the American Bar Foundation (Silverstein, 1965) indicates that poor, black, and uneducated defendants in the United States did not get equal treatment in the criminal justice system. Silverstein examined data on over 11,000 criminal cases across the country and found that blacks, persons of low socioeconomic status, and people with low educational achievement typically received unfavorable treatment at all stages of the judicial process—from getting a preliminary hearing through to the sentencing process. Blacks, being disproportionately poor and uneducated, often lost on all three counts.

In the most recent large scale study, a team from Rand Corporation (Petersilia, 1983) examined 1980 data from the computerized information system kept by the California Bureau of Criminal Statistics. This database tracks every offender's process from arrest to sentencing. The Rand group also used self-reports obtained from about 1400 men in prison in Texas, California, and Michigan. These researchers, too, found that, holding other factors constant, minorities received longer sentences and served longer in prison than whites.

The archival research on disparities in sentencing provides more consistent evidence for racial discrimination than does the simulation research. There is some indication, however, of an egalitarian trend. Hindelang (1969) found evidence of racial discrimination in his review of the early archival studies but less in more recent research. He suggested that the later research was more methodologically sound, and, therefore, nonracial variables (e.g., prior convictions) were better controlled for equality of comparison. Pruitt and Wilson (1983) examined Wisconsin state court records for three time periods and found racial discrimination affecting both decision to imprison and length of sentence only at the earliest time period (1967–1968), not at the later ones (1971–1972, 1976–1977). In addition, in a reanalysis of several studies of sentencing, Hagan (1974) reports that when the type of crime was controlled for and only first offenders were considered, no differences in sentencing between blacks and whites were observed. In noncapital crimes in which the defendant had a prior record of offenses, however, blacks received longer sentences than whites. Summarizing the research on race and sentencing, Greenberg and Ruback (1982) state

> On the basis of the available data, it is too early to conclude whether the defendant's race directly affects the sentencing decision, although it does seem that if the effect exists, it is not very strong. However, it may be that the defendant's race *indirectly* affects sentencing in that blacks and other minority group members are more likely to be arrested and prosecuted and therefore are more likely to have a criminal record (Black, 1971; Chambliss & Seidman, 1971). And it is this prior criminal record that, in turn, affects the judge's sentencing decison. (p. 196)

Nevertheless, overall the archival research suggests that Bell's (1973) words may still be true—"[T]here's little reason for blacks to trust the judicial system" (p. 193)—in America.

In addition to what the research on sentencing shows about racism, there is ample documentation of continued underrepresentation of minorities on juries (Benokraitis, 1982; Nemeth, 1981; Simon, 1980; Zeisel, 1980). In fact, the exclusion of blacks from juries, particularly in cases involving black defendants, has been the basis for legal appeals to the United States Supreme Court. In one case (Swain v. Alabama, 1964), Swain, a black man convicted of raping a white woman, presented evidence that of the eight black men who served on the panel of potential jurors, none served on his trial jury, primarily because of legal challenges by the prosecuting attorney. In addition, Swain showed that no black had served on a jury involved in a black person's criminal trial since 1950, even though several blacks had regularly appeared on jury panels. The Supreme Court ruled that a defendant "is not constitutionally entitled to a proportionate number of his race on the trial jury" (p. 202). Furthermore, the Court supported the system of peremptory legal challenges, "challenges without cause, without explanation and without judicial scrutiny," and concluded that this system "provides justification for striking any group of otherwise qualified jurors in any given case, whether they be Negroes, Catholics, accountants or those with blue eyes" (p. 212). In a reversal of Swain v. Alabama (1964), the Supreme Court recently moved to protect the rights of black defendants by placing limits on the exercise of peremptory challenges. The decision forbids the use of those challenges to eliminate jurors solely on the basis of their race (Taylor, 1986).

This important criminal law ruling resulted from the Supreme Court's examination of the case of Batson v. Kentucky (Taylor, 1986). James Batson, a black man convicted of robbery by an all-white jury, argued that jury selection procedures that allowed the prosecuting attorney to eliminate blacks from the jury pool deprived him of his constitutional right to a trial by a cross-section of the community. The prosecutor used four of his six peremptory challenges to exclude all potential black jurors. The Supreme Court justices have sent the case back to the Kentucky courts with the directive that the courts must ascertain whether the exclusions were racially motivated. If so, Batson's conviction should be reversed. A result of this decision is that "henceforth, prosecutors who persist in challenging blacks can themselves be challenged to explain—or abandon—their tactics" (Newsweek, 1986, p. 70).

This Supreme Court decision addressed one longstanding form of institutional racism in the legal system. Nevertheless, institutional racism not only has been inherent in the courtroom, but also has permeated the entire criminal justice system (Bell, 1973; Hilliard, 1978; Reasons & Kuykendall, 1972.)

THE *VOIR DIRE* PROCEDURE AND SOCIAL PSYCHOLOGICAL IMPLICATIONS

This section of the chapter is based on Clara Mayo's experience as an expert witness on defense motions requesting changes in standard *voir dire* procedures in a number of cases involving black defendants. Criminal defendants are entitled to be tried by a "fair and impartial jury." The courts have interpreted fairness as "free from prejudice," which presumably includes racial prejudice as well as prejudgments of the particular legal issue at hand. In fact, a recent ruling by the California Supreme Court broadened the scope of *voir dire* questions to allow inquiry into matters about which "the local community or the population at large is commonly known to harbor strong feelings" (Carlson, 1981, p. 10). This ruling suggests that expert testimony should be permitted to show the prevalence and intensity of racial prejudice.

The task of the expert witness who seeks to persuade the court that social psychological research can be helpful in assessing racial prejudice among jurors involves a conceptual analysis of the *voir dire* process and a search through the social psychological literature on racial prejudice to find the "best fit" between knowledge and application. To the extent that expert testimony merely contributes to the proceedings in a particular case, it falls within what Haney (1980) has described as "tinkering" in established legal forms. To the extent to which such testimony sets a prededent for more attention to racial attitudes in *voir dire* in general, it moves toward the use of psychological research and theory to effect desirable change in the legal system.

Before we describe the application of racial attitude research to the *voir dire*, we briefly describe that process. Jury selection involves a questioning period, known as the *voir dire*, in which prospective jurors are asked about possible prejudgment and bias in the specific case (Bonora & Krauss, 1983). The term, *voir dire*, roughly meaning "to speak the truth" (Suggs & Sales, 1978), refers to a process intended to ensure the selection of a fair and impartial jury.

The judge in all federal courts and most state courts has discretion over the scope, format and content of the *voir dire* examinations (Bonora & Krauss, 1983). There is substantial variation in who conducts the *voir dire,* under what conditions potential jurors are questioned, and how much of a role attorneys have in the process.

First, differences exist in the extent to which attorneys may participate in asking questions of potential jurors. In a survey of federal judges, Bermant (1977) found that about 75% of them allow no oral participation by counsel in criminal cases. Data on state courts are scanty, but it is clear that even in states where attorney participation in the *voir dire* is statutory, judges vary greatly in their implementation of the statute (Bonora & Krauss, 1983). Although the trend appears to be toward judge-conducted *voir dire* in the state courts (Bermant, 1977), attorneys and the judge, the judge alone, or attorneys alone may conduct the *voir dire.*

Second, the number of people questioned at the same time also varies. The *voir dire* may take place with an entire panel of potential jurors being addressed en masse, often 50 people at once. Sometimes an individual or a small group may be questioned in front of the rest of the panel. Less frequently, small groups or individuals are questioned outside the presence of other potential jurors (Bonora & Krauss, 1983).

Based on their response to the *voir dire,* prospective jurors may be designated as members of the jury or as alternates, or they may be dismissed by challenges. There are two types of challenges: *for cause* and *peremptory.* Either attorney in the case may challenge an individual for cause if the attorney can demonstrate that the potential juror is biased against one side or the other or has already prejudged the case. Challenges for cause are unlimited in number, but the judge rules on the merit of each. Also, Suggs and Sales (1978) make the point that successful challenges for cause are relatively difficult to obtain. Peremptory challenges, on the other hand, are limited in number and generally require no justification or explanation to the court.

Shifting focus, we now consider the social psychological context of the courtroom during the *voir dire.* This phase of jury selection is aimed at determining individuals' qualifications or fitness for the jury task. Potential jurors understand they will be included or dismissed based on their responses to particular questions. They know they are being evaluated and are the focus of attention of an audience consisting of other potential jurors, the judge, attorneys, the defendant, courtroom personnel, members of the general public, and sometimes media representatives.

From a social psychological perspective, the *voir dire* is a special kind of interview, and as in any interview situation, the quality of information obtained depends largely on the conditions under which the interview is conducted, the motivation of the interviewee, the type of information sought, and the perceived goal of the interview (Cannell & Kahn, 1968). In situations in which individuals are aware of being evaluated, they become especially concerned with their performance. In short, they are likely to experience evaluation apprehension (Rosenberg, 1965). Because the demand characteristics (cf. Miller, 1972) of the *voir dire* suggest that appearing fair and impartial is the appropriate behavior in this setting, potential jurors will strive to appear so. Such dynamics bode ill for the accurate assessment of individuals' racial attitudes even among dominative (Kovel, 1970) or "old-fashioned" (Chapter 4) racists.

APPLICATION OF EMPIRICAL LITERATURE

DIFFICULTY IN MEASURING RACIAL ATTITUDES

In addition to the social psychological context in which it occurs, the *voir dire* process typically presents several problems in format, which interfere with the accurate assessment of racial attitudes. These arise from the *role* or position of the questioner vis à vis the potential juror, the *size of the group* to which questions are addressed, and the *structure* of the *voir dire* questions themselves.

First, the role of the judge has an effect on how the potential jurors respond to questions. Research in social psychology is rich in evidence that interviewer characteristics often bias interviewee responses (cf. Cannell & Kahn, 1968). In particular, where interviewers are of higher social class (as judges are), interviewees may be more inclined to experience evaluation apprehension and give socially desirable responses. In addition, the power of the judge in the courtroom, which is conveyed in both direct and subtle ways to jurors, may incline them further to give socially desirable responses, among which is the denial of racial prejudice. Judges, however, often think that their power and status give jurors an added incentive to answer honestly. The research on this issue suggests that judges may be mistaken. Marshall and Smith (1984) sent a questionnaire to 267 former jurors within 2 days of their completing jury service. Marshall and Smith found that jurors who reported feeling self-conscious and anxious when questioned by the judge also reported that they did not answer questions as honestly as those who felt more comfortable during the *voir dire*. Because it is not now socially acceptable to admit to having racist thoughts or intentions, the status and power of the judge probably puts increased pressure on some potential jurors to lie in order to maintain face. Other surveys of ex-jurors indicate that some degree of dishonesty prevails in the *voir dire*. Broeder (1965) conducted posttrial interviews with former jurors who said they had sometimes deliberately made misleading statements during the *voir dire*. Shatz (1977) describes her experience during *voir dire* in which she was less than honest because she felt a conflict between the legal requirement to set aside her feelings and the pressure of her own conscience and principles. In another instance, she evaded answering a *voir dire* question. Furthermore, according to Chester (1970), the wish to serve on a jury resulted in her responding to the *voir dire* in a manner intended to please the district attorney. The influence of class and status is only partially minimized when lawyers participate in the *voir dire*. However, three interviewers may uncover biases better than one (Padawer-Singer & Singer, 1974). Resistance to including counsel in the *voir dire* centers on the greater amount of time that is consumed and on the possibility of influencing jurors during an adversarial *voir dire* (Bermant, 1977).

A second matter of the *voir dire* format on which social psychological research has a bearing is the size of the group in which jurors are questioned. Frequently, racial prejudice is assessed by addressing the entire jury pool of 50 or more people with a single question, such as, "If there is any among you who by virtue of knowing the defendant to be of the Negro race would be prevented from reaching fair verdict, so indicate at this time." In order to respond affirmatively, a prospective juror would have to rise among a group of strangers and acknowledge him or herself to be racially prejudiced. There is ample research to indicate that people are unlikely to single themselves out in this way (see Hare, 1976). The expert witness is on solid ground in advising the court that individual questioning of jurors is more likely to uncover potential prejudice. Not only is the quality of information suspect when *voir dire* about racial attitudes is conducted in the presence of a large group, but also it has the added disadvantage that prospective jurors learn from one another what the "right" and "wrong" answers are (Bonora & Krauss, 1983). There is also the further danger that one respondent's explicitly biased answers may taint the entire group, necessitating the summoning of a new group of potential jurors.

There is one other aspect of *voir dire* format to which social psychological research findings may be addressed. The structure of *voir dire* questions is typically close-ended. This practice is believed to save time and to absolve the questioner from deciding what answers constitute prejudice. A prospective juror who is placed in the position of saying either "yes" or "no" as to whether a defendant's race would prevent that juror from reaching a fair verdict is presumed to be offering unambiguous evidence of partiality or impartiality (Fram, 1982). Social science testimony concerning the inclusion of some open-ended questions on racial matters can focus on such advantages as reducing acquiescence sets and making available information on dimensions of racial attitudes of which potential jurors may be unaware (Cannell & Kahn, 1968). Generally, courts have been receptive to this sort of testimony, within the limitations imposed by constant time pressures. Courts have been less open to testimony concerning the wording of questions themselves. This lack of receptivity may derive from the legal profession's view of its own greater expertise in matters of question formulation. Recent findings, however, regarding the lack of comprehension by jurors of many judges' instructions (e.g., Charrow & Charrow, 1979) may persuade the courts that typical *voir dire* questions, replete with double negatives, technical legal terms, and multiple ideas, are poorly understood by prospective jurors (Monahan & Loftus, 1982).

The Nature of Racial Attitudes

Beyond presenting social science evidence about measurement problems, expert testimony can be helpful in conveying to the court relevant information about the nature of racial attitudes. Specifically, the expert can give information about the *pervasiveness* of racial attitudes, their *diffuseness,* and their *multidimensional* quality.

Research concerning the pervasiveness of racial attitudes (e.g., Allport, 1954; Brigham & Weissback, 1982) is important because of the frequent assumption in *voir dire* that racial attitudes are at issue only in cases involving a racial incident (Alvarez, 1982). That race is a salient feature in person perception (e.g., Allport & Postman, 1947) and that attributions are affected by knowledge of race are worth conveying to the court. Duncan (1976), for example, had white college students watch a videotape (that they thought was live) in which either a black or a white male shoved another man. When they watched a white do the shoving, participants saw it as "playing around," but when they saw a black do the shoving, they labeled it as violent. (See also Schofield, Chapter 8.) Furthermore, personality characteristics were attributed as the cause of the behavior of blacks, whereas more situational attributions were perceived as the cause of the behavior of whites. Added to the perceptual and attributional differences involving race, it is generally assumed in *voir dire* that if asked directly, "Are you racially prejudiced?" persons under oath will respond truthfully. Expert testimony could point out features of the *voir dire* that make such admissions difficult and cite evidence that people are often unaware of their racial prejudice, which can be expressed in diffuse, subtle, and indirect ways.

The diffuseness of racial attitudes makes it possible for jurors to be convinced that they are impartial with regard to race while in fact they hold a variety of prejudicial assumptions. Numbers of studies of unobtrusive measures of discrimination and prejudice show that antiblack sentiments are more prevalent than survey data suggest. (See Crosby, Bromley, & Saxe, 1980, for a review.) There is evidence that, for various reasons, prejudiced individuals are unaware of their biases, and, if asked, would attribute their behavior to reasons other than antiblack prejudice. (See Chapters 3 and 4.)

Finally, as Woodmansee and Cook (1967) have shown, racial attitudes are multidimensional. For example, people who oppose affirmative action legislation are not necessarily the same people who resent working with blacks. Such research findings could be useful in persuading the court to ask more than one or two questions in assessing racial attitudes of prospective jurors.

EMPIRICAL ANALYSIS OF *VOIR DIRE* QUESTIONS

In the preceding section of this chapter, our aim was to show how research findings on racial attitudes could be applied to the *voir dire*. *Voir dire* proceedings can also contribute to social psychological understanding of racial attitudes.

With that goal in mind, we undertook an empirical study of *voir dire* racial attitude questions accepted and rejected by the court to ascertain whether differences exist in the underlying structure of such questions. We sought to understand what assumptions about the nature of racial attitudes are made by judges. For example, are some questions rejected by judges because they seem to be too personal and hence too conflict-producing to ask?

With the assistance of the National Jury Project, we obtained a pool of 27 questions submitted to state courts for *voir dire* in criminal cases involving black male defendants. We randomly selected for further study, from these 27, 10 accepted and 10 rejected questions (see Table 1). In the interest of completeness, we sought a parallel set of questions submitted for *voir dire* by prosecutors and found that the state proposed no questions on racial attitudes in these cases involving black defendants. The lack of such questions indicates either that the

TABLE 1   Accepted and Rejected Questions on Racism

Accepted

1. Do you realize that the presumption of innocence applies to a black defendant as well as a white defendant?
2. Do you feel that a black defendant is more likely guilty because of his color?
3. Can you fairly and impartially decide this case on the basis of the evidence and law, disregarding the race of the defendant?
4. Have you, your children, or your friends been affected by the racial tension in the public schools?
5. Has racial conflict affected your neighborhood or any of your former neighborhoods?
6. Do you think that black people are more likely to commit crimes than white people?
7. If two witnesses give conflicting testimony and one is black and the other is white, in your opinion, would you be more likely to believe one or the other?
8. Will you be influenced in any way, either pro or con, by the race of the defendant?
9. Would you be able to give a black man accused of murdering a white man the same benefit of the doubt as you would give a white man accused of murdering a black man?
10. What does racial prejudice mean to you?

Rejected

1. How do you feel about black people living in your neighborhood?
2. How would you describe your experience with black people at your job?
3. Other than physically, how do you think black people differ from white people?
4. What is your view of interracial dating and marriage?
5. Do you think that black men are more likely to rape white women than black women?
6. Have you ever had a black person in your home?
7. What comes to mind when you hear that a black man has been accused of assaulting a white woman?
8. Do you think life in this community is different for black people than it is for white people? How?
9. Do you belong to any organizations which have expressed views on racial issues?
10. If black people moved into your neighborhood would you be more afraid of crime than you are now?

prosecution had no interest in prospective jurors' racial attitudes or, more likely, that prosecutors assume that the prevailing public racial attitudes pose no problem for the prosecution's case.

In order to examine the underlying structure of the defense-proposed *voir dire* questions accepted or rejected by the court, we submitted them to a multidimensional scaling procedure. Multidimensional scaling is a method for measuring—in this particular instance—the participants' judgments of similarity and dissimilarity among the 20 proposed *voir dire* questions. Relationships among the questions are revealed by their proximity to one another on a spatial map. As with factor analysis, the researchers must, however, interpret the meaning of the relationships among the questions.

PROCEDURE

To generate data for this multidimensional scaling, we asked 43 white introductory psychology students (14 men and 29 women) at Boston University to evaluate the degree of similarity among our *voir dire* questions. The final analysis was based on data from 40 respondents, three protocols being discarded as incomplete. Participants were volunteers and received course credit for their participation.

The *voir dire* questions were presented in paired format, with the order of questions randomly determined and pages randomly sorted in each respondent's booklet to control for practice or fatigue effects. Each of the 20 *voir dire* questions was paired with every other question, yielding 190 paired comparisons which students rated for degree of similarity–dissimilarity on seven-point Likert-type scales.

Participants filled out the questionnaires in three group settings on two separate days. They spent 20 to 45 minutes filling out the scales with most people taking about 30 minutes. When the participants arrived, the study was described briefly as one in which, "We are interested in the issue of selecting jurors in criminal proceedings involving black defendants. In this study we are comparing questions asked of potential jurors with those that were not allowed to be asked. What we want to find out is whether systematic patterns underlie what is and is not asked potential jurors with regard to their racial attitudes." Participant questions were invited before and after the study, and study results were mailed to participants who requested them.

RESULTS AND DISCUSSION

The multidimensional scaling procedure was used to generate solutions involving one to four dimensions. A two-dimensional solution was accepted as an adequate representation of the participants' perceptions of the similarity among the *voir dire* questions.[1] The interpretability of additional dimensions was low. We interpreted the first dimension as legal–attitudinal versus personal–experiential. This dimension correlated significantly with the status of the questions—that is, with whether questions were accepted or rejected by the judge

[1] The two dimensional nonmetric solution described here had a stress value of .19 (using Kruskal's formula; Young's stress equalled .25).

(point-biserial correlation = .45, $p < .05$). *Voir dire* questions which dealt with the prospective jurors' attitude toward the law and criminal acts were more likely to be accepted by the court than were questions asking about jurors' personal experience with black people. Typical questions from the legal–attitudinal end of the dimension are "Can you fairly and impartially decide this case on the basis of the evidence and law, disregarding the race of the defendant?" and "Do you realize that the presumption of innocence applies to a black defendant as well as a white defendant?" Representative questions from the personal–experiential end of that dimension are "Have you ever had a black person in your home?" and "How would you describe your experience with black people at your job?"

What does this dimension tell us about the underlying assumptions guiding judicial acceptance or rejection of *voir dire* questions? That judges were more willing to ask people about their racial attitudes involving applications of the law rather than about their experiences with and feelings about blacks suggests that it is this bias concerning application of the law that needs to be identified in the *voir dire*. It can be argued, however, that to reject questions dealing with a prospective juror's life experiences with black people is to reject information concerning prejudices likely to be triggered when evaluating evidence to reach a verdict. This is especially important given clear research evidence that direct questioning substantially underestimates the degree of antiblack prejudice that exists among American whites (Crosby et al., 1980). Hence, direct *voir dire* focused on legal matters has limitations for exposing racial bias, but broad-ranging questions are more likely to elicit such bias.

Considering now what this scaling dimension can tell social psychologists about racial attitude assessment, we note that attitude scales commonly used in the field do not include items about crime. For example, the 110 item Woodmansee and Cook (1967) scale delineates 11 dimensions of racial attitude and contains not one item dealing with crime and law. Given the results of the present study and other evidence of the association of race and crime in the public mind (e.g., Allport & Postman, 1947), it may be worth considering whether such content may constitute yet another aspect of the multidimensionality of racial attitudes.

Another distinction between accepted and rejected questions which is pertinent to our earlier comments about *voir dire* question format is the fact that 9 of the 10 accepted questions were close-ended—that is, required a yes–no reply. Of the 10 rejected questions, only 4 were close-ended. This structural dimension overlaps with the foregoing attitudinal dimension. In other words, legal–attitudinal questions are more often framed in a close-ended fashion and person–experiential in open-ended formats. A hierarchical regression analysis holding question form constant renders that correlation between the attitudinal–personal dimension and acceptance or rejection of questions nonsignificant. If, indeed, question format was found to be the stronger factor in determining judges' acceptance of questions, close-ended experiential questions might be tried, although they may be generally less informative and more time-consuming for the court. Similarly, open-ended questions in legal–attitudinal domains might be suggested, thus placing both alternatives before the court.

The second dimension yielded by the multidimensional scaling procedure was interpreted as an evaluative one with negatively worded questions contrasted with neutral ones. The point-biserial correlation between this dimension and the accepted–rejected status of the *voir dire* question was .34, not statistically significant. Therefore, this dimension does not distinguish between accepted and rejected questions. Nonetheless, it is a salient feature of the dimensional space for the respondents who judged the questions on their similarity. An example from the negative end of the evaluative dimension is "If black people moved into your neighborhood would you be more afraid of crime than you are now?" An example of a neutrally worded question is "Other than physically, how do you think black people differ from white people?"

Interpretations of the dimension are not self-evident. It may represent no more than the commonly identified evaluative component in attitude measurement whereby prejudice is regarded as a negative affective stance toward some group or person. Whatever the interpretation, it is interesting to note that the contrast to negativity in the dimension is neutral rather than positive. Apparently, no questions that assess positive racial attitudes are posed in the *voir dire* (or for that matter, in most racial attitude scales; cf. Chapter 2). For example, the Woodmansee and Cook (1967) measure uses items concerned with Negro superiority as a type of lie scale. This area, too, may be fruitful for further research, especially considering the fact that a small number of black prospective jurors are occasionally found even in predominantly white jurisdictions.

CONCLUSION

Our review of the literature on verdicts and sentencing shows that racism in America has not disappeared. Rather, over the years, the nature of discriminatory behavior and prejudiced attitudes has become more subtle (see chapters by Gaertner and Dovidio and by McConahay). Thus we find some evidence, but not a massive amount, of antiminority feelings in the simulation research. In most of these studies, we believe that subjects were really responding to questions about their attitudes regarding blacks or whites as criminal defendants. The jurors did not deliberate with others. Their verdicts had no consequences. There was little realism in the simulation. Thus, subjects could afford to be egalitarian.

Nevertheless, the more realistic simulated jury research (Bernard, 1979; Lipton, 1983), showed that *deliberation* has a substantial effect on jurors' verdicts. Also, in the real trials from which the archival studies came, jurors' verdicts had important consequences. In actual trials, blacks and other minorities were found guilty more often and sentenced more harshly than whites. These findings suggest that when it matters, racism appears.

In our discussion of the application of the findings of the empirical literature on the jury selection process, we have tried to show that social psychologists can contribute substantially to ensuring fairer jury trials for black and other minority defendants. Much remains to be done, however. Continued research on the *voir dire* process and on prejudice, discrimination, and racism will advance our knowledge—hence, the potential for effective application. We mentioned earlier that racial attitude scales have not included items about crime and law and that legal or criminal content may indicate other aspects of the multidimensionality of racial attitudes. However, in our review of the literature on racial bias in verdicts and sentencing, we called the simulation studies "veiled attitude surveys." This research demonstrates that at least for some portions of the population, blacks are seen as more guilty than whites by virtue of their race. Obviously, research on this issue would be particularly pertinent to the *voir dire* and would tell us more about racial attitudes in general. Also, the type of crime is rarely examined in the research literature. The idea of Sunnafrank and Fontes (1981)—that certain crimes may be stereotyped as typically committed by a black or a white person—is a valuable one. The relationship between a racially stereotyped crime and verdict may give us more understanding of how the legal and psychological aspects of juror thinking are related.

Other possible research concerns the format of questions asked in the *voir dire*. We found that legal–attitudinal questions, which were usually accepted by judges, predominantly required a yes or no answer, whereas questions based more on experiences, typically rejected by judges, were more often framed in open-ended formats. To examine if, indeed, it is the question format which determines judges' acceptance of questions, it would be useful to formulate questions based on experiences in a close-ended format. Perhaps the answer to a question such as, "Have you ever had a black co-worker in your home?" might be less informative to the court than a similar open-ended question. However, the response would probably be more telling than if no experience-based questions were asked at all.

In our judgment, social psychological research is relevant and useful in a courtroom. But there is still a reluctance on the part of many judges and attorneys to accept it. For example, the third author was recently asked to act as an expert witness in a case involving an interracial couple in which the wife became sterilized as a result of a poorly developed birth control device. To us, it seemed obvious that the research involving sexuality across race would be important in selecting a jury for this trial. There is research in sociology and social psychology that applies directly to this situation and that could be used to document the need for questions related to race during the *voir dire*. Stember's (1976) book on sexual racism and Hernton's (1965) work, *Race and Sex in America*, document the negative ways in which whites perceive issues of sexuality between blacks and whites. In a classic laboratory experiment, Schulman (1974) demonstrated that college students were likely to punish a black stimulus person for sexual encounters with a white. Unfortunately, the judge in the case ruled that it was unnecessary to consider hearing an expert witness describe such research, and unnecessary to ask potential jurors questions regarding their attitudes toward interracial dating or marriage, or interracial children. Yet these matters were potentially relevant to whether jurors could be impartial.

The court's decision in this case suggests the need for applied psychologists to present their work more clearly and to wider audiences so that judges and lawyers can become convinced of psychology's potential to contribute to the fair and impartial operation of the criminal justice system. The law may not see color, but jurors and judges and lawyers do. Research has shown that a substantial proportion of jurors do not believe that defendants in criminal cases are innocent until proven guilty (Bonora & Krauss, 1983), and our analysis suggests that minority defendants are seen as even less innocent than others. The biases in the way that people judge others outside of the courtroom are not left on the courthouse steps when they go in (Rokeach & Vidmar, 1973).

ACKNOWLEDGMENTS

Portions of this paper were presented at the American Psychological Association meeting in Los Angeles, August, 1981. The authors are grateful to Martin Guyotte and Gerard Smits for statistical consultation.

Stephanie Nickerson thanks her father, Eugene Nickerson, for his careful reading of earlier drafts of this chapter.

REFERENCES

Allport, G. W. (1954). *The nature of prejudice*. New York: Doubleday.

Allport, G. W., & Postman, L. J. (1947). *The psychology of rumor*. New York: Holt, Rinehart & Winston.

Alvarez, N. L. (1982). Racial bias and the right to an impartial jury: A standard for allowing voir dire inquiry. *Hastings Law Journal, 33*, 959–983.

Barnett, J. J., & Feild, H. S. (1978). Character of the defendant and length of sentence in rape and burglary crimes. *Journal of Social Psychology, 104*, 271–277.

Bell, D. A., Jr. (1973). Racism in American courts: Cause for Black disruption or despair? *California Law Review, 761*, 165–203.

Bermant, G. (1977). *Conduct of the voir dire examination: Practices and opinions of federal district judges* (Report FJC-F-77-7). Washington, DC: Federal Judicial Center.

Bernard, J. L. (1979). Interaction between the race of the defendant and that of the jurors in determining verdicts. *Law and Psychological Review, 5*, 103–111.

Benokraitis, N. (1982). Racial exclusion in juries. *Journal of Applied Behavioral Sciences, 18*(1), 29–47.

Black, D. (1971). The social organization of arrest. *Stanford Law Review, 23*, 1087–1111.

Bonora, B., & Krauss, E. (Eds.), (1983). *Jurywork: Systematic techniques* (2nd ed.). New York: Clark Boardman.

Brigham, J., & Weissbach, T. (Eds.). (1972). *Racial attitudes in America: Analyses and findings of social psychology*. New York: Harper & Row.

Broeder, D. W. (1965). Voir dire examinations: An empirical study. *Southern California Law Review, 38*, 503–528.

Bromley, S., Saxe, L. & Crosby, F. (1977, April). *Black and white racism: An unobtrusive experimental assessment*. Paper presented at the annual meeting of the Eastern Psychological Association, Boston.

Bullock, H. A. (1961). Significance of the racial factor in the length of prison sentences. *Journal of Criminal Law, Criminology, and Police Science, 52*, 411–417.

Cannell, C. F., & Kahn, R. L. (1968). Interviewing. In G. Lindzey & E. Aronson (Eds.), *The handbook of social psychology* (Vol. 2, pp. 526–595). Reading: MA: Addison-Wesley.

Carlson, W. (1981, June 2). A ruling on questions to jurors. *San Francisco Chronicle*, p. 10.

Chambliss, W. J. & Seidman, R. B. (1971). *Law, order, and power*. Reading, MA: Addison-Wesley.

Charrow, R. P., & Charrow, V. R. (1979). Making legal language understandable: A psycholinguistic study of jury instructions. *Columbia Law Review, 79*, 1306–74.

Chester, G. (1970). *The ninth juror*. New York: Random House.

Crosby, F., Bromley, S., & Saxe, L. (1980). Recent unobtrusive studies of black and white discrimination and prejudice: A literature review. *Psychological Bulletin, 87*, 546–563.

Duncan, B. (1976). Differential social perceptions and attributions of intergroup violence: Testing the lower limits of stereotyping of blacks. *Journal of Personality and Social Psychology, 34*(4), 590–598.

Faranda, J. A., & Gaertner, S. L. (1979, April). The effect of inadmissable evidence introduced by the prosecution and the defense, and the defendant's race on the verdicts of high and low authoritarians. Paper presented at the annual meeting of the Eastern Psychological Association, New York.

Feild, H. S. (1979). Rape trials and jurors' decisions: A psychological analysis of the effects of victim, defendant, and case characteristics. *Law and Human Behavior, 3*, 261–284.

Foley, L. A., Chambin, M. H., & Fortenberry, J. H. (1979, August). The effects of race, socioeconomic status, and personality variables on jury decisions. Paper presented at the annual meeting of the American Psychological Association, New York.

Fram, S. J. (1982). Restricting inquiry into racial attitudes during the voir dire. *American Criminal Law Review, 19*(4), 719–750.

Gerard, J. B., & Terry, T. R. (1970). Discrimination against Negroes in the administration of criminal law in Missouri. *Washington State University Law Quarterly*, 415–437.

Gerbasi, K. S., Zuckerman, M., & Reis, H. T. (1977). Justice needs a blindfold: A review of mock jury research. *Psychological Bulletin, 84*, 323–345.

Gleason, J. M., & Harris, V. A. (1975). Race, socio-economic status, and perceived similarity as determinants of judgments by simulated jurors. *Social Behavior and Personality, 3*(2), 175–180.

Gray, D. B., & Ashmore, R. D. (1976). Biasing influences of defendants' characteristics on simulated sentencing. *Psychological Reports, 38*, 727–738.

Greenberg, M. S., & Ruback, R. B. (1982). *Social psychology of the criminal justice system*. Monterey, CA: Brooks/Cole.

Hagan, J. (1974). Extra-legal attributes and criminal sentencing: An assessment of a sociological viewpoint. *Law and Society Review, 8*, 357–383.

Haney, C. (1980). Psychology and legal change. *Law and Human Behavior, 4*, 147–199.

Hare, P. (1976). *Handbook of small group research* (2nd Ed.). New York: Free Press.

Hernton, C. (1965). *Sex and racism in America*. Garden City, NY: Doubleday.

Hilliard, T. O. (1978). Psychology, law and the Black community. *Law and Human Behavior, 2*(2), 107–131.

Hindelang, M. E. (1969). Equality under the law. *Journal of Criminal Law, Criminology and Political Science, 60*(3), 306–313.

Howard, J. C. (1975). Racial discrimination in sentencings. *Judicature, 59*, 120–125.

Kalven J., Jr., & Zeisel, H. (1966). *The American jury*. Boston: Little Brown.

Kovel, J. (1970). *White racism: A psychohistory*. New York: Pantheon.

Landy, D., & Aronson, E. (1969). The influence of the character of the criminal and his victim on the decisions of simulated jurors. *Journal of Experimental Social Psychology, 5*, 141–152.

Lipton, J. P. (1983). Racism in the jury box: The Hispanic defendant. *Hispanic Journal of Behavioral Sciences, 5*(3), 275–290.

Marshall, L., & Smith, A. (1984). *The social psychology of jury honesty during voir dire*. Unpublished manuscript, Boston University, Department of Psychology.

Mayo, C., & LaFrance, M. (1980). Toward an applicable social psychology. In M. Saks & R. Kidd (eds.) *Advances in applied social psychology* (Vol. 1, pp. 81–96). Hillsdale, NJ: Erlbaum.

Miller, A. G. (Ed.). (1972). *The social psychology of psychological research.* New York: The Free Press.

Miller, M., & Hewitt, J. (1978). Conviction of a defendant as a function of juror-victim racial similarity. *Journal of Social Psychology, 105,* 159–160.

Monahan, J., & Loftus, E. F. (1982). The psychology of law. *Annual Review of Psychology, 33,* 441–475.

Myrdal, G. (1944). *An American dilemma: The Negro problem and modern democracy* (Vol. II). New York: Pantheon.

Nemeth, C. (1981). Jury trials: Psychology and law. In L. Berkowitz (ed.), *Advances in experimental social psychology* (Vol. 14, pp. 309–367). New York: Academic Press.

Nemeth, C. H., & Sosis, R. H. (1973). A simulated jury study: Characteristics of the defendant and the jurors. *Journal of Social Psychology, 90,* 221–229.

Newsweek. (1986, May 12). Integrating the jury box. 70.

Padawer-Singer, A., & Singer, A. (1974). Voir dire by two lawyers: An essential safeguard. *Judicature, 57,* 386–391.

Petersilia, J. (1983). *Racial disparities in the criminal justice system.* Santa Monica, CA: The Rand Corporation.

Pruitt, C. R., & Wilson, J. Q. (1983). A longitudinal study of the effects of race on sentencing. *Law and Society Review, 17*(4), 613–635.

Reasons, C. E. & Kuykendall, J. L. (Eds.). (1972). *Race, crime and the law.* Pacific Palisades, CA: Goodyear.

Rokeach, M., & Vidmar, N. (1973). Testimony concerning possible jury bias in a Black Panther murder trial. *Journal of Applied Social Psychology, 3,* 19–29.

Rosenberg, M. J. (1965). When dissonance fails: On eliminating evaluation apprehension from attitude measurement. *Journal of Personality and Social Psychology, 1,* 28–42.

Schulman, G. I. (1974). Race, sex and violence: A laboratory test of the sexual threat of the Black male hypothesis. *American Journal of Sociology, 79*(3), 1260–1277.

Shatz, D. (1977). The trials of a juror. *New York State Bar Journal, 49,* 8-201, 232–236.

Silverstein, L. (1965). *Defense of the poor in criminal cases in American state courts.* Chicago: American Bar Foundation.

Simon, R. J. (1980). *The Jury: Its role in American Society.* Lexington, MA: Lexington Books.

Stember, C. H. (1976). *Sexual racism: The emotional barrier to an integrated society.* New York: Elsevier Scientific Publishing Company, Inc.

Suggs, D., & Sales, B. D. (1978). The art and science of conducting the voir dire. *Professional Psychology, 9,* 367–388.

Sunnafrank, M. & Fontes, N. E. (1981). General and crime related racial stereotypes and influences on juridic decisions. *Cornell Journal of Social Relations, 17*(1), 1–15.

Swain v. Alabama (1964). *United States Reports, 380,* 202–247.

Taylor, S., Jr. (1986, May 1). High court limits excluding blacks as jury members. *New York Times,* 1, B8.

Thornberry, T. P. (1973). Race, socioeconomic status and sentencing in the juvenile justice system. *Journal of Criminal Law and Criminology, 64,* 90–98.

Ugwuegbu, D. C. E. (1976). Black jurors' personality trait attributions to a rape case defendant. *Social Behavior and Personality, 4,* 193–201.

Ugwuegbu, D. C. E. (1979). Racial and evidential factors in juror attributions of legal responsibility. *Journal of Experimental Social Psychology, 15*, 133–146.

Weiten, W., & Diamond, S. S. (1979). A critical review of the jury simulation paradigm: The case of defendant characteristics. *Law and Human Behavior, 3*, 71–93.

Wilson, D. W. & Donnerstein, E. (1977). Guilty or not guilty? A look at the "simulated" jury paradigm. *Journal of Applied Social Psychology, 7*(2), 175–190.

Wolfgang, M. E., & Riedel, N. (1973). Race, judicial discretion, and the death penalty. *American Academy of Political and Social Science, 407*, 119–123.

Woodmansee, J. J., & Cook, S. N. (1967). Dimensions of verbal racial attitudes: Their identification and measurement. *Journal of Personality and Social Psychology, 7*(3), 240–250.

Zeisel, H. (1980). Forward. *Law and Contemporary Problems, 43*(4), 1–7.

RACISM: A CULTURAL ANALYSIS OF THE PROBLEM

James M. Jones

Department of Psychology
University of Delaware
Newark, Delaware 19711

INTRODUCTION

This chapter takes the view that despite the fact that pollsters report that racial attitudes of white Americans are becoming more tolerant, racism continues to be a problem in America. Racism is a problem because there continue to be major disparities between black and white citizens which reflect the fact that historical biases have not been ameliorated; there are substantially lower participation rates for black Americans in major sectors of American commerce, education, political, and legal activities which suggest that blacks are still not participating as full citizens in this society; there is evidence that the more positive racial attitudes reported by pollsters do not reflect the ongoing white antipathies toward blacks demonstrated by ingroup preference and self-interest.

A review of current statistics on racial disparities in health, education, and welfare and related life circumstances reveals the substantial black–white gaps that since the mid-1960s have not diminished in spite of absolute gains for blacks. Consideration of aspects of black culture will suggest that while discrimination on the basis of race (skin color) has been legislatively extirpated, continued biases associated with cultural aspects of black life abound.

Given the fact of a multicultural population, group differences are a reality with potential to be a major source of strength to the fabric of this society. However, for this to happen, we need to find ways to make people in power appreciate this potential and utilize and/or share their power in ways that ensure broader contributions and participation of racial and ethnic minority segments of the population.

279

This chapter is organized to explore these observations and arguments. Using the black–white relationship as a model of the problem, the first section explores statistical evidence for the continuing, and in some cases widening, gap between the well-being of whites and blacks. The second section considers ways of understanding the causes of the problem (systemic bias versus individual inadequacy) and the differential remedies these causes imply. The third section examines an approach to black culture which emphasizes its multidimensionality as well as its evolutionary character. Aspects of black culture offered as guides to this discussion are organized around the acronym *TRIOS*, standing respectively for *T*ime, *R*hythm, *I*mprovisation, *O*ral Expression, and *S*pirituality. Following the discussion of TRIOS, the chapter considers the relative effects of skin color and culture as the basis of contemporary racial disadvantage. The role of power in maintaining racial disadvantage is also discussed. Finally, it is suggested that the amelioration of racial bias requires a more inclusive multidimensional view of psychosocial characteristics and their corresponding cultural determinants, and the dynamics of intergroup relations that follow from perceived ingroup similarity and outgroup differences.

A LOOK AT THE PROBLEM

There is factual, as well as presumptive, evidence that race, gender, age, and ethnicity all influence behavioral outcomes in this society. The central concern of this volume is with ways in which outcomes are *negatively* influenced by these factors. These negatively influencing factors are

Prejudice:
  The prior negative judgment of the members of a race or religion or the occupants of any other significant social role, held in disregard of the facts that contradict it . . . an affective, categorical mode of mental functioning involving rigid prejudgment and misjudgment of human groups. (Jones, 1972, p. 61)

Discrimination:
  Those systematically differential behavioral outcomes associated with social categories. It is seen as following from the prior negative judgments characteristic of prejudice.

Racism:
  Results from the transformation of race prejudice and/or ethnocentrism through the exercise of power against a racial group defined as inferior, by individuals and institutions with the intentional or unintentional support of the entire culture. (Jones, 1972, p. 172)

While each of these negatively influencing factors creates problems of opportunity for groups in this society, the remedies implied by each vary. For example, it is usually considered that prejudice, being a *prior judgment,* only requires one to bring the prejudiced person in contact with the victim to learn about the group characteristics, to reduce stereotypes, and to rely on more individuating information in making judgments about a specific member of that group (Deutsch & Collins, 1951; Lockesley, Ortiz, & Hepburn, 1980). Discrimination, on the other hand, is the behavioral consequence of such negative judgments and its remedy is often quota-based programs of equal opportunity and affirmative action. Racism, too, has several different characteristics, one of which is *institutional racism,* which does not require proof of intention to discriminate and may be remedied by affirmative action programs. The most intractable, yet possibly most critical, is *cultural racism,* which requires a new look at cultural assumptions and their manifestations in social organization.

In the following pages, I summarize some of the evidence for the negative consequences of being black in this country. I consider a number of explanations of these disparities in a later section. Although I am concerned with racial bias here, it is obvious that in many cases, the disparaties have economic foundations to them. I do not here claim that racial disparities now are wholly independent of economic considerations. In this light, I agree with Wilson (1978) that economic class is a powerful determinant of outcomes for all citizens of this country. I do not, however, argue that economic condition is more or less important than race, but suggest that the race/culture intersection defines a critical dimension of racism in contemporary society.

HEALTH

Table 1 summarizes trends in mortality for black and white Americans. A black child born in 1982 is nearly twice as likely to die in infancy as a white child (1.94 times). This likelihood is *greater* than it was in 1950 (1.64 times)! In spite of this early risk, by the teenage years, racial differences in mortality rates are small. The death rates for black males nearly equals that for white males (142 vs. 145 per 100,000 population), and the rate for black females is slightly more than for white females (55 vs. 50 per 100,000 population). However, the racial disparity grows exponentially for both males and females during the young adult decades of ages 20s, 30s and 40s, where the death rate for blacks is 1.44, 2.77, and 2.16 times that for whites among

TABLE 1   Mortality Health Statistics for Black and White Americans

Infant mortality (1950–1981): deaths/1,000 live births				
	1950	1960	1970	1982	Percentage
Black	43.9	44.3	32.6	20.0	−54.4
White	26.8	22.9	17.8	10.5	−60.8
Black–white ratio	1.64	1.93	1.83	1.94	

Death rates by all causes (1980): deaths per 100,000 population, by age group							
	15–19		20–24		30–34		40–44	
	B	W	B	W	B	W	B	W
Male	142	145	360	250	410	148	802	370
Female	54.6	50.3	101	54.6	148	78	390	170

Visits to physician (1981): millions			
	Office	Emergency room	Phone
White	633 (75%)	99 (11.7%)	112 (13.3%)
Black	71 (64%)	33 (30.0%)	6 (6.0%)
Black as a percentage of the total	10.1	25	5.1

Disability days lost: millions			
	1970	1979	1980	1981
White	2,526	3,468	3,518	3,622
Black	365	585	580	575
Black as a percentage of the total	12.6	14.4	14.1	13.7

Note. From the Statistical Abstract of the United States. 104th Edition. U.S. Department of Commerce, Bureau of the Census. U.S. Government Printing Office. Washington, D.C. 20402. 1984.

men; and 1.85, 1.90 and 2.29 times that among women. That is, the mortality rate for blacks in the 30- to 40-year age group is 2.47 times as great as for whites. Mortality rates for black infants, by contrast are only 1.94 times that for white infants. Thus, while racial differences in infant mortality are highly publicized, having survived infancy, a black person is at *increasing* mortality risk relative to whites as he or she gets older!

Of some modest interest is the additional observation that 30% of the visits blacks make to the doctor are made in the emergency room of hospitals (contrasted to 11.7% for whites). Disability days lost on the job might be viewed as an indication of overall illness rates. Here, blacks lose slightly more days than whites as a percentage of the total population. However, when factoring in the high unemployment rate for blacks, it is probably even larger.

EDUCATION

In education, differences continue but have been reduced more than some other areas (see Table 2). In 1982, 51.6% of all black people were enrolled in school compared to 47.9% for whites. More significant is the number of years of schooling completed. In 1960, blacks had completed an average of 8.0 years, or elementary school education. By 1982, this figure had risen to 12.2, or slightly more than a high school education. The increase in the number of high school graduates also shows a major increase from 10.1% to 54.9% of the black population. However, in 1982, this is still some 16% less than the percentage of white high school graduates.

The figures for illiteracy are most promising. In 1979, the illiteracy rate for black and white young people ages 14 to 24 was identical (.2%). Illiteracy rate gaps show consistent diminution from 1959 to 1979 and from young to old. This difference does not reflect, however, new forms of literacy in languages, business, and computers.

CRIME

The crime statistics from Table 3 speak for themselves. Blacks are arrested at a rate more than twice their percentage of the population, and at a higher rate in 1982 than in 1974. Though it has declined modestly from the 7.05 figure of 1975, the homicide rate among blacks is still over five and a half times that for whites. The victimization rate is also higher for blacks, though not as great as the homicide difference. Blacks are in jail at a rate nearly four times their numbers in the population and are executed at a rate more than five times their percentage (see also Chapter 9). In fact, more than half of all executions from 1930 to 1982 were of black people.

It is important to make note of the well-known disparity between blacks and whites in the types of crimes committed. White-collar

TABLE 2 Education Statistics for Black and White Americans

	School enrollment (percentage of the population)			
	1960	1970	1980	1982
White	56.4	56.2	48.9	47.9
Black	55.9	57.4	53.9	51.6

	Amounts of schooling, persons aged 25 and older			
	1960	1970	1980	1982
White				
Years completed	10.6	12.1	12.5	12.6
Percentage of high school graduates	41.1	52.3	68.6	71.0
Black				
Years completed	8.0	9.8	12.0	12.2
Percentage of high school graduates	20.1	31.4	51.2	54.9

	Illiteracy (percentage of the population)					
	1959		1969		1979	
Age	B	W	B	W	B	W
14–24	1.2	0.5	0.5	0.2	0.2	0.2
25–44	5.1	0.8	1.3	0.4	0.5	0.2
45–65	11.3	1.8	5.5	0.7	2.6	0.5
65+	25.5	5.1	16.7	2.3	6.8	0.8

Note. From the *Statistical Abstract of the United States.* 104th Edition. U.S. Department of Commerce, Bureau of the Census. U.S. Government Printing Office. Washington, D.C. 20402. 1984.

crimes, which are associated with white people, are more difficult to detect, are less frequently prosecuted and are, generally, regarded not so much as crimes as ingenuity gone awry. E. F. Hutton and General Dynamics' Mr. Paul Thayer recently have been publicly exposed for major white collar crimes involving millions of dollars. A total of 4 years in jail (for Mr. Thayer) and a modest fine for E. F. Hutton is the sum total of the penalties. Thus, the significant disparities reflect, as much as anything else, socioeconomic differences in circumstances related to criminal behavior as well as social values implicated in their prosecution.

TABLE 3 Crime-Related Statistics for Black and White Americans

	Arrests							
	1974		1977		1980		1982	
	n	%	n	%	n	%	n	%
White	4,112	72.5	6,429	73.6	7,146	75.1	7,070	71.8
Black	1,562	27.5	2,308	26.4	2,375	24.9	2,777	28.2

	Homicide rate per 100,000		
	1975	1977	1980
White	11.9	11.5	14.1
Black	83.9	72.0	80.1
Black–white ratio	7.05	6.26	5.68

	Victimization rate against persons/1,000		
	1975	1977	1980
White	34	32	33
Black	42	41	50
Black–white ratio	1.23	1.28	1.51

	Jail inmates: 1978	
	n	%
White	89,418	58
Black	65,104	42

	Executions (1930–1982) for crimes							
	Murder		Rape		Other		Total	
	n	%	n	%	n	%	n	%
White	1,676	51	48	10.6	39	55.7	1,760	46
Black	1,631	49	405	89.4	31	44.3	2,067	54

Note. From the Statistical Abstract of the United States. 104th Edition. U.S. Department of Commerce, Bureau of the Census. U.S. Government Printing Office. Washington, D.C. 20402. 1984.

INCOME

Table 4 shows what is widely known: Blacks have lower incomes than whites. The median income for blacks in 1982 was $11,968, while for whites it was $21,117. This figure represents a 1.9% decline in income for whites, but a 4.5% decline for blacks. So, blacks are, relative to whites, *worse* off now than 15 years ago! In 1967, 41.7% of blacks earned less than $10,000. In 1982, that figure had risen to 42.6%. In 1967, only 5.3% of blacks earned more than $35,000, while in 1982, this figure had risen to 8.6%. The corresponding figures for whites were 16.8% in 1967 and 23.5% in 1982. The black–white gap *increased* over the 15 years from 11.5% to 14.9%!

Much discussion centers around single-parent households. The Moynihan Report (U. S. Department of Labor, 1965) attributed the poor economic plight of blacks to this trend. However, in 1982, the black–white gap in income is constant whether speaking of a married-couple household, a male-headed household, or a female-headed household. In fact, the *gap* is least for female-headed households.

Finally, it is interesting to note that in 1982 there were both more blacks and more whites below the poverty line than there were in 1967. However, one is still three times as likely to be in poverty if one is black than if one is white.

One final income-related observation: of 9,833,000 businesses identified in 1977, only 231,000 of 2.3% were black-owned. The $633 billion GNP of American business is contrasted with $8,645,000 for black-owned businesses or one hundredth of 1% (.01%).

SUMMARY

The problem, then, is that being black in this society puts you at risk on almost every indicator of well being and opportunity we can calculate. It is often argued that class not race is the major determinant now of opportunity and achievement. However recent data provided by the College Entrance Examination Board (1985) shows that SAT scores for blacks coming from families earning over $50,000 per year are still *lower* than SAT's of whites coming from families earning less than $6,000 per year. Similarly, income disparities between blacks and whites are *greatest* for income levels above $35,000 per year. So, while we certainly agree that being born black into poverty in the inner city truncates opportunities considerably in this society, relative

TABLE 4 Income Earning for Black and White Americans, 1967–1982

	Individual income: % earning each amount							
	1967		1977		1980		1982	
Annual income	B	W	B	W	B	W	B	W
$10,000	41.7	21.3	38.5	20.2	42.0	21.3	42.6	21.6
20,000	32.8	28.3	28.9	23.7	27.1	24.6	27.0	25.5
35,000	20.2	33.6	22.8	32.6	20.5	29.8	21.7	29.3
50,000	3.8	10.1	6.7	13.8	7.7	14.8	6.4	13.9
60,000	1.5	6.7	3.1	10.1	2.7	9.5	2.2	9.6

	Median household income (constant dollars)			
	1967		1982	
	B	W	B	W
Household	12,504	21,535	11,968	21,117
Percentage of change			-4.3	-1.9
Family				
Married			19,638	25,513
Male head			14,865	21,117
Female head			7,921	13,076
Nonfamily				
Male			8,345	13,832
Female			4,812	7,808
Multigroup			12,354	22,824

	Poverty level (percentage below)							
	1967		1977		1980		1982	
	B	W	B	W	B	W	B	W
	34.7	10.0	31.3	8.9	32.5	10.2	35.6	12.0

Note. From the Statistical Abstract of the United States. 104th Edition. U.S. Department of Commerce, Bureau of the Census. U.S. Government Printing Office. Washington, D.C. 20402. 1984.

opportunity and achievement continue to be unevenly distributed across racial and ethnic groups after taking socio-economic status (SES) origins into account. This is the problem. While people of widely varying points of view might agree that the preceding disparities are the problem, they will strongly disagree on both the causes of the problem and the approaches to solutions implied by them. The next section reviews different interpretations of the causes of racial disparities and the implications of these interpretations for understanding contemporary race relations.

WAYS OF UNDERSTANDING THE PROBLEM

The title of this volume, *Prejudice, Discrimination, and Racism*, identifies three critical, highly associated but clearly separable, aspects of race relations in the United States. Historically, psychology, particularly social psychology, has focused its attention on prejudice: a faulty generalization from a group characterization (stereotype) to an individual member of the group, irrespective of either (1) the accuracy of the group stereotype, or (2) the applicability of the group characterization to the individual in question. This prevailing approach clearly emphasizes individual characteristics of judgment and information-processing tendencies and capabilities (see Chapter 5). The resultant attitudinal biases have historically been associated with both a negative motivation to harm dissimilar others or a positive motivation to help similar others.

A significant body of persuasive evidence has accumulated in the past few years suggesting that prejudice has a general cognitive information-processing basis (see Chapters 5 and 6) which is exploited by the realities of interracial dynamics in this society. The illusory correlation idea (Hamilton & Gifford, 1976) offers a basis for associating negative traits with blacks; the cognitive complexity idea (Linville & Jones, 1980) sets conditions for both the negative bias against blacks as well as potential for positive bias based on interracial contact and group boundaries; Brewer (1979) has presented strong evidence for the inclusionary dimension of prejudice (ingroup favoritism).

Additional evidence has shown that actual perceptual and behavioral bias against blacks continues to be widespread in spite of attitudinal surveys suggesting that racial attitudes are becoming more positive. Crosby, Bromley, and Saxe (1980) have presented persuasive evidence for bias against blacks in helping, aggression, and nonverbal indicators of hostility. Gaertner and Dovidio (Chapter 3) argue persuasively for the continued biases of whites who are well intentioned. McConahay (Chapter 4) makes a similar argument citing the displacement of conventional negativity to contemporary symbols of racial disaffection (busing, affirmative action, etc.).

The notion of prejudice is concerned with individual cognitive judgments and the affective tone attached to them. Yet, the statistics summarized in the previous section are clearly aggregated for blacks as a group. Can one reconstruct these group outcomes on the basis of individual antipathies? I believe not. The wide range of differences in disparate outcomes across regions of the country, age groups, economic, political and educational strata, and so on are more parsimoniously explained by a patterning of systemic responses to black Americans. The first idea we should consider is *discrimination*.

Discrimination refers simply to differential treatment of individuals on the basis of their social category by people or the institutional policies they create and enforce. As we noted earlier, discrimination may be thought of as the behavioral consequences of prejudice. In this regard, it was institutional racism (the institutionalized form of racial discrimination) that led President Lyndon Johnson to issue Executive Order 2301 establishing affirmative action as a remedy for discrimination. Because President Johnson viewed racial discrimination as an institutional problem, the remedy was not required to meet an *intentionality* criterion. That is, evidence of racial disparities, such as those described earlier, was ipso facto evidence of discrimination and institutional culpability, and affirmative action was seen as both a necessary and appropriate remedy.

President Johnson was persuaded by the report of the Kerner Commission (National Advisory Commission on Civil Disorders, 1968) that the problem of black Americans was caused by white racism and, further, that white racism was found in institutional practices and was responsible for the pages of statistics showing the disadvantaged plight of black Americans. While the fact of negative disparities for black Americans was persuasive for President Johnson, President Reagan's administration takes an opposite view.

The Reagan administration's approach to affirmative action, led by the Head of the Division of Civil Rights in the Justice Department, Bradford Reynolds, rests on two major points. Before a remedy for alleged institutional discrimination can be considered, according to this view, the aggrieved party must prove

1. The discrimination was intentional, and
2. The accuser was him or herself *personally* discriminated against.

The first point significantly reduces the scope of remedies of racial discrimination since only in those cases where intent can be proven is any remedy required. The second point further restricts the domain of discrimination remedies because only if a specific case of discrimination can be documented is any remedy required, *and only for the documented case!* Therefore, the aggregate basis for determining the existence of discrimination with corresponding widespread group remediation (i.e., quota-based affirmative action) would no longer serve to eliminate restrictive practices. Therefore, one could characterize President Johnson's policies as consistent with the traditional liberal view that poverty and dependency reside in causes external to the victims; whereas, President Reagan's rings a more conservative theme suggesting that a person's disadvantage is not caused by differential treatment, but by the victim's personal inadequacies.

In the first section of this chapter, I reviewed data which revealed racial disparities on several meaningful indices of life in America. However, just as the philosophies of the administrations of Presidents Reagan and Johnson clearly illustrate, an understanding of and reaction to these disparities depend largely on the perceived locus of causality. Figure 1 depicts these two contrasting viewpoints or models for understanding the source of these racial disparities.

The critical starting point is the fact of racial disparities, found in the middle of the models. Moving from here to the top, we have Model 1, which presumes that racial disparities result from systemic or structural features of the nation's institutions (and the persons who run them). These systemic features may be the result of individuals who act in prejudicial ways, the historical legacy of denial, oppression, and legislative, judicial, educational, and economic arrangements which thwarted and suppressed black Americans (often by design). This system-blame point of view is associated with Allport's (1954) telescopic model of prejudice occurring at increasingly macrosystemic levels of society and Jones' (1972) analysis of institutional and cultural racism. Although the system-blame approach is generally at a molar level of social analysis, it does not preclude the more molecular approaches of traditional social psychological analyses which focus on individuals and attitudes and behaviors because it also recognizes the *prejudice–discrimination* link.

Moving to the bottom of Figure 1, we arrive at another perception of causes of racial disparities. In this view, there is an implicit assumption that the system (both structure and function) is an opportunity-based meritocracy. Failure to benefit from or be successful in the

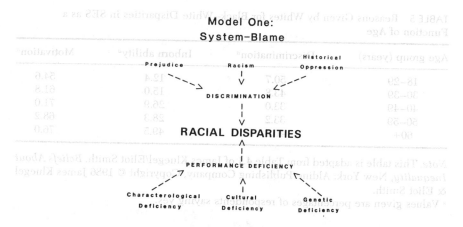

FIGURE 1. Models of racial disparities.

system can only be attributed to inadequacies in the individual. This individual-blame point of view accepts the idea that blacks are worse off than whites as a group, but attributes this disparity to inferior performance of blacks, which is in turn attributed to their inferior character, culture, or genes. When a society espouses meritocratic bases of outcome predicated on a belief in equity (outcomes proportional to inputs) then such disparities can be fully justified on the basis of presumed deficiencies.

A possible midway position between Models 1 and 2 acknowledges past discrimination but not contemporary bias. This view is expressed in two forms: (1) there is no contemporary inequality of treatment, therefore, no needed remediation; and (2) contemporary inequality is only due to historical inequities, and discrimination against whites is inappropriate because it attempts to remedy a past wrong with a contemporary one.

Most distressing is the evidence that the general tendency among white Americans is to view racial disparities from the perspective of Model 2. Kluegel and Smith (1986) have presented substantial and convincing data that show white Americans believe racial disparities in SES are due primarily to lack of motivation among blacks, that there are no structural impediments to SES advancement for blacks, and that the system is an opportunity structure open to *anyone* with the individual characteristics to get ahead.

TABLE 5   Reasons Given by Whites for Black–White Disparities in SES as a
Function of Age

Age group (years)	Discrimination[a]	Inborn ability[a]	Motivation[a]
18–29	50.7	12.4	54.6
30–39	43.8	15.0	61.8
40–49	33.0	26.9	71.0
50–59	33.2	28.3	68.2
60+	40.4	49.5	76.0

Note. This table is adapted from Table 4.1 of James Kluegel/Eliot Smith, *Beliefs About Inequality,* New York: Aldine Publishing Company, Copyright © 1986 James Kluegel & Eliot Smith.
[a] Values given are percentages of respondents saying yes.

Based on white respondents' answers to questions about causes of SES differences between blacks and whites (see Table 5), the following profile emerged: In the age range 40–60 years where we might presume the highest concentration of people with power and influence to occur, only 33% believe discrimination is a cause of SES differences between blacks and whites, while 70% believe motivational factors are responsible. While the profile improves significantly for younger white Americans, they too feel motivation is a more prevalent cause than discrimination for black–white SES disparities. This blame-the-victim approach (cf. Caplan & Nelson, 1973; Ryan, 1971) is consistent with a general tendency to make dispositional attributions for the behavior of others and to commit the "fundamental attributional error" (Pettigrew, 1978; Ross, 1977) by discounting environmental influences on behavior.

Obviously the remedy to black–white disparities will vary depending on whether one believes Model 1 or Model 2 gives the best accounting. However, the two approaches are not mutually exclusive. That is, historically, the systems of discrimination and oppression (systematic banking and real estate practices of red-lining, the separate but equal doctrine legalized by the *Plessy v. Ferguson* decision of 1896, and employment discrimination) not only created the conditions of racial disparities summarized previously, but also contributed substantially to the creation of a ghetto environment in which basic opportunities were not available.

Being in a restricted, disadvantaged, and unpredictable environment offers minimal advantage to institutionalized education, offers little employment, and maintains a reward structure that encourages certain forms of lawlessness and family disintegration. The more suc-cessfully one adapts to this environment and its requirements for suc-cess, the less likely one is to develop attributes that are functional in the broader society. Thus, the intersection of Models 1 and 2 can be conceived as a sinister double-bind, such that short-term adaptation may lead to long-term disadvantage. This problem is further exacer-bated by the prevailing notion that the circumstances of disadvantage and truncated opportunity are actually *caused* by those who are vic-timized by it.

There is ample evidence that Americans' belief in the principle of equity translates further to a belief that this a *just* society (Lerner, 1980). This leads to a general individual-blame orientation, as we have already seen from the Kluegel and Smith (1986) data. But it also further underscores the double-bind. Blacks have less of nearly every tangible evidence of socioeconomic success than whites. There are the differential outcomes of living in this society. To maintain one's belief in equity (and justice), the differential outcomes *must* be bal-anced by perception of differential *inputs*. The lesser inputs of blacks are inferred by whites to be lower motivation and deficiencies of character and ability (see Model 2). Thus, whites are in positions of power, which enable them to define what shall constitute acceptable inputs, and further, are and have been in positions to structure black environments such that adaptation to them decreases the likelihood of developing those characteristics rewarded by the supposed meritoc-racy within the broader society.

The preceding double-bind for black Americans, fueled by a power differential and sustained by white's self-interest is the heart of the notion of *cultural racism*. In this view, the maintenance and func-tioning of opportunity structures (i.e., formal institution of education and training, employment and informal associations that facilitate ac-cess to opportunity) in this country is predicated on ceratin values of individuality, future-orientation, written and material approaches to accomplishment which define appropriate inputs. If a person does not or cannot operate within this framework, he or she is either obliged to operate within another opportunity structure (usually at variance with the prevailing societal one) or is at a disadvantage within the majority context. If a group has evolved from a cultural legacy and tradition at variance with this framework, it too is at a collective disadvantage or must develop alternate routes to the mainstream opportunity struc-ture. That is, this group must find ways to use the cultural legacy instrumentally to gain the opportunity for development, growth, and accomplishment in this society. In the following section, I discuss one approach to racial disparities that is based on this view of cultural racism.

BLACK CULTURE: THE TRIOS APPROACH

Racism as an explanation for racial disparities is associated with the system-blame approach. Individual racists are presumed to develop and maintain racially biased systems, while institutions operate in such a fashion that blacks receive less of the positive outcomes dispensed, and more of the negative sanctions. The authorizing, enabling, and guiding force behind both individual and institutional forms of bias is the cultural context with its assumptions of value, opportunity, accomplishment, and merit.

Black motivational and ability deficiencies are offered as explanations for racial disparities by individual-blame proponents, based in part on the notion that blacks have inherent (genetic or cultural) tendencies and/or capacities that put them at a disadvantage in an open, competitive meritocracy. The cultural perspective on black–white disparities suggests that negative adaptations to slavery and oppression have left blacks with behavioral, cognitive, and attitudinal characteristics that run counter to the norms of this society.

The cultural approach taken here is conceived to have two principle components.

REACTIONARY COMPONENT

This approach suggests that black Americans lost whatever culture they may have had in Africa and that such as there is any black culture at all, it consists in the collective adaptations blacks have made to a racist and oppressive society. Because many of these so-called adaptations are considered maladaptive in the larger society, a culture of poverty or cultural disadvantage perspective describes this conception.

EVOLUTIONARY COMPONENT

This view suggests that black culture represents the unfolding of a cultural core laid in an African past and characterized in function, if not form, across the cultures of the African diaspora.

The comprehensive system-blame point of view expressed here is that the system of government that unfolded from the cultural legacy of British colonial racism and imperialism accomplished the intricate patterns of racist control by

1. Oppressing and dehumanizing blacks in ways that created a hostile, pernicious, and largely untenable environment to which they as a group had to adapt—to which adaptation now is characterized within the reactionary perspective of black culture.[1]

2. Establishing a cultural context in which certain attributes and values (among them white skin) were held up as the standard of conduct and competence against which all alternatives were judged deficent. Beginning with skin color, the black presence and cultural style was viewed as a persistent and deficient alternative.

If one believes that black culture has a significant evolutionary component deriving from an African legacy just as black color clearly derives from that same legacy, then black Americans are disadvantaged not only by the color of their skin, but also by the content of their character. This, in my view, is the problem of cultural racism.

There is one other perspective that needs to be considered. Cole (1970) suggested that black culture consists in three parts:

A. *Mainstream Experience.* Blacks, as with all citizens of this country, participate in the American Way. Differences exist, to be sure, but we all "die and pay taxes," although some die sooner and some pay proportionately more in taxes!

B. *Minority Experience.* The sense of being a numerical political or power minority is shared with other groups, such as, at varying times, ethnic groups, poor people, women, older people, et cetera. When one is in such a situation, the concerns with powerlessness, discrimination, and disadvantage lead to common experiences.

C. *Black Experience.* Those experiences peculiar to being black in this society, comprising both reactionary and evolutionary components, represent aspects of black culture that do not include features common to others. Cole (1970) suggests these features include *soul* (defined as long suffering) and *style* (described as the individual patterns of expressions).

Thus, black culture and black personality that derives from that culture are multifaceted over both time and modality. That is, the reactionary–evolutionary distinction implies that elements of black culture have emerged and been elaborated over different historical

---

[1] It should be noted that reaction to such oppressive circumstances also has been a source of strength and resilience for black people.

eras and circumstances, and the three-tiered dimensions of main-stream, minority, and black cultural components combine in differing ways across people and groups. These multidimensional bases of black cultural experience can be construed with the overall require-ment of living in and adjusting to a multiracial society, and the facets of individual and collective adaptation both drive behavior and re-spond to it. That is, individual and collective behavioral styles both express the preferences of blacks and inform the mode and nature of adaptation to the environmental realities.

The challenge for a black person is, in this view, to determine how to integrate the necessities of adapting to an often oppressive and discriminatory system, and the desire to be expressive of those values, beliefs, and preferences that are the legacy of centuries of cultural evolution. The notion of *biculturality* is a way of identifying the dy-namic of this integrative process, with the challenge of rationalizing the demands of functional instrumentality and preferred expressive-ness. That they often conflict makes the problem all the more difficult.

In the following section, I review the *TRIOS* concept as one ap-proach to bicultural integration. The concept attempts to specify di-mensions of human experience on which there may be evolutionary cultural differences between an African and European tradition, and for which adjustments and accommodations to the instrumentality–expressiveness issues must be made. The long view of TRIOS should be as a balancing of human attributes that follow from cultural func-tion and structure evolving over time. The patterning of these attrib-utes within people and across groups will describe new ways of per-ceiving and evaluating inputs to a meritocratic society.

TRIOS

TRIOS is an acronym standing for five dimensions of human experi-ence: time, rhythm, improvisation, oral expression, and spirituality. The concepts emerged from my analysis of racial differences in sports performance (Jones & Hochner, 1973), African religion and philoso-phy (Jones, 1972; Mbiti, 1970), Trinidadian culture (Jones & Liver-pool, 1976), and psychotherapy with black clients (Jones & Block, 1984). For a detailed review of the development of the TRIOS ideas, see Jones (1979).

These five dimensions reflect basic ways in which individuals and cultures orient themselves to living. They refer to how we experience and organize life, make decisions, arrive at beliefs, and derive mean-ing. TRIOS is important because on these dimensions of human expe-

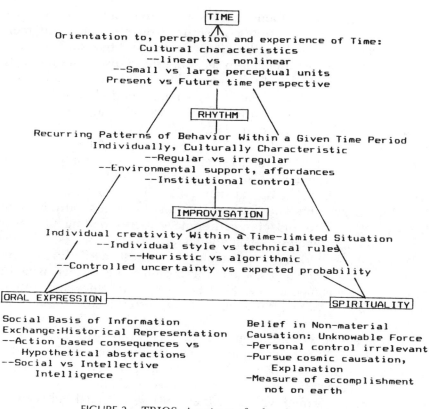

FIGURE 2.   TRIOS: A quintet of cultural concepts.

rience, we will find divergences between the Euro-American and Afro-American perspectives. The culture in which we live has evolved from the Euro-American perspective, but both have interacted and necessarily share in the fabric of contemporary culture.

TIME

The cornerstone of TRIOS is Time. Figure 2 depicts time at the apex of the TRIOS configuration because time is integral to all of life, to being. To paraphrase Descartes, *tempis fugit, ergo sum*. Time is an important concept for understanding racism for several reasons.

1. Cultures differ significantly in how they organize, perceive and value time. One of the enduring findings in psychology is the relationship between future time perspective (FTP) and achievement attitudes and behavior. Future time perspective is defined as the length of the future time span that is conceptualized (Wallace, 1956). De

Volder and Lens (1982) found that among a group of high school boys, grade point average and study persistence were associated with more positive regard for goals in the distant future and that studying hard was perceived as instrumental to reaching these distant future goals. Leshan (1952) found that the stories told by middle-class adolescents described action that took place over a longer period of time (e.g., 4 months) than the action in stories told by lower-class adolescents (e.g., 30 minutes). The literature on delay of gratification (Mischel, 1958, 1961a, 1961b) concerns the temporal span within which certain levels of inducement retain their reward value. It was proposed in the original studies conducted in Trinidad that Trinidadians of African descent had a shorter temporal span for reward than Trinidadians of East Indian descent. This finding has now been generally extrapolated to other race and class differences corresponding to black–lower-class deficiencies in delay behavior.

While ample evidence accumulates to suggest that failing to conceptualize goals, behaviors, and rewards along an ever-increasing future time dimension puts one at risk for successful achievement, there is also evidence that FTP is a particularly westernized cultural manifestation. For example, Levine, West, and Reis (1980) examined a variety of differences between Brazilian and American (Californian) attitudes toward time and found consistent differences such that Brazilians could be described as less interested in and responsive to temporal accuracy (as measured by public clocks and an individual's watch), less concerned with timeliness in interpersonal behavior (as measured by concern with being on time or late), and more impressed with people who were *not* punctual (indicated by ratings of success of people who always came late).

In addition to showing, generally, that Brazilians have a different conception of behavioral enactment and evaluation of punctuality, Levine and Bartlett (1984) have shown that the time sense may combine with *individuality* to produce the westernized sense of FTP. That is, Levine and Bartlett measured pace of life in a large and a middle-sized city in each of six countries and found it was possible to order the six countries by the speed with which people walked and made change in the post office, and maintained accurate clocks. From fastest to slowest pace of life, the authors reported the following order: Japan, England, United States, Italy, Taiwan, and Indonesia. The authors went on to propose that if coronary risk associated with a sense of time urgency was associated with pace of life, the incidence of coronary heart disease should follow the same order. The generalized relationship of coronary heart disease and pace of life did not obtain.

Japan, which had the fastest pace of life, had a lower coronary heart disease rate than the United States, England, and Italy. The authors speculate that the Japanese interest in group efficiency, production, and achievement may be the critical contrast with the more individualistic orientation of, say, the United States. Thus, the value of individualism may combine with FTP and time urgency to produce the achieving attitudes and behaviors we find in published literature and in everyday life.

Finally, it should be noted that in African philosophy, temporal perspective is decidedly not future oriented, and in fact, Swahili language does not even have a word for future (Mbiti, 1970). Rather, time is reckoned from the present, *sasa*, to the past, *zamani*, with meaning reserved only for events that take place in the present or the relatively near future.

2. The basis for FTP is a linear view of the movement of time. The linear assumption makes the future the inevitable point toward which the present moves. The present becomes a way station, a context for the development of strategies to move toward the future and to influence the nature and content of future outcomes. By contrast, a nonlinear perspective concentrates on what Ornstein (1977) calls the extended present. Events happening now are valued for their intrinsic worth, not for their instrumental value toward achieving a future goal, as Devolder and Lens (1982) found with white high school students.

Zimbardo, Marshall, and Maslach (1971) actually tested differences between people with a hypnotically induced extended present and those who were normally time-oriented. They found that in addition to using fewer future-tense verbs, these present-people were less responsive to social constraints (for example, experimenter directions) and less able to draw on idealized or abstract representations of forms necessary to execute drawings. While role-playing extended present subjects were able to replicate the verb-tense pattern, they were not able to mimic hypnotically induced subjects in these other ways.

The epitome of the nonlinear perspective is given by a popular expression in Trinidad, "Any time is Trinidad time!" One might describe the approach to time in Trinidad as cyclical moving forward each year to the point of Carnival, at which time culture returns to a common beginning advanced only slightly from the previous year. There is forward movement, but it is slow and maintains a powerful air of sameness.

3. One might describe the future–linear temporal approach as a structural one, and contrast it with the present-oriented–nonlinear approach, which is functional. A "second in time" is officially mea-

sured by 1,192,631,700 cycles of the frequency associated with the transition between two energy levels of the isotope cesium 133. This precise temporal structure defines the context within which behavior is played out. Thus, an appointment is defined by the time for which it was set, and failure to respond to that time makes one *late*. A functional approach to time reckons time as a consequence of behavioral enactments. So a party that begins at 9:00 P.M. only does so within a structural frame of temporal reference. Within a behavioral or functional frame, it begins when people arrive.

The point of this is simple. When people whose values and experiences appear to place them at opposite ends of the FTP spectrum attempt to interact or communicate, it is very likely that they will behave differently, bring different expectations and assumptions to the interaction, derive differential meaning from certain events, and evaluate the other differently as a result of the interactions. If one of the interactants has a power advantage over the other, it is quite likely that such differences will have a negative effect on others' outcomes. In this society, linear perspective is normative and valued, and deviations often put one at risk.

RHYTHM

Rhythm refers to a recurring pattern of behavior within a given time frame. Rhythm is associated with a flow of energy which drives behavior. When things seem to "click," we say "we're on a roll." In sports, momentum describes a steady acceleration of competence and execution. Building energy or rhythm requires that effort or behavior is synchronized with environmental forces through which is must operate. Thus synergy is a positive state associated with movement and flow between person and environment.

When preferred or natural rhythms of people are blocked repeatedly, performance, and often mental health, suffers. For example, sports teams that play in order not to lose usually do not win (Atkinson, 1974). People who are unable to relate their own behavioral patterns to outcomes (particularly success outcomes) often become disengaged from activities around them and depressed (Seligman, 1975). Boykin (1983, 1985) has shown more specifically that performance tasks in traditional school settings require a cognitive and behavioral approach that may be at variance with the rhythmic proclivities of urban lower-income black (and, to a lesser extent, white) children. He developed four different cognitive–perceptual tasks (crossing out a certain number in a table of random numbers, for example) and presented them to fourth- and sixth-grade children in one of two formats. In the *fixed* format, tasks were presented in order with five types of each task presented before proceeding to the next task. In the second or *variable* format, tasks and types within tasks were presented in random order. A second variable rhythmic stimulation, or *verve*, was included (indicated by a variety of self-report measures of home stimulation—music, TV watching, houshold density, etc.). Boykin was able to show that task performance was greater for white than black children under the *fixed* format presentation, but that there was no difference under the *variable* format presentation. Moreover, this Race by Presentation Format interaction was greater for sixth than for fourth graders, such that black sixth graders in the variable format condition performed best of all! In addition, in the variable-format condition, "verve" was positively correlated with success for black, but not white, children.

Any source of regularity produces a rhythm. Thus I am not rehashing the old stereotype that blacks have rhythm and whites do not. Rather, all people and groups have preferred behavioral patterns and these are influenced by level of stimulation and related environmental affordances (McArthur & Baron, 1983). To the extent that institutions are conceived from the perspectives of white middle-class rhythms and associated affordances, blacks and other groups are likely to be at risk in attempting to interact constructively with the institution.

IMPROVISATION

Webster's Seventh New Collegiate Dictionary (1965) defines *improvisation* as

1. composing, reciting or singing on the spur of the moment;
2. making, inventing or arranging offhand.

The first definition implies a kind of expressiveness, while the latter emphasizes inventiveness or creativity. Both definitions implicate immediacy or time pressure. Thus, we might define improvisation as expressive creativity under pressure of immediacy. The expressiveness aspect gives improvisation its personal mark or character, while the inventiveness must itself be goal-directed or problem-solving. Thus, improvisation includes both expressive and instrumental features. That form of individual expressiveness that characterizes improvisation we might consider *style*.

Inventiveness under time pressures is the *instrumental* manifestation of improvisation. Given the sudden imposition of a needed or desired goal, how does one achieve it without prior planning? To achieve goals in such situations, one must have available a repertoire of relevant skills and the presence of mind to organize and implement them effectively. In fast-paced athletic events where uncertainty and surprise are essential strategies, one is continually faced with situations calling for improvisation.[2]

Improvisation is by no means limited to music and sports. Viewed as a means toward achievement, then traditional achievement goals must be viewed in relation to the systematic, predictable routes available to reach those goals. For black Americans, these routes have not been generally available, and improvisation is often the adaptive and necessary alternate approach. For example, one of the most successful black businessmen in this country, John Johnson, owner and publisher of *Ebony* magazine, among many other ventures, tells of the early days of his business in Chicago. As his magazines grew and his need for corporate office space grew, he faced the problem that real estate agents would not sell good space to a black man. Fully aware of this reality, Mr. Johnson represented himself as an assistant to a powerful white businessman for purposes of evaluating potential properties, and finally selected an appropriate one for his business. Finding alternate routes to common goals in this society is a legacy of racial bias.

Improvisation, then, is an achievement behavior. Its context is usually a moment in time, and its character includes both characteristic expressiveness of the performer (style) and creative use of available structures, resources, ideas, and so on. This characterization of improvisation can be expressed more formally as follows:

$$\text{Goal attainment} = f\left(\frac{\text{performance}}{\text{capacity}} + \frac{\text{individual}}{\text{attunement}} + \frac{\text{situational}}{\text{affordances–demands}}\right)$$

Performance capacity refers to the level of skill or ability possessed by the performer and the appropriateness of those skills to the goal at

[2] Worth and Markle (1970) called such activities "reactive" and hypothesized that blacks would excel at them. Data from Jones and Hochner (1973) supported the notion of black superiority at improvisational performance by showing blacks to be better hitters in baseball and relatively better shooters from the field in basketball. It was also shown that white professional basketball players shot free throws with greater accuracy than blacks. This reliable finding is interpreted to suggest that the conspicuous absence of improvisational opportunity may have a dampening effect on black performance.

hand. *Individual attunement* refers to those sensibilities or predilections that characterize a person and his or her preferred mode of expression. Attunements are based, in part, on experience and ecological adaptation. *Situational affordance–demands* influence which skills and individual characteristics will likely be selected and/or effective.

Traditional achievement behavior seeks to control the situational affordances–demands such that they are in line with and draw on those performance capacities most highly developed in the person. Thus, control of the environment and situation are critical to achievement in the traditional view. Improvisational achievement, on the other hand, accepts (indeed *seeks*) the challenge of performing skillfully in an environment whose demands and affordances are not necessarily known in advance. These, then, represent two *styles* of achievement, *both* of which require skills for success. The former tries to anticipate and control the future and prepare the skills presumed to be most effective for those anticipated future situations. The latter develops skills through ongoing performance and rehearsal, thus building a repertoire available to be called on instantaneously when an unpredictable situation demands.

In the lexicon of achievement and the contexts in which it is discussed, planful, future-directed behavior is developed, prescribed, and trained. Improvisational achievement is rarely mentioned, and when it is, it usually carries pejorative connotations. Playground basketball is seen as undisciplined; jazz is seen as an emotional expression a cut below classical Western music; reflective problem solving is seen as superior to impulsive style. Traditional achievement is accomplished through practice, hard work, and discipline, while improvisational achievement is perceived to be raw ability, or worse, luck. This culture values work, effort, and discipline even more than ability (Weiner, Frieze, Kukla, Reed, Rest, & Rosenbaum, 1972). Stylish behavior is often called hot-dogging, and improvisation is relegated to present-based behavior often described as an inability to plan or maintain future-oriented directions.

The point made here is that improvisation is a historical legacy of black culture following in part from a present-oriented cultural style, in part from a context of oppression in which the future was unreliable, unpredictable and not guaranteed to occur at all, much less to occur with certain predictable features. Thus, an improvisational style for black people is both preferred (by many) and demanded as a consequence of survival. It represents, in other words, both evolutionary and reactionary ingredients of black culture.

Oral Expression

Oral expression is the social basis of information exchange. If important information is communicated orally between people and over time, then interpersonal relationships will be important, as will social knowledge and judgment. The broad implication of this view is that all forms of performance, judgment, and accomplishment will evolve from a basic social foundation.

In the midst of a literate culture in which written expressions of intelligence, opinion, ability, and accomplishment tend to define the meritocracy, *oral traditions often put one at a disadvantage*. If this disadvantage is not taken into account, egregious errors in evaluation occur and products of oral traditions are at risk. For example, Cole, Gay, Glick, and Sharp (1971) attempted to demonstrate similarities in memory capacities between Africans (e.g., the Kpelle in Liberia) and Americans. Assuming categorization to be a general mnemonic strategy, they found that Africans were systematically and invariably less successful at memorizing certain information, no matter what structural mnemonic aids were given. However, when the context in which memory operates in Africa was considered, and the to-be-remembered words were embedded in a folk-story, African-American differences disappeared. If the educational system fails to recognize the contextual basis of memory and the oral style of information exchange, some children will be at risk in assessments of their functional intelligence.

Another consequence of oral traditions is that language plays a critical role in information exchange and social relations. Because of its centrality, all features of language are important, including linguistic, paralinguistic, and nonverbal. All context-based language features of communication and expression imply a social reality. Formal systems and institutions are notable for their lack of social context. Further, the approach to language and communication is more often literal. Hence, opportunities for the effective use of nonverbal and paralinguistic aspects are reduced.

Yet, the oral tradition is more than mere verbal interchange. According to Jahn (1961), the word, or *nommo* (in Bantu), is life itself. The *nommo* is the life force, the spiritual–physical fluidity that gives life to everything. A newborn child does not have being until he/she is given a name by the father and that name is *pronounced!* The word embellishes and completes creation. It accompanies acts and gives them meaning. The fabrications of a goldsmith are not a creative success without the verbal incantations that accompany the work, as Leopold Senghor, the late president of Senegal, notes:

The prayer, or rather the poem that the goldsmith recites, the hymn of praise sung by the sorcerer while the goldsmith is working the gold, the dance of this myth at the close of the operation, it is all—poem, song, dance—which, in addition to the movement of the artisan, completes the work and makes it a masterpiece. (1956, p. 56)

With this profound significance of the word, of speaking meaning into action and its products, it is important to trace the form and function of such origins in the evolution of a culture. The intersection of African–American culture surely must contain elements of each. Our failure to recognize this near certainty, and to develop strategies for understanding the resultant dynamics in performance, preference, belief, and collective action is a major omission in our efforts to come to terms with racial–cultural bias.

SPIRITUALITY

I define *spirituality* as a belief in nonmaterial causation. According to Jahn (1961) African philosophy contains four primary categories within which all being is subsumed. They are

    I. *Muntu*—human being
   II. *Kintu*— thing
  III. *Hantu*—place and time
  IV. *Kuntu*— modality

Everything there belongs to one of these four categories and must be conceived not as substance but as a force! *Ntu* is the universal force to which prefixes accord specific manifestations. Thus, spirituality is merely the force that resides in all beings, things, places—times, and modalities. While we tend to reserve force for *origins* in Western thought, it is present in all categories of being in traditional African thought.

Not only is *muntu* but one force in the world, but *muntu* includes the dead as well as the living, *orishas, loas*, and ancestors. If the force in all being is capable of exerting influence, then the material (*kintu*) is but one source of causation; living and dead, place and time, and modality all contain force. This is the essence of a spiritual orientation as here conceived.

If force is related to causation and causation to control, then one of the clear consequences of spirituality is a lessened sense of personal control. Apart from the mystical and religious practices and beliefs we associate with the concept of spirituality, the more practical and pervasive implication is for direct personal control of self-relevant events. Literature in psychology attests to the role personal control plays in performance, sense of well-being and achievement in this society. The locus-of-control construct (Rotter, 1966) establishes the principle that being a cause is critical to self-worth and accomplishment. DeCharms (1966) is even more explicit with his theory of personal causation in which one is either an origin or a pawn. The field-independence construct of Witkin, Dyk, Faterson, Goodenpugh, and Karp (1962) is yet another approach with the same theme.

To the foregoing constructs of causation, we can add the compelling findings of Langer and her colleagues (see Langer, 1983), which show the lengths to which people will go to maintain belief in the value of being in control. For example, bingo cards that one selects are judged to be more valuable than those that are arbitrarily provided. Langer and Rodin (1976) made the more profound observation that elderly nursing-home patients who were given some control over their lives (as simple as having plants to water and care for) were happier and lived longer than patients who were not offered this small control over their lives.

If, by tradition, philosophy, and religious practice, a people believes that causation and control are at best shared with other forces in the universe, then personal worth will be less highly associated with control. Perhaps it is a belief in and value placed on personal control that lies behind the capacity to engage in such controlling activities as the exploitation of slavery, colonialism, and continuing more subtle forms of racism, discrimination, and prejudice.

Thus, to understand the dynamic implications of spirituality is to understand the operation of psychological control and the philosophical context within which it resides. There are positives and negatives in every systematic position, especially as it unfolds in behavior sanctioned by culture. We have, it seems, accepted and taken for granted the notion that we are, can be, and should be in control of ourselves and the world around us. This belief has obvious positive consequences, but may have negative consequences as well. One of them, as alluded to earlier, may be the problem this volume addresses.

CONCLUSION: MULTIDIMENSIONAL APPROACH TO CULTURAL DIVERSITY

On the basis of the preceding discussions, the problem of racism can be summarized:

Blacks are collectively living in a worse environment and benefiting less from the wealth and opportunity that this country offers than are whites. The descriptive statistics presented in the first section of this chapter clearly support this view. One of the problems further implied by these data, though, is the extent of class differences among blacks and the extent to which racism and class-based disadvantage are a singular problem. This is the essential view advanced by Wilson (1978). While it is true that significant class differences exist among blacks, the disparities between black and white do not diminish very much as one moves up the economic spectrum. For example, the SAT score differences between black and white high school students continue to show differences in favor of whites even when white students from low-income families (less than $6,000) are compared with black students from high-income families (over $50,000).

Whites believe that there are very few, if any, *structural* barriers to black opportunity, and, therefore, disparities are due mainly to motivational or ability deficiencies among blacks. This perception leads to a further negative evaluation of blacks which systematic research in social psychology (e.g., Crosby et al., 1980; Gaertner & Dovidio, 1981; Gaertner & McLaughlin, 1983; McConahay & Hough, 1976) has shown to be manifested in a variety of more-subtle ways than attitude surveys typically discern.

There is a strong ethnocentric bias in this country which generally accepts unquestioningly the superiority of traditional values of Euro-American origin. To the extent that those adaptive and evolutionary values of Afro-Americans are at variance with the majority view, blacks will be in a difficult position. When this home-court advantage is further supported by the power to define the inputs or instrumentalities comprising a meritocratic equity-based system of rewards, then blacks and all other groups are required to develop strategies that will confer efficacy on preferred patterns of behavior and developed abilities.

Blacks are in a double-bind, in that those behaviors that may be adaptive to negative circumstances (such as those associated with economically depressed urban life exacerbated by systematic racism and oppression) present modest short-term gains but long-term losses in the ability to negotiate the success parameters of the larger society. There are enough exceptions to this generalization that we may, at the same time, look for those positive consequences of adaptation to the local environment for successful functioning in the larger context.

The power to define which instrumentalities (inputs) will be useful in realizing the meritocratic opportunities in this society rests with people who often believe that blacks are not only different but also deficient and that those differences constitute a legitimate basis for differential outcomes.

How might one conceptualize the problem in such a way that potential solutions are conceivable? I would see the problem from two perspectives:

A. From a system-blame perspective, it is necessary to reduce barriers to opportunity that emanate from the operation of systematic disadvantage associated with discrimination. Thus, the first approach to the problem is to reduce discrimination against blacks. This is hardly a novel idea, but one for which there is important and exciting work being done that lends substantial weight of social and behavioral science findings to the effort. The basic discrimination problem can be conceived as follows: Human tendencies toward social categorization lead to ingroup preference, which leads to outgroup discrimination. Thus, discrimination against blacks is the indirect result of social categorization. There are two general methods for reducing the categorization effects:

1. Reduce the salience of group boundaries, which leads to a wider conception of ingroup and a smaller conception, correspondingly, of outgroup. (see Chapter 11).
2. Increase the salience of individual variability by demonstrating the individuating information about people rather than category-based information (see Chapter 7).

The former approach emphasizes ways in which people are similar and draws upon human categorization tendencies to strengthen intergroup relations by using the resultant ingroup biasing effects across a wider selection of categorical groups. Recent work by Gaertner and Dovidio (see Chapter 11) has followed this course with promising results.

The latter approach, on the other hand, emphasizes the difference between people and by so doing highlights the fact that we are all different and, therefore, it is more diagnostic to learn about a given person than to assume the categorical information is applicable and appropriate. Work by Lockesley and her colleagues (Lockesley, Hepburn, & Ortiz, 1982; Lockesley, Ortiz, & Hepburn, 1980) and, more recently, analyses by Miller and Brewer (cf. Chapter 7) have developed this idea into a conception that promises to reduce group boundaries by increasing perceived variability within and across groups.

B. A second approach is to acknowledge the possibilities of group differences and, rather than perceive any and all differences as problematic, try to discern ways in which differences make a positive contribution to the aggregate set of capacities in the total social and cultural fabric of a multicultural society. To do this, we clearly need to think differently about human diversity than we do now (also see Chapter 8). We readily accept in principle the notion that diversity is good. Yet when it comes to practicality, the question always becomes what value or instrumentality does such a difference have for important goals in this society?

First of all, when one experiences multiple cultural components in his or her own daily life tolerance for diversity and respect for difference tend to follow. The result is potentially a society in which diversity is itself a virtue and accepted as commonplace. One societal advantage is the notion that evolution of a species is made better by the variability of adaptation incident to diversity of population. There are several models in social psychology that suggest that diversity of opinion, for example, improves group decision making (Janis & Mann, 1977). Latané and Wolf (1981) also suggest that minority influence may be critical to reverse the tendency for majorities to stagnate with their self-contained positions. Nemeth (1979) goes further by suggesting that the mere presence of a minority in a group task process will often serve to introduce more creative thinking among the majority members.

Second, one consequence of the individualistic, time-urgent perspective is higher risk of coronary disease. However, even though pace of life was shown to be greater in Japan, coronary risk did not increase (Levine & Bartlett, 1984). Thus, collective action and cultural norms of functional inclusiveness (working together toward common goals) may well be an antidote to the negative consequences of individualistic competitiveness. The model of cultural diversity and bicultural adapation with the emphasis on the cultural evolution of a group value system that downplays individualism and control and emphasizes nonmaterial control and human comparability is one approach.

The emphasis on the written word in our culture permits a certain abstraction of human experience. Shall we send a memo or stop by and chat with an employee or colleague or have an all-hands meeting? Increasingly good management is seen as including personal and social skills perhaps associated with an oral approach to interpersonal relationships. The aloof and powerful manager is giving way to the sensitive and accessible colleague.

The approaches to living envisioned by the TRIOS model represent not simply a basis for describing racial–cultural differences between black and white Americans. Rather, it is an attempt to systematically review aspects of racial difference in which the orienting premise does not put blacks at a deficient starting point, and further, to elaborate the range of human behaviors deemed important in this society. In fact, I argue, the dimensions of TRIOS are important to any functioning society. Biculturality, thus, is a two-way street. While blacks have and must necessarily develop the same skills that whites must and do in this society, whites should recognize the salience of the flip side of traditional cultural truisms. It would be a worthwhile exercise to make a list of positive and negative expressions of characteristics assumed to be traditional in the Euro-American and Afro-American adaptations of living in the United States. Also, we can learn from the experiences of people who are socialized and forced to adapt to fundamentally different environmental circumstances. How does a person, born and raised in an urban ghetto of the northeast or a barrio of the southwest or an Appalachian mountain village of West Virginia convert an ecological–economic disadvantage to an occasion for growth and development? What skills and abilities go into converting expressive qualities and localized instrumentalities into a wider set of opportunities and accomplishments? Do we have any understanding, and how might we advance our own appreciation of differences by learning of what they consist? It is often argued that increased tolerance for others often accompanies the experience of intolerance at the hands of others. Learning, therefore, to understand and truly appreciate cultural diversity and the variety of circumstances from which individuals and groups evolve in this society is a backdrop for both the means of reducing social categorization and its corresponding discriminatory effects.

TRIOS is offered as a set of ideas that may have currency for such an expanded appreciation of cultural diversity. It is not meant as a simple portrayal of black people as African people—rather, a look at dimensions of human experience that are real, evolutionary, and valid as legitimate human responses to survival in an oppressive environment and the inexorable processes of evolution.

Elsewhere (Jones, 1983), I have suggested that culture, not color, is the better way to approach matters of race in this society. The color approach emphasizes differences that are clear and undeniable. However, the important differences (those associated with culture and character) are not addressed by the focus on skin color. Thus, when we talk about blacks, for example, or whites, what are we saying? Perhaps little more than that skin color has been the organizing principle or schema for much of race relations in the United States for over three centuries.

The cultural approach, by contrast, emphasizes the content of experience and its historical antecedents as a basis for coming together, sharing cultures, and recognizing the contributions different cultural groups make to our national culture. In this view, culture represents a way of bringing people and groups together, of both acknowledging boundaries (of ethnicity and culture) and transcending them by embedding them in the broader cultural concept.

As a problem, the fusion of color (perceived to be negative and often tied to presumptions of genetic inferiority in blacks) with culture as an inadequate expression and/or adjustment of blacks to contemporary modern society produces a context for the expressions of prejudice, discrimination, and racism. However, the approach here advocated would eliminate this negative association and offer in its place a positive multidimensional view of incorporation and inclusion. I hope that some of the ideas presented here will, in the long run, prove positive and effective in making this a better and stronger society for all of our citizens.

REFERENCES

Allport, G. W. (1954). *The nature of prejudice.* Reading, MA: Addison-Wesley Publishers.

Atkinson, J. W. (1974). The mainsprings of achievement-oriented activity. In J. W. Atkinson & J. O. Raynor (Eds), *Motivation and achievement.* Washington, DC: Hemisphere.

Boykin, A. W. (1983). The academic performance of Afro-American children. In J. Spence (Ed.), *Achievement and achievement motives* (pp. 323–371). San Francisco: W. H. Freeman and Company.

Boykin, A. W. (1985, March). *Developing a paradigm to examine culture heuristically.* Invited address at the Annual Meeting of the Eastern Psychological Association Convention, Boston.

Brewer, M. B. (1979). In-group bias in the minimal intergroup situation: A cognitive-motivational analysis. *Psychological Bulletin, 86,* 307–324.

Caplan, N., & Nelson, S. D. (1973). On being useful: The nature of consequences of psychological research on social problems. *American Psychologist, 28,* 199–211.

Cole, J. B. (1970). Culture: Negro, black and nigger. *Black Scholar, 1,* 40–44.

Cole, M., Gay, J., Glick, J. & Sharp, D. (1971). *The cultural context of learning and thinking.* New York: Basic Books.

College Entrance Examination Board. (1985). *Equality and excellence: The educational status of Black Americans.* New York.

Crosby, F., Bromley, S., & Saxe, L. (1980). Recent unobtrusive studies of black and white discrimination and prejudice: A literature review. *Psychological Bulletin, 87,* 546–563.

DeCharms, R. E. (1966). *Personal causation.* New York: Wiley.

Deutsch, M. & Collins, M. E. (1951). *Interracial housing: A psychological evaluation of a social experiment.* Minneapolis: University of Minnesota Press.

De Volder, M. L., & Lens, W. (1982). Academic achievement and future time perspective as a cognitive-motivational concept. *Journal of Personality and Social Psychology, 42,* 566–571.

Gaertner, S. L., & Dovidio, J. F. (1981). Racism among the well-intentioned. In J. Bermingham & E. Clausen (Eds.), *Racism, pluralism, and public policy: A search for equality* (pp. 208–222). Boston: G. K. Hall.

Gaertner, S. L., & McLaughlin, J. P. (1983). Racial stereotypes: Associations and ascriptions of positive and negative characteristics. *Social Psychology Quarterly, 46,* 23–30.

Hamilton, D. L. & Gifford, R. K. (1976). Illusory correlation in interpersonal perception: A cognitive bias of stereotypic judgments, *Journal of Experimental Social Psychology, 12,* 392–407.

Jahn, J. (1961). *Muntu: An outline of the new African culture.* New York: Grove Press.

Janis, I. L., & Mann, L. (1977). *Decision making.* New York: The Free Press.

Jones, J. M. (1972). *Prejudice and racism.* Reading, MA: Addison Wesley.

Jones, J. M. (1979). Conceptual and strategic issues in the relationship of black psychology to American social science. In A. W. Boykin, A. J. Franklin, & J. F. Yates (Eds.), *Research directions in black psychology* (pp. 390–432). New York: Russell Sage Foundation.

Jones, J. M. (1983). The concept of race in social psychology: From color to culture. In L. Wheeler & P. Shaver (Eds.), *Review of personality and social psychology,* (Vol. 4, pp. 117–149). Beverly Hills, CA: Sage Publications.

Jones, J. M., & Block, C. B. (1984). Black cultural perspectives. *Clinical Psychologist, 37,* 58–62.

Jones, J. M., & Hochner, A. (1973). Racial differences in sports activities: A look at the self-paced versus reactive hypothesis. *Journal of Personality and Social Psychology, 27,* 86–95.

Jones, J. M., & Liverpool, H. (1976). Calypso humour in Trinidad. In A. Chapman & H. Foot (Eds.), *Humour: Theory and research* (pp. 259–286). London: John Wiley, Ltd.

Kluegel, J. R. & Smith, E. R. (1986). *Beliefs about inequality: Americans' views of what is and what ought to be.* Chicago: Aldine Publishing Co.

Langer, E. J. (1983). *The psychology of control.* Beverly Hills, CA: Sage.

Langer, E. J., & Rodin, J. (1976). The effects of choice and enhanced personal responsibility for the aged. A field experiment in an institutional setting. *Journal of Personality and Social Psychology, 34,* 191–198.

Latané, B., & Wolf, S. (1981). The social impact of majorities and minorities. *Psychological Review, 88,* 438–453.

Lerner, M. J. (1980). *The belief in a just world: A fundamental delusion.* New York: Plenum.

Leshan, L. L. (1952). Time orientation and social class. *Journal of Abnormal and Social Psychology, 47,* 589–592.

Levine, R. V., & Bartlett, K. (1984). Pace of life, punctuality, and coronary heart disease in six countries. *Journal of Cross-Cultural Psychology, 15,* 233–255.

Levine, R. V., West, L., & Reis, H. (1980). Perceptions of time and punctuality in the United States and Brazil. *Journal of Personality and Social Psychology, 38,* 541–550.

Linville, P. W., & Jones, E. E. (1980). Polarized appraisals of out-group members. *Journal of Personality and Social Psychology, 38,* 689–703.

Lockesley, A., Hepburn, C., & Ortiz, V. (1982). Social stereotypes and judgments of individuals: An instance of the base-rate fallacy. *Journal of Experimental Social Psychology, 18,* 23–42.

Lockesley, A., Ortiz, V., & Hepburn, C. (1980). Social categorization and discrimination behavior: Extinguishing the minimal intergroup discrimination effect. *Journal of Personality and Social Psychology, 39,* 773–783.

Mbiti, J. (1970). *African philosophy and religions.* New York: Doubleday.

McArthur, L. Z., & Baron, R. M. (1983). Toward an ecological theory of perception. *Psychological Review, 90,* 215–238.

McConahay, J. B., & Hough, J. C. (1976). Symbolic racism. *Journal of Social Issues, 32,* 23–45.

Mischel, W. (1958). Preference for delayed reinforcement: An experimental study of a cultural observation. *Journal of Abnormal and Social Psychology, 56,* 57–61.

Mischel, W. (1961a). Preference for delayed reinforcement and social responsibility. *Journal of Abnormal and Social Psychology, 62,* 1–7.

Mischel, W. (1961b). Delay of gratification, need for achievement, and acquiescence in another culture. *Journal of Abnormal and Social Psychology, 62,* 543–552.

National Advisory Commission on Civil Disorders. (1968). *Report of the National Advisory Commission on Civil Disorders.* New York: Bantam Books.

Nemeth, C. (1979). The role of an active minority in intergroup relations. In W. G. Austin & S. Worchel (Eds.), *The social psychology of intergroup relations* (pp. 225–236). Monterey, CA: Brooks/Cole.

Ornstein, R. E. (1977). *The psychology of consciousness.* New York: Harcourt Brace & Janovich.

Pettigrew, T. F. (1979). The ultimate attribution error: Extending Allport's cognitive analysis of prejudice. *Personality and Social Psychology Bulletin, 5,* 461–476.

Ross, L. (1977). The intuitive psychologist and his shortcomings: Distortions in the attribution process. In L. Berkowitz (Ed.), *Advances in experimental social psychology* (Vol. 10, pp. 173–220). New York: Academic Press.

Rotter, J. B. (1966). Generalized expectancies for internal versus external control of reinforcement. *Psychological Monographs, 80* (1, Whole No. 609).

Ryan, W. (1971). *Blaming the victim.* New York: Pantheon.

Seligman, M. E. P. (1975). *Helplessness: On depression, development and death.* San Francisco: W. H. Freeman.

Senghor, L. (1956). L'esprit de la civilisation ou les lois de la culture négro-africaine. *Présence Africaine,* VIII-X. Paris.

U.S. Department of Commerce, Bureau of the Census. (1984). *Statistical Abstract of the United States,* 104th Edition. Washington, DC: U.S. Government Printing Office.

U.S. Department of Labor. (1965). *The Negro family: The case for national action.* Washington, DC: U.S. Government Printing Office.

Wallace, M. (1956). Future time perspective in schizophrenia. *Journal of Abnormal and Social Psychology, 52,* 240–245.

Webster's Seventh New Collegiate Dictionary. (1965). Springfield, MA: G. & C. Merriam Company, Publishers.

Weiner, B., Frieze, I., Kukla, A., Reed, L., Rest, S., & Rosenbaum, R. M. (1972). In E. E. Jones, D. E. Kanouse, H. H. Kelley, R. E. Nisbett, S. Valins, & B. Weiner (Eds.), *Attribution: Perceiving the causes of behavior* (pp. 95–120). Morristown, NJ: General Learning Press.

Wilson, W. J. (1978). *The declining significance of race.* Chicago: University of Chicago Press.

Witkin, H. A., Dyk, R. B., Faterson, H. F., Goodenpugh, D. R. and Karp, S. A. (1962). *Psychological differentiation.* New York: John Wiley Publishers.

Worthy, M., & Markle, M. (1970). Racial differences in reactive versus self-paced sports activities. *Journal of Personality and Social Psychology, 10,* 439–443.

Zimbardo, P. G., Marshall, G., & Maslach, C. (1971). Liberating behavior from time-bound control: Expanding the present through hypnosis. *Journal of Applied Social Psychology, 1,* 305–323.

PREJUDICE, DISCRIMINATION, AND RACISM: PROBLEMS, PROGRESS, AND PROMISE

Samuel L. Gaertner

Department of Psychology
University of Delaware
Newark, Delaware 19711

John F. Dovidio

Department of Psychology
Colgate University
Hamilton, New York 13346

INTRODUCTION

The analyses offered in this volume address many issues regarding the progress that has been made toward the elimination of prejudice, discrimination, and racism. There is indeed reason to be optimistic. A significant reduction of blatant forms of racism has occurred over the past 125 years, and particularly over the past 40. Nevertheless, the analyses presented within several of the preceding chapters suggest that racism at the individual, institutional, and cultural levels remains more deeply embedded than is indicated by recent opinion surveys. The contributions to this volume therefore give cause to remain seriously concerned, but also provide some reasons to be cautiously optimistic, about the level and nature of racism in the United States.

REASONS TO BE CONCERNED

Towards the Elimination of Racism, which was edited in 1976 by Phyllis Katz (see also Katz & Taylor, in press) is a book whose title aroused expectations yet to be fulfilled. Chapters 1 and 10 in the present volume, for example, indicate that the quality of life among black Americans has improved over the past few decades, but that the gap between blacks and whites in areas of health and employment has remained intact or even widened. While the opinion polls show that white America's attitudes toward blacks have become more tolerant over the past 40 years (see Chapter 1), meaningful proportions of the

315

white population continue to embrace the old-fashioned form of bigotry. For example, 16% of the whites sampled in the 1980s, compared with 54% in the 1950s, claimed that they would not vote for a *qualified* black candidate for president. Although this represents a substantial reduction in prejudice, it is important to note that 16% of approximately 170 million adults is still a significant social fact. Furthermore, white supremist groups, like the Ku Klux Klan, continue to flourish and, by some indicators, seem to be attracting increasing numbers of supporters.

Also, the work regarding ambivalent, aversive, and modern forms of racism (presented in Chapters 2, 3, and 4) suggests that white America's racial attitudes are actually more negative than is indicated by public-opinion-poll methodologies. Although we generally trust the genuineness with which people express their opinions on questionnaires and survey instruments, the accuracy with which they interpret their race-related feelings, beliefs, and behaviors as nonracist is questionable. Crosby, Bromley, and Saxe (1980) conclude that white America, although generally complying with a nonbigoted ideology, has not truly internalized feelings and beliefs commensurate with their espoused attitudes. Because the old-fashioned form of racism, the type that is typically tapped by opinion polls, is evolving into more subtle, more rationalizable, and less overtly negative forms, many whites appear (and may actually believe that they are) nonprejudiced and nondiscriminatory. Schofield (Chapter 8) points to the problematic consequences of consciously trying to maintain a colorblind ideology in the absence of further, more complete interracial acceptance. Nickerson, Mayo, and Smith (Chapter 9) describe the negative impact of racism for blacks in the courtroom. In addition, people who exhibit more subtle, modern forms of prejudice may, during periods of anger or stress, regress to more primitive, old-fashioned types of racism (Kovel, 1970; Rogers & Prentice-Dunn, 1981). Therefore, the fact that interracial behavior is being governed by egalitarian norms in the present does not guarantee that the direction of future change will continue to be positive.

In considering evidence of racism in America, perhaps we are placing too much faith in the findings of experimental research which primarily used the familiar, but not necessarily representative, university undergraduate. Nevertheless, evidence of prejudice among our college samples suggests the pervasiveness of racism in the general population. Given that prejudice and educational level seems to be inversely related (e.g., Adorno, Frenkel-Brunswik, Levinson, & Sanford, 1950), our detection of even subtle forms of racial bigotry among these well-educated and generally more egalitarian samples must be considered in an assessment of the degree of racism still prevalent in the United States. Furthermore, it is from the ranks of these college populations that our teachers, judges, and leaders of public and private institutions responsible for formulating and administering social policy are recruited.

Due in part to the 1964 Civil Rights Act and the 1972 Equal Employment Opportunity Act, black men and women are represented today in occupational roles from which they were formerly excluded. While this achievement would otherwise give cause only for optimism, the increased visibility and distinctiveness of blacks in these positions may contribute to the distorted impression that the presence of blacks is actually higher than indicated by the statistical evidence. Unfortunately, this mistaken impression could support arguments both that racism in this country is largely a problem of the past requiring whites to make no further adjustments and that those blacks who have not already moved into mainstream America are probably intellectually or motivationally deficient. Indeed, Kluegel and Smith (1982) report national survey data revealing that 73% of white adults see the current opportunity of blacks as equal to or greater than that of the average white American. Furthermore, Kluegel and Smith's findings reveal that while prejudice scores among whites drop dramatically with decreases in respondents' age, there is no corresponding trend toward increased recognition of structural (i.e., institutional) limits to opportunities for blacks. Additional analyses indicated that those whites who deny the continued existence of structural barriers to black opportunity are most likely to assume that the causes of poverty, unemployment, and dependency among blacks reside within the character of the individual. Thus, even though prejudice scores may decline, even younger members of the white population perceive the circumstances of blacks in a manner that could justify resistance to programs that provide increased opportunities to blacks (also see Chapter 10).

The contributions of Hamilton and Trolier (Chapter 5) and Linville, Salovey, and Fischer (Chapter 6), which detail the role of cognitive processes in the development, operation, and maintenance of stereotypes, represent a substantial reason for continued concern. The cognitive perspective partially ties stereotyping and the consequences of stereotypic thinking directly to normal, apparently inescapable human functioning. Thus, this perspective offers a less hopeful prognosis for the elimination of racism than does the work that links prejudice and stereotyping to psychopathological processes (for example,

as does the research on the authoritarian personality). That is, causes
that reside in defective functioning can usually be assumed to be less
frequent and more amenable to intervention than those that result
from normal, more universal functioning. The problem is further compounded by the fact that cognitive, categorical distinctions are generally accompanied by needs for self-esteem and desires for positive
distinctiveness which lead to more positive feelings about ingroup
members relative to outgroup members (e.g., Brewer, 1979; Tajfel &
Turner, 1979, 1986). Here too, racism may be partially rooted in normal rather than aberrant human functioning.

Eliminating prejudice by reducing the salience of cognitive, categorical boundaries (see Chapter 7), although a theoretically promising
approach, is particularly difficult when race is involved. Categorical
boundaries between blacks and whites cross-cut several dimensions
of social relations: socioeconomic status, residential distribution, linguistic expression, and cultural values (Chapter 10). Racial group
boundaries, therefore, are more likely to be salient factors in intergroup interactions than are other types of categorical distinctions that
involve fewer dimensions (Brewer & Miller, 1984). Furthermore, the
importance of perceptually distinctive physical cues for social categorization processes are particularly troublesome because of their primacy in information processing. Campbell (1958) notes that as a result
of the evolutionary process, "we have the marvelously effective mechanism of vision which, within a limited range of entities, analyzes
entitativity [the degree of having the nature of an entity] so rapidly and
vividly that all other inferential processes seem in contrast indirect,
ponderous, and undependable" (p. 17). Therefore, the role of physical
cues in maintaining categorical distinctions, in combination with the
additional intergroup differences, is a considerable obstacle to overcome for strategies designed to eradicate prejudice, discrimination,
and racism.

Another major cause for concern involves the inability of researchers and practitioners to generate effective social technologies for reducing prejudice that can withstand the hostile circumstances within
which they often must be implemented. School desegregation is a
case in piont. Allport (1954), Amir (1976), Cook (1984, 1985), and
Stephan (1985) have listed features of an intergroup contact situation
that are necessary to promote favorable intergroup attitudes. That intergroup contact under these conditions would increase intergroup
tolerance and acceptance is referred to as the *contact hypothesis* (Allport, 1954). The lists include cooperative rather than competitive in-

teractions; cooperative interactions involving similar levels of competence between groups; cooperative tasks with outcomes that are positive; interactions among members who do not possess qualities stereotypically associated with their group membership; situations that provide strong normative and institutional support for the contact; similarity of beliefs and values between the groups; opportunities for intimate, self-revealing, personal contact; contact that has the potential to extend beyond the immediate situation; contact that is voluntary and extends over a lengthy period; contact that occurs in a variety of contexts with a variety of ingroup and outgroup members; and contact involving equal status both within and outside the initial contact situation. Clearly, the incongruity between the circumstances we know to be necessary for intergroup contact to promote intergroup acceptance and those circumstances within which desegregation must usually be implemented is a substantial cause for concern. Indeed, we can almost be assured that if we encounter a natural situation containing many of the factors specified by the contact hypothesis, intergroup acceptance probably preceded the construction of the contact situation. Furthermore, although school desegregation has never been either uniformly implemented or implemented fully in accord with the contact hypothesis, the results are not as promising as we would wish. Despite some evidence suggesting that under appropriate circumstances interracial contact can reduce prejudice (McConahay, 1981), children do not necessarily show reduced levels of racial prejudice and increased interracial acceptance within desegregated schools (Stephan, 1978). Even when some of the appropriate circumstances are present, intergroup acceptance rarely generalizes beyond the immediate contact situation (Brewer & Miller, 1984).

Overall, individual and social factors continue to conspire to create and perpetuate racism in the United States. Together, normal cognitive mechanisms for processing categorical information, the primacy of distinctive physical features in the perception of social entities, the historically racist culture of the United States, the contemporary failure to appreciate cultural values and styles that depart from traditional Anglo-Saxon ideals, the subtlety of current racial attitudes, the tokenistic representation of blacks in mainstream America, and the failure to develop technologies that effectively reduce prejudice within the contexts in which they must operate, all present formidable challenges to the goal of eliminating racism in this society. While it would be inappropriate not to acknowledge the pervasiveness of these challenges to a future in which prejudice, discrimination, and racism are no more than history, it would be irresponsible to ignore events in this country that give reason to view the future with optimism and renewed commitment.

REASONS TO BE OPTIMISTIC

It is clear that the laws and norms of our country have changed so dramatically, particularly within the past 40 years, that there is reason to be optimistic about the possibility of even further progress toward the elimination of prejudice, discrimination, and racism. At the societal level, the days of open discrimination sanctioned by law are at the present time behind us. It is now illegal to discriminate on the basis of race. At the individual level, racial attitudes have changed. Espoused racial prejudice among whites has significantly declined, and stereotypes of blacks are more positive than ever before (see Chapter 1). Furthermore, many whites vigorously aim to present themselves as nonprejudiced and adopt a colorblind perspective (see Chapter 8) in interracial interactions. Our own work (Chapter 3), along with that of Katz, Wackenhut, and Hass (Chapter 2) and McConahay (Chapter 4), suggests that, although the attitudes of many whites are not entirely nonprejudiced, many people genuinely reject self-attributions of bigotry and seem to bend over backwards at times to avoid acting inappropriately in interracial contexts. Furthermore, the work of Katz and his colleagues suggests the existence of positive feelings toward blacks that are independent of whites' egalitarian values. McConahay's assessment (see Chapter 4) thus appears valid and encouraging. He states that "there are grounds for limited optimism for the long-range future so long as the norm that 'nice people can't be racists and racists can't be nice people' establishes the climate for creative ambivalence."

In addition to changes in attitude, there is a pattern of events in this decade that gives reason to be optimistic about progress toward the elimination of racism. In politics, increasing numbers of blacks have been elected, partially due to the support of white voters, to serve in important public offices (for example, as mayors of major cities such as Atlanta, Chicago, and Philadelphia). Reverend Jesse Jackson's candidacy had a significant impact on the presidential politics of 1984. In the media, blacks are portrayed more frequently than ever before in positions of responsibility and leadership, often without making race a salient feature of the characterization or story line (e.g., the Bill Cosby

Show). In terms of formal recognition, the legislation to establish a national holiday to honor Dr. Martin Luther King, Jr., can be interpreted as representing a symbol of our nation's progress toward its espoused commitment to freedom and equality. A national holiday dedicated to Dr. King is a national achievement that will have continued impact on future generations. The effects of black role models in politics, in the media, and as national heroes can have important positive consequences on the attitudes of both black and white people.

As noted earlier in this volume (Chapter 10), employment and educational opportunities have improved significantly for blacks. Black men and women are more frequently represented in occupational roles from which they were previously excluded (although not yet proportionate to their numbers in the population). More blacks than ever before are attending colleges and pursuing postgraduate education. Futhermore, in some states (e.g., Massachusetts) the public education curriculum has formally been expanded to include multicultural education. Multicultural education involves the recognition of cultural diversity and the integration of these values into students' classroom experiences. While the greater achievement of blacks in employment and education probably represents in part the results of affirmative action and other formal policies, it would be a mistake to ignore the fact that the removal of barriers limiting blacks' educational opportunities and occupational roles is also due in part to the conscious attempts by whites to behave in accord with their nonprejudiced, nondiscriminatory ideals.

The commitment of social science to understanding the causes of racism and the progress that has been made in identifying factors that promote interracial acceptance are additional reasons to be optimistic. Although the factors proposed by Allport (1954), Amir (1976), Cook (1984, 1985), and Stephan (1985) as necessary for intergroup contact to increase intergroup attraction are rarely pre-existing and are difficult to introduce in most actual interracial contact situations, their specification itself is a significant achievement. In addition, the recent surge in research on cognitive processing of information regarding ingroup–outgroup categorization has focused social psychology's attention on theoretical issues that are important to understanding racial prejudice (see Chapters 5 and 6). The analysis provided by Brewer and Miller (1984; also see Chapter 7) theoretically integrates past achievements involving the contact hypothesis with work on social information processing and with the study of intergroup behavior in general. Together, these lines of inquiry offer a valuable perspective on increasing interracial acceptance.

In summary, there are several reasons to be optimistic about future progress toward a fully egalitarian society. Changes in laws, declines in expressions of prejudice, and improvements in the sociopolitical status of black men and women indicate that society can change in significant ways. The presence of black role models in the media, the formal recognition of Martin Luther King and his contributions, and the celebration of cultural diversity in the classroom suggest that blacks have earned some degree of respect within the dominant white culture. Furthermore, the commitment of social scientists to the study of racism encourages confidence in continued progress toward the elimination of prejudice, discrimination, and racism. In the next section, we examine some current theoretical trends in intergroup behavior that ultimately could facilitate the development of methodologies to promote more harmonious interracial relations.

TOWARD THE ELIMINATION OF RACISM: THE STUDY OF INTERGROUP BEHAVIOR

Within the literature on intergroup behavior, there is general agreement that factors which increase the salience of group boundaries increase the degree of intergroup bias (e.g., Brewer, 1979; Wilder, 1978, 1986; Worchel, 1979, 1986). Basically, with increased awareness of the intergroup boundary there is enhanced appreciation of ingroup–outgroup or we–they categorizations. This enhanced appreciation transforms a person's perceptions and behaviors from an interpersonal to an intergroup level of responding. At the intergroup level, people act in terms of their social identity, more faithfully conforming to the group's norms and also treating others in terms of their corresponding group memberships rather than their personal identities (see Brewer & Miller, 1984; Brown & Turner, 1981; Miller & Brewer, Chapter 7; Sherif, 1967). Outgroup members, in particular, become depersonalized, undifferentiated, substitutable entities (Park & Rothbart, 1982; also see Chapter 6). In addition, with increased boundary salience, an individual's motivation for maintaining positive self-regard initiates social comparison processes that result in increased positive evaluations for ingroup relative to outgroup members (Tajfel & Turner, 1979, 1986; Turner, 1975).

There has also been some convergence of opinion regarding the possible utility of disrupting the categorization process so as to degrade the intergroup boundary and thereby promote intergroup acceptance and more personalized interactions and evaluations. While decreasing the salience of intergroup boundary is the common goal, various strategies have involved personalizing interactions (Brewer & Miller, 1984); forming new groups with crossed-category member- ships (Deschamps & Doise, 1978); individuating outgroup members (Wilder, 1978); and creating one, superordinate group (Turner, 1981; Worchel, 1979, 1986). In Chapter 7, Miller and Brewer describe three general models of the process of intergroup contact effects (see also Brewer & Miller, 1984). The first model views structural aspects of the contact situation (e.g., cooperative interdependence) as a fundamental causal factor that directly mediates perceptual, attitudinal, and behav- ioral changes. The second model, which is based on cognitive disso- nance and self-perception theories, views personalized interaction as the result of changes in affect that occur to justify positive patterns of interaction during the contact situation. That is, positive interaction (e.g., cooperation) with a disliked group can create cognitive disso- nance, which in turn can motivate the development of more positive intergroup attitudes. These more positive attitudes then lead to more individualized interactions. The third model, which is based on Ta- jfel's (1969) work on social categorization and is one that represents Miller and Brewer's approach, hypothesizes the opposite sequence. Changes in categorization are prerequisite to changes in affect as well as to changes in the nature of intergroup interactions. Brewer and Miller's (1984; see also Chapter 7) analysis suggests that the features specified by the contact hypothesis as instrumental in promoting in- tergroup acceptance are effective because they reduce the salience of the intergroup boundary and promote personalized interactions be- tween the memberships. Given that interracial contact situations can- not often realistically be expected to include many of the prerequisite features, Brewer and Miller's theoretical integration is especially valuable. This perspective can contribute to the identification of alter- native features that also reduce the salience of the group boundaries and facilitate personalized interactions, but which can more realisti- cally be expected to be introduced in interracial contact situations. This framework can also help identify features of existing contact situations that should be eliminated because they increase the sali- ence of the group boundaries and thereby inhibit the development of more positive, personalized intergroup relationships.

Recently, in the context of group mergers, we have been investigat- ing the possibility of replacing the salience of the intergroup bound- ary with the perception of common membership within a superordi- nate entity. We suggest that superordinate goals successfully reduce intergroup conflict (Sherif & Sherif, 1969) because they increase the likelihood that members of these groups will perceive themselves as belonging to one group rather than to two (see Turner, 1981; Worchel, Axsom, Ferris, Samaha, & Schweitzer, 1978). Strategies that increase the salience of a common or superordinate group are hypothesized to reduce the salience of prior group boundaries and thereby contribute to the development of a general sense of unity and identity.

In addition to reducing the salience of the previous group boundaries, increasing the salience of the superordinate group, and each member's identification with and commitment to it, can also harness ingroup forces (both cognitive and motivational) that can further increase the likelihood of more differentiated, personalized, and positive interactions among the members. Thus, it is proposed that features of contact situations that emphasize a common, superordinate entity (e.g., a town, neighborhood, or school) can take advantage of the ingroup forces which would otherwise contribute to the development of intergroup bias and redirect these forces toward the elimination of social conflict. Ingroup membership, for example, influences how the prevailing intergroup events are cognitively processed. Information about ingroup members is coded and stored in memory using more complex, differentiated classifications than is information concerning outgroup members (Park & Rothbart, 1982; also see Chapters 5 & 6). Also, Tajfel (1970) proposed the existence of an implicit norm to favor ingroup members, and Brewer's (1979) review of the literature indicates that intergroup bias often represents a pro-ingroup rather than an anti-outgroup orientation. Brewer (1979), in particular, suggests that the critical aspect of ingroup–outgroup categorization is that when people are classified as ingroup members they are moved closer to the self. Therefore, ingroup members are perceived to be less differentiated from the self than are outgroup members. Morever, people believe that ingroup members share more of their own attitudes than do outgroup members (Allen & Wilder, 1979; Stein, Hardyck, & Smith, 1965), and belief similarity, in turn, is a powerful determinant of interpersonal attraction (Byrne, 1971). Ingroup categorization also influences prosocial behavior. People are more helpful toward ingroup than outgroup members (Hornstein, 1976; Piliavin, Dovidio, Gaertner, & Clark, 1981) and are more likely to be cooperative and exercise more personal restraint in their use of an endangered common resource when they are interacting with ingroup than with outgroup members (Kramer & Brewer, 1984). Thus, there is considerable evidence suggesting the possibility that as a person's status changes from outgroup to ingroup membership, people's attitudes and behaviors toward them become more differentiated and favorable, conditions which can facilitate personalized interaction. Therefore, we believe that strategies of intergroup contact that emphasize the salience of the superordinate group can utilize ingroup forces productively to promote intergroup acceptance and personalized interactions between the memberships.

Consistent with this perspective, Slavin and Madden's (1979) review of school practices that improve race relations revealed that participating on interracial sports teams and in cooperative learning groups were among the activities most related to positive interracial attitudes (see also Cook, 1984; Johnson, Johnson, & Maruyama, 1984). Although it is not clearly understood why cooperative interaction facilitates intergroup acceptance, it is possible that intergroup cooperation not only reduces the salience of the intergroup boundary but also contributes to members' perceiving the existence of one entity rather than two (see Campbell, 1958; Turner, 1981). Although intergroup cooperation has positive benefits, it is not always easy to induce cooperation among groups. Imposing a superordinate group identity, however, has been shown to increase the likelihood of cooperative, self-restrained behavior among individuals (Kramer & Brewer, 1984, in press), and therefore this strategy may have additional potential for changing the nature of intergroup relationships. That is, emphasizing a common, superordinate identity may facilitate the induction of cooperative interaction between groups that may otherwise be independent or competitive.

When interracial behavior is considered, the problems associated with reducing the salience of intergroup boundaries and increasing the awareness of a superordinate entity are compounded by the number of convergent cultural, social, and physical boundaries that differentiate the groups. It is not likely that the members would or could forsake their previous subgroup identities completely or permanently, nor is that necessarily desirable (see Chapter 10). Nevertheless, an increased salience of the superordinate group even for temporary periods may permit positive bonds to develop through the perforated boundary and thus change the basis for future interaction. Furthermore, subgroup and superordinate group identities can be salient simultaneously. For example, members of a household constitute a family, but they can also categorize themselves as parents and children without losing awareness of their superordinate connection. The formation of a superordinate group thus does not require each constituent subgroup to forsake its identity entirely.

An important theme in the chapters by Schofield (Chapter 8) and Jones (Chapter 10) is that in integrated settings the adoption of a colorblind perspective is usually associated with the requirement that the behavior of blacks must conform to the prevailing norms of white, middle-class culture. Failure of blacks to adapt to this expectation typically prevents them from attaining their desired rewards from the meritocracy. This requirement to conform devalues black culture, and thus black people, and also precludes the opportunity for the total aggregate to profit from diversity. Relatedly, Schoennauer's (1967) analysis of corporate mergers and acquisitions indicates that an inter-action pattern that requires one company to forsake its identity and culture for that of the other company is most frequently associated with crisis situations (i.e., losses of capital, reduced sales, and in-creased resignations). Successful mergers were associated with an in-tegration pattern in which in the first stage the two management teams joined together without either company being required to conform to the style of the other, followed by a second stage in which the merged company developed a culture that represented a blend of the two corporate cultures or combined each into a pattern in which new values, norms, and procedures emerged.

From our superordinate or merged group perspective, the research challenge is to discover techniques and strategies that induce the members of separate groups to conceive of the aggregate as one entity, and then to examine whether this perception facilitates cooperative-ness, acceptance, and personalized interactions between the member-ships in ways that may even generalize beyond the immediate super-ordinate group context. An initial test of this approach (Gaertner, 1985) examined the way physical arrangements of the memberships in space (in terms of the seating patterns) affect the degree to which two groups perceive themselves as one unit rather than two. The idea that the arrangements of people or objects in space can influence the man-ner in which elements are perceptually organized is derived from some basic postulates of Gestalt psychology (i.e., laws of similarity, proximity, and common fate; see Campbell, 1958). Perhaps, in addi-tion to other strategies, approaches that engage the visual system to induce the perception of one entity would be particularly effective with groups that are physically differentiated. Thus, if Campbell's (1958) assumption that visual processes analyze entitativity rapidly and vividly compared to other perceptual and inferential processes is valid, then these forces too may be used productively toward the elimination of a problem that they may have helped to perpetuate. It was expected that the manner in which people from different sub-groups are dispersed in space (e.g., around a conference table, class-room, or city) would influence their conceptual representation of the aggregate as either one group, two groups, or separate individuals and consequently their degree of intergroup bias.

In this study, two groups of four students (two males and two females) met in separate rooms to reach consensus on the best solution to the Winter Survival Problem (Johnson & Johnson, 1975). This task requires participants to imagine that their plane had crashed in northern Minnesota in the winter and to rank-order 10 items (e.g., a gun, newspaper, candy bar) in terms of their importance to the group's survival. Following the group discussion and consensus, the two groups (AAAA and BBBB) were merged together in a single room around a hexagonal table. Using color-coded identifications, subjects were arranged in one of three seating patterns (see Figure 1): Segre-

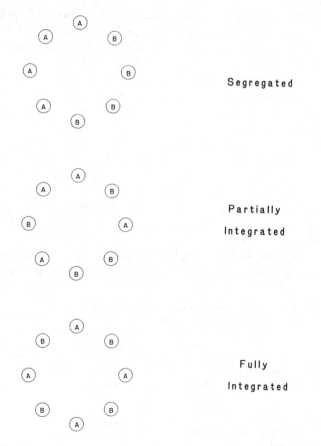

FIGURE 1. Seating arrangements of members of the two groups in the Segregated, Partially Integrated, and Fully Integrated conditions.

gated, Partially Integrated, and Fully Integrated. The subjects were then asked to reach consensus again on the Winter Survival Problem. Next, questionnaires were administered to assess each participant's impression of his or her group experience. For example, subjects were asked whether the merged group felt like one unit, two units, or separate individuals and whom they would vote for to be leader if the survival problem were real rather than hypothetical. It was predicted that as the seating pattern varied from Segregated (a pattern which physically emphasized subgroup boundaries) to Partially Integrated to Fully Integrated (a pattern which physically degraded subgroup boundaries) there would be decreased salience of the premerger group boundaries resulting in a greater sense of unity and decreased intergroup bias.

The results indicated that with greater integration in seating, participants more frequently experienced the merged aggregate as one unit rather than two and showed less ingroup bias in their choice for leader (see Table 1). Similarly, this pattern of reduced ingroup favoritism as a function of seating integration characterized participants' perceptions of the relative value of members' contributions to the solution and their ratings of friendliness between and within subgroups. When the group was used as the unit of analysis, the results also revealed that the Fully Integrated, relative to the Segregated, seating pattern increased feelings that the merged entity was one unit and reduced ingroup bias in leader selection. Furthermore, subjects' individual solutions to the Winter Survival Problem at the end of the experiment suggested that participants in the Fully Integrated condition tended to internalize the merged group's solution more than did subjects in the Segregated condition.

Further evidence of the positive effects of seating arrangement is revealed in an internal analysis that examined the consequences of

TABLE 1   The Effects of Seating Arrangement during the Merger

	Segregated (15 groups)	Partially integrated (15 groups)	Fully integrated (16 groups)
Do you feel that this group acted more like:			
One unit	51.7%	63.5%	65.6%
Two units	37.9%	27.8%	21.9%
Separate individuals	10.3%	8.7%	12.5%
Voting for leadership of merged group:			
Voted for previous ingroup member	62.2%	59.5%	48.8%

members conceiving the merged unit as one entity rather than as two groups. In this analysis, the impression of one unit or two was treated as an independent variable. The results revealed that subjects who conceived of the aggregate as one unit perceived the merged group as more cooperative, democratic, pleasant, close, and successful than did subjects who saw the group as two units. In addition, participants who perceived the merged group as one unit were more satisfied with the group atmostphere, believed that members worked better together, and had greater confidence in the group's solution. Although it is not a statistically reliable effect, subjects who perceived the merged group as two units tended to show an ingroup favoritism effect: They liked people who were formerly from their subgroup more than people formerly from the other subgroup. This bias did not exist among subjects who saw the merged group as one unit.

We are currently pursuing additional work on group mergers, which is leading us to business, educational, military, church, and medical settings. The intent of this research is to study group mergers in a variety of settings to identify strategies that increase the effectiveness of the merger process and may have trans-situational properties. Also, in the laboratory, we are investigating how physical factors (e.g., colored unifroms) and social variables (e.g., having the merged group adopt the name or territory of one of the subgroups; see Gaertner & Drout, 1984) affect perceptions of unity in intergroup contact situations. In addition, we plan to assess the consequences of superordinate group membership on interracial behavior, particularly related to the subtle forms of racism discussed earlier in this volume. Optimistically, shared group identity and the development of a sense of partnership can eliminate manifestations of even these more subtle, indirect, and rationalizable forms of racism. Given that the degradation of an intergroup boundary is the common focus of various current investigations into the reduction of intergroup bias in general, there is reason to be encouraged that diverse strategies such as personalizing interactions (Brewer & Miller, 1984; also see Chapter 7), forming new groups with crossed-category memberships (Deschamps & Doise, 1978), individuating outgroup members (Wilder, 1978); and creating a superordinate group can all contribute to an understanding of some of the causes of intergroup conflict and potentially lead to the development of an array of techniques that can be implemented within interracial contact situations.

In general, we believe that racism cannot be fully understood without considering basic perceptual, cognitive, interpersonal, intergroup, social, historical, and cultural factors. Although the theoretical analyses discussed throughout this volume do not address all the issues involved in prejudice, discrimination, and racism, they do contribute to a fundamental understanding of these phenomena. As Miller and Brewer (1984) observe, "Though we do not believe that any social phenomenon such as desegregation can be fully understood outside its historical and social context, we do see some advantage to 'stepping back' from particular instances and immediate political issues to assess similarities and regularities that appear across events that may occur in different times and places but that nevertheless share important commonalities . . . . The purpose of such an abstraction is to contribute to the development of a social science theory of intergroup behavior and attitudes, which can in turn inform public policy in relevant instances" (pp. 1–2). Thus, despite reasons to be concerned about the progress of race relations, there are also significant reasons for optimism. Progress toward understanding racism has been made at a level of theoretical development that goes significantly beyond mere intuition. By understanding the causes of racism, innovative steps toward the elimination of racism can be taken using strategies and methods that rely on processes that may be as fundamental as those that appear to be involved in the development of prejudice, discrimination, and racism.

ACKNOWLEDGMENT

We would like to thank Jeffrey Mann for his helpful comments on an earlier version of this manuscript.

REFERENCES

Adorno, T. W., Frenkel-Brunswik, E., Levinson, D. J., & Sanford, R. N. (1950). *The authoritarian personality*. New York: Harper & Row.

Allen, V. L., & Wilder, D. A. (1979). Group categorization and attribution of belief similarity. *Small Group Behavior, 10*, 73–80.

Allport, G. W. (1954). *The nature of prejudice*. Reading: MA: Addison-Wesley.

Amir, Y. (1976). The role of intergroup contact in change of prejudice and ethnic relations. In P. A. Katz (Ed.), *Towards the elimination of racism* (pp. 245–308). New York: Pergamon Press.

Brewer, M. B. (1979). In-group bias in the minimal intergroup situation: A cognitive-motivational analysis. *Psychological Bulletin, 86*, 307–324.

Brewer, M. B., & Miller, N. (1984). Beyond the contact hypothesis: Thereotical perspectives on desegregation. In N. Miller & M. B. Brewer (Eds.), *Groups in contact: The psychology of desegregation* (pp. 281–302). Orlando, FL: Academic Press.

Brown, R. J., & Turner, J. C. (1981). Interpersonal and intergroup behavior. In J. C.

Turner & H. Giles (Eds.), *Intergroup behavior* (pp. 33–65). Chicago: University of Chicago Press.

Byrne, D. (1971). *The attraction paradigm*. New York: Academic Press.

Campbell, D. T. (1958). Common fate, similarity and other indices of the status of aggregates of persons as social entities. *Behavioral Science, 3,* 14–25.

Cook, S. W. (1984). Cooperative interaction in multiethnic contexts. In N. Miller & M. B. Brewer (Eds.), *Groups in contact: The psychology of desegregation* (pp. 155–185). Orlando, FL: Academic Press.

Cook, S. W. (1985). Experimenting on social issues: The case of school desegregation. *American Psychologist, 40,* 452–460.

Crosby, F., Bromley, S., & Saxe, L. (1980). Recent unobtrusive studies of black and white discrimination and prejudice: A literature review. *Psychological Bulletin, 87,* 546–563.

Deschamps, J. C., & Doise, W. (1978). Crossed category group memberships in intergroup relations. In H. Tajfel (Ed.), *Differentiation between social groups* (pp. 141–158). London: Academic Press.

Gaertner S. L. (1985, March). *When groups merge: Reducing the salience of group boundaries.* Paper presented at the American Educational Research Association Annual Meeting, Chicago.

Gaertner, S. L., & Drout, C. E. (1984, April). *When groups merge: The effects of territorial occupancy.* Paper presented at the Annual Meeting of the Eastern Psychological Association, Baltimore.

Hornstein, H. A. (1976). *Cruelty and kindness: A new look at aggression and altruism.* Englewood Cliffs, NJ: Prentice-Hall.

Johnson, D. W., & Johnson, F. P. (1975). *Joining together: Group theory and group skills.* Englewood Cliffs, NJ: Prentice-Hall.

Johnson, D. W., Johnson, R. T., & Maruyama, G. (1984). Goal interdependence and interpersonal attraction in heterogeneous classrooms: A metanalysis. In N. Miller & M. B. Brewer (Eds.), *Groups in contact: The psychology of desegregation* (pp. 187–212). Orlando, FL: Academic Press.

Katz, P. A. (Ed.) (1976). *Towards the elimination of racism.* New York: Pergamon Press.

Katz, P. A. & Taylor, D. A. (Eds.). (in press). *Eliminating racism: Means & controversy.* New York: Plenum.

Kluegel, J. R., & Smith, E. R. (1982). Whites' beliefs about blacks' opportunities. *American Sociological Review, 47,* 518–532.

Kovel, J. (1970). *White racism: A psychohistory.* New York: Pantheon.

Kramer, R. M., & Brewer, M. B. (1984). Effects of group identity on resource use in a simulated commons dilemma. *Journal of Personality and Social Psychology, 46,* 1044-1057.

Kramer, R. M., & Brewer, M. B. (in press). Social group identity and the emergence of cooperation in resource conservation dilemmas. In H. Wilke, C. Rutte, & D. Messick (Eds.), *Experimental studies of social dilemmas.*

McConahay, J. B. (1981). Reducing racial prejudice in desegregated schools. In W. D. Hawley (Ed.), *Effective school desegregation.* Beverly Hills, CA: Sage.

Miller, N., & Brewer, M. B. (1984). The psychology of desegregation: An introduction. In N. Miller & M. B. Brewer (Eds.), *Groups in contact: The psychology of desegregation* (pp. 1–8). Orlando: Academic Press.

Park, B., & Rothbart, M. (1982). Perception of out-group homogeneity and levels of social categorization: Memory for the subordinate attributes of in-group and out-group members. *Journal of Personality and Social Psychology, 42, 1051–1068.*

Piliavin, J. A., Dovidio, J. F., Gaertner, S. L., & Clark, R. D., III. (1981). *Emergency intervention*. New York: Academic Press.

Rogers, R. W., & Prentice-Dunn, S. (1981). Deindividuation and anger-mediated interracial aggression: Unmasking regressive racism. *Journal of Personality and Social Psychology, 41*, 63–73.

Schoennauer, A. W. (1967, Jan.-Feb.) Behavior patterns of executives in business acquisitions. *Personal Administration, 22*–32.

Sherif, M. (1967). *Group conflict and co-operation*. London: Routledge and Kegan Paul.

Sherif, M., & Sherif, C. W. (1969). *Social psychology*. New York: Harper & Row.

Slavin, R. E., & Madden, N. A. (1979). School practices that improve social relations. *American Educational Research Journal, 16*, 169–180.

Stein, D. D., Hardyck, J. A., & Smith, M. B. (1965). Race and belief: An open and shut case. *Journal of Personality and Social Psychology, 1*, 281–289.

Stephan, W. G. (1978). School desegregation: An evaluation of predictions made in Brown v. Board of Education. *Psychological Bulletin, 85*, 217–238.

Stephan, W. G. (1985). Intergroup relations. In G. Lindzey & E. Aronson (Eds.), *The handbook of social psychology* (3rd ed., Vol. 2, pp. 599–658). New York: Random House.

Tajfel, H. (1969). Cognitive aspects of prejudice. *Journal of Social Issues, 25*, 79–97.

Tajfel, H. (1970). Experiments in intergroup discrimination. *Scientific American, 223*, 96–102.

Tajfel, H., & Turner, J. C. (1979). An integrative theory of intergroup conflict. In W. G. Austin & S. Worchel (Eds.), *The social psychology of intergroup relations* (pp. 33–48). Monterey, CA: Brooks/Cole.

Tajfel, H., & Turner, J. C. (1986). The social identity theory of intergroup behavior. In S. Worschel & W. G. Austin (Eds.), *Psychology of intergroup relations* (2nd ed., pp. 7–24). Chicago: Nelson-Hall.

Turner, J. C. (1975). Social comparison and social identity: Some prospects for intergroup behavior. *European Journal of Social Psychology, 5*, 5–34.

Turner, J. C. (1981). The experimental social psychology of intergroup behavior. In J. C. Turner & H. Giles (Eds.), *Intergroup behavior* (pp. 1–32). Chicago: University of Chicago Press.

Wilder, D. A. (1978). Reduction of intergroup discrimination through individuation of the out-group. *Journal of Personality and Social Psychology, 36*, 1361–1374.

Wilder, D. A. (1986). Cognitive factors affecting the success of intergroup contact. In S. Worschel & W. G. Austin (Eds.), *Psychology of intergroup relations* (2nd ed., pp. 49–66). Chicago: Nelson-Hall.

Worchel, S. (1979). Cooperation and the reduction of intergroup conflict: Some determining factors. In W. G. Austin & S. Worchel (Eds.), *The social psychology of intergroup relations* (pp. 262–273). Monterey, CA: Brooks/Cole.

Worchel, S. (1986). The role of cooperation in reducing intergroup conflict. In S. Worchel & W. G. Austin (Eds.), *Psychology of intergroup relations* (2nd ed., pp. 288–304). Chicago: Nelson-Hall.

Worchel, S., Axsom, D., Ferris, F., Samaha, C., & Schweitzer, S. (1978). Factors determining the effect of intergroup cooperation on intergroup attraction. *Journal of Conflict Resolution, 22*, 429–439.

INDEX